AMERICAN WEIGHTLIFTING

AMERICAN WEIGHTLIFTING

GLENN PENDLAY

with James McDermott and Mike Prevost

ON TARGET PUBLICATIONS

Aptos, California, USA

American Weightlifting
Glenn Pendlay
with James McDermott and Mike Prevost

Foreword by Donny Shankle
Introduction by Trey Goodwin

Main Photographers:
Micah Gilbert Photography & Design
Derek Selles

ISBN-13: 978-1-931046-07-7 Paperback
ISBN-13: 978-1-931046-08-4 Hardcover
First printing May 2022

On Target Publications
P O Box 1335
Aptos, California 95001 USA
otpbooks.com

Library of Congress Cataloging-in-Publication Data

Names: Pendlay, Glenn, author. | McDermott, James Anthony, II, 1986–
    co-author. | Prevost, Michael C., 1967– co-author.
Title: American weightlifting / Glenn W Pendlay III, with James Anthony
    McDermott II and Michael C. Prevost.
Description: Aptos, California : On Target Publications, [2021] | Includes
    index. | Summary: "American Weightlifting covers the coaching practices
    and programming of one of the top USA Weightlifting coaches, Coach Glenn
    Pendlay"— Provided by publisher.
Identifiers: LCCN 2020055603 | ISBN 9781931046077 (paperback)
Subjects: LCSH: Weight lifting—United States—Coaching. | Weight
    lifting—United States—Training. | Weight lifting—United States.
Classification: LCC GV546.3 .P44 2021 | DDC 796.410973—dc23

LC record available at https://lccn.loc.gov/2020055603

CONTENTS

GLENN PENDLAY, REST IN PEACE

Photo 1—Glenn Pendlay

Glenn Pendlay was good at everything he tried, but he was especially good at seeing what weightlifters needed to do to become better lifters. He had an eye for perfection and a thirst for knowledge that propelled him to the top levels of coaching weightlifting. There was nothing he wouldn't do to get better at coaching and supporting his athletes.

Through those efforts, Glenn changed the face of American weightlifting and the athletes he coached now continue his legacy. He was a visionary, and he pulled a lot of people into that vision with him.

From an early age, Glenn was fascinated with sports, lifting weights, and the pursuit of strength. In fact, when he was about 12, he used a posthole digger to rig up a squat rack using six-foot wooden posts so he could squat.

Through those early years, Glenn tried relentlessly to gain great strength, but lacked the resources to accomplish that goal. Everything changed when Glenn attended Kansas State University, and met Alan Myers in the campus weightroom. Alan introduced him to the sport of powerlifting, and the two started training together in the early mornings. Under Alan's guidance, Glenn began to make progress in his

strength gains; he put on muscle and increased his bodyweight from 200 pounds to more than 300 over the following five years. The two trained heavy sets of five repetitions for most lifts, a rep number his future athletes would come to know well.

Glenn's original intention was to obtain a degree in education and become a high school teacher. In 1992, that plan—and the course of Glenn's life—abruptly changed after a meeting with legendary Russian weightlifting coach Alexander Medvedev when he traveled to Moscow to attend the Junior World Powerlifting Championships.

After the event, Medvedev invited him to stay in Moscow and train under his guidance. Medvedev, through an interpreter, taught Glenn how to snatch and clean and jerk, and shared his thoughts on the science behind training for weightlifting.

This was Glenn's first exposure to the role science played in the process of the human body adapting to gain strength. He was hooked, and absolutely had to learn more.

Photo 2—Glenn and Alexander Medvedev, August 11, 1992

Upon returning to the United States, Glenn promptly changed his education major to exercise physiology. The stage was set, and he embarked on a persistent pursuit to gain knowledge about the human body and its ability to adapt to the stresses placed upon it.

Over the next few years, Glenn slowly transitioned as an athlete from powerlifting to weightlifting. This was no quick switch, because Glenn always saw things through to the end. He had goals in powerlifting, and wasn't about to abandon them.

His time in the sport helped him build what he considered "decent" levels of strength. As a younger lifter weighing 275 to 285 pounds, he benched pressed just over 500 pounds without a specialized bench shirt. He was able to perform multiple reps at 425 pounds on the strict barbell row—what many now refer to as "The Pendlay Row." Someone once bet against him being able to curl 235 pounds; he did it for eight reps.

Everyone who knew Glenn was aware of how much he loved squats. While powerlifting, he squatted 606 pounds for 10 reps, and box squatted 800 pounds to a box height set below parallel. He also back squatted 500 pounds for 20 reps.

As a weightlifter, Glenn front squatted 550 pounds, push pressed 440 pounds, and high-bar back squatted 600 pounds. As the story goes, he stood up so explosively out of that 600-pound squat that he launched the bar over his head and to the floor in front of him. He'd heard that a Russian weightlifter, David Rigert, had done this in training before a major competition. Being curious—and competitive—Glenn wanted to see if he could accomplish the feat.

In one of his most memorable weightlifting meets, Glenn made six of six attempts with a best snatch of 160 kilos, best clean and jerk of 190, and totaled 350 kilos. This was done after a full day of coaching 19 of his athletes. Only a few years into training as a weightlifter, Glenn snatched 170 kilos and cleaned 210.

Glenn earned his master's in the field of endocrinology, where he studied how different levels of stress affect the endocrine system, and how that in turn affects the body's adaptation to stress. His research led to multiple papers in peer-reviewed journals, working not only with weightlifters, but also athletes involved in cycling, skiing, track and field, football, and many other sports.

Wherever Glenn went, success in weightlifting followed—first in Wichita Falls with the Wichita Falls Weightlifting team, then in California at California Strength, on to South Carolina with MuscleDriver USA (MDUSA®), and finally back in his hometown of McPherson, Kansas, with the Mac-Town Barbell Club. Beginning in the mid-1990s, Glenn coached over 100 national champions at all levels of the sport: 10-year-old school-age national champions, senior world team members, a Pan American medalist, master's world champions, and a world record holder.

Photo 3—Glenn at work

His athletes also competed successfully in team championships, including six men's collegiate national team titles in seven years, and three junior national team titles. During his career, Glenn became a USA Weightlifting Senior International Coach (Level 5), which is the highest accreditation one can receive in the United States. In 2004, he was named the AAU Coach of the Year. He was appointed as head coach for five USA World Championship teams, as well as multiple Pan American teams. Glenn never stopped coaching weightlifting full time.

Glenn loved to write. He had an immense talent for explaining complicated subjects, boiling them down to something easily digestible. He did that with his article, "The Life of a Samurai" posted on his WordPress blog on July 22, 2017. In the post, he discussed how living the life of Samurai meant devoting one's life to mastering one thing. The Samurai devoted their lives to mastering the sword and combat. Glenn's "one thing" was weightlifting.

The level of Glenn's passion and love for weightlifting is something most in the world will never fully comprehend. In his quest to produce bigger totals in American weightlifters, to grow the sport of weightlifting in the United States, and to hopefully see an American winning gold at the Olympics was second to none. Glenn gave up a lot in pursuit of his "one thing," including business ventures and personal relationships. He wholeheartedly believed that succeeding at doing one thing really well was the right answer—that if he did that, his life would have been a success.

Photo 4—Glenn using the coach's head tilt while watching a lift. Photo courtesy of Mark Hazarabedian.

Glenn was diagnosed with Stage IV metastatic cancer in 2019 at the age of 48. A few quick months later, in his home town and surrounded by his family, Glenn Pendlay passed away peacefully.

Many who knew Glenn personally agree that when he set his mind to do something, there wasn't much that could stop him. He had an unparalleled level of determination with the right ratio of stubbornness. He spent his final days doing what he dedicated his life to: programming workouts for his athletes, having discussions about weightlifting, and traveling to the gym to support and coach his weightlifters. In fact, he refused pain medications that would sedate him so he could continue coaching training sessions.

Glenn left behind a storied career in academics and sports. This book, *American Weightlifting*, is a culmination of the knowledge he acquired, experiences he lived, and his philosophies about training. Flipping through these pages was a dream he had for decades. Over the years, it too was often put on the backburner while he devoted more time to coaching his athletes and, he felt, rightly so.

When he came back to the project during his final years, he often said, "This is how people will remember me when I'm gone." He was worried people would forget about him, that the old California Strength and MDUSA videos would receive fewer plays, and that Pendlay equipment would gather dust in back corners of gyms.

Glenn often wondered if weightlifting—his one thing—would move on, leaving his memory behind.

That won't happen—not if the people who loved him have anything to say about it.

Glenn was generous with his time, shared his knowledge and resources with anyone who asked because he wanted to help make American weightlifting better. He wanted to grow the sport. His goal was for this book to serve that purpose.

It's now up to each of us to keep Glenn's legacy and memory alive.

Accomplishing that task is relatively simple: Share Glenn's "one thing" and spread his love of weightlifting. If you see young kids or beginner lifters needing help, help them. If they're using a Pendlay bar or plates, take a moment to tell them where the name came from and that "Pendlay" is not just another brand, but a person who would have loved to see them lifting weights.

Finally, when in doubt, do what Glenn would have wanted you to do: Put another kilo on the bar, and keep chasing new personal records.

Photo 5—Glenn and Jon North
Photo courtesy of Mark Hazarabedian.

Photo 6—The Glenn Pendlay

FOREWORD
DONNY SHANKLE

The first time I met Coach Pendlay was at my first national weightlifting contest. When I learned I'd be training under him, I was excited anyone would be willing to teach me. What I didn't know was that I'd be training under the greatest of weightlifting coaches, and that he'd also turn out to be one of my greatest friends.

Coach Pendlay was a large man at 350 pounds when I met him, and everyone felt his strength in his presence, which was somehow both intimidating and welcoming. People trusted him without knowing him, and his athletes felt as though the worst thing in the world would be to disappoint him. This is an inherent feature the best coaches possess, and he was one of the best.

Our first conversation is still clear in my mind. I told him I knew everything I needed to know about what it would take to get better. All I needed from him was help in getting stronger. My stubbornness continued for years, but Coach looked past that and taught me everything he knew. I really can't think of a better example of the mentor and protégé relationship than our own.

Before being my coach, and later my friend, he was my teacher. The best coaches are teachers first. Through being an athlete and a teacher, they learn the virtue of patience. This patience comes in handy when you're teaching a sport that will take at least a decade to gain proficiency. The way I teach today is largely influenced by how Coach Pendlay taught: always from the top down and make sure the lifter first learns the proper positions.

Coach was always present for me. When I needed money for gas to get to the gym, he helped. When I couldn't stand up because my knees hurt too much, he picked me up…and filled my hand with Ibuprofen. When I needed guidance, he directed me to a storehouse of books he'd read.

Along with our shared enjoyment of reading, we had the most insightful conversations on our long road trips to competitions. During these lengthy drives, we'd listen to CDs on how to speak Russian; we'd talk politics and touched on every subject you can imagine. I was learning so much, so fast.

And I was winning.

Training with Coach Pendlay always included snatching and cleaning and jerking. He kept the training simple and directed toward making personal records. By keeping it focused on two objectives, he put his genius into the training. He understood the importance of the mind in the gym, and how important it is to be aggressive.

At one point, I trained under another famed coach, Ivan Abadjiev, and gave Coach Pendlay a call after weeks of getting hammered in the gym. I asked him what I needed to do to get through the training. His response was something I'll never forget: "Get aggressive, Donny. You always lift at your best when you get aggressive."

That was all he said, and all I needed to hear. This thought has continually helped me to confront head-on any amount of difficulty in training, and in life.

There wasn't a better coach to have in the warm-up room than Coach Pendlay. His presence was felt by other coaches and his athletes were immediately a step ahead of the other competitors. A warm-up platform was always found first, and all we had to do was concentrate on making our attempts. Coach was fantastic at making sure we were ready when it was our time to lift. The attempts were laid out, and as long as we did our part and made our lifts, he'd load the bar with what was necessary to win.

This is an often-overlooked quality at the heart of weightlifting. Winning gold is all that matters. I can't tell you how many times Coach reiterated that if we wanted to win, we had to make our lifts.

The importance of being strong, as well as being consistent, was always addressed in the training hall and competition warm-up room.

This is how you'll win.

Coach Pendlay will always be more than a coach to me. I'm honored to have lifted for the man, and known him as a friend. "It is what it is" is something he'd say, meaning there's no point dwelling on what can't be changed—a stoic response if there ever was one, but full of wisdom.

This advice came in handy, especially during those brutal times in the squat rack. I remember one squat session when I went down, shaking uncontrollably after making a personal best front squat in front of him. He just stared at me; I didn't know what he was thinking, but I knew I'd get no sympathy.

Another time, I jerked a world record from the blocks, and he came over…wanting me to go for more. Neither of us knew when I'd be in such top form again, so that was the time to strike. He wanted me to keep going after more.

These are key things I learned from Coach that carry over into all of my life's ventures. Be aggressive and passionate about what you want. Immerse yourself in study, and sharpen your mind when you're not lifting. Acknowledge the unavoidable, but don't let it deter you from being disciplined in and out of the gym. Never let go, and always keep chasing as long as you keep believing.

These are not things you learn from someone who's "just a coach." These you learn from a virtuous and learned human being.

I'll forever work hard to do Coach justice when I teach what he taught me. My demeanor in the gym when I coach is similar to the way he coached me. I say little, and watch everything. I let the weightlifter's confidence come out on its own, and modestly do my part as an observer.

In *American Weightlifting*, Coach outlines a simple yet thorough accumulation of his weightlifting knowledge. The joy I felt in seeing on paper the lessons and principles I learned through firsthand experience brought back a flood of indelible memories.

There's no better work on the subject of weightlifting than Coach Pendlay's book. This isn't written by a pretender or an embarrassing armchair guru. This comes from a man who produced champions. I'm proud to be among them.

Thank you, Glenn.

Photo 7—Donny Shankle, 200-kilo clean

INTRODUCTION
TREY GOODWIN

I frequent gyms around the country, and see equipment everywhere boasting the Pendlay logo. I enjoy popping into random CrossFit® gyms to satisfy my craving for weightlifting, and typically find myself lifting a Pendlay® bar with Pendlay weights, surrounded by folks wearing bearded T-shirts. I lose myself in the moment and envision Glenn Pendlay's face staring back at me. I hear my coach, my mentor, and my friend yelling for me, "C'mon Trey, big pull!"

The muscle memory and speed are surprisingly still there, and is enough for an onlooker to ask, "Where did you learn how to do that?"

I found Coach Pendlay in the summer of 2000 at a small gym in Wichita Falls, Texas, and began training with him while preparing for Texas high school football and powerlifting meets. I realized early on that there was something special about him as a coach. He took me from a small-town young man with some natural strength and a desire to be the best, to a decorated athlete with honors in various high school sports, earning the title of a Texas High School All-State powerlifter. Still wanting more, I continued to trust him with my weightlifting career, making the 45-minute drive each night to train with him.

Later that fall, I asked Glenn to speak to my high school football team at one of our team breakfasts. He made the drive from Wichita Falls to Electra and spoke to us about what it takes to be a champion—specifically, what separates a good athlete from an elite athlete. The points Glenn made in that speech were cemented in my mind, and still resonate with me today.

I utilized many of the work ethics and values of leadership, time management, commitment, extra effort, and goal setting he imparted to eventually become an elite athlete under his direction.

I continued to employ these principals throughout my college studies, earning degrees and certifications,

and I still uphold them today in my career in the oil and gas industry.

Glenn prided himself in understanding the research and science behind strength. Through administering science-based programming tailored to fit each individual lifter, our Wichita Falls Weightlifting Team became the best in the nation. Additionally, our team had some of the brightest kinesiology minds, people who came from all over the country vying for spots to learn under Glenn while completing their studies, knowing that no other university program could compare to his.

While attending my first year of college at Midwestern State University, our team, under Glenn's direction, participated as subjects of several strength and conditioning scientific studies, which eventually were published. Our names were never displayed, and we were simply referred to as Test Group A and Test Group B, Test Subject, or whatever else they chose to call us. We'd often joke that we felt like lab rats at times, wondering if this was where the term "gym rats" was coined.

There were periods of 8 to 10 weeks when we'd arrive in the early morning hours to get blood drawn in order for specific tests to be done. Through separating our red and white blood cells and various other complex tests, Glenn was able to efficiently gauge how certain workouts effected individual lifters and their testosterone levels.

It was through tests such as these, along with programming and research that he came to know the intricate details of each lifter on our team. Through Glenn's understanding of how and why our bodies worked differently from one another, he was able to design and tailor each of our programs to target our personal strengths and weaknesses.

Under Glenn's supervision and incorporation of his scientific program design, our team flourished as we watched each other grow physically and mentally.

Our strength intensified, as did our competitive edge that came as we began to embrace the ability to perform beyond anything we thought possible. I saw myself soar in competition, winning various national championships, earning the status of Collegiate All American, representing the United States in international competitions, and competing in two Olympic Team Trials. I wasn't alone—many of the members of Glenn's Wichita Falls Weightlifting team gained their own notoriety as elite weightlifters.

After winning the bronze medal at the Senior National Championships in Chattanooga, Tennessee, in 2003, Glenn approached my parents to discuss with them, along with me, the next step in my weightlifting career. He wanted me to spend the summer training at the US Olympic Training Center in Colorado Springs, Colorado. At the end of the summer, I was invited to become a permanent resident at the Olympic Training Center. It was the chance of a lifetime.

Leaving my home weightlifting team and Glenn's program was difficult, especially at a time when the program was excelling and growing, cultivating as well as drawing tremendous talent. One thing was apparent: The reason I'd achieved the strength and technique to acquire a spot at the Training Center was due to the expertise of Coach Pendlay.

After my time at the Olympic Training Center, I continued lifting under Glenn's supervision at a distance while completing my degree at Oklahoma State University. Within a three-week period of time, I graduated, competed in my second Olympic Team Trials, and got married. Although I continue to lift on my own, I hold Glenn and the talent he helped to build in me close to my heart.

Now, years later in gyms filled with Pendlay tools of the trade, I'm proud to be a name-dropper in that moment when I'm asked, "Where did you learn how to do that?" I tell them Glenn Pendlay was my coach and that he taught me techniques that will never leave me.

It's then that I'm taken back to the morning in the fall of 2000 to a little high school football breakfast in Electra, Texas, where Glenn spoke to my heart and mind. I hear his voice speak directly to me, telling me what it takes to be a champion.

Who else can give a speech on what it takes to be a champion but champions themselves, a title that will always befit Coach Pendlay.

Photo 8—Trey Goodwin snatching 140 kilos
Photo by Bruce Klemens

Prior to working with Glenn, I coauthored the book *The Dark Orchestra* with Jon North. After publishing that book, Travis Cooper tagged me in a post on Facebook in the Weightlifting Friends group after Glenn posted, "Can anyone give me the name and email of the guy who helped Jon North with his book?" I couldn't believe GLENN PENDLAY was looking for me, but I was excited to find out why.

Soon enough, we were talking on the phone, and he explained that seeing text on a computer screen was difficult after having a stroke. He needed someone who knew weightlifting, had experience writing books, and could help him build the *American Weightlifting* manuscript.

Photo 9–Glenn coaching me through jerk steps
at a seminar held at Albany CrossFit

Over the next few years, I got to know Glenn well. He flew to New York twice for seminars I either took or assisted with, and I flew to Kansas several times to work on the book.

To say I learned a lot from Glenn is an understatement—his generosity knew no limits. Whether it was elaborating on a concept we were discussing for the book, or giving me his opinion on how to fix an error one of my athletes was consistently making, he was always eager to share his knowledge. I'll always admire that about him.

He had a passion for weightlifting that was immeasurable and contagious. His example made me want to take athletes to weightlifting meets; to produce champions who win gold medals and set American records; to make athletes stronger and push them in training; to do things to help grow the sport we love.

Glenn was my mentor and one of the most intelligent people I've ever met. I dearly miss talking to him every day (at 8:00 a.m. his time, 9:00 a.m. my time) about politics, food, nature, guns, and of course, weightlifting.

As were so many others, I was heartbroken when Glenn passed away on September 5th, 2019. I'm humbled he trusted me to finish his book and will be forever grateful for his friendship and all he taught me. That's why I promised to share the knowledge he shared and to keep pushing athletes to make new PRs in the gym or on the competition platform.

It's up to us to keep his legacy alive, and to make sure his work is not forgotten. If you're a coach, use the methods in this text to help your athletes continue to make progress and find success. If you're an athlete, use the lessons to perform self-analysis to see if you could be doing better. Then, put another kilo on the bar to go for a PR, or sign up for a weightlifting meet. It's what Coach Pendlay would have wanted.

Regardless of who you are, if you see people lifting with a Pendlay bar or plates, let them know "Pendlay" isn't just a brand name on the equipment, but that Glenn Pendlay was a good man who did a lot to advance the sport of weightlifting in America.

For over a decade, publishing this book was a major dream of his. He often spoke about wanting to write the book he wished he'd had when he was a beginner. I'm so pleased to have had the opportunity to play a part in making that dream come true. I hope this book helps you with your training, and gives insight into the immense genius behind one of America's greatest weightlifting coaches.

At the time of his passing, I had almost all of this material from Glenn. The text is written in first person because the collection was nearly complete when he died.

This is his material as given to me.

Some weightlifters make the snatch and the clean and jerk look so breathtakingly easy. Caleb Ward is a perfect example. From his first warm-up set with an empty bar, through each progressive weight increase and up to a new personal record, his technique on each repetition looks identical to the one that came before. His movement is precise, consistent, and I'd even go so far as to say "beautiful." Anyone who loves weightlifting would agree.

James Moser is another lifter who, like Caleb, moves with exemplary technique, and is the most efficient lifter I've ever seen put a barbell overhead and flirt with the American record in the snatch. Both Travis Cooper and Jared Fleming possess this same level of technical mastery in the clean. But, where Ward and Moser were both forced into extreme efficiency in their lifts due to not being brutally strong, Cooper and Fleming are very strong lifters who still lift with great, even beautiful style.

We can watch Caleb or James snatch, and can appreciate the lift for its aesthetic appeal. Then, we can watch Travis and Jared clean and jerk, and appreciate each lift for its power. We can also watch Donny Shankle perform any lift and appreciate the ferocity with which he approaches the bar and his pulls. Down to our bones, we can feel the wave of emotions Jon North brings with him to the platform and yearn for the next time we have the opportunity to pick up a barbell.

I've been particularly lucky to have coached outstanding athletes like these and others whom you may not have heard of but will in these pages. This book is my attempt to provide a roadmap for lifters who want to be the next Ward or Moser, or the next Cooper or Fleming, the next North, even the next Shankle…or even surpass them.

I don't intend this book to serve as an all-encompassing encyclopedia of the sport of weightlifting—Arthur Drechsler already wrote that book. Instead, this is an attempt to document what I've learned about American weightlifters living and training in the United States.

The chapters on learning the snatch, the clean, and the jerk outline a method of teaching the lifts that I slowly gravitated to over my 25-plus years of coaching. It worked for the lifters I coached, from football players doing the lifts to get stronger for their sport, to those dedicated to weightlifting. This method worked for rank beginners as well as to experienced and accomplished lifters.

It's simple—maybe even the simplest way of teaching I've encountered.

And that's why it works.

Photo 10—Donny Shankle lifting at the Wichita Falls Athletic Club

The chapters on programming outline what I found to work for lifters of varying skill levels. For the beginners, it borrows heavily from my experiences with Caleb Ward and others like him whom I coached from their first weightlifting workout to the end of their careers.

The program in the beginner's chapter is meant to flow seamlessly from the initial learning of the lifts because in weightlifting, there's no definitive line between learning the lifts and training the lifts.

The intermediate programming chapter covers training for lifters of that level. These might be the most rewarding athletes to coach. Gains do not come quite as fast as they do for beginners, but you can start to see glimpses of the lifters they will eventually become, and that's incredibly rewarding.

Finally, we get to the advanced programming chapter, which was difficult to write. Many who exist on the periphery of the sport assert that there are no advanced American weightlifters. I point to James Moser and say if you don't think he's an advanced lifter, you don't know much about weightlifting.

There are various reasons we in America are no longer at the pinnacle of the sport; some of them are worth talking about—which we will in the text—but many aren't. It's my belief that with the renewed popularity of weightlifting in the USA, we'll continue to find athletes who combine the technical precision of Ward, the absolute fearlessness of Moser, the brute strength of Cooper and Fleming, the passion of North, and the ferocity of Shankle. These new lifters will move to the top of the podium at world championships and the Olympics.

As a bonus, I've included chapters of my thoughts about implementing Louie Simmons's Westside Barbell™ Method to weightlifting, and how to properly use strength training for sports athletes.

I have a tremendous amount of respect for Louie and feel he is misunderstood by many weightlifters and coaches. My goal is to shed some light on how his training system can be a valuable resource to American weightlifting.

The chapters on training for athletes outline the methods I've used over the years to prepare kids for sports such as football, track and field, and wrestling. Sports seasons are fast-paced and at times emphasis isn't placed on the weightroom. I feel that's a mistake that could hinder a young athlete's long-term performance levels. My goal in these chapters is to provide insight into how I train athletes using year-round programming for preadolescent kids, preteens, and teenagers.

My hope is that the information here helps new strength coaches use their time with athletes more effectively and gives established coaches an idea or two, with the end result being longer and more prosperous athletic careers.

I intend for this book to be useful to both coaches and athletes. My instructions throughout the text are geared toward the individual athlete. We're having a conversation in a similar way that we would if I were this athlete's coach. However, other coaches can certainly use this text for their own learning or to benefit their athletes.

If even a few tips help American weightlifters and their coaches, I'll be satisfied.

SECTION A
LEARNING THE LIFTS

Learning the lifts is a career-long process. There's no definitive line between learning the lifts and training the lifts. Learning is a part of training, and training is a part of the learning process that'll go on for as long as you're in the sport. This reality needs to be taken to heart, but unfortunately, it's overlooked by many beginners.

You'll never be done "learning the lifts."

The primary goal of this first section is to start the process of learning the snatch, the clean, and the jerk, which we'll do by introducing my Three Step Top-Down Method. This method has been interwoven into two subsequent sections: *Training for American Weightlifters* and *Essentials for American Weightlifters*, and will become the foundation for all the programming and training you'll do. We'll finish the book with a section on how to use this knowledge to program for general athletic development.

Photo 11—Caleb Ward snatching while teammates
Donny Shankle and Jon North watch.
Photo by Greg Everett

In Chapter 1, you'll learn the Three Step Method of performing the snatch with an empty barbell—the first step in your training. Once you've learned the clean and the jerk, the next step will be to progress into Chapter 5, where you'll learn the basics of how to write a weightlifting program.

From there, you'll move into a comprehensive breakdown of a beginner program. The Three Step Method will follow you there—and to the other programs, as each of the three steps will become an integral part of your training. Approaching your training in this way ensures that the process of learning the lifts coincides with increasing strength in those lifts.

I've found that pursuing an endless quest to learn the lifts is the best way to produce world-class results. Caleb Ward, Travis Cooper, Donny Shankle, and Jon North all practiced the basics daily, and their impressive lifts are a testament to this pedagogy. If the basics worked for them, they can indeed work for you if you train intelligently.

Avoid the big mistakes countless athletes make:

- Resist increasing the weight on the bar too quickly.

- Embrace being a beginner, and stay one for as long as possible while learning all you can.

- Stick close to the competition lifts in your training instead of overemphasizing methods intended for advanced athletes.

- As a beginner, you don't need variety; you need to perfect your movement patterns and get brutally strong.

Training is a continuation of the learning of technique; there's no break between the two, regardless of your training age or skill level.

A BRIEF SYNOPSIS OF EACH CHAPTER

CHAPTER 1
LEARNING THE SNATCH

In this initial chapter, we'll dive into the intricacies of the snatch, an often-daunting movement for beginners. I'll demystify this by teaching the reasoning behind different aspects of the learning process.

As an athlete, you should be invested in all aspects of your training, including the history of the sport that affects why we perform movements as we do today, and why a coach wants things to be done a certain way.

Ask yourself: Do you know why more full snatches instead of power snatches should be done when learning? Can you find the best grip width for yourself without a coach reminding you every session?

Do you have an understanding of the importance of various positions of the lift, as well as strategies to improve them should you lack flexibility?

Well, you should, and in time, you will. The answers to these questions will be covered in this chapter, in addition to a comprehensive breakdown of the Three Step Method.

This chapter can be used as a reference before training sessions. By continually reminding yourself of the basics and practicing them with attention to detail, you'll build the efficient motor patterns necessary to express your athletic potential. Not only that, but you'll be a knowledgeable athlete as well, which is just as important.

CHAPTER 2
LEARNING THE CLEAN

Chapter 2 will continue the learning progression started in Chapter 1. It's often said that learning the clean comes much easier to athletes after initially learning the snatch. I found this quirk to be true. Because of that, I highly recommend taking your time when learning the snatch. Here, you'll learn about the front rack position, front squats, and the application of the Three Step Method when learning the clean.

CHAPTER 3
LEARNING THE JERK

In this chapter, I'll outline how to properly perform the jerk, which you'll eventually put together with the clean. You'll discover different aspects of the pressing motion, be provided with a method for determining the correct split stance, and learn the progression I use to teach the jerk.

The jerk is often regarded as the most difficult of the competition lifts to learn. Not everyone will be successful in their initial attempts at doing the splitting motion while simultaneously moving the barbell overhead.

However, "difficult" doesn't mean "impossible," so be patient. Work on the split for several months to give it a chance. Then, if it's still not working out and you've exhausted all resources, you can switch to power jerking. At that point, you'll work on and use everything in the aforementioned progression up to the power jerk.

CHAPTER 1
LEARNING THE SNATCH

I believe in teaching the full snatch from the beginning rather than starting with the power snatch. For the uninitiated, the full snatch entails receiving the bar in a deep overhead squat, while the power snatch limits the depth of the catch well above a full squat.

Although the power snatch is easier to teach and probably faster to learn, starting with this version of the lift will waste time in the long run. Beginners can get away with so many errors in the power snatch that the entire lift must be relearned when transitioning to a deeper receiving position. Compounding this, multiple practice sessions over days and even weeks will be spent engraining incorrect positions and bad habits that will ultimately need to be broken. Suffice it to say, it's simpler and better to learn the full lift from the beginning.

The only exception to this occurs when a beginner has a severe lack of flexibility and is unable to safely or comfortably perform an overhead squat. Even then, doing overhead squats until the athlete gains enough flexibility is still a better option than starting with the power snatch.

It's common for a beginner not to be able to receive the bar in an extremely deep position. It's normal for beginners to catch it a little high and ride it down into a deep squatting position. As long as lifters can descend into a deep position from wherever they catch the bar without having to take a step or losing their balance, it's okay to proceed.

Beginners who learn via the power snatch often end up for a long time able to power snatch much more weight than they can squat. In fact, learning to do the power versions of either the snatch or clean too soon is one of the best ways to hold a lifter back or prematurely stall progress.

Always teach or learn the full movement from the start, and you'll be way ahead in the long run.

THE LEARNING PROCESS

Ensuring that you're practicing and patterning the correct body positions is the most important aspect of the learning process. Lifting heavier and heavier weight with less-than-optimal biomechanics will reinforce incorrect movement patterns and set you back in the long run.

The rhythm of the lift is the second most important aspect. The bar should start fast off the floor, and get faster as the lift progresses before finishing even faster. The phrase "Fast, Faster, Fastest" is an easy way to remember this concept. Although the bar should be lifted as fast as possible, beginners can't follow correct rhythm if they make the initial pull off the floor too quickly.

When initially learning the lift, during the pull off the floor beginners are limited to a bar speed they can increase during the later parts of the lift. This necessitates many beginners purposefully pulling off the floor with a much slower bar speed than their actual capability.

For a beginner, it's more important to increase speed throughout the lift to achieve the correct rhythm than it is to pull quickly off the floor. Beginners need to crawl before they walk—and learn to start the pull slowly enough that the speed can be increased as the lift progresses. But make no mistake: The ultimate goal is to pull as fast as possible.

After rhythm, the overall speed of the lift is the next most important aspect of learning. Not only should the movement of the body impart tremendous speed to the bar, but the body itself—feet, knees, hips, torso, and arms—should also move with urgency.

Finally, once you've addressed the optimal body position, rhythm, and overall speed of the lifts, strength is the last thing to worry about: how much weight is on the bar.

Many beginners obsess over the weight on the bar, but won't spend much time practicing position, rhythm, and speed. If you initially concentrate on practicing these three aspects, you'll increase the weight on the bar much faster than if weight is the priority.

I had my first experiences teaching beginners how to perform the lifts in the mid-'90s, in Kansas working with high school football players, then a few years later in Texas working with more football players and their coaches. Trying to teach 30 15-year-olds to snatch is challenging, and it forced me to simplify my teaching method until it was easy to understand.

That early experience was key in developing my Three Step Top-Down Method, simply because several other methods I initially tried didn't work. The Top-Down Method proved to be easy to understand and learn, and it's what I've used ever since…and what we'll expand upon shortly.

I'm not in favor of using a PVC pipe to initally learn the lifts. Using no weight is almost as harmful as too much. An empty 20-kilo bar is enough weight for most men, while a 10- to 15-kilo bar will be useful for women and kids.

Additionally, I don't believe in practicing with an empty bar for an extended period. You should start increasing the weight as soon as you can, but only if the added weight doesn't interfere with the correct movement pattern. Most male athletes who attend my seminars can perform a decent snatch with a load of 50 to 60 kilos after a morning of instruction, female and youth lifters a bit less.

Practicing the snatch for two or three hours seems to be the perfect amount of time for an initial learning session. That's long enough to understand what to do, but not so long that frustration sets in.

SLOW DOWN AND DO IT RIGHT

Most people reading this know how to type. But ignore that for a moment, and imagine you're just now being presented with a QWERTY keyboard, and are asked to type a simple sentence. How would you do it? You'd use the hunt-and-peck method.

What if a great typing teacher had 60 minutes to teach you to put your fingers on the middle line, index fingers on the letters F and J, and type properly?

You'd be able to type a sentence faster and more error-free than just hunting and pecking.

But if there was a world championship of typing, no one would be hunting and pecking. The upper limit of human genetic potential to type fast is simply higher when using all your fingers than when using only two of them. If you want to be the best typist in the world, or just the best typist you can be, you'll put your fingers on the keys properly, look away from the keyboard, and practice.

In the same way, you must use your body properly while cleaning or snatching a bar or your ultimate potential will be lower than it could have been. There's a period while learning to move well that you'll actually be able to lift less using good technique than when using bad technique.

Most people can move an empty bar slowly through the correct positions from the shins to the hips within a short time of being taught the positions, and can properly extend and catch the bar soon after. But as you speed up the movement and add weight, all beginners reach a point when they miss the proper positions, and form deteriorates away from the form that will yield the highest potential weight.

This point of deterioration can't be accurately predicted for a beginning lifter. It varies person to person and day to day for the same person. Given a specific day and a particular lifter, the deterioration might happen at 30 kilos or 100, at 50% of maximum…or 80.

At some point, your best lifts will be achieved with a movement pattern basically the same as the movement pattern that will ultimately let you lift the highest potential weights. When you deviate from this movement pattern, you'll miss; when you maintain it, you'll make the lifts.

If you're not there yet, stop adding weight and moving faster when you miss your positions—don't wait until you're missing lifts. Slow down and practice doing it correctly.

This is frustrating, but millions of people have done it as they learned to type. Frustrating or not, you can certainly do it when learning to lift.

The need to slow down while learning sometimes leads to confusion. And that's exacerbated by the instructions given to achieve a proper rhythm in the lift. For a good lifter, the best rhythm is fast, faster, fastest: fast to the knees, faster up the thigh, then fastest during the second pull and the pull under. Your aim should be to have the bar and your body start the lift fast…and get faster as the lift proceeds.

But that's not how it goes with a beginner. When beginners pull too fast off the floor, they miss the positions. Or, they'll hit the right position at the knee, but have to slow down while pulling the bar up the thigh to "find" the correct position at the hip. Neither is helpful in developing good technique.

I tell those just learning the lifts to pull slowly off the floor, speed it up gradually as the bar comes up the thigh, then explode and catch when they feel the bar hit the right place on the hip on the snatch or upper thigh on the clean.

First, concentrate on the correct positions, even if you have to go slowly—even if you literally have to pause the bar at the knee and at the hip to make sure it's right. Then we'll look for the correct rhythm, taking out the pauses and speeding up as the lift proceeds, even if the actual speed has to start slow to maintain the position. Finally, you'll gradually add speed, but not so fast that position or rhythm are compromised. That doesn't mean pulling slowly is right for a lifter past the learning stage. You'll pull fast from the floor…just maybe not today.

CHOOSING THE CORRECT GRIP WIDTH

Before you start lifting, spending a few minutes at the outset to find the optimal grip width for the snatch will give you one less thing to worry about during the learning process. Each time you practice the snatch, you'll know exactly where your hands should be on the bar, saving wasted time adjusting and readjusting each session.

To find your best grip, stand upright with the bar in both hands, and begin to widen your hands evenly from both ends until the bar rests comfortably in the crease of your hips.

Then, to ensure the bar is in the correct place, bend your knees while also bending slightly forward at the hips. You should continue to keep the bar close to the body by actively applying rearward pressure on the bar using your arms and upper back. If you gripped correctly, the bar should slide into the crease of the hips below the bony protuberance of the pelvis, but above the thighs.

If your grip is too narrow, the bar will hang too low, and you'll feel it slide down your thighs. Conversely, if your grip is too wide, the bar will be too high on the stomach and won't descend into the hip crease.

Experiment with different grip widths until you find the grip that places the bar optimally in the hip crease. Although this grip may be changed later when you're more experienced, it's the most appropriate starting grip to learn the lift.

Photo 1.1—Correct grip width

Photo 1.2—The grip is too narrow

Photo 1.3—The grip is too wide

THE HOOK GRIP

Photo 1.4—Grabbing the bar

Photo 1.5—Tuck the thumb

Photo 1.6—The hook grip

The normal grip we use to pick up every-day objects places the thumb on top of the fingers. By simply making a fist as you read this, you'll see your thumb naturally covers the fingers.

To employ the use of the hook grip, the opposite should occur—the thumb is covered by the fingers and pinned between them and the barbell.

In addition to finding the correct grip width, I want you to learn to make use of the hook grip. It's long been known that a weak or loose grip limits the speed and power an athlete can put into a lift.

This is the body's neurological failsafe to prevent injury. If the barbell pulls the hands open and rolls into your fingertips during a snatch, the body hits the brakes and limits your ability to pull underneath the weight.

This is why the hook grip is so useful. It creates a stronger connection to the barbell by using the thumb as a "strap." That will greatly limit the potential for the bar to slide from the hands and will allow for greater velocity to move it overhead.

Beginners often find the hook grip uncomfortable. I promise that with continued practice, it will become second nature in no time and there will come a time when you can't imagine doing a snatch or clean without it. This is simply a growing pain every new weightlifter must endure.

I encourage you not to take the seemingly easy way out in the beginning by avoiding discomfort. That will only stunt your progress in the long term, and at some point, you'll need to return to this basic aspect of technique to make progress again.

The hook grip should be used on the snatch, the clean, and all pulling variations. I don't recommend the hook grip for the jerk or pressing exercises, as it could put unnecessary pressure on the wrist and hands.

Some lifters release the hook grip when receiving the snatch, and others don't. It's a personal preference and is something that should happen naturally.

THE OVERHEAD POSITION

Photo 1.7—Correct overhead position

Not only will the grip width affect the barbell's positioning on the legs and thighs as you learn and perform the snatch, but it will also influence the final overhead position. Your grip width should be wide enough so the barbell hits four to five inches overhead in the top position. Too narrow of a grip will put the bar higher, which could negatively affect balance, while too wide could put the bar closer to the head than desired. The barbell being too close to the head could put the lifter in a precarious position when missing a lift, potentially leading to injury. And, if the bar touches the head during a competition, the lift doesn't count.

The full receiving position for the snatch ideally involves an athlete being in a deep squat with the torso as upright as possible, and the arms fully locked out to support the barbell overhead. The shoulders can be either internally or externally rotated—this is individual and is based on each person's genetics.

The head should be in front of the barbell—so much so that if the barbell were to fall straight down, it would just barely graze the back of the head and fall to the upper back. The barbell should be resting in the palms with the wrists fully cocked back.

That position is the one I've found to work best for my athletes, but again, it comes down to individual preference. Many lifters struggle to keep the barbell in the palms while maintaining the wrist position due

to a lack of flexibility. Because of that, the bar will rest in the upper hand and fingers. That lack of flexibility is something that should be improved.

GAZE AND THE PRESSING ERA

The position of the eyes and the gaze of a lifter should be set straight ahead; avoid looking up. Looking up has the tendency to prompt lifters to tilt the head back, which could negatively affect the balance overhead. It also lends itself to using more of the upper body to move the weight, as opposed to using the powerful hips and legs.

The cue to "look up" is used by many coaches and is ultimately a remnant from the pressing era of weightlifting during the 1950s and '60s when the Olympic press was a competitive lift. At that time, the rules of the sport also didn't allow lifters to make bar-to-body contact on the snatch or clean, which led to the need for using more of the upper body.

Not allowing contact necessitates a lot more use of the upper-body musculature, which is obvious to anyone attempting a heavy snatch or clean with no bar-to-body contact. In addition to the press being a third competition lift, more use of the upper body led to weightlifters having much more upper-body development during the press era than they do now.

Looking up during the press, jerk, or snatch might not have been a bad thing for those who had that higher level of upper-body development. It wasn't uncommon in that era for lifters to press more than they could snatch.

The lifts themselves have also evolved—modern lifters use less upper-body musculature, and the lifts are now determined predominantly by hip and leg strength. Today's lifters lift more weight using modern techniques in the snatch, clean, and jerk than those of the press era.

As a community, weightlifting is still dealing with the ramifications of the pressing era. Lifters during that time who eventually found their way into coaching taught what they learned as athletes. A lifter learning in the 1990s would most likely have had a 40- or 50-year-old coach who came from the press era.

This was a time when the internet and social media didn't exist. The exchange of information was slow, mainly coming from books or person to person—there were no YouTube channels, and seminars were sparse. We had to read! Coaches in this country were few and far between; their gyms were isolated islands where beliefs and philosophies on technique were the way it was at each barbell club.

A person who started lifting as of 2010 or later will more than likely be less affected by the pressing era and its cues, such as looking up or using the upper body to lift. Those philosophies aren't completely gone, since some of those older coaches are still around, and their athletes, who may now coach themselves, are still teaching what they learned.

But now more information is available; there are no more "islands of lifting" and people can research multiple techniques from anywhere in the world, and at the click of a button can watch videos and listen to countless podcasts. Slowly, as the generations age, we'll eventually move past the older ways and continue to evolve the sport as the way we exchange information also evolves.

Looking up was once a good thing because of the demands of the sport at the time. But now, we must practice and learn to use the hips and legs more than the upper body. So, keep the eyes looking forward.

Do what feels right in the other positions. As a beginner, it will take trial and error to discover what's ideal for you. Experiment with different grip widths, stances, and positions to find what leads you to success in heavy lifting.

CORRECTING THE OVERHEAD POSITION

Not everyone is as blessed as lifters like Travis Cooper, Caleb Ward, or Kevin Cornell, who all had beautiful squat positions and exceptional shoulder flexibility. In fact, most of us need to work diligently to meet the high flexibility demands of the snatch.

Fortunately, there are numerous exercises to refine the final overhead position of the lift. Improvements here will also benefit the clean and the jerk, which we'll discuss in the second and third chapters.

The overhead position of the snatch demands a high degree of flexibility in the ankles and hips to allow the body to be upright in the squat, and in the shoulders to help keep the bar locked in its proper placement.

Your base is always a good place to start in your flexibility efforts. If you can't squat low, fixing your shoulders isn't going to help, but fixing your squat could fix your shoulder position. A house is only as strong as its foundation.

Here are just a few of the many exercises I use to improve flexibility.

SQUAT HOLD

Photo 1.8—Holding the bottom of a squat

For a weightlifter (or any athlete looking to perform at a high level), the bottom of the squat should be a position you could rest in comfortably. If you're stiff as a board and squatting below parallel is difficult, spending time in the bottom position is the most basic way to work on that.

Start small with 15- to 30-second holds, and work your way up from there. While at the bottom of the squat, put your elbows between your thighs, and push the knees out. Lift your chest as high as possible to maintain posture.

If this is still too difficult, hold onto a dumbbell or a kettlebell by pinning it to your chest, or hold the uprights of a squat rack for support. Then, slowly wean yourself from that extra assistance over time.

As your comfort level in the squat improves, you can hold at the bottom for longer periods of time. Shoot for between two and five minutes.

ACHILLES TENDON STRETCH

Photo 1.9—Stretching the Achilles tendons with a bar

Once you're able to hold the bottom of the squat without lifting your heels off the floor, you can progress to this stretch, which will target the calves and Achilles tendons. With an empty barbell in your arms, move into a deep squat, and then rest the bar across your lower thighs just above the knees.

Use the leverage you have with the barbell to lift your chest, and sit with good posture. You won't need a lot of weight—an empty bar will go a long way.

Just as with the squat holds, start with sets of 15 to 30 seconds, then try to work your way up to a minute. Travis Cooper and Jon North were quite fond of using this exercise regularly in their warm-up routines. If you can correctly perform it, do the same.

SHOULDER DISLOCATES

Dislocates with a dowel or PVC pipe are great for improving flexibility in the chest and shoulders. To perform dislocates, grab a dowel using a wide grip. Bring the bar up over your head and allow it to fall behind you, aiming to touch your lower back. Then reverse the movement. As you perform the exercise, keep your elbows straight. If they bend, take your hands out wider.

Avoid hyperextending at the spine to cheat the range of motion. Brace your abdominals and stand with good posture.

As you gain flexibility, to increase the difficulty, you can narrow the grip. Perform sets of 15 to 20 reps as part of your warm-up routine.

Photos 1.10–1.16—Shoulder dislocate sequence

SOTS PRESS

The Sots press is an exercise popularized by the retired Soviet weightlifter Viktor Petrovich Sots. It's an excellent tool to challenge both strength and flexibility while in a deep squat position. You can perform this exercise by holding a barbell on the front of the shoulders with a narrow grip (what you would use to press or jerk), or behind the neck with a snatch-width grip.

In either variation, squat down while holding a barbell on your shoulders using the desired grip, then use the upper body and arms to press it overhead. It's easier said than done—this might be something to work up to after starting with a dowel. Start with three sets of five reps during your warm-up, and as your ability improves, slowly add weight.

Work on your limitations. Everyone needs a little something different, and there are countless resources to pull from to put your body in better positions. Kevin Cornell was able to Sots press 115 kilos from the front using a clean grip.

Becoming more like Travis, Caleb, and Kevin is a good goal: flexible enough to hit efficient positions for the sport...and strong in those positions. In weightlifting, you don't receive any extra points for being overly flexible—you need just the right amount of flexibility. If you have too much, you risk losing force production and strength.

Intend for this flexibility work to complement and supplement your training, while learning the lifts gets the majority of your attention.

Photos 1.17–1.18—Sots press, clean grip

Photos 1.19–1.20—Sots press, snatch grip

THE THREE STEP TOP-DOWN METHOD

This method starts with the simplest movement: snatching from the hips. Snatching from the hips involves an explosive jumping motion, then catching the bar in a squat.

Snatching from the knees adds a little more complexity—moving the bar from the knees and up to the hips with hip extension, followed by an explosive jumping motion and catch of the bar. Snatching from the floor adds even more complexity—extending at the knees to move the bar off the floor, hip extension to move the bar from the knees to the hips, and then the same explosive jumping motion, followed by catching the barbell.

We start simple, and then each step adds complexity. For easy reference, notice that each step is labeled as:

o **Pendlay Step One—**
Snatching from the hips

o **Pendlay Step Two—**
Snatching from the knees

o **Pendlay Step Three—**
Snatching from the floor

It's okay to take multiple workouts to learn to snatch from the hips. After you learn that, you can progress to the knees. Take as long as you need to learn from there before progressing to the floor. The majority of lifters learn from the hips, knees, and floor in the same workout, but some take longer.

Remember, you can always go backward. Once you start lifting from the floor, if you're not getting into the correct position at the hips, go back and practice lifting from the hips. If you can't get into correct positions when the bar arrives at the knees, go back and practice lifting from the knees again.

These three steps will become the foundation for training the lifts in the programming chapters. Each position—hips, knees, and floor—will have their own personal records and training sessions. It's in this manner that you'll continually learn how to lift, how to train, and how to increase strength all at once.

THE THREE STEP TOP-DOWN METHOD: THE SNATCH

PENDLAY STEP ONE—SNATCHING FROM THE HIPS

After finding your optimal grip width, the next step calls for a snatch executed with the bar starting in the hip crease. To do this, stand upright with the bar and flex the knees about four inches, all while keeping your weight toward your heels.

Photo 1.22—Bar is held at the crease of the hip

Photo 1.21—Bar held correctly to begin step one

Continue to exert rearward pressure using your arms and upper back to keep the bar tight in the crease of the hip. Next, with no counter-movement or further bending of the hips or knees, forcefully extend the hips and knees, and allow the bar to immediately move overhead via the momentum generated by that short, quick movement.

The bar should finish in an overhead position that's at least even with the ears or slightly behind. At this point, the less you think about the bar path, the better. Many beginners try to overanalyze and over think the lift, which slows down the movement and creates confusion. You're trying to learn an extremely fast and explosive movement, and trying to remember a long list of cues will cause you to move slower.

Photo 1.23—Side view of step one: Slight knee bend, vertical torso, shoulders neutral

This short, explosive movement is the heart and soul of the snatch. As a lifter, you'll succeed or fail largely based on how quickly and forcefully you execute this small movement. I can't emphasize this enough: If you're unable to produce force from this position, you won't become a great weightlifter.

Conversely, if you're adept at producing force with the bar in the hip crease, that's as close as you can come to a guarantee of success in weightlifting.

MOVING THE FEET

That explosive upward movement should immediately be followed by a quick adjustment of the feet into a stance that allows a comfortable descent into the bottom position of the snatch or overhead squat.

Many people find it easier if the feet are "stomped" down with an audible clap of the shoes on the platform. This was a technique that Joe Mills, one of the greatest American weightlifting coaches to ever live, used with his athletes at the Central Falls Weightlifting Club in Rhode Island. In fact, many referred to the sound his athletes made as the "Central Falls stomp." I didn't have the opportunity or pleasure to know Joe Mills, but I greatly admire him.

I wholeheartedly agree with and teach the un-weighting of the feet during the transition from pulling the bar, to going under it, to aggressively returning the feet to the platform. The sound it makes is an audible cue that the transition from pulling to moving under was aggressive and forceful.

The feet leaving the platform is advantageous for most lifters, but as little time as possible should be spent in the air. The quicker you can get your feet back down, the more time you have to tighten everything from your shoulders and arms to your hips and hamstrings in preparation for catching the bar.

There's no clear line between pulling up on the bar and pulling yourself down into the receiving position. These happen as part of the same movement. This movement starts with an explosive extension of the hips and legs to propel the bar upward, and progresses to pulling the body down with the traps, shoulders, and arms.

Many lifters think of the traps and the shrugging motion as part of pulling the bar up, but it's mostly used to *pull the body down*. Extending the pull and attempting to get the bar higher by using the shrug and the shoulders and arms to try to pull the bar up are common mistakes made by beginners. This is a fool's errand that only accomplishes delaying the move into the receiving position, and results in the bar crashing onto the arms and wrists. The explosive extension at the top of the pull just takes a fraction of a second, and inside that instant, the lifter's body stops moving up and starts moving under the bar.

A small part of the shrug and the arm flexion and shoulder action can happen when the feet are still on the floor. This transfers upward motion to the bar. But most of it should happen when the lifter's feet are off the floor, and contributes to pulling the body down.

Correctly timing this change from pulling up on the bar to pulling the body under is one of the most important aspects of both the snatch and the clean. That's one of the reasons I advocate movement of the feet, with an energetic return of the feet to the platform. The sound created is audible evidence that the feet left the platform for an instant, and almost always coincides with the change between pulling the bar up to pulling the body down. The descent under the bar happens extremely fast, and much of it happens with the feet off the floor. The quicker the feet return to the platform, the better.

Many find it comfortable to widen the stance as the feet are slightly repositioned. Make sure your chest stays up as you reposition your feet. You should be looking straight ahead, with your chest pointed at the wall in front of you, not toward the floor.

ONE FLUID MOVEMENT

This portion of the lift can be learned slowly, but you should still emphasize creating a single fluid movement. The start and end of the various components of step one—the forceful extension of the knees and hips, the repositioning of the feet, and the overhead squat—should be indistinguishable to the naked eye.

It'll take a bit of practice to make these separate movements flow together, but keep at it until they're convincingly seamless. At that point, you'll have all the tools needed to execute a successful snatch starting with the bar in the hip crease.

To simplify the movement even further and speed up the learning process, the aforementioned cues and instructions can be condensed into one simple mantra: *Jump and catch.* Repeat this as a way of eliminating the urge to overanalyze the movement at this early stage in the learning process.

Jump and catch.

Jump and catch.

Try to avoid consciously thinking about what your hips, knees, and feet are doing or where the bar is going. There should be no extra movement or thought between accelerating the bar through the hip crease and catching the bar overhead with the arms locked. These two movements should happen almost simultaneously with the feet slapping the platform as the elbows lock out the bar overhead. Spend as long as needed on this first step, because if this step isn't fully ingrained in your memory and motor patterns, you have little chance of success in the subsequent steps. Although this initial step usually can be taught in a 30-minute session, use as many practice sessions as necessary to make this movement both automatic and fast.

Do not move on until you perfect this first step.

PENDLAY STEP TWO—SNATCHING FROM THE KNEES

Steps two and three begin by revisiting the position you learned in step one. This will ensure that as you start snatching from lower positions, you'll retain that quick, forceful movement you developed at the hip crease.

For step two, again start by grabbing the bar with your optimal grip width and standing upright with the arms hanging straight down in front of the body. As in step one, begin by flexing the knees about four inches, or until the bar slides into the crease of the hip. At this point, your weight should still be toward your heels, and your arms straight with the elbows rotated rearward until they're pointing toward the ends of the bar.

While continuing to apply pressure on the bar, bend only at the hips, and allow the bar to slide down just slightly below the kneecaps at about the position of the patellar ligament.

As you flex the hips, the knees should naturally move slightly backward in relation to the feet, without any change in the degree of knee-joint flexion created in step one. The actual knee angle as measured from the bottom of the hamstrings to the top of the calf muscle remains the same as you transition between steps one and two.

Once the bar is just below the kneecaps, the arms should be vertical, with the shoulders slightly in front of the bar. Your weight should remain toward your heels throughout this movement. This is the correct position to snatch with the bar starting at the knees.

Executing the upward phase toward the hip crease requires a reversal of the movement used to bring the bar down the thighs. The bar should move up the thighs in the same way it came down.

With the knee angle remaining unchanged, start extending at the hip joint until the bar returns to the crease of the hip in an identical position to that achieved in step one.

As you do this, continue to exert rearward pressure on the bar with your arms so the bar maintains contact with the thigh and doesn't swing out in front of you. Once the bar is again in the crease of the hip, repeat the "jump and catch" you learned in step one by forcefully extending the hips and knees, quickly repositioning the feet and descending smoothly into the overhead squat.

You should be able to go from step one to step two and back again with the weight staying toward the heels the entire time. Shorter lifters may feel the weight more on the mid-foot when the bar is at the hips, but you shouldn't feel the weight on the toes.

This transition between the knees and the hip crease can be performed slowly at first to ensure the correct body positions at each step. When you become skillful at transitioning between these positions, you can then emphasize creating a fast and fluid movement from beginning to end.

Photo 1.24—Bar is held correctly to begin step two

Photo 1.25—Side view of step two:
The shoulders should be slightly ahead of the bar

PENDLAY STEP THREE—SNATCHING FROM THE FLOOR

Photo 1.26—Bar is held correctly to begin step three

Photo 1.27—Side view of step three

Once you're comfortable snatching from the knees and hip crease, the final step is to move the bar to the floor. Start again at step one with your optimal snatch grip, with the bar at arm's length in front of the body. While maintaining rearward pressure on the bar, flex the knees four inches until the bar rests in the crease of the hip.

Bend at the hips and allow the bar to slide down the thigh, stopping at about the position of the patellar ligament just below the kneecaps.

Keep the back extended or arched, not rounded.

After revisiting the positions in steps one and two, lower yourself farther by bending at the knees using a squatting motion until the bar reaches the middle of the shins, or if you have plates on the bar, to the point where the plates reach the floor.

If you correctly executed the descent, your arms should be hanging straight down when viewed from the side, not angled forward or backward. The knees should barely be visible in front of the arms, and the hips should be back, just above the knees.

During the bar's descent, your weight should shift toward the heels as the bar is lowered from the hips to the knees, and then toward the mid-foot as the bar nears the floor.

KNEES—HIPS—KNEES

Just as in step two, the bar should move up the body in the same way it came down. To reach the floor, you will first flex the knees, then bend at the hips before finally bending again at the knees. You'll stand in the reverse order. With the empty bar at the middle of the shins—or if the bar is loaded, the plates are on the floor—extend the knees and drive your weight from the mid-foot back toward the heels as the shins become more vertical.

When the bar passes the knees, extend the hips until the bar again reaches the now-familiar hip crease. Finally, explosively extend the knees and hips to drive the bar overhead, reposition the feet, and descend into the overhead squat.

With these three steps, you now have all the body positions you need to successfully snatch.

To cement your understanding of the body positions during the snatch, let's take another look at the lift from the perspective of the knees and their movement in relation to the feet. In step one, the flexed knees move forward over the feet. In step two, the knees move back when you flex the hip joint. In step three, the knees move forward again as you flex them to bring the bar to the floor.

When you execute the full lift, the knees move backward as you extend them to raise the bar off the floor before shifting slightly forward as you bring the bar to the hip crease. During the final extension, the knees again extend and move rearward.

This backward, then forward, then back again movement is called the "double knee bend." Done at full speed, this happens fast. Many people can't see it even if it's pointed out to them.

In my opinion, this is why no one should purposefully concentrate on doing it, and this is one of the things this teaching method will help you do automatically. Don't *think* about the double knee bend. If you learn the lift the way I describe, it will happen automatically. If you think about it, you'll only slow yourself down.

Photo 1.28—Proper start position from the floor

*Photo 1.29—Side view of the start position:
When the plates touch the ground, the knees
should be barely visible inside the arms*

CLOSING THOUGHTS

Although these three steps are simple and easy to learn, many people rush through them and practice the positions incorrectly or even out of order. It's crucial to learn every step in the original sequence—move the bar correctly on the way down every time, pausing at each position.

If you rush through the steps and don't pause on the way down, how much useful time do you spend in each of the important positions? Barely any.

Conversely, if you pause briefly in each position on the way down as well as on the way up, you'll have accumulated 15 to 20 brief pauses in every position by the time you start lifting from the floor. That will exponentially increase the motor learning of the correct biomechanics while lifting and lowering the bar. In fact, through some odd magic in the nervous system, repeating the act of lowering the bar along the correct path is almost as valuable as raising the bar from the floor.

It certainly makes learning the lifts easier.

The lift should happen naturally, and your body should have a certain amount of looseness as you do it. Tightening up too much won't work. You can't move quickly when you're tense. If you feel tense, take a short break, relax, and try again.

I rarely use PVC pipe or anything lighter than a bar to teach the lifts. The lifts are easier to learn with some weight. A bar is usually a good starting point. At some point in the learning process, a little additional weight helps.

If more weight is needed, step two is usually the correct place to add it.

Photos 1.30–1.38—Full snatch sequence

After you've completed the teaching progression of the snatch, it's time to address the clean. Sometimes the clean can be approached in the same workout as the snatch, but if you have any doubt, address it in a later session. Better to go slower than risk a bad habit creeping into your movement by trying to do too much too fast.

We work on the snatch first instead of starting with the clean because learning the clean first doesn't seem to have much positive carryover to the snatch. On the other hand, if you learn the snatch first, it has significant carryover, and seems to make learning the clean much easier.

The pull for the clean is almost identical to the pull for the snatch; thus, the Three Step Top-Down learning process is nearly identical for both lifts. In fact, most of what you practiced in the snatch will transfer to the clean, which usually means the clean can be learned in about half the time it took to learn the snatch.

As with the snatch, you'll start by learning the full clean; don't waste time trying to learn the power clean first. Avoid the instant gratification that comes with catching weights in a high receiving position and continue to teach your body to catch the bar in a deep squat.

The main differences between the snatch and clean are their grip widths and the final position of the bar during the catch, as well as small differences in bar position during the pull. While the snatch uses a wide grip and finishes above the head via the overhead squat, the clean requires a much narrower grip, and finishes in the rack position on the shoulders via the front squat. For this reason, most people find the clean simpler and easier to learn. The snatch is largely self-correcting. If you don't do it right, you'll probably drop the bar. The learning curve tends to be quick when you start dropping the bar because you figure out in a hurry how to keep it overhead.

With the clean, however, it's possible to make much larger mistakes and still complete the lift. Because of this, I'll start this chapter discussing front squats and the front-rack position, both of which might not cause misses if done incorrectly but will certainly create bad habits that will compound over time.

THE FRONT-RACK POSITION

Photo 2.1—Front rack position: Notice his hands aren't closed around the bar—open or closed, either is fine

Photo 2.2—Close-up of the front rack position

Supporting the bar on the shoulders is likely to be an awkward position for most beginners. Since this rack position is critical to the success of the clean, it should be practiced before starting the Three Step clean progression. This will ensure that you understand where the bar should sit during the front squat, and will reveal flexibility deficiencies that may prevent you from racking the bar.

Start by placing the bar on the front of your shoulders so it sits loosely in the hands with the elbows pointing in front of the body. Push the shoulders forward and up, so the bar rests on the deltoids and touches your neck.

You can adjust your grip in this position by sliding your hands evenly along the bar until they're slightly outside the shoulders. The ideal clean grip for most people is two to three inches wider than the shoulders, which should ensure that your hands don't touch your shoulders when the bar is racked. If the grip is too wide, you'll encounter difficulty rotating your elbows forward under the bar during a clean.

If you've correctly racked the bar, the upper arms should be almost horizontal, parallel to the floor. The bar shouldn't sit on the clavicle bone or be supported by the wrists. In fact, the shoulders should receive the majority of the bar's weight, with the hands and wrists acting only as loose stabilizers.

Even when possessing enough flexibility for a solid rack position, beginners often try to keep holding the bar in the hands and on the wrists instead of on the shoulders. That causes the elbows to droop toward the floor, which in turn allows the bar to slide lower on the chest. Although this lower bar position may not cause problems with lighter weights, it will be impossible to successfully catch a heavy clean in a deep front squat with the elbows pointed toward the floor. It's imperative that you learn how to comfortably support the bar on the shoulders and not in your hands.

Don't worry if you have difficulty pointing the elbows forward. It'll just take a little work and determination to develop a more comfortable rack position.

CORRECTING THE FRONT-RACK POSITION

Even more than the overhead position in the snatch, the front-rack position in the clean can be particularly troublesome for people who lack sufficient upper-body flexibility. Continuing to work on the flexibility exercises outlined earlier is a good place to start. But if you have the foundation of a good squat and still struggle with the front rack, there's one exercise that will go a long way toward building a better receiving position for the clean.

Front-Rack Stretch

This exercise is best performed with a coach or partner, but I'll also describe how it can be performed solo. First, bring a barbell to your shoulders and assume the front-rack position. Try to keep a closed fist with as many fingers as possible on the bar, and let it rest in your palms. Your partner—who is about to invade your personal space—will then duck down so your elbows rest on his or her shoulders, with your partner's hands on the barbell just outside your hands. From there, the partner begins to stand, driving your elbows up while simultaneously pressing the bar down on your shoulders.

This stretch can be performed with or without the use of a squat rack. To use a squat rack, your partner will again duck under your elbows, place the hands on the bar just outside of your hands, and begin to stand. The bar remains in the rack, and your partner helps by pushing the bar into the rack while standing up.

You'll want to have a constant stream of communication when performing this stretch. Your partner should push the bar down into your shoulders, not forward into the throat where it could impact your breathing. If you feel like you're about to pass out, stop and reposition. After holding the stretch at the top for a few seconds, your partner would then lower down to ease off before rising again to see if both of you can push the stretch farther.

If you lack a partner to help with the stretch, you only need to make a few alterations. First, place a second barbell in the squat rack, and then put the first on your shoulders in the front-rack position, keeping the aforementioned position with your hands. Then, step forward to the rack, and rest your elbows on the second barbell. From there, bend at the hips and knees to squat down to sit into the stretch.

Try not to allow the barbell to lift off your shoulders; if you need to add a little weight to help with this, go for it.

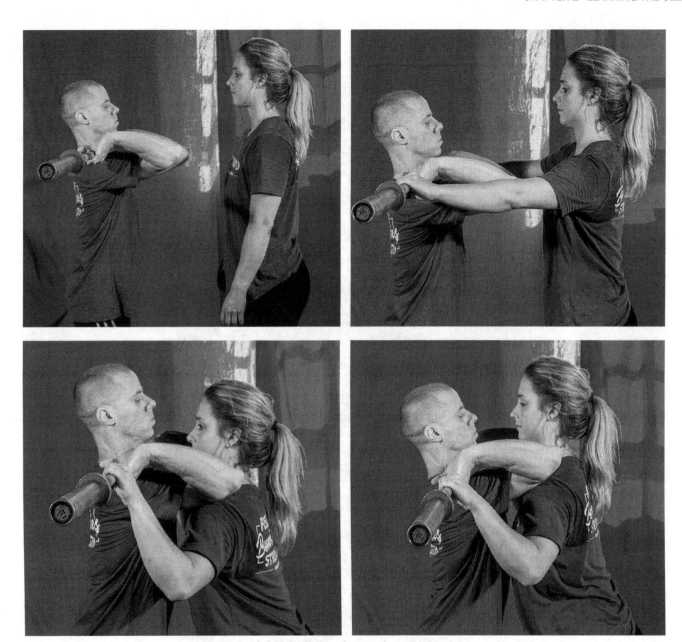

Photos 2.3–2.6—Partner front rack stretch sequence

FRONT SQUATS

Next, we'll build upon the front-rack position by adding front squats. As mentioned, to properly perform the clean, you need the ability to move quickly and fluidly into the rack position while descending into a deep squat. To safely accomplish that goal, we'll isolate the front squat to build positional awareness along with the torso and leg strength needed to clean heavy weights.

When preparing to front squat, take a stance that's about shoulder width, and as you go down, break first at the knees. Try to keep your hips as tucked as possible. As you descend, actively push the elbows up as hard as you can. Push them up even farther than you think you need to; they can't be too high. You should feel like you're doing most of the work with your quads, and your torso should remain upright.

If you feel yourself starting to kick the hips out too far behind, stop the movement. You might get away with that with a light weight, but eventually, you'll have enough weight on the bar that kicking the hips backward will cause you to drop the bar off your shoulders.

While learning, exaggerate the upright nature of the lift. There will be a time when it's fine to figure out how bent over you can go and still keep the bar on your shoulders—but learning the clean is not the time for that.

Photo 2.7—Front squat start position

Photo 2.8—Front squat bottom position

THE THREE STEP TOP-DOWN METHOD: THE CLEAN

PENDLAY STEP ONE—CLEANING FROM THE HIPS

After getting comfortable with the rack position, you'll now start cleaning from the hips, much as you did with the snatch. However, unlike the snatch, you won't be able to use the hip crease as a positioning landmark because the bar hangs several inches lower due to the clean's narrower grip.

The optimal position for the bar during step one is somewhere on the upper thigh, depending on your arm and torso length. To find this position, stand straight with your shoulders neutral, and bend the knees about four inches. For most athletes, this will put the bar somewhere between the hip crease and a position about one-third of the way down the thigh.

This position should feel comfortable and natural, much like it did for the snatch. If you have a long spine or short arms, or both, the bar will sit closer to the hip crease. If you have long arms, the bar will rest even lower on the thigh. Some athletes with extremely long arms might have more success with a slightly wider grip to get the bar closer to the hip crease.

Much like the snatch, the elbows should be rotated to point toward the ends of the bar with the arms extended almost vertically. If needed, pull the bar rearward against the thigh using your shoulders and upper back.

Now, explosively extend your knees and hips to propel the bar upward while simultaneously moving your feet into a stance that allows for a comfortable descent into the front squat. Following this violent extension, keep the bar as close as possible to your torso before receiving the bar at the neck in your now-familiar rack position.

Try not to overthink the bar path from the thighs to the neck. If you keep the bar close and aim for the rack position, the path of the bar will take care of itself. You're trying to learn an extremely fast movement; too much instruction or feedback can be just as harmful as too little.

Make sure your chest stays upright as you rack the bar, and your elbows at the finish are pointing out in front of you.

The bar landing on your shoulders should coincide with the repositioning of the feet, much like the elbows in the snatch locked the bar overhead at the same instant the feet hit the platform.

While many find it easier if the feet are stomped down with an audible clap, be careful to avoid spending too much time in the air to do that, which would cause the bar to crash down on you.

Photo 2.9—Correct grip width with the bar one-third down the thighs

Besides preparing you for the front squat, proper movement of the feet in the clean is integral to ensuring the correct usage of the arms following the extension of the knees and hips.

Photo 2.10—Side view with the bar held on the thighs

Picking your feet up off the floor is important because it prevents you from using your arms to reverse curl or upright row the bar into the rack position. When your feet are airborne, it's much harder to apply force to the bar using a curling or rowing motion. Properly moving the feet often fixes these faults without having to address arm movement.

Photo 2.11— Bar held correctly to begin step one

Photo 2.12—The shoulders are neutral, knees slightly bent, and the bar is held high on the thighs

One Fluid Movement

The final part of the lift includes a quick and smooth descent into the front squat, while keeping the elbows and chest up and the eyes forward.

This part of the lift can be learned slowly at first, but I want you to place emphasis on creating a single fluid movement.

The start and end of the various components of the clean—the forceful extension of the hips and knees, the movement of the feet, and the front squat—should be indistinguishable to the naked eye. As you practice more and begin using heavier loads, you'll quickly realize it's easier to squat under the bar than it is to pull the bar high enough for a power clean. If squatting under the bar doesn't feel natural, force yourself to finish every lift with a full front squat until the descent under the bar becomes automatic.

That "jump and catch" cue can be used effectively here to reduce a litany of instructions into its most basic components: jumping and catching.

Practice this simple drill until it becomes automatic and you'll no longer hesitate at each segment of the movement. Try to avoid consciously thinking about what your knees, hips, and feet are doing or where the bar is going.

PENDLAY STEP TWO—CLEANING FROM THE KNEES

Steps two and three begin by revisiting the position you learned in step one. That will ensure that as you start cleaning from lower positions, you'll retain that quick and forceful movement at the hips.

Photo 2.13—Bar held correctly at the patellar ligament to begin step two

For step two, stand upright with the bar held in front using a clean grip, and bend your knees about four inches until the bar slides below the hips to the top of the thighs.

Photo 2.14—The knees have moved back until the shins are vertical

Continue to point the elbows toward the ends of the bar, and keep the bar tight to the thighs by applying rearward pressure through the shoulders and upper back.

While keeping your weight toward your heels and with your back arched, bend forward at the hips and allow the bar to slide just below the kneecaps near the patellar ligament. Your arms and shins should be roughly vertical, and the knees should be slightly flexed, just as they were in step one. You should now be in the correct position to clean with the bar starting at the knees.

Executing the upward phase toward the hips requires only a reversal of the movement you used to bring the bar down the thighs. The bar should move up the same way it came down with the knee angle unchanged. Start by extending at the hip joint until the bar returns to the top of the thighs in an identical position as that achieved in step one.

Once the bar is again at the top of the thighs, repeat the "jump and catch" cue from step one by forcefully extending the knees and hips, quickly repositioning the feet, and racking the bar in the front squat.

As you continue practicing, remember to always start at step one and move down the thighs.

Repeating this top-down process will ensure that each time you bring the bar up toward the hips, you'll be passing through the correct positions.

As you learned in the snatch, the short and violent extension of the knees and hips is the key to success in weightlifting.

PENDLAY STEP THREE—CLEANING FROM THE FLOOR

Now that you're successfully cleaning from the knees and hips, the final step is to move the bar to the floor. Start again at step one with your optimal clean grip and with the bar at arm's length in front of the body.

While maintaining rearward pressure on the bar, flex the knees four inches until the bar slides below the hip crease to the top third of the thigh. Now, bend at the hips and allow the bar to slide down the thigh, stopping at the patellar ligament just below the kneecaps. Keep your back extended or arched.

After revisiting the positions in steps one and two, continue to lower yourself by bending at the knees using a squatting motion until the bar reaches the middle of the shins, or if you have plates on the bar, until the plates reach the floor.

As the bar starts to approach the middle of the shins, you should feel your weight shift forward from your heels toward the mid-foot.

Photo 2.15—Bar held correctly at the mid-shin to begin step three

Photo 2.16—Side view: After the bar passes the knee, the knees are flexed farther until the bar is where it would be if the plates were touching the floor

Photo 2.17—This is the correct start position from the floor: Shoulders neutral, head and eyes looking neither up nor down, knees slightly in front of the arms with the elbows rotated out

Photo 2.18—Side view of the start position

If you correctly executed this descent, your arms should now be hanging straight down when viewed from the side, not angling forward or back. The knees should be visible in front of the arms, and the hips should be just below the knees.

During the bar's descent, your weight should shift at first toward the heels as the bar is lowered from the hips to the knees, then toward the mid-foot as the bar nears the floor.

KNEES—HIPS—KNEES

As with step two, the bar should move up the body in the same way it came down. To reach the floor, you first flexed the knees and then bent at the hips before finally bending again at the knees. You'll stand in the reverse order: With the empty bar at the middle of the shins or with a loaded bar's plates on the floor, extend the knees and drive your weight from the mid-foot back toward the heels as the shins become more vertical.

When the bar passes the knees, extend the hips until the bar again reaches the first position at the top of the thigh. Explosively extend the knees and hips to drive the bar into the rack position, reposition the feet, and descend into the front squat.

With these three steps, you now have all the correct body positions needed to clean successfully.

CLOSING THOUGHTS

Just as with the snatch, when practicing the clean from the floor, it's often advantageous for beginners to move slowly at first, or even with short pauses at the knees or thighs to cement the correct body positions at each step.

You can also move back and forth between difficult positions, such as from the knees to the floor and back again. However, the overall goal is to create one fluid movement starting from the floor and finishing in the rack position without any pauses.

Photos 2.19–2.27—Full sequence of the clean

CHAPTER 3
LEARNING THE JERK

Of the three distinct movements in weightlifting, the jerk is the most difficult to learn for most people. That might be because the jerk is the quickest movement, or the issue could stem from the shoulder flexibility required to perform it efficiently. People often claim great jerkers are born not made, and I tend to agree with that sentiment. Although for some lifters, the jerk comes naturally and they can easily jerk a weight they can clean, others struggle endlessly to master this short yet technical overhead movement.

In learning the jerk, we utilize many accessory exercises, such as the press (also known as the military, overhead, or strict press), the push press, and the power jerk.

To understand the potential to put maximal weights overhead with the jerk, let's compare it to the press and push press. The press uses only arm and shoulder strength to move the bar from the shoulders into a locked-out position overhead. The push press uses leg drive to initiate the movement and arm strength to lock it overhead. The jerk (either power or split versions) not only uses leg drive and upper-body strength, it also relies heavily on a speedy descent of the body under the bar as it moves upward. This combination of movements—a powerful initiating leg drive, a strong push from the upper body, and a rapid drop under the ascending bar—will result in moving the most weight overhead.

Learning to execute these three components fluidly and with the right timing will be the most difficult part of the learning process.

STEP ONE—THE PRESS

Mastering the press is the first step in learning the jerk. To perform this movement, bring an empty barbell to the front-rack position, and place the hands just outside your shoulders.

As in the clean, the bar should rest on top of the deltoids, not on the clavicle, with the elbows held in front of the bar. The shoulders should bear the full weight of the bar, while the hands and wrists provide loose support.

With the bar positioned on your shoulders, press it straight overhead. The elbows will flare out to the sides—take care not to allow the bar to excessively loop out and around your head, which can occur as the bar passes your face. You'll need to tuck the chin slightly backward to avoid hitting it or allowing the bar to loop around it.

You're now learning the path the bar must travel toward its final overhead position. Allowing the bar to loop out around the head creates an inefficient bar path that will haunt you later when performing the jerk. Develop the habit of moving your head out of the way by tucking the chin; that practice will save a lot of heartache.

Once the bar has cleared your head, move your head forward again so the bar finishes at least behind the ears, if not completely behind the head.

Practice this with an empty bar until you can raise and lower the bar with no fear of hitting your chin or head.

Photo 3.1—Press starting position

Photo 3.2—Pressing motion

Photo 3.3—Press lockout and overhead position

STEP TWO—THE PUSH PRESS

The push press is the second step in learning the jerk. This movement builds on the press by adding a "push" from the legs—what's commonly called the "dip and drive."

To start, stand with the bar in the same rack position used for the press, with the knees slightly unlocked. With your weight on your heels, flex your knees about four inches before immediately reversing that movement and explosively extending the knees and

hips. Keep your chest and torso vertical in the downward and upward phases of the dip and drive.

This upward explosion is nearly identical to the violent extension of the knees and hips you practiced during step one of learning the snatch and the clean. This leg and hip drive should propel the bar upward. As the bar's speed slows during its ascent, your arms and shoulders need to start pressing, exerting upward pressure on the bar to complete its path overhead.

Once the bar clears your forehead, move your head forward through the space created by your outstretched arms to position it in front of the bar. Don't allow yourself to lean back when driving the bar overhead; this could throw you off balance and potentially cause injury.

You might tend to drive up to your toes when doing the push press, and it's okay for that to happen. Just as in the pull of the snatch or clean, don't purposefully extend up to the toes, but it might happen as a natural follow-through of the "jump" motion. Your body will be moving upward, and that momentum doesn't instantly stop.

Purposefully attempting to rise on the toes is likely to lead to overthinking, which in turn will slow your movement. If this rise happens without conscious effort, let it be. If it doesn't happen, that's even better.

Photo 3.4—Push press starting position

Photo 3.5—Push press dip position

Photo 3.6—Push press drive and pressing motion

Photo 3.7—Push press lockout and overhead position

STEP THREE—THE POWER JERK

After practicing the mechanics of the dip and drive together with the press, you'll begin to incorporate the drop under the bar that's necessary to complete a power jerk.

The setup and leg drive are the same as for the push press, with the only difference being that as the bar moves overhead, you'll move your body underneath.

Do this by re-bending your knees and hips while continuing to forcefully extend the arms against the bar. You're simply adding another dip to the end of the dip and drive used in the push press, such that the power jerk becomes a "dip–drive–dip."

The feet can stay where they are, but most people find it more comfortable to move into a slightly wider stance as they lock out the bar overhead. As in the push press, make sure your chest and torso stay vertical, and that you don't drive the bar forward as you go overhead.

This descent under the bar is necessary because of the rules of competitive weightlifting that state that a press-out is not a legal movement in the sport. Instead, the bar must immediately travel from the rack position to a locked-out position overhead without a visible pressing of the bar.

Once the barbell is locked in the overhead position, the elbows must stay locked until you bring your feet back underneath you or, if in competition, you receive the "down" signal from the front referee. Since this rapid lockout is expected in the sport, dropping under the bar is what you'll learn and practice.

Most lifters are either natural push pressers or natural power jerkers. As the weight gets near maximal, some will naturally want to drop under the bar even when doing a push press, while others will naturally want to press the bar for the power jerk. It's much better to instinctively move under the bar as the weight becomes heavier.

Most good jerkers want to move under naturally, and probably couldn't do a heavy push press with no downward body movement even if they wanted to.

Photo 3.8—Power jerk starting position

Photo 3.9—Power jerk dip position

Photo 3.10—Power jerk drive

Photo 3.11—Power jerk catch position

Photo 3.12—Power jerk full lockout

STEP FOUR—BUILDING THE SPLIT POSITION

The power jerk requires a lot of shoulder flexibility. The bar is harder to balance securely once you've received it overhead. That's because the feet are in line, and aren't providing a big base of support. If you drive the bar just a little too far forward or backward, it's likely to come down.

For this reason, about 90% of lifters are able to jerk more in a split stance. Splitting the feet provides a much larger base of support, and makes it easier to balance the bar overhead. It also doesn't require as much shoulder flexibility as a power jerk. Most people will be able to lift more weight and successfully complete more attempts with split feet.

Although the power jerk is a more simple movement, every beginning lifter should learn to split. You'll likely find you can lift more with a split, and if you spend your first year or two trying to power jerk, you'll be behind the curve when finally forced to use a split to jerk the weights you can clean.

Almost anyone who's been around weightlifting for the past 10 or 15 years can name at least one advanced lifter who wasn't forced to learn the split as a beginner, and later was unable to consistently jerk the weight he or she was able to clean. Often,

odd-looking leg geometries end up becoming ingrained habits, and the risk of injury is increased.

To find your correct split position, start by drawing a line on the floor in front of you. Moving heel to toe, walk two full foot lengths forward. Then, make a horseshoe-shaped mark on the floor to indicate where the forward foot will land. This measurement is a rough estimate of the length of your split jerk.

Look for a position that puts the front shin vertical and the back thigh near vertical—not precisely, but closer is better. Some adjustments may be necessary based on what feels comfortable in the final position.

Photo 3.13—Starting line

Photos 3.14–3.16—Walk heel to toe to find split stance length

Photo 3.17—Full split position

When performing the split jerk, with the toes placed on the line drawn on the floor, the front foot will move forward roughly one-and-a-half feet, while the back foot moves back about a foot. The weight distribution between both limbs should ideally be 60% on the front leg and 40% on the back leg. Ultimately, there's no way to tell precisely, but it should be a little more on the front than the back.

I can't stress enough the importance of bending the back knee to place the thigh at a near-vertical position. With the back knee straight, the overhead position will change in relation to the height of the barbell—and it'll be different from one lift to the next. If the back knee is down and the thigh vertical, it allows you to move under the bar without needing to adjust your overhead position in relation to the height of the barbell. That will lead to a more consistent placement of the feet and leg geometries when performing the split jerk as well.

Horizontal displacement due to a straight back leg when moving the bar overhead is the kiss of death in the split jerk. Legendary American weightlifter Norbert "Norb" Schemansky famously said, "If your jerk is done correctly, you should be able to jerk on ice." This means no horizontal pressure. The pressure on the feet should ideally be up and down as they move off and to the floor. Perfect balance is the ideal and is something to work toward.

STEP FIVE—SPECIAL JERK EXERCISES

The first four steps to the progression emphasize the pressing motion, overhead position, using the legs to move the barbell off the shoulders, and finding the correct split stance. Step five aims to fine-tune the split position by spending more time there to build positional awareness, confidence, and the ability to make adjustments. After spending time with the press from the split and the jerk from the split outlined in step five, you'll be ready to move to step six and put it together into the full split jerk movement.

PRESS FROM THE SPLIT

The press from the split is a great exercise to begin learning the split position. With a barbell held in the front rack, arrange your feet in a split position and perform a press to lockout, then lower the bar to prepare for the next repetition.

Photo 3.18—Press from the split start position

Photo 3.19—Pressing motion from the split stance

Photo 3.20—Press from the split lockout

You should be holding the bar on your front deltoids exactly as you did for the press, push press, and power jerk—nothing changes.

The bar should be pressed straight up until it clears the chin and face. Then, bring the head forward so the bar ends up locked out behind. Some coaches argue that the bar only needs to be behind the ears; it certainly needs to be behind the ears, but behind the head is even better.

Just as in the snatch and the clean, pausing in positions provides strength gains, confidence, and refined motor patterns. This is a major benefit provided by the press from the split exercise.

Too many athletes neglect spending valuable time holding the split stance and as a result, it feels foreign with heavy weights overhead. In the pauses, coaches can study and correct an athlete's position, which is difficult to do at full speed.

This exercise should be done with light weight relative to strength. The main goal is to keep the leg geometry from changing as the bar is pressed up and brought down.

When you can keep the legs in the same position for several sets of five repetitions, you can move on to the jerk from the split.

JERK FROM THE SPLIT

This exercise is almost the same as the press from the split, but adds a small foot movement.

Photo 3.22—Jerk from split position dip

Photo 3.23—Jerk from split position drive

Photo 3.21—Jerk from split start position

Photo 3.24—Jerk from split receiving position and lockout

Start the exercise with your feet in the same position as the press from the split, but initiate the movement with a modified dip and drive. Move the back knee slightly downward, and allow the front knee to flex a little. Quickly move upward by extending the knees.

As you dip, don't allow the front shin to move forward. In fact, neither knee should move, except for a slight up and down movement. Keep the rear foot up on the toes. Both feet should come slightly off the floor immediately after the upward drive, and the feet should be quickly returned to the same spot as the bar is caught on locked arms. The feet should make an audible sound as they return to the floor.

When this exercise is done correctly, the legs maintain the same geometry after the feet return to the floor as before the initiation of the lift. If you do a set of five, the geometry of the legs should look the same after the fifth rep as they looked on the first.

STEP SIX—THE JERK

Once you feel comfortable in the split position with the bar overhead, it's time to practice the full jerk. Start with the bar in the rack position and the feet hip width apart, although some athletes prefer a slightly wider stance. Execute your normal dip and drive, and quickly move your feet into the split position. The rear foot should move back about a foot, while the front foot moves forward about a foot-and-a-half. The feet should land at the same time, or the back foot slightly ahead of the front foot.

Make sure the front foot is flat on the floor, while the back heel is off the floor. The back knee should be bent and pointed down with the back thigh near vertical. The front shin should be vertical. At this point, you should be in your split stance with the bar comfortably balanced overhead. Finally, bring the feet back together with the bar motionless overhead.

How you execute this recovery is as important as the initial split—many lifts have been dropped because the lifter incorrectly recovered. First, move the front foot of the split back under the body before bringing the back foot forward and in line with the front foot.

Moving the back foot forward first can cause the bar to drift forward of your center of mass, resulting in either chasing the bar forward or dropping the bar in front. Always begin your jerk recovery by moving the front foot backward.

Photo 3.25—Jerk start position

Photo 3.26—Jerk dip position

Photo 3.27—Jerk drive

Photo 3.28—Jerk receiving position

Photo 3.29—Jerk recovery, front foot back first

Photo 3.30—Jerk finish position and lockout

CLOSING THOUGHTS

The snatch always receives a lot of attention when beginners first start weightlifting. A good deal of work is put into the clean as well, but one could argue that practice with the snatch definitely influenced the smooth transition of understanding the clean. However, the jerk isn't afforded that benefit, and as a result, it can be frustrating to learn.

The overall goal is to build a strong and well-balanced position you can confidently split into rep after rep. To accomplish that goal, you're going to need to devote just as much time practicing the jerk as you do the other two movements.

Here are a few strategies that can help you lay the foundation of a future world-class jerker:

o   Draw the lines on the floor that you learned on step four of the learning progression. Practice hitting the marks every single rep until you arrive at the point when you no longer need the visual cue.

o   Spend more time in the split position by adding the press from the split exercise to your training in one of two ways. First, perform a few sets of 10 reps with an empty barbell at the start of your training sessions as part of a warm-up. Second, add two or three sets of five to 10 reps at the end of a training session. Add weight to the exercise as long as you're able to maintain proper leg geometries in the split position.

o   Put all of the focus on the jerk by training it separately from the clean on at least one training session per week. In the coming chapters, you'll see examples of this and the previous idea.

Some people eventually discover the split jerk doesn't work well for them and gravitate to the power jerk. That's okay, but I encourage you to give the split jerk a few months of solid training and practice before making that decision.

At that point, if your natural ability is better suited on the power jerk, so be it, but at least we exhausted all options for the split before jumping ship.

SECTION B

TRAINING FOR AMERICAN WEIGHTLIFTERS

As I mentioned earlier, there's no definitive line between learning the lifts and training the lifts. That statement will start to make even more sense as we discuss how to integrate the snatch, clean, and jerk into structured training programs.

I intend to teach you how to seamlessly blend learning and training of the lifts with the goal of long-term progress. With that, I'll start to introduce special strength exercises and methods that'll facilitate progress on the lifts.

In the coming pages, you'll read about programming for beginners to advanced lifters, youth to masters lifters, and everyone in between. Every athlete is in the pursuit of continual progress on the lifts, but they all require different programming considerations to reach their ultimate potential.

This section is a culmination of all I've learned from programming for lifters of various populations. My hope is that coaches will use this information to help their athletes, and for athletes to gain a better understanding of the training process.

Photo B1—Everything a weightlifter could possibly need

A BRIEF SYNOPSIS OF EACH CHAPTER

CHAPTER 4
CULTURAL DIFFERENCES IN PROGRAMMING

It's the responsibility of athletes to be fully immersed in their sports. They must educate themselves on the history and understand how the values of other countries differ from their own. It's a mistake to ignore history and the way other cultures operate. Not repeating the same mistakes is a valuable part of learning that history.

In this chapter, I outline why copying the training systems of other countries didn't work for the USA, how American values affect our participation on the world stage, the role played by performance-enhancing drugs (PEDs) in the sport, and what we need to do to find success as "clean" athletes.

CHAPTER 5
HOW TO WRITE A WEIGHTLIFTING PROGRAM

Here I provide a general outline of how to write a weightlifting program. I discuss the three main goals of a weightlifting program, choosing the structure of the workouts, choosing a weekly or monthly training plan, and determining the number of repetitions for exercises.

In addition, I also detail training cycles and their application in the program. The subsequent chapters on programming expand on the information based on the skill level of the lifter.

CHAPTER 6
PROGRAMMING FOR BEGINNERS

There has always been negativity associated with being labeled as a "beginner." You know what? I get it. As a newcomer to the sport, your head is swirling with questions from the moment you step in the gym: "How often should I be squatting?" "What days do I train the snatch and clean and jerk?" "When should I do my first competition?"

It can be overwhelming and frustrating when all you want to do is lift heavy…but your technique doesn't allow for that yet. My goal with this chapter is to answer these questions and many others, along with providing a blueprint to help guide your training leading up to your first weightlifting meet.

The early days of a lifting career will be some of the most productive and enjoyable. The programming described in this chapter is intended to flow seamlessly from the initial learning of the lifts. Here, you'll learn how to begin to work toward both technical mastery in the lifts, and gain optimal strength, utilizing exercises such as the back squat, deadlift, and push press.

CHAPTER 7
PROGRAMMING FOR INTERMEDIATES

In the beginner programs, we laid the foundation of strength and technical mastery. Once the initial gains period has slowed or stalled, it may be time for a lifter to progress to intermediate-level programming.

This chapter outlines additional training days and methods that will continue to drive progress, such as complexes, lifting from blocks, timed sets, and the Texas Method.

I also introduce new assistance exercises into the programming, such as pulls ending with a shrug, high pulls, panda pulls, and power variations of the lifts.

Training as an intermediate will start to become more individualized from one training cycle to the next. I'll show you how to properly navigate this phase of your training career.

CHAPTER 8
PROGRAMMING FOR ADVANCED WEIGHTLIFTERS

Many people dream of one day calling themselves an advanced athlete, but don't know what it takes to be one. In this chapter, I detail what's required to perform at the periphery of the sport.

You'll learn even more about the need for recovery, the training schedule of advanced lifters training under me at Cal Strength and MDUSA, and the absolute need for individual training programs, along with examples from around the country.

In addition to that, you'll discover information about advanced training methods that can be used to drive progress on the snatch and clean and jerk.

CHAPTER 9
WESTSIDE FOR WEIGHTLIFTERS

I've long held a tremendous amount of respect for Louie Simmons. I firmly believe that with an open mind, members of the weightlifting community can learn a lot from him and the Westside Method. In this section, you'll learn about Westside Methods, including the Conjugate System, using bands and chains, the Repetition Method, the Max-Effort Method, and their applications to the sport of weightlifting.

The programming presented here is advanced in nature and in many ways is an extension of the concepts discussed in Chapter 8. True beginners should first follow the programming presented in Chapter 6. Intermediate-level lifters whose progress begins to stall can progress to the beginner Westside programming presented in this chapter.

CHAPTER 10
PROGRAMMING FOR YOUTH, JUNIOR, AND MASTER WEIGHTLIFTERS

People still think of weightlifting as a dangerous activity. That couldn't be further from the truth. In fact, weightlifting is an inclusive sport that welcomes participation from athletes of all ages. It can provide young children with activity, teens with goals and character-building, and those at the later stages of life with an athletic and competitive outlet. Here I present a case for the merits of weightlifting for all, and my thoughts on training and programming for all members of the aforementioned age groups.

CHAPTER 4
CULTURAL DIFFERENCES IN PROGRAMMING

American athletes and coaches have largely based their training on eastern European models from decades ago. However, it's not ideal to copy the training systems of other countries that are different from the USA in every conceivable way. Many of those countries had socialist or command-based societies where a top-down centralized approach with all the programming originating from the national head coach was more acceptable.

Countless athletes were placed into these systems with a few rising to the top. The emphasis was always on how the best lifters performed and how a country compared to other countries. In the 1970s, success in athletics was often seen as a validation of the political system. Even the great super heavyweight Vasili Alexeyev spoke about "defending the honor" of Soviet athletics and the Soviet system.

The emphasis wasn't on the individual, but instead on the overall system. The measurement of success was based on the team, the country, and the system producing results and succeeding against other countries with different systems. Because only the star athletes won medals, the success of the system was mostly graded on how well the top one percent performed.

Most competitive athletes were supported by their governments. This helped enforce adherence to the training system by denying support to athletes who didn't conform.

The USA is a more individualistic society, where we're used to more personal freedom and choosing our own paths. Here, athletes and coaches make their own decisions, and use training systems different from one another. For Americans, the emphasis of training and the measurements of success are based on individual athletes achieving close to their absolute maximal potential.

This applies to those who are born to be champions, and those who will never achieve stardom or anything beyond basic competence. The difference in approach between our society and others may seem slight—and in both cases the goal is to win gold medals—but when looked at through the eyes of athletes or coaches, the difference is monumental.

Late starters picking up the barbell for the first time in their 20s, 30s, or even 40s, or someone switching from a fitness program like CrossFit at these ages, will need different training than a future star who picked up the sport as a teenager. The variations will be apparent in both the amount and in the structure of the training.

For coaches, the difference may be even greater than for athletes. In many countries, the programs don't originate from personal coaches in a gym with individual athletes; they come from higher up the food chain. The job of a personal coach is to find a way to modify the programming to fit the athletes. As any coach will tell you, the difference between modifying a program that was written by others and creating a program specifically designed for an athlete is huge.

Until recently, the concept of recreationally taking up this sport later in life was unheard of in many countries. The idea of recreational weightlifting was born in the USA. We pursue the sport not because we have to, but because we enjoy the challenge that comes in achieving difficult goals.

Coaches in the United States can only achieve success by working with a wide variety of athletes. They can't limit their coaching to those who started early and have the talent to progress to the national or even the world stage. For those reasons, a top-down, command-based approach that rewards conformity to a centralized system won't work in the USA.

The American society and training system strives to bring out the best performance in each athlete, and allows freedom of choice.

THE SOVIET APPROACH

Periodization was one of the most significant concepts to come out of Eastern Europe. The Russian physiologist, Leo Matveyev, was one of the first to popularize it; it was then expanded upon by Romanian sport scientist Tudor Bompa and others. Periodization is a system that organizes training so athletes arrive at peak performance levels for the biggest competitions. The programming is progressive, and cycles through different periods in which certain aspects of training are the primary focus.

When reading about the periodized approach in the USSR and Eastern Europe, everything is recorded as an average of a group of lifters. If you read that a group of three "Class One" weightlifters did on average 33% of their jerk volume with power jerks, remember that no individual lifter might have actually done a third of the training using power jerks. Two lifters might have done no power jerks, and one lifter might have done nothing but power jerks. The average of the three might have been 33%, but that doesn't mean doing a third of the jerk training volume with power jerks would be ideal.

This data might point you in the right direction, but it doesn't give specifics as to what had actually worked for a lifter, or what might work in the future. For American coaches primarily concerned with optimizing training for a specific lifter, knowing the training averages for a large group of athletes is often not particularly helpful.

In training, the devil is often in the details, but the periodized approach assumes a lot. Periodization seeks to supply an adequate stimulus to cause adaptation, but not so strong as to overwhelm the ability to adapt. This is relatively easy for a beginner, but gets harder as athletes get close to their ultimate potential.

The timeline of progress is individual. One athlete might adapt quickly at the beginning of the training, and then just as quickly grind to a halt—often this can be explained by lifestyle, but not always. Another athlete might start with slower adaptation, but the increases in strength and the weightlifting total continue steadily for years.

The more detailed the training plan and the longer the plan continues, the further from reality it becomes.

And this is without considering the amount of genetic variation in athletes. Classic models of periodization might work better in homogeneous societies with less variability in genetics and lifestyle. But in the USA, with what are surely the most varied genetics of any country on the planet, as well as the greatest freedom and choice of lifestyle, trying to shoehorn individuals into a plan that lasts a year or longer is speculation based on unwarranted assumptions.

Often, when looking at the spreadsheet of a program written to conform to a periodization model, the prescription of exercises, sets, reps, and percentages looks more like manual labor than actual results-producing training. It's as if someone had a volume quota on certain exercise classes to be met during that week of the overall plan…like the tail wagging the dog.

Our goal is to make progress on maximum snatches and clean and jerks done in competition. The training process itself should be subservient to this goal, and not become a goal itself.

Periodization is widely used in American weightlifting—many of the programs used by or written for our athletes fall into the category of "periodized" programs. Periodization itself isn't the problem; it's good science when applied correctly. It supplies the needed variation and points training toward peak performance on a future date. All athletes need this.

However, the way periodization has been applied in the United States is often as a cookie-cutter program using a spreadsheet to be disseminated to many athletes. This has led to less-than-optimal results. We copied something written decades ago, or created variations on a theme that were usually no better than the original…and often worse. I'm reminded of another quote by Alexeyev when asked in an interview what he thought about other weightlifters copying his program: "Theirs, however, is a copy—not the original. Even though the copy may be a good one, it will always be a step away from the original."

Although easy to distribute to large groups of lifters, these programs rarely take into consideration individual needs, starting points, and rates of adaptation. Spreadsheet programs designed to be distributed to multiple athletes often don't account for the point of technical mastery or the level and rate of strength development an individual possesses.

Instead, athletes are shoehorned into a program designed for the average lifter or a peer group of similar lifters. An athlete might start at an advanced stage of strength, but at a beginning stage of technical mastery. Another lifter could have intermediate levels of technical mastery, but beginning levels of strength development. They don't need the same training, and it would be a mistake to use the same generic program.

Lifters need a systematic approach that encompasses both technical mastery and strength, and maximizes the potential of every athlete. We have to spend less time imitating and more time innovating.

THE BULGARIAN APPROACH

One Eastern European country was successful without using classical periodization as was practiced in the USSR. Bulgaria was the country, and Ivan Abadjiev was the head coach. As a tiny country with a small population, they performed head and shoulders above the norm, and sometimes even better than the USSR.

Bulgarians certainly used variation in training, but it was different from the highly structured approach popularized by Matveyev and Bompa. A lot of information is available on how the Bulgarians trained, but much of it is contradictory. Any accurate outline of Bulgarian training must include information from Abadjiev himself, as well as both European and American athletes who trained under him.

The Bulgarians based training around max-effort singles in the snatch, clean and jerk, and front squat. They achieved variety not through a litany of special exercises, but through periods comprised of difficult workouts and easier workouts, difficult weeks and easier weeks, difficult months and easier months.

During a difficult workout, they'd lift to maximum for a single, reduce the weight a small amount to perform a double or another single, and then work back up for more attempts at maximal weights. On difficult weeks, they'd go to maximum more often during a workout, and there would be more workouts where their maximums were challenged.

Several Bulgarian nationals and other European athletes who lifted at training camps in Bulgaria indicated that injured Bulgarian athletes unable to perform the competition lifts would perform exercises such as deadlifts, military presses, push presses, and back squats—all with significant volume. They did everything from maximal singles to sets of 10. These injured athletes trained several times per day, often maxing out on these exercises at each session, and eventually, when the injuries healed, returned to normal training.

These strength exercises weren't done in a progressive fashion. Several of the lifters who did this mentioned that training when injured was significantly harder than training uninjured. Was it punishment, or meant to encourage them to get back to normal training on the snatch and clean and jerk? Or was the strength work part of an overall plan that took periods of injury into account and sought to use these to their advantage? Abadjiev never fully explained this aspect of his athletes' training when discussing the Bulgarian system.

Donny Shankle, who trained under Abadjiev for a while, told me that when he asked him what he should train one day, Abadjiev turned the question around and said, "I don't know; what do you think you can do?" In talking to other American lifters who trained with Abadjiev, this seems to have been the norm. He aimed to push each lifter to perform as close to the limit as possible almost every single day.

The Bulgarian system is tailored for those who're anatomically and physiologically suited for the demands of the sport. It works well for the top one percent of athletes destined to be champions, but it's a frustrating system for those who aren't.

For an athlete suited for the sport who has the time to train and is willing to take anabolics, the system works. For those who don't fit the mold, it often doesn't. When Abadjiev came to the United States to coach at California Strength and was told that American athletes couldn't use anabolics, Abadjiev said, "Then why am I here? This is a waste of time."

His approach is elegant because it focuses exactly on what's needed—the snatch and clean and jerk—but it's also limited and caters to athletes built to withstand this demanding type of training, and who are willing to do anything to succeed. It needs modifications to be successful for a wider range of athletes.

AN AMERICAN APPROACH

I didn't develop my approach to weightlifting in a vacuum. In Moscow in 1992, Alexander Medvedev was the first person to show me how to snatch. He also gave me copies of his book, *A System of Multi-Year Training in Weightlifting*. The text was in Russian, and I had to buy the translated version from Bud Charniga before I was able read it. I read everything I could get my hands on about weightlifting, and this included information on Abadjiev and the Bulgarian approach. Even then, I could see there were drawbacks in either of these schools of thought if they were to be copied verbatim in the United States.

I tried to follow both of these approaches in my own training. First, I tried the program outlined by Medvedev for an extended period. Then I tried Abadjiev's approach, which I also attempted to follow for several years that included the time I was at my athletic peak as a weightlifter. It became apparent that the only way I could reach my potential as a weightlifter was to go beyond just copying, and to form an approach more appropriate for athletes in the US. Anything that will work for Americans has to be more individualized than what can be achieved by copying another country's method.

Other American coaches successful in raising the performance of athletes to high levels also had a huge influence on my personal training program and my overall training philosophy.

John Thrush wrote a training program for me early in my career. The program he gave me for my own use actually ended up being closer to the programs I eventually developed than either the Russian or Bulgarian models. John is a very smart guy, whom I probably haven't given enough credit for the influence he had on my training and coaching. John Coffee also helped me develop as a lifter and a coach. Both Thrush and Coffee have proven their ability to develop high-level weightlifters in the USA. It's an unfortunate reality that because both were coaching in an environment that limited or eliminated the use of PEDs, neither is given the same level of respect as that received by the top coaches of other countries.

Lon Kilgore is the person who without a doubt had more influence than anyone on me as an athlete and a coach. Dr. Kilgore is a scientist first and a weightlifter second, but he loves the sport and has been continuously involved in weightlifting from his teenage years to the present. If I were to call anyone a mentor, it would be Lon. He has a bias toward the Russian periodized system because of its base in science, but he doesn't let this blind him to other approaches.

When developing my approach over the years, I was heavily influenced by well-established and successful schools of weightlifting and the American coaches who mentored me. The periodized model as outlined by Matveyev, Bompa, and Medvedev is simply good science. There's beauty in the simplicity and specificity of Abadjiev's Bulgarian method. The training philosophies of other American coaches showed me that an original system that didn't follow a European model verbatim was possible.

I've also had numerous opportunities to converse with coaches and athletes from other countries, some who were extremely accomplished, and some who weren't. Informal meetings and conversations with a variety of people participating in the sport from different areas of the world can be a valuable educational experience. Everyone looks at the sport through a different lens; getting information from a wide variety of people including athletes, coaches, and administrators gives us a more realistic view.

I remember an accomplished European lifter with whom I had the good fortune to spend an hour at Worlds one year. I also had the opportunity to talk at length with one of his coaches. However, it wasn't until I spoke over beers one night with a couple of the lifters who trained with him that I gained a complete picture of his training and formed an idea of what made him a champion.

The inability to put the information into proper perspective is one of the downfalls of getting information from lifters you don't know. For instance, I attended a coaching symposium at the Olympic Training Center in Colorado Springs, where the top coaches of an African nation gave a lecture on their national training program. The program was based on the Bulgarian style of training, and they even had a former high-level Bulgarian lifter overseeing their training. It became apparent that the "Bulgarian System" being described was not what I or others had previously known.

Being under the assumption that the Bulgarians went to max several times per day, attendees were puzzled when no maximal lifting was prescribed in the program—instead only submaximal percentages were done for multiple reps.

After a little digging and a lot of conversation to get across the language barrier, the coach finally confirmed that maximal lifts were indeed done each training session, and that the percentages were based on the maximal lifts done at the beginning of that particular workout. The language barrier made it difficult for us to understand, but to the coaches presenting the material, going to maximum was a given and didn't need to be described.

This experience sticks with me as an example of how people from various cultures can draw completely different meanings from the same information. To get a realistic view of what's done in other countries or even nearby gyms other than your own, don't take things at face value; you have to dig deeper. Talking to an athlete about the training is often not enough, but once you talk to the coach and several teammates who are together in the gym daily, you can start to form a realistic picture.

STRENGTH AND PERFORMANCE-ENHANCING DRUGS

Of all the physical qualities needed by a weightlifter, strength is the most basic. It's also the quality that has the most potential to be influenced by training, and is also the most influenced by the use of PEDs. While strength can serve as a substitute for many things, there's simply no substitute for strength. Make no mistake, strength enhancement is the reason weightlifters use steroids. As some are fond of pointing out, there's no such thing as "technique steroids." These drugs serve one purpose: They make athletes stronger. And weightlifting is a strength sport.

For lifters using PEDs, there's a wide range of modalities that can increase strength. Strength gains come from either high or low volume, or high or low intensities. As long as lifters put in the work, they'll get stronger.

In the United States, we have the US Anti-Doping Agency overseeing drug testing of athletes. This No Advanced Notice (NAN) program makes it difficult for athletes to take PEDs and get away with it. However, countries with no NAN program have an advantage that not only manifests in competition, but in the way they can program training as well. We've all read about how lifters from certain countries don't need to do specialized strength work in the squat. With the added advantage of PEDs, the snatch and clean and jerk become sufficient in building strength. That ability to focus soundly on the competition lifts in training over athletes who will need to spend more time on back squats, presses, and deadlifts is another reason the gap in results between clean and doping countries is so wide.

Many American coaches copy the programs of countries that don't have an effective NAN program, but they don't get the same results because they're missing that important element. Without drug use, many traditional weightlifting programs won't produce the same results.

In the USA, we'll never be able to get away with widespread PED usage. Our culture won't allow for the use of steroids by weightlifters. In an interesting cultural phenomenon, we tolerate it for sports like baseball and football, but not weightlifting. Turning a blind eye to drug use would be the fastest way to completely kill the sport in this country.

When drug use is tolerated in any capacity, it quickly becomes necessary to take drugs to win. At the youth level, parents are already apprehensive about weightlifting because of the lack of opportunities for scholarships or high-paying athletic jobs in the sport. Parents instead push their kids to the more popular activities; if it were a requirement to use PEDs to find success, parents simply wouldn't allow their children to participate. A different approach is vitally important for American lifters: We have to learn how to get brutally strong without drugs.

TRAINING AS A CLEAN ATHLETE

In a perfect world, strength gains would come from simply training the competition lifts. The Bulgarians based their entire training program around the competitive lifts and front squats, and for them, this method worked.

However, a program based mostly on singles done in front squats and complex movements like the snatch and clean and jerk makes it difficult for lifters not using PEDs to achieve maximal strength. Building a big total for a drug-free athlete is a long and slow process that requires precise programming not only on the competitive movements, but also on the movements used to build strength.

With the current reliance on spreadsheet programs applied to large groups of lifters, we've forgotten the concept of progressive resistance. Performing an exercise like the squat for a set of five with 100 kilos prepares a person to do the same exercise for five reps with increased weight in a subsequent workout.

Very small increases each workout compound over a period of months and years. This concept is effective for strength exercises like squats, deadlifts, and push presses. Progress on these slower lifts is more reliable and consistent than on the competitive lifts.

For the faster competition lifts, this concept is harder to apply because of the increased technical demands. Every weightlifter knows that progress on the snatch and clean and jerk isn't steady or dependable. You may hit a new PR clean and jerk of 100 kilos and then go through an extended period when there's seemingly no progress until finally you have a breakthrough and clean and jerk 105.

In my approach to programming, I believe performing strength exercises that closely mimic the movements of the competitive lifts so increased strength on those movements can be used as a barometer of progress. If the strength exercises like the squat, deadlift, and push press are performed in this way, the strength gains in these exercises are more likely to carry over to the competitive movements. The carryover to the competition lifts will never be 100%, but there will be carryover.

And whether the carryover is 90% or 50%, even 50% of something is better than 100% of nothing. Whatever the carryover, increasing the squat and snatch-grip deadlift by 50 kilos will increase the max snatch.

We'll work to keep the carryover high by keeping the bar speed and movement patterns of the strength exercises as close as possible to the competitive lifts.

For example, you'll assume the same position you'd use on a snatch-grip deadlift as you would a snatch, and you'll be moving similarly and at comparable speeds to the competitive lifts when possible.

There will be repetitions performed with a lower bar speed than that of the competitive lifts and with slightly different motor patterns due to the amount of weight being lifted or the number of repetitions. It will be hard to execute the double knee bend on the fifth rep of a five-rep maximum (5RM) set of snatch-grip deadlifts or snatch pulls with a shrug.

It will also be difficult to make sure the bar breaks from the floor with the hips in precisely the same place on each of those repetitions. But in all cases, we won't let the perfect be the enemy of the good. As you get stronger, some portion of that strength will transfer. We'll try to keep the transfer as high as possible while continually increasing strength.

Gaining strength is an integral part of the training process; improving technical mastery is the other part of the equation. In weightlifting competition, we test via a max single on the snatch and a max clean and jerk. In training, everything is judged by how it will affect the max singles done in competition.

The first program I implement for beginners uses singles in the snatch and clean and jerk, and I stay as close as possible to that model. If an athlete can make continual progress in the competition lifts while sticking with only high-intensity singles in training, there's no reason to stray from this plan. For most, however, a certain amount of variety in the training stimulus leads to faster progress.

An athlete might need variety purely for mental reasons. The reason for the variety need isn't important as long as progress is made on the competition lifts.

CLOSING THOUGHTS

Both the periodized philosophy that originated in the USSR and the Bulgarian approach created champions and produced world records. We know these training systems worked for lifters taking PEDs. Whether these approaches can produce champions and world records without drug usage has always been unclear.

An effective training system in the USA has to produce high performance in a drug-free environment.

We can't depend on a training volume that's so high it can turn weightlifting into manual labor.

We also can't base our training programs on constant max-effort singles and lifts, because that method seems to work for only a small segment of the population.

An American system needs to work for a variety of ability levels and training situations. Using derivatives of the snatch and clean and jerk in addition to the actual competition lifts enables more lifters to build technical mastery. Strength exercises and rep schemes other than maximal front squat singles allows more drug-free athletes to build the strength required for peak performance.

CHAPTER 5
HOW TO WRITE A
WEIGHTLIFTING PROGRAM

The huge volume of training systems and trying to choose between them was one of the things that intimidated the hell out of me back in the early 1990s.

Bulgarian. Russian. Max every day if you want to progress. Going to max too often stunts progress. Pulls are key. Pulls are useless. The Hatch system. The Calpian system. The Greek system.

How do you choose?

Even the most productive coaches argue endlessly about what's right and wrong. How in the world is a beginner to know?

A Bulgarian lifter made me stop and think about this when he asked, "Why does everyone in the US argue about which training system is best? We all do the same system. We snatch, we clean and jerk, and we squat. The rest are just useless details."

If you put three weightlifters training the snatch in a group of 100 "regular" trainees in a gym, will it be hard to spot the weightlifters? Will it matter if one of them is doing snatch pulls, or one is power snatching? Will it matter if one is going to maximum, then dropping down to do lighter doubles, and the other is working with percentages, starting with a series of doubles at 80 and 85 percent, then ending with singles at 90, 92.5, and 95 percent?

No. It won't matter at all. One would instantly know the weightlifters. What they're doing is alike enough and different enough from what all the other trainees are doing to immediately know they're all doing the same sport, something different from the others.

This is a similar situation to learning to play the piano. The most important element of learning to play the piano is to sit down at the piano and make an attempt to hit the right keys at the right time with the right fingers.

Strumming a guitar won't do it; running or lifting weights or perfecting your jump shot won't do it—only sitting in front of that piano will do it. Sure, there are good piano instructors and bad piano instructors, but isn't the particular method or drill irrelevant compared to just sitting in front of a piano and hitting keys instead of working on your jump shot?

The most important thing about the training of a weightlifter is to train the snatch, the clean and jerk, and squat. The rest are just details...and knowing that makes the whole process a lot less intimidating.

EXPOSING THE FINE DETAILS OF PROGRAMMING

The goal of this chapter is to demystify programming and training for weightlifting. To do that, I'll dismantle the training system I developed over the last several decades of coaching. With any luck, beginners reading this won't be as intimidated like I was in the 1990s when presented with all the different styles and training methodologies to wade through.

First, we'll take a look at a typical training week from the Cal Strength and MDUSA days. This will be useful for beginners to see the structure of a full weightlifting program and join in the discussion of its inner workings. I want you to know what we did in training and why each of the elements was important. With this working knowledge of how the program is outlined, the finer details will start to make more sense.

From there, I'll present basic information on how anyone with just the knowledge described in this chapter could structure workouts, choose a weekly and monthly training plan, select repetition ranges, and evaluate progress on the snatch, clean and jerk, and strength lifts.

I'll also go into detail on the finer points of training, such as how strength and technique on the lifts affect one another, specificity and adaptation, and how someone who already has a strength training background can transition into weightlifting.

This is the first part of a comprehensive breakdown of programming and training for weightlifting using my system. The analysis will continue across the following programming chapters.

Photo 5.1—Jon North preparing to snatch

A LOOK BACK AT CAL STRENGTH AND MDUSA PROGRAMMING

THE SNATCH AND CLEAN AND JERK

The backbone of our program in the Cal Strength and MDUSA days involved three main workouts: Monday, Wednesday, and Friday afternoon. These were our three heaviest workouts on the snatch and clean and jerk. Friday was always the competitive lifts, while the other two days might have included variations, like lifts off a box or from the hang. But, whatever the variant, these were definitely the three heaviest workouts, the sessions where we expected lifts over 90 percent.

The emphasis was usually to get to the heaviest possible single on the lifts, then do back-off sets. The set and rep counts of the two lifts changed depending on the lifter and the particular needs, but they were always to go heavy on the competitive lifts or close variations.

We did a morning workout Monday through Friday. These workouts were normally not as heavy, and concentrated more on doubles rather than singles. We often did the power versions of the lifts on these workouts, and went to max. But max on a power version is usually only 80 to 90 percent of a full lift. And

when we did the full lifts or a variation, we usually didn't go heavier than what the athlete could do for a power version.

STRENGTH EXERCISES

We finished the workouts with an overhead strength exercise. Push presses were the most widely used, but based on the individual lifter, it might have been presses, push presses, power jerks, or jerks. Those workouts added a lot of the overall training volume; to address the individual needs of the athletes, the exercises were more variable than in the afternoon.

Squatting was usually programmed with one thing in mind: whatever will keep the squat moving upward but giving the least interference with the rest of training. Often a program like the Texas Method can work, as will be discussed in Chapter 7, but we add one more session to accomplish this: a Saturday session when squatting is prioritized and is done first, followed only by overhead strength work, like pressing or push pressing, or jerk practice.

I planned a volume workout on Monday, a light workout on Wednesday, and an intensity day on Saturday, always trying to make some sort of PR. The first two squat sessions could be done in either the morning or the afternoon sessions, whichever best fit that particular lifter.

When we arrived at the point that Texas Method squatting wasn't increasing the squat, we switched to something different. This was sometimes something that might at least temporarily interfere with the competitive lifts. The squat has to move up.

There are a lot of options; the Smolov program is one we used. It's a four-day-a-week program of back squats, and is high enough in volume that it needs to be done during the Monday, Wednesday, or Friday morning training sessions during the week, and on Saturday. Another option is frequent max-effort front squats. Find what works to get your squat up. There isn't a single best way; just find what works.

The squat has to move up…or you need to find another way.

PROGRAMMING SIMPLIFIED

Nothing generates controversy in the world of weightlifting more than programming, except for proper technique, who coached whom, and drugs. But all that aside, there are plenty of arguments about how to program, and I'd like to present some simple steps that should allow just about anyone to write a decent program, no controversy needed.

STEP ONE

Do enough snatching to make progress on the snatch. Seems simple enough, doesn't it? It *is* simple, but there are qualifications to help with the decisions.

Beginners can usually become steadily better at the snatch with only two or three snatch sessions a week. As you progress, you'll probably find that adding sessions helps keep the progress moving. But don't dismiss snatching three times a week as only for rank beginners; plenty of people have snatched big weights training the lift three times a week. Start with two or three snatch sessions a week, and use common sense as a guide.

When you snatch, what exactly do you do? There are many snatch variations to choose from. Use the competition-style lift as your default position, and if there aren't special considerations, do full snatches from the floor.

But there are many reasons you might want to do something else for one or more of your snatch sessions. If your technique is bad, or you're just learning the lift, you might want to include partial lifts, such as the snatch from the hips or from the knees. Variations like this are simple, make it easier to do at least part of the lift correctly, and help reinforce good technique.

There are many variations. Educate yourself on the possibilities, and include those you think will help. Keep in mind that the default should always be the actual competition lift, and barring a good reason, those should make up the bulk of your training.

STEP TWO

Do enough clean and jerks to make progress on the clean and jerk. The advice for the snatch applies here, but remember that the clean and jerk is two movements that can be separated.

As with the snatch, if there are no special considerations, do the whole lift as it's done in competition. But if your technique is bad or you're just learning,

you can simplify it to make it easier to learn good technique on one part of the lift at a time.

You can do cleans by themselves, or jerk from a rack or block without first cleaning the weight. Separating the lifts this way often makes it easier to work on a deficiency. But even if you find this useful, try to do the clean and jerk in the competition style at least once a week.

STEP THREE

Get stronger.

Squats are the most important strength exercise for weightlifters. Other valuable choices include front squats, push presses and presses, RDLs, and pulls with a snatch or clean grip. But squats are the most important and can be sufficient by themselves.

There are a million strength programs. Most will be successful if you put in the work, but squatting two or three times a week for multiple sets at a medium-rep range of four to six is popular in weightlifting and general strength training circles for a reason. Let that model form the foundation of your default strength program unless there's a good reason to do something different. There you go: the backbone of a weightlifting program.

Common sense should eventually allow you to fill in most of the rest of the details yourself, but a few hints might help things along.

CHOOSING THE STRUCTURE OF YOUR WORKOUTS

Doing the snatch first, then the clean and jerk, and finally the squat is the most popular way to structure a workout. When one specific way of doing things is the most popular by lifters from around the world over many decades, you should pay attention. There's a reason it's popular.

In this case, snatches don't seem to interfere with what you can accomplish in the clean and jerk or squat if done after snatching, but heavier exercises seem to impede the snatching if done first. Once you're in decent shape, the competitive exercises hinder the squats less when squats are at the end of the workout than squats interfere with the competitive exercises if squats are done first.

Some people do front squats with a low volume prior to the competitive lifts, and it seems to work just fine. If your leg strength is a serious weakness, experiment with this. But if there are no special considerations, the order of snatch, clean and jerk, and then squat will probably work for you.

Within one movement, you can structure the lifts however you want, or at least any way that leads to gradually increasing the weights over time. One popular way is a series of singles, doubles, or triples within a workout, all at the same weight, but trying to increase the working weight over time.

Another option is to just work up to a daily max, then add volume to the workout by either taking weight off and working back to another max a time or two, or by adding a few doubles or triples or even more singles a few kilos lighter than your best for the day.

Something in between will also work—anything where you're challenging yourself and gradually increasing the weight over time.

CHOOSING THE WEEKLY OR MONTHLY PLAN

The simplest weekly program is to snatch, clean and jerk, and squat three non-consecutive days per week. Snatch or clean and jerk variations can be substituted for the competition exercises if there's a good reason, but don't get too far from doing heavy competition lifts on a regular basis.

Setting aside Friday, or your third workout of the week, for going as heavy as possible for singles on the competition lifts is a worthwhile strategy. The first two training days of the week can be used for doubles or triples (if you do them) or variations of the lifts (if you do them). Using at least one workout per week as a test day for the competitive lifts can keep you grounded in what's really important, namely… snatching and clean and jerking more weight for one rep at a time.

Planning your training over a month, or even several months, can be as simple or as complicated as you want to make it. People—especially beginners—have been plenty successful with virtually no planning, just continually challenging themselves to beat PRs in the various training lifts.

But often enough, people can't deal with the mental and physical boredom of doing the same thing all the time, so some variation is useful. There's nothing wrong with paying extra attention to pushing the squat up at certain times of the year, limiting the volume of the snatch and clean and jerk to help accomplish this.

It's viable to focus more on variations of the lifts and doubles and triples when distant from a competition, then gradually concentrating more on the competition lifts for singles as the contest approaches.

However, if you opt for variety, don't stray from the basics too far or for too long.

CHOOSING THE NUMBER OF REPS

For the snatch and clean and jerk, anything above three reps should eventually be self-correcting. Most people who try sets of five on the clean and jerk with any decent load quickly abandon the notion that the competitive lifts can be trained with higher reps. Accomplished lifters use sets of one to three almost exclusively, and singles or doubles are far more popular even than triples.

There's no magic rep scheme. Some people train productively using doubles and triples. Some use nothing but singles. Mix things up a little, and even include sets of five on the hang snatch every once in a while for a change of pace.

There's no right or wrong answer.

Photo 5.2—Jared Fleming, the focus of a champion

WHAT ARE TRAINING CYCLES?

Training cycles are discrete periods of time when you'll be setting a goal and trying to reach that goal by the end of the cycle. I recommend starting with training cycles that are about eight weeks in length. Eight weeks is a long enough time to see positive changes, but not so long that you lose sight of the goal. Training cycles introduce variation into training, which is why I'm not a big proponent of training cycles longer than 12 weeks. When you do training cycles longer than 12 weeks, you eventually lose the variation that makes training cycles advantageous in the first place.

Each training cycle has a beginning, which is normally a week or two of lighter or less stressful training. That's followed by the main work period, normally consisting of four or five weeks of hard training. Next, we have a peaking period of slightly decreased training stress, and finally, a competition.

A training cycle is a form of periodization where training changes throughout the cycle in a specific way that gives the athlete the best chance to perform at a high level the day of the competition.

For your first training cycle, or even your first few cycles, the week-to-week variation will be minimal. As you progress through many training cycles, the week-to-week variance increases. The time it takes to get to full intensity and training load at the beginning of the cycle will lengthen, and the time it takes to peak at the end of the training cycle and to reach full capabilities in competition will also increase.

The period at the beginning of the cycle can range from less than a week to one or two weeks. The peaking period at the end of the cycle can go from less than a week to two or three weeks. This means that as you progress as a lifter, training cycles out of necessity get longer. That's the natural progression as performance rises, and beginners PR all the time for a litany of reasons, while intermediate and advanced lifters see fewer PRs in training.

The 10th training cycle in your career should have a more dramatic drop in volume than the initial cycles, and a rise in intensity as that cycle progresses. The training load will no longer be the same for each week of training. Much as how the Texas Method varies intensity and volume throughout the week, as we'll discuss in detail, a training cycle will eventually vary volume and intensity. The beginning of the cycle will be higher in volume, while the end will be higher in intensity.

PERCENTAGES IN TRAINING

Most weightlifting programs rely on percentages to determine the weights used on various days.

However, for many athletes—especially novice or advanced—percentages shouldn't be the last word in choosing weights.

It's typical for a novice to be able to max out with a 70-kilo snatch that's ugly and all over the platform, but still make the lift. This same person might not be able to do 60 kilos for several sets or reps with consistently good form.

Sixty kilos is about 85% of 70, but it's common for a training program to call for several doubles at 85%. Practicing with a weight like 60 kilos, which would ensure rep after rep of bad form, wouldn't be the best choice. If 35 kilos is the most at which an athlete can show consistently good technique, that should be the main training weight even though it is only 50% of max.

The lifter should continually attempt to raise the weight at which he or she can show good form. There will be periodic attempts with higher weights—and even attempts with new maximums regardless of how ugly.

But there should always be more "perfect" lifts than ugly, no matter how low that takes the weight.

An advanced lifter is at the other end of the spectrum. Caleb Ward has the most consistent technique of any lifter I coached and is a good example here. For him, doing anything up to 90% is about as challenging as getting out of bed in the morning. Holding his training weight down because he's only supposed to hit a certain percentage would decrease the training effect of his workouts.

Percentages are good guidelines, especially for average lifters who are neither novice nor advanced. However, guidelines shouldn't be blindly followed without regard to the individual athlete.

You should never make 100% of your lifts in any session. If you do, it says one thing:

You're training too light.

Many people talk endlessly about the evils of too many misses, and there's no doubt, lots of misses are a bad thing.

But making all your lifts is probably even worse. It means you don't have the guts put weight on the bar.

Putting 100 kilos on the bar is absolutely the necessary first step in snatching 100.

Have the courage to load the weight.

Of weights you load on the bar, you should make about 85% of those lifts. I've put this number between 70% and 95% at various times when I was in different moods. But 85% is a good middle ground.

If you usually make too many more than this, you may be training too light. If you make too many fewer, you may be training too heavy and not developing good motor patterns as quickly as you could.

This applies mostly to singles and doubles on the snatch and clean and jerk, but when using a rep max of three or five reps on, say, the squat, when do you call it quits? There's no hard and fast rule. If you're doing a 5RM, rep number five is picture perfect, and your name isn't Caleb Ward, you're training too light.

Form breaks down with heavy weight. And for a normal human, it's impossible to be moving picture perfect on the last rep of a 5RM…period. On the other hand, if rep number one is dangerously bad, take weight off the bar. Most 5RMs will break down to some extent between reps two and four.

Every weightlifter should remember this: The whole point of weightlifting is to lift the most weight. Err on the side of *going for it!*

Don't fail for lack of trying.

STRENGTH VERSUS TECHNIQUE

Although in the sport of weightlifting, this debate of strength versus technique is ridiculous and has been recognized as such from the start, it still persists. Wherever there's a shortage of experience and common sense, this rears its ugly head. This commentary will be yet another attempt to slay this beast, and no doubt, it will again fail.

Let's imagine that the level of a lifter's strength and technique are both illustrated by having a certain number of pebbles. Suppose one could have between zero and 100 strength pebbles. Zero indicates an inability to do a squat with bodyweight, no bar or weight added. One hundred indicates a complete and total realization of any and all strength possible given the genetic potential.

The technique, pebbles, operates along the same lines; it's the person with the most total pebbles who will lift the most weight. Now to make this realistic, let's add a couple more conditions.

First, let's assume that as you accumulate pebbles, whether strength or technique, each pebble of that particular variety becomes harder and harder to pick up and hold onto.

It's relatively easy to pick up the first 20 strength pebbles, and even easier to retain them. This might represent going from not being able to squat bodyweight unassisted, to being able to squat with a 150-pound bar. It's very easy to achieve that, and given any level of activity or training, it's also easy to maintain.

But with each accumulated pebble, picking it up becomes harder, as does retaining it, so much so that picking up the last 10 is more difficult than the first 90. After all, isn't going from a 500-pound squat to 600 harder and more time consuming than getting up to 500 pounds in the first place? It certainly is for most people.

Second, suppose that once either strength or technique gets a certain amount ahead of the other, further increases are useless and don't count.

You might have the most beautiful pull in the world, and a transition going under the bar that's poetry in motion, but if you're not strong enough to stand up with the weight, it's wasted.

And if you're pulling the bar in a manner that makes biceps strength the limiting factor, is increasing the squat going to help you? Are your biceps ever going to be strong enough to break a world record?

Think about these conditions and what they mean. If your imagination is lacking, let me help:

o   To lift the largest weights, it takes a high level of strength *and* a high level of technique.

o   A relative lack of either quality makes subsequent focus on the other quality inefficient and self-limiting.

o   Achieving a balance of both qualities is always the easiest and fastest way to a given level of performance.

o   We should all be trying to increase both qualities with a focus on whichever is the most lacking.

o   There's no reasonable argument to be made that either quality should be prioritized to the point of letting the other fall behind.

There it is, simple and logical.

And it'll make no difference whatsoever to those engaged in this silly debate.

STRENGTH INCREASES DRIVE LONG-TERM PROGRESS

While in a high-volume squatting or strength phase, the snatch and clean and jerk are likely to temporarily go down. When people recover from the intense strength work, the lifts usually take a jump…and recover more than the lost ground.

While practice on the snatch and clean and jerk is important, strength increases are the real driver of long-term progress in weightlifting. The competitive lifts are often talked about in terms of the relationship with the squat, and it's safe to say no one will ever snatch or clean and jerk more than they squat. Both competitive lifts will always be a percentage of your squat, and that percentage will never be equal to or greater than 100%. The maximal efficiency a lifter can achieve is thought to be approximately 65% for the snatch and 85% for the clean and jerk.

As strength increases, so does the potential for a big total in weightlifting. But, the temporary decrease in numbers of the competitive lifts while on an intense strength cycle makes some coaches shy away from programming a lot of strength work. While some of the weightlifting programs I see are great, there are some that have a real lack of strength training to go along with the technical work. This is a great way to drive progress in the lifts for a brief time, but it falls short over the long term.

If you're following an online program, ask yourself what percentage of the work is geared toward strength development, and what percent is geared toward technical improvement. Look at the amount of time you spend on the snatch and clean and jerk versus the amount of time you spend squatting and other strength work for a good way to quantify this. If you're spending an hour training the snatch and

clean and jerk, and only half that long doing strength work, something is wrong.

During most phases of training, you should spend at least as much time on squatting and other strength exercises as on practicing the snatch and clean and jerk and other related lifts. Make sure the coach who's writing your programming isn't sacrificing long-term progress for short-term gains.

Photo 5.3—Travis Cooper preparing for a clean and jerk in training

SPECIFICITY VERSUS ADAPTATION

We know how to make the body adapt: Simply do an exercise you haven't done before. Or do several sets in a rep range outside your norm. You'll get sore, but over the next few days, the soreness will go away, and when you repeat the exercise, you'll have less soreness each time. Eventually you'll have none. The body has adapted.

As weightlifters, we do the same exercises over and over, which isn't exactly ideal for adaptation. But if all you do is snatch and clean and jerk with near-maximal weights, it *is* ideal for specificity. Every adaptation the body makes will be perfectly suited to the task of heavy snatches and clean and jerks.

If you add heavy squats to the mix, it'll surely help make your legs strong. But, the increased leg strength won't be perfectly suited to the snatch and clean and jerk.

Squats don't occur at the same speed as the snatch; the force curve isn't the same as the force curve in a snatch, and the range of motion in the squat isn't the same as in a snatch.

It's the same with every assistance exercise we do. Training other than heavy singles in the competition lifts allows us to greatly increase the body's adaptations, but those assistance exercises also cause the adaptations to be less than perfectly suited to that of maximal lifts in the snatch and clean and jerk.

There's a tradeoff between adaptation and specificity; what's great for one is bad for the other.

TRANSITIONING TO WEIGHTLIFTING FROM A GENERAL STRENGTH BACKGROUND

I have some thoughts about the best way for an experienced weight trainer to transition into the sport of weightlifting. The guy or gal who already has a reasonable amount of basic strength and a bit of muscle to go with it will transition well.

These folks are often frustrated by normal beginner routines. They're used to training hard, and because they probably start with the ability to snatch or clean and jerk only very low percentages of their squat, deadlift, or bench press, they don't think they're getting much of a workout.

This can be frustrating for a person used to pushing to the limit several times a week on general strength exercises. And their strength and size, especially in the upper body, often temporarily regresses when they start Olympic lifting because the majority of the work they're doing is technically challenging, but isn't challenging from a muscular perspective.

This isn't a problem for a typical beginner with little or no weight training experience. For this person, snatches and clean and jerks, along with a bit of pressing and squatting, will add strength and muscle, even with weights limited more by technique than by strength.

But for people with a big bench, a big squat, and two or three years of hard training under their belts, it's unlikely this will be the case. These people might be well served by an introduction into the sport that's a little different.

This would be something that lets them transition a bit slower from their old style of training, and allows them to maintain and hopefully even improve

basic strength and muscle size as they learn to do the snatch and clean and jerk.

I've used a program that accomplishes this well. The foundation of this program was the programs written by Dr. Mike Stone in the 1980s, and the template, with a few minor changes, is still in use today. I've used the program here and there from the late 1990s with various lifters ranging from those transitioning from powerlifting to weightlifting, to competitive lifters who want a rest cycle after a major contest, and want to temporarily back off a bit on the competitive lifts but still maintain progress when it comes to overall strength.

This is a four-day-a-week program; the premise is simple, as is usually the case with good programming. Two days a week, we practice the snatch and clean and jerk, and two days a week, we squat and press. And honestly, that's all that's important. However, I'll supply some details because no one would pay much attention to a programming commentary made up of just two sentences.

The best way to set this up is with snatches and clean and jerks on Monday and Thursday, and squatting and strength work on Tuesday and Saturday. This doesn't mean it's the only way to do it, but it's worked for me.

"Practice" for the snatch and clean and jerk means just that; there's no magic rep scheme. If you normally train for 90 minutes, aim to practice for 90 minutes, split between the two lifts. For example, if you lack mobility, much of the time initially might be taken up by work on mobility.

In some circumstances, the time working on the snatch might initially be taken up simply trying to attain an overhead squat position. It's possible the bulk of the time in the gym on these days might just be an empty bar in hand. But, people get better as time goes on, and at some point, they'll gradually start to handle more challenging weights.

Use common sense when doing these workouts; challenge yourself, but don't do so much as to interfere with the strength training.

When it comes to squatting and pressing, if you can't figure this out for yourself, you aren't really in the target population for this program. If you are, you've already raised your squat at least a hundred pounds and probably more. Use your head, and do what's needed to keep gaining. Experiment with adding front squats if you haven't already.

Most people who do general strength routines use the bench press in their programs; whatever has been working, keep it up. But consider adding an emphasis on overhead work, such as presses and push presses, and begin to deemphasize the bench press.

When would you advance beyond such a routine? The need for a hybrid program fades when a lifter is snatching 50% or clean and jerking 65% more than the back squat. Let common sense be your guide. At some point, the weights on the snatch and clean and jerk will be heavy enough, and will no longer simply be practice; it'll be real training.

If you had two or three years of strength training behind you before you started weightlifting and have taken the time to achieve decent form and weights on the competitive lifts using this routine, you should be equipped with enough experience and knowledge to know where to go from there.

MEASURING PROGRESS

The first step in evaluating training is pretty simple. If you're a beginner, are the weights increasing on the snatch, clean and jerk, squat, and your other strength lifts? If they are, good, keep training. If not, something might need to be changed.

A change doesn't mean starting a whole new program. It could be as simple as switching from singles to doubles or triples for a training cycle or two. It could mean changing to a variation of the snatch or clean on a training day to work on a weak point. It could even mean adjusting the repetitions, restarting a linear progression, or changing the training method of a strength lift as mentioned earlier.

As you develop from a beginner to intermediate and eventually advanced lifter, progress might become more difficult to gauge. With sufficient training under your belt, there are expectations I've outlined on what strength levels should look like when comparing one lift to another.

As an intermediate to advanced lifter, adjusting the training based on the information you find becomes

more individual. You'll need specific exercises or methods that we'll cover in the following chapters. Right now, let's discuss the evaluations. Further along in the text, we'll cover the exercises and strategies that can be used to improve the areas where you're lacking in strength and technique.

FRONT SQUAT

The front squat should be roughly 90 percent of your back squat. Most lifters I've coached have been close to this benchmark.

If you're back squatting 182 kilos, theoretically, your front squat should be around 165 kilos. Of course, there are individual differences between lifters—falling within a range of 155 kilos and 175 kilos is appropriate.

CLEANS

Most technically proficient weightlifters can clean around 90 percent of their front squats. That puts a person with a 165-kilo front squat cleaning around 148 kilos. I've coached some who could clean 100 percent and others who fell in the 80 to 85 percent range. So, 90 percent is what I would ultimately expect as a good result; if you're falling way below that benchmark, there's likely a technique problem that needs to be sorted out.

POWER CLEANS

Depending on your technical efficiency and strength, being able to power clean 90 percent of your best clean is normal. I expect a lifter with a 148-kilo clean to be power cleaning around 132 kilos.

CLEAN AND JERK

Plain and simple, you should be able to jerk what you can clean, so this is the same answer as the clean number. Ideally, clean and jerk numbers are between 90 and 100 percent of the front squat. That might put someone who back squats 182 kilos to clean and jerk 165 kilos, maybe more if really efficient and fast.

SNATCH

Snatching 80% of your clean and jerk is a fairly good ratio. If you're back squatting 182 kilos and have a 165-kilo clean and jerk, that would put your snatch at 118 kilos. I've read research proposing that basing the snatch on the back squat is more accurate.

The figure described was that the snatch should be between 60 to 65 percent of the back squat. That puts a person squatting 182 kilos with a snatch between 109 and 118 kilos. I personally think 65% is more realistic, but I'll let you be the judge.

OVERHEAD SQUAT

The overhead squat is a little trickier. It's not something I outright program often, but inquiring minds might want to know. You should be able to overhead squat a bit more than your snatch, but I've coached multiple lifters who have overhead squatted near or even more than their best clean and jerk.

Let's take a look at some of these numbers and discuss a reasonable benchmark.

Damon Kirkpatrick and Ben Preda overhead squatted 183 kilos when their best clean and jerks were 167 and 166 kilos, respectively.

Donny Shankle overhead squatted 191 kilos when he was clean and jerking around 200 kilos.

Justin Brimhall overhead squatted 170 kilos at a bodyweight of only 75 kilos.

I personally overhead squatted 183 kilos. I don't remember my clean and jerk at the time, but I'm proud of it all the same.

Ultimately, I'd say a lifter back squatting 182 kilos who can clean and jerk 165 kilos and snatch 118 kilos should be able to overhead squat between 118 and 148 kilos.

There you have it: general guidelines on measuring the rate of progress you're making in training.

BEGINNING AS A WEIGHTLIFTER

No one wants to be labeled a "beginner" and no one wants to do a beginner program. But skipping ahead to an intermediate or advanced program won't make anyone progress faster either. In fact, it'll slow down progress, and could even decrease the long-term potential for attaining a high total.

The first six months of a weightlifting career are when an athlete should be building good motor patterns that will last throughout a career. These months

are also when people build most of the work capacity that will become valuable in the years to come.

The drop-out rate is high, but if lifters make it through the first four weeks, they're usually able to stick with it for the long term and go on to become intermediate and even advanced lifters.

They end up winning…first on the local level, then the national level. Do you have what it takes? Let's find out.

SUCCESS IN WEIGHTLIFTING

Success in weightlifting is defined by snatching and clean and jerking more weight. It's that simple.

It isn't defined by having a huge squat or carrying an impressive workload in training. Those can certainly contribute to increasing the competitive lifts, but don't let them become the ends unto themselves.

If you follow these basic recommendations and use common sense, you'll have plenty of tools to design a good beginner's program. This is far from an exhaustive treatise on programming, but as your need for more advanced strategies and fine-tuning grows, so will your experience and knowledge.

Keep a workout log, and take good notes. When you change your program, change one thing at a time, and give the change a reasonable amount of time to work before you abandon it. Approach things in a systematic way, and with every week and every success or failure, you'll add to your knowledge of how your body reacts to training, and what you need to do to snatch and clean and jerk more.

CLOSING THOUGHTS

We've worked to demystify programming and hopefully made it a little less intimidating. Where do we go from here? We dive deeper. Now that you have a macro view on my personal training system, we'll dismantle and discuss each component to gain a micro view.

In the coming chapters, you can expect to learn about individual exercises, training methods, and view sample programming from the perspectives of beginner, intermediate, and advanced weightlifters.

The most important elements in the training of a weightlifter are to train the snatch, the clean and jerk, and the squat. This fact should never be forgotten as you progress through different training levels.

Should you become lost along the way having added too much to your training, you can always return to this baseline and start to make progress again.

Finally, I leave you with two quotes. Both come from men who made a significant impact on American weightlifting, and both will become more meaningful as your knowledge and experience in the sport grows.

"The worst program in the world, if you believe in it 100%,
is better than a great program you don't believe in."
~ Lynn Jones

"I can tell you everything I know about weightlifting in 15 minutes.
But it will take you 15 years to understand what I'm talking about."
~ Joe Mills

CHAPTER 6
PROGRAMMING FOR BEGINNING WEIGHTLIFTERS

Your first training program will begin two processes that will continue throughout your career: building strength and obtaining technical mastery in the competition lifts. Sometimes these aspects of the program will seem to interfere with each other, while other times they'll complement and even build off one another. Gaining strength should improve positions in the lifts, and improved positions will make technical mastery easier to obtain.

Many beginners assume that a couple months of practice will be enough time to master the lifts. It won't be. That's one of the many frustrating aspects of the sport.

All athletes continue to make mistakes throughout their careers, but as they improve, those mistakes will become less significant. Even after a lifter has trained for 10 years and has won national championships, there are still new levels of weightlifting skill to be acquired. Yet I often hear people who've been lifting for a short time comment that they've "learned the lifts," or even that they've mastered them. However, after a year in the sport, they've barely even begun this process.

In that way, weightlifting is similar to the game of golf. You never really master it; your mistakes just get smaller. I've heard golf enthusiasts talk about how frustrating and maddening the game can be, which sounds a lot like weightlifting. The perfect lift is like the perfect golf swing. You can chase it, study it, and work toward it for years. Suddenly, seemingly by accident, it happens. The pull feels effortless, the bar drops into the perfect position, and the lift is over before you know it.

This perfection is fleeting. Usually, the next lift is not quite right, and you feel as though you've added 40 kilos to the bar while the weight was unchanged.

Photo 6.1—Travis Cooper has always been a big squatter. He's done more than 600 pounds in the 77-kilo weight class.

Learning and mastering the lifts is a never-ending process. Even after breaking an American record, the lifts still have the ability to humble you and make you feel like a beginner again. To use the golf analogy again, the week after a pro wins the Masters, he can be found on the course working on his putting.

The idea of "mastering" the lifts is inconceivable because you'll never be done learning. There's no point at which you can boast, "I've learned all I can learn." I don't mean to scare you away from weightlifting; I just want to encourage you to relish the journey that training will become because you'll never reach a final destination.

As you begin training, always remind yourself that no one has become a great weightlifter in just a few weeks or months—no one. If you dream about becoming a great weightlifter and want to find success, you *must* train for the long haul. It absolutely won't happen overnight.

As soon as you can snatch and clean and jerk a bar, I want you to sign up for a local meet. You won't be very good at this meet. However, it will give you an excellent opportunity to grow as a weightlifter.

This includes everything from your preparation for the meet, your experience there, and the increased motivation after it. Far too many people delay their first meet for reasons that are more psychological than having to do with the lifts.

But you can't actually call yourself a weightlifter until you enter a weightlifting competition.

A BEGINNER'S FIRST PROGRAM

Every beginner should start with three days of training per week. Beginners are typically enthusiastic and want to jump immediately into training six days a week, or even do two training sessions a day. While I understand the excitement these athletes feel as they start weightlifting, it's a mistake to give into the temptation of training too often.

Most people will do better, learn the lifts faster, and make more progress during their first year of training if they initially train three days per week. Trying to do too much too soon leads to frustration and injuries. Too much too soon is the single biggest reason people quit the sport before accomplishing anything of note.

American Fred Lowe made three consecutive Olympic teams (1968, 1972, and 1976), and he never trained more than three days a week. The best modern lifters train more than this, and most of them even train twice a day, but many people underestimate the effectiveness of a three-day-a-week program.

A lot can be accomplished with three weekly training days; elite athletes build up the capacity over years to handle the workload of training five or six days per week or even twice per day.

Jumping into training programs with that many training sessions when you're not ready won't lead to more progress. It will lead to more injuries.

Elite weightlifters slowly build their lives around weightlifting over years or even decades. They often don't have families to support and they sacrifice their social lives to train.

Photo 6.2—James Tatum warming up his snatch at the 2015 World Championships in Houston, Texas

Very few athletes who are training full time also hold down a full-time job. At the elite level, *the training* is a full-time job. But, every elite lifter started where you are now, awkward lifts done in relatively few training sessions per week. Start slow and you'll progress faster and with fewer injuries than if you try to become a full-time weightlifter overnight. Save the sacrifices for later, when more frequent training will actually lead to better results.

For beginners, I prefer to program eight-week training cycles. These cycles are a basic form of periodization, a way to organize multiple weeks or months of training. Eight weeks is long enough to make measurable progress, but not so long that your needs change mid-cycle. A training cycle adds structure, specific goals, and a timetable for achieving them. Without these, weightlifting is just an activity or recreation. With these, it becomes a sport.

In this book, I'll assume you're preparing for a competition in eight weeks. Depending on where you live, you may not have a local competition to train for and will have to make up one if that's your situation. Set a date on your calendar eight weeks out that will simulate competition, even if only in your head. This date on the calendar is designed to motivate you, and give you the opportunity to experience the gradual building of excitement, pressure, and maybe even fear that accompanies competition preparation.

ESTABLISHING BASELINES

Weightlifting competition is centered on maximal singles in the snatch and clean and jerk—that's why training those lifts and their variations is based on one-repetition maxes (1RMs). When learning to snatch and clean and jerk, you'll establish a separate 1RM from the hips, from the knees, and from the floor.

For the strength exercises, you'll set a baseline rep maximum for each exercise in the program. This includes a 3RM for the front squat and a 5RM for the back squat, snatch-grip deadlift, and push press. Once these baselines are set, there's no need for anything beyond doing a kilo more than the previous week or workout. You should expect to increase the weight on each exercise virtually every workout.

When increasing weights from one workout to the next, smaller jumps are better than bigger jumps. Consistently increasing the weight even by a small amount is more important than getting every kilo you possibly can in a specific workout. Small, steady increases that allow your body to adapt to an ever-increasing load are sustainable, while large increases each workout usually are not.

With the strength exercises, sets of three to five reps provide a balance between increasing neural efficiency and building muscle that makes the process of increasing strength more sustainable than it would be at either a lower or higher number of reps per set. I don't recommend higher reps with strength exercises, such as sets of 10, because there's too much of an endurance component instead of a stimulus that promotes strength increases.

Higher-rep sets are also more difficult to recover from, and interfere too much with the training of the competition lifts.

Using rep maximums eliminates the need to interrupt training to judge progress by going for maximum singles. A maximal set of three to five reps, or whatever number of reps you're using at the time, is a natural part of the training process, and training doesn't have to be interrupted to test strength and judge progress.

Not having to interrupt the training process to test saves time, so more productive work can be done in a training cycle. Strength training is largely independent of technical training to ensure that no matter where lifters are in terms of technical mastery, they're continually building strength.

After the first eight-week program, you'll likely need more variation and will get it through the second beginner program. Do the second beginner program immediately after the first, as it's geared toward the slower rate of progress you'll probably be making in your third and fourth months in the sport.

When you get to the intermediate stage, you'll likely need even more variation. The programs in the intermediate chapter will provide that.

PURSUING TECHNICAL MASTERY

Learning how to snatch and clean and jerk is your first priority when becoming a weightlifter. This was covered in Chapters 1, 2, and 3, where you practiced my Three Step Top-Down learning progression.

It was also in those chapters where we began the discussion of the lack of a clear line between learning and training. The snatch and clean and jerk chapters focus on learning.

Here in the beginner chapter, the focus is now on training. But, learning occurs in every training session, and that will never change.

We'll utilize the positions of the Top-Down Method (hips, knees, and floor) with progressively heavier weights. Snatching and cleaning from the hips, knees, and floor, and building bar speed from a dead stop in all three positions are powerful strength stimuli in addition to building technical mastery.

Beginner lifters should train these positions for a minimum of one training cycle. Some might use all three positions longer, while others might begin lifting only from the floor once the first cycle is complete. The duration of the transition from doing the lifts at the hips and knees to doing them all from the floor is individual.

A typical training week should consist of a day reserved for each position: On Mondays, lift from the knees; Wednesdays from the hips; and Fridays from the floor.

Photo 6.3—Jon North
I can't find a better example of a well-executed finish than this

I recommend this method for a couple reasons.

Lifting from the floor is the most important position because that's what we do in competition, but the pull from the floor is also complex and difficult to do correctly. There's nothing more frustrating for a beginner than repeatedly missing a snatch from the floor, even though the weight isn't challenging.

At this point in the learning and training process, lifting from all three positions each week takes pressure off athletes to constantly add weight from the floor because they can challenge themselves a little more from the other positions. Greater skill at the higher positions translates to heavier weights, which can go a long way in preventing boredom and frustration. This allows athletes to progress slower from the floor to develop good lifting habits with weights that are more appropriate for their skill level.

While building good habits from the floor, lifting from the hip and knee positions provides an outlet

where athletes can challenge themselves with weights that feel heavy. For people just learning the lifts, the hip position is often where they can lift the most weight. The motor patterns of this position are less complex and more quickly mastered than lifting from the knee or especially from the floor. As people gain skill over time that changes, and eventually, lifts from the floor can usually be done with more weight than the other positions.

Additionally, human beings simply like variety. All weightlifters have certain exercises they like and others they dislike. If you force yourself to practice each position throughout the week, there will be one that becomes your favorite—most likely because you do your best lifting and lift the most weight from that position. This planned variety will help keep training interesting and give you more opportunities to attempt PRs in training.

Keeping track of different records is motivational because it gives you a number to shoot for and surpass almost every workout. Keep records for the positions and other variations of the competition lifts you use in training, including lifts performed from low, medium, and high lifting blocks. Lifting from blocks that place the bar at the knee or even at the hip is almost identical to lifting from the hang at those positions. There are small differences, enough to warrant keeping records from blocks, as well as records from the hang.

For most lifters, the hang positions work very well, but for some, the blocks are a great tool, and can be a worthwhile substitution. When using blocks, the bar should ideally be at the same height as when doing a lift from the hang at that position. If it is, the lifts are interchangeable in your programming at this level.

The final reason to use all three positions during a training week is to purposefully vary the physical workload. Lifts from each position stress the body in a slightly different way. Lifts from the hips are the least stressful for most lifters because of the short pull. They provide an easier workout between the two more difficult and stressful workouts on Monday and Friday.

Varying the stress of training from day to day makes it easier for the body to adapt to training and to increase performance over time.

This format also allows you to drill the hip and knee positions to optimally prepare for Friday, when you'll have a chance to set a new record on the most important position: from the floor—the only one you'll do in competition.

Most weightlifting competitions occur on the weekend and thus, on non-competition weeks, many coaches, including me, have come to view the end of the training week as an opportunity to go heavy on the competition lifts.

At California Strength, we referred to this day as "max-out Fridays." The tradition started when I was coaching Donny Shankle and Jon North, and the tradition was carried on by Travis Cooper, James Tatum, Kaleb Whitby, and Mike Szela.

Be careful not to unintentionally turn Monday and Wednesday into max-out days. Planning to take Friday as a heavy day—and regularly doing so—can take some of the pressure off of constantly trying your best weights in each workout.

If you know you're going to try a PR on Friday, it's easier to hold yourself back a bit earlier in the week. Sometimes you'll be able to get very good work in with more moderate weights when you don't have to worry about going heavy because you know you'll be going heavy on Friday.

To ensure your body is fresh for the most technical part of the training session, you'll snatch and clean and jerk before you squat. Your goal should be to complete three to five good reps for each lift at a weight that's challenging enough to promote adaptation or improvement. Including warm-ups and lighter weights, you'll probably finish each training session with a total of about 15 to 20 snatches and about 15 clean and jerks.

As long as you did the prescribed number of lifts on Monday and Wednesday, there's no harm in letting Friday's session become a max-effort day where you work up and try to hit your best weight. In fact, I encourage this because it helps mentally; it gives you something to look forward to all week.

Don't skimp on warm-up lifts, as they're a great opportunity to hone your technique and prepare for your working weights. If you plan to snatch 100 kilos during a training session, don't load the bar directly to 100. Warm up with a 20-kilo bar for a few reps, then perhaps 50, 70, 80, 86, 92, and finally 96 kilos as your last warm-up.

These warm-up numbers are based on a 100-kilo snatch to make it easy to convert these weights to percentages of whatever your work set number is for the day. The jumps between warm-up sets get smaller with the smallest jump being immediately before the first work set.

As a beginner, keep your training simple, and focus on the competition lifts. Lifts done from the knees or hips are simpler movement patterns, and allow beginners to lift challenging weights before perfecting the movement from the floor. Lifting from the hip or knees uses the same technique as a lift from the floor, but starting from a higher position.

There will be time later to add more variety. Things like complexes or power versions of the lifts will be useful as an intermediate lifter. Right now, as a beginner in your first couple of training cycles, your priority should be to practice technical mastery in the lifts.

PURSUING STRENGTH

Technical mastery is not easily measured or graded because of its ambiguous nature. Strength, on the other hand, is tangible. If your squat improves from 205 kilos to 210, the progress can be seen, measured, and recorded.

Strength training takes place against a backdrop of ever-improving technical mastery. As proficiency in the competition lifts increases, so does the contribution to strength training. If your max snatch isn't representative of your maximal strength in the snatch pulling motion, work on the snatch may not be a meaningful part of your strength training. For example, if a lifter has a max snatch-grip deadlift of 200 kilos and a max snatch of 50 kilos, the snatch won't contribute to strength increases in a meaningful way.

If this lifter increases the snatch to 100 kilos, training in the snatch itself becomes a more meaningful part of gaining strength in the snatch pulling motion. If the same lifter increases the snatch to 150 kilos, the snatch becomes an extremely important part of strength training.

This is why it's important that beginners don't base their strength training on the competition lifts; they don't yet have the technical mastery for those lifts to be an effective part of strength development.

Strength is the biggest challenge for American athletes—and indeed athletes from any country with a legitimate NAN program—but the weightlifting movements aren't particularly good strength builders. The competitive lifts are too fast and the motor patterns too complex, both of which lower their strength-building potential.

As the skill level of an athlete increases, the competition lifts contribute more to strength development, but they'll never be on the same level as movements with simple movement patterns, such as squats and deadlifts. This is why we use squats to build the snatch, but we don't use the snatch to build squats.

Squats, deadlifts, and other basic strength exercises should be the core of any strength program because they generate a large amount of muscular tension… and they build strength. A fast movement won't generate as much muscular tension as a slower movement done with heavier weights.

Attempting to move the bar as fast as possible increases the muscular tension and strength-building potential of an exercise. However, performing the same exercise with a heavier weight will always be more effective in building strength, even if the bar moves slower.

Since strength is the biggest obstacle for any lifter not using PEDs, it makes sense to prioritize strength exercises in training. If you can't snatch-grip deadlift the world record snatch or front squat the world record clean and jerk, significant gains in strength are absolutely necessary and should be high on your list of priorities.

Increasing the strength of US athletes is an important part of raising our performance to world record levels. A good strength program takes the rapid progress beginners can make into consideration by allowing for strength increases nearly every workout. It will also recognize the slowing of strength gains over a career by assuming that measurable progress slows from each workout to each week, month, or training cycle.

Photo 6.4—Kevin Cornell racking a 150-kilo clean during training

Photo courtesy of Mark Hazarabedian

THE BACK SQUAT

Photos 6.5–6.9—The back squat sequence

The back squat is indispensable for weightlifters. Many people assume squats are simply for leg strength, but when back squatting, the back, the hips, the stabilization muscles of the torso, and all other postural muscles are developed.

The muscles of the torso have to be strong to support the heavy loads the sport demands, whether the weight is held overhead as in the snatch, on the chest in the clean, or overhead in the jerk.

The placement of the barbell on the traps or upper back allows a lifter to perform more repetitions and support more weight for a longer period than any other exercise. This challenges the body in a way other exercises simply can't.

For most beginners, it takes a while to learn sufficient technique in the clean and jerk, and especially the snatch, to feel like they're challenging their strength levels. In the meantime, the back squat is the lift that will allow you to challenge your strength levels.

This will change, but there's no doubt that back squats drive progress, and will raise your potential in the snatch and the clean and jerk. I consider the back squat the real foundation for a weightlifting total.

If your goal is to clean and jerk 100 kilos, your back squat 1RM will need to be somewhere around 125 before that's possible. If you're an extremely efficient lifter, you might manage a 100-kilo clean and jerk with a 115- to 120-kilo back squat.

The more efficient your snatch, the more you can snatch in relation to your back squat. If your technique is inefficient or if you have limitations, such as a lack of mobility in certain joints, you may have to back squat far more. A lifter with those limitations and a 125-kilo back squat will probably be able to snatch around 75 to 80.

Just as with the clean and jerk, mobility limitations that make catching the bar overhead difficult may mean you have to back squat significantly more to snatch the same weight.

Photo 6.10—James Tatum ready to back squat 240 kilos

The beginner program contains two back squat days and one front squat day per week. Most lifters will only need to front squat once weekly because each clean or clean and jerk involves a front squat, decreasing the need for extra front squatting.

Both the back squat and the deadlifts use more total muscle mass than the front squat, and more weight on the bar. Thus, they're both better overall strength exercises than the front squat.

The back squat also transfers to the front squat much more than the front squat transfers to the back squat. For these reasons, doing two back squat workouts per week and only one front squat workout is the right balance for most beginners.

There's controversy about the proper way for a weightlifter to squat—everyone seems to have an opinion, and most have a strong opinion. However, actually doing the back squat and squatting deep is far more important than the style used.

Now, the back squat is only a training exercise for weightlifters. The important part is that it makes the legs, hips, and back stronger so you can apply that new strength to the snatch and clean and jerk.

Performance

When preparing to back squat, set up a squat rack with a barbell at roughly chest height. Depending on the style of squat rack, this may need to be adjusted higher or lower so you can clear the hooks holding the bar.

Stand facing the squat rack and place your hands on the bar so they'll be just outside your shoulders when the bar's on your back. Those with limited shoulder flexibility may need to take the hands wider.

Duck and wedge yourself under the bar, placing it high on the upper traps. The bar should be resting on the muscles of your traps and shoulders. Some may find this uncomfortable if lacking the natural padding and the bar is resting on bony prominences. If that happens, lower the placement of the bar slightly so it doesn't rest on bone or the neck.

Stand tall and walk the weight out of the rack. Take a stance of about shoulder width, and as you go down, break first at the knees. Try to keep your hips as tucked in as possible.

During the movement, keep the eyes and gaze fixed straight ahead. Avoid looking down or kicking the hips too far back during the squatting or standing motions. The angle of the torso won't be as upright as it is in the front squat, but maintain your torso as upright as possible.

THE DEADLIFT

Many non-lifters assume that since the deadlift more closely mirrors the movement of the snatch and the clean than does the back squat, the deadlift is the more important strength exercise. But the proper performance of the snatch and clean pull with a double knee bend before the final extension employs an upright torso near the top of the pull where most of the power is generated.

The final extension is actually closer to a jumping or squatting motion than a deadlifting motion. Although the deadlift is a great strength exercise, it doesn't correlate as well with the snatch or clean and jerk than the back squat.

Deadlift capability is negatively correlated with the length of the athlete's spine. Athletes with a long spine are usually weaker at the deadlift. On the other hand, spine length is usually at least somewhat positively correlated with performance in weightlifting, which is another reason high performance in the deadlift isn't predictive of high performance in the snatch or clean.

Photos 6.11–6.13—The deadlift sequence

None of this means the deadlift is not a great whole-body strength builder; it is. In fact, the deadlift is of particular benefit for those who aren't good at it for anatomical reasons. An athlete with a long spine will have trouble at the bottom of the pull as the bar moves off the floor. Thus, there's nothing as effective as deadlifts to build strength off the floor.

The deadlift must be trained with both a lower volume and a lower frequency because it's particularly stressful on parts of the body without a good blood supply, such as the lower back. The lower back is comprised of a lot of connective tissue, tendons, and ligaments, as opposed to the thighs that contain more vascular tissue. Additionally, much of the lower back's use is through static contraction, which doesn't increase blood flow.

The muscles of the thighs can be trained with more volume and frequency, and they recover relatively quickly. The thighs are constantly in use, even just walking, and this helps with blood flow.

For beginners, I recommend one weekly work set of three to five reps of the deadlift; do this on Wednesday. Wednesday is when you'll front squat, which isn't as stressful as the back squat, so the extra stress of the deadlifts is less likely to cause overwork that day.

Beginners will do snatch-grip and clean-grip deadlifts using the same motion as the pulling portion of the snatch and the clean. These are done with weights calculated from the max that can be moved through this portion of the lift with the hips and shoulders in the same relationship as in the snatch and the clean, with the back straight or even arched.

The same motion includes executing a double knee bend when possible, and using a short explosive

vertical shrug at the top. Snatch-grip and clean-grip deadlifts build strength, and also a powerful stimulus for ingraining the correct pulling motion and rhythm.

How the weight is calculated is the only difference between the snatch-grip and clean-grip deadlifts and the snatch and clean pulls. Pulls are calculated from the maximal snatch or clean, and for a beginner, these maximal weights are limited by a lack of technical mastery.

Deadlifts, however, are calculated from the maximum weight that can be moved through that same range of motion, and isn't limited to a weight you can move under and catch.

For a beginner, the differences in weight between pulls and deadlifts can be large, but these differences become smaller as the skill level of the athlete increases, and can eventually disappear.

Performance

To perform the deadlift variations, stand in front of a loaded bar and begin by bending at the knees and hips until you're able to grab it using either a snatch grip or clean grip. I recommend using a double-overhand hookgrip as long as possible.

If grip strength is a limiting factor, you may choose to use lifting straps. With a clean grip, most lifters will be able to perform most or all of the sets with a hook grip, but for the snatch, many will be forced to use straps. A mixed grip with one hand pronated and the other supinated could be used as a last resort.

The starting position and foot placement should be identical to that of the snatch or clean. This is crucial because we're training strength in those positions.

Initiate the lift by pushing your feet "through the floor" as you stand. Brace your abdominals while working hard to maintain a strong posture. As you stand, engage the lats to keep the barbell tight against your body. Ideally, the bar should travel in a nearly vertical line from the starting position to the hips.

I can't emphasize this enough: Attempt to perform a double knee bend and a shrug just as you would for a snatch or clean pull.

Finally, return the bar to the floor by lowering it through that same vertical line.

PRESS AND PUSH PRESS

Some lifters develop into great snatchers and jerkers with no direct overhead work outside of snatching and jerking. But many athletes find that extra overhead work in addition to the competition lifts helps build a big total.

While the press would seem to be the most basic way to increase overhead strength, it's difficult in the wrong parts of the overhead range of motion. When pressing with either a clean grip or snatch grip, the movement is difficult right as the bar comes off the shoulders or neck, and gets easier as it progresses to the lockout.

That's the opposite of where a weightlifter needs to build strength in the shoulders and arms.

In the jerk, the force needed to move the bar off the shoulders or neck is mostly supplied by the hips and legs. The arms are only needed to hold the lockout. If they're used before the lockout, it's very little…or should be.

In the push press, like the jerk, the legs supply most of the force to move the bar off the shoulders or neck, and as the bar slows, the arms supply an ever-increasing proportion of force until lockout, where the arms and shoulders hold the bar in the locked-out position. Because of this, the push press, unlike the press, develops strength where a weightlifter actually needs it: the lockout.

Performance

See "Chapter 3: Learning to Jerk," pages 53–55, for performance instruction of the press and push press.

POSTERIOR-CHAIN STRENGTH EXERCISES

In addition to the snatch-grip and clean-grip deadlifts, it may also be useful to incorporate other posterior-chain strengthening exercises, such as the death march, suitcase deadlifts, one-arm kettlebell swings, pull-ups, rows, and exercises like glute ham raises, back extensions, or hip extensions that make use of the glute-hamstring developer (GHD), one of the most underutilized pieces of equipment in any gym.

At least, it was before the advent of CrossFit, which increased the popularity of the GHD.

Each of these exercises has a place in training based on the needs of an individual athlete.

BACK EXTENSION

The back extension strengthens the spinal erectors, and it does so in a unique way, making it an extremely useful exercise. It's an exercise *every* weightlifter should do.

There are other exercises that train the erectors, but with most of them, the lifter is only required to maintain an isometric contraction—exercises such as Romanian deadlifts and hip extensions fit this description. The back extension is one of the only exercises that works the erectors both eccentrically and concentrically.

Think about this: If you wanted to build 20-inch arms, you wouldn't consider limiting the training of your biceps and triceps to isometric contractions. If people did that, no one would develop big arms. Yet, many assume isometric contractions are all they need for the erectors.

Training the erectors eccentrically and concentrically leads to the muscles becoming much bigger and stronger, which is vital for a weightlifter.

I've witnessed the erectors of lifters I've coached becoming noticeably larger over a period of several weeks. I can't remember ever seeing this kind of visually noticeable muscle growth in conjunction with any other muscle group or exercise.

Photos 6.14 and 6.15—The back extension sequence

Performance

Most people will use a GHD to perform this exercise. Adjust the GHD so the knees are bent and the belly button is on the pad, allowing spinal flexion and extension without movement of the hip or knee joints. Round your back until your spine and torso are as flexed as possible. Reverse the movement to full spinal extension to complete the repetition.

If you're a handy person, you could get creative and build equipment that might work better. I built a back extension bench at California Strength that put the thighs about 30 degrees away from vertical—in my opinion, the perfect angle.

HIP EXTENSION

Hip extensions—also known as a back raise—work all the muscles involved in the extension of the hips, including the glutes and hamstrings. It's particularly valuable when there's a reason an athlete can't do exercises like the deadlift. The hip extension can be performed with a barbell, holding plates or dumbbells, and even with just bodyweight.

Do these at the end of a session for sets of 10 repetitions; however, including them in the warm-up is also useful. If done at the end of a workout, push the weight up and treat them with the same respect and effort as you do squats and deadlifts.

I once asked Donny Shankle what assistance exercises he felt helped him the most, and he said other than squats, back and hip extensions were the most valuable. These exercises were good for Donny because he has a long torso, which makes it hard for him to stay out over the bar while keeping his back arched and pulling the bar off the floor. Donny reminded me that his best snatches and cleans in training always came when he was at PR levels on the back and hip extensions.

Performance

The hip extension is usually done on a GHD that puts the legs parallel to the floor, while keeping the torso at parallel with the hips extended. There are also commercially available hip extension benches that put the legs at 45 degrees.

Keep a rigid, arched back, flex at the hips stretching the hamstrings, and lower the torso. Go as far as you can until you run out of room because the GHD blocks your path or your back starts to round. Then, extend the hips until the torso is at the starting position—parallel to the floor or 45 degrees from vertical, depending on the bench.

Be sure to raise your torso back up to a consistent starting height for each repetition. As you start to fatigue, this will become progressively more difficult.

Photos 6.16 and 6.17—The hip extension sequence

GLUTE HAM RAISE

Photos 6.18–6.23—The glute-ham raise sequence

The hamstrings are a muscle group that crosses both the hip and knee joints. Because of that, they're dynamic, and can be trained in a multitude of ways. The vast majority of exercises performed by weightlifters challenge the hamstrings from where they cross the hip joint.

Good mornings, hip extensions, kettlebell swings, and Romanian deadlifts are examples of such exercises. The beauty of the glute ham raise is that it challenges the hamstrings from the knee joint—the other joint they cross.

I can't stress enough how important it is to have a balanced, strong, and injury-free posterior chain. If you can deadlift a house, but can't perform 10 glute ham raise reps with bodyweight, you're leaving serious strength on the table...and leaving yourself open to potential future hip or knee injuries.

Performance

The setup for the glute ham raise is identical to the hip extension. Lying face down on the GHD with the hips and torso parallel to the floor, lower the torso by flexing at the hip and stretching the hamstrings. Flex the hamstrings to extend the hip and raise the torso back up to parallel.

Continue flexing the hamstrings to raise the thighs to near vertical, with the knees at a 45-degree angle. Finally, you'll extend the knees to return to the starting position.

I prefer to have athletes do this exercise with momentum and with a barbell on their backs if warranted.

PROGRAMMING STRENGTH EXERCISES

Each week, every lifter should do strength exercises for squatting, pulling, and overhead strength. A week of strength work for a beginner will look like the following chart.

MONDAY		
Exercise	Sets x Reps	Weight
Back Squat	3 x 5	-
Push Press	3 x 5	-
WEDNESDAY		
Exercise	Sets x Reps	Weight
Front Squat	3 x 3	-
Deadlift (Snatch or Clean Grip)	1 x 5	-
FRIDAY		
Exercise	Sets x Reps	Weight
Back Squat	3 x 5	-

As a beginner, you'll simply be trying to add a small amount of weight each time you train the back squat, front squat, push press, or deadlift. Start with a weight that allows you to complete the prescribed reps without a significant slowing of the bar.

After a workout or a couple of workouts, you'll become impatient, and will want to raise the weight too quickly. Everyone is tempted to do this. Let me be the voice of reason: You'll squat more, and do it sooner if you progress slowly.

If you give your body a chance to adapt, you can often make linear progress for months. I've seen people make progress every single back squat workout for more than six months.

On the other hand, if you get too greedy and try to ramp up the weight faster than your body can adapt, you'll stall after a few weeks. Make haste slowly! If there's any doubt about what weight to use, always choose the lighter weight. There's absolutely no disadvantage in starting your linear progression at a lighter weight, and progressing at a slower rate.

Progress is the lifeblood of a weightlifting program. It will keep you motivated, and we therefore want to keep it going for as long as possible. Workout-to-workout increases in weight with the strength exercises should start at no more than five percent.

As the weeks and months go by, the increases will become smaller. Thus, every lifter should own fractional plates to move the weight up by a smaller amount than is possible with regular plates, especially for movements that train the smaller muscle groups such as the press and push press.

If you back squat 50 kilos for three sets of five on your first training day, you should try between a kilo and a 2.5-kilo increase the next session, with another similar increase the training session after that…and so on.

The front squat will have its own starting weight and progression, which will most likely be lighter than the back squat. For example, the same person who started the back-squat progression with 50 kilos might start the front squat progression with 30 kilos for three sets of three, and then increase the weight to 31 kilos the following week.

These guidelines also apply to the push press and the deadlift. Workout to workout, make increases no greater than five percent, but no less than the minimum allowed by your equipment. Use common sense when planning the increases. Prolonging the linear progression is essential, but the weight has to be meaningful enough to stimulate an adaptation. Make sure your front squat weights rise fairly quickly beyond your best weight in the clean, and that your back squat weight is even heavier. This ensures strength building from the outset.

The capability in the snatch and clean and jerk will vary from workout to workout. This is entirely normal. You may have a Monday when snatches feel great, and you make a significant PR, followed by two or three training sessions when you can't match your best lifts. The lifts should trend upward, but the rate of increase will never be steady—there will be peaks and valleys.

With strength exercises, however, the progress should be more predictable. If you're performing your strength work correctly, each increase in your squat, deadlift, or push press *will* raise your potential in the snatch and clean and jerk. Remember this when you're having a bad day or week with the competition lifts.

If you follow this linear progression, your squat weights should move up every session for at least the first four weeks. At some point, the squats will stall, and you'll fail to complete the prescribed reps during a session. When that occurs, take about 10% off the bar and restart the linear progression.

For example, if you fail to complete all three sets of five at 110 kilos, during the next squatting session, drop the weight to around 95 to 100, and begin the linear progression again. If you have doubts as to how much to decrease the weight, opt for the lower choice. That should allow you to continue your progression past the original weight at which you failed.

After you've reset once, you should be able to continue linearly past your first reset weight, but eventually, you'll run into another strength wall. If you're no longer making progress on the squat while on the first beginner program, you might be ready to move to the second. If you're already on the second beginner program, you might be ready to move to the intermediate program.

If at least one of your other strength lifts—like the deadlift or push press—or your competition lifts are still moving up, it might be best to stay on the beginner program until you can no longer make progress of any kind. However, the point comes for every lifter when more and faster progress can be made on the intermediate program, and only you and your coach will know precisely when that is.

Don't sacrifice form to increase the weight on the bar. Squat as deep as possible and keep your chest up and your back tight. Don't mistake sloppiness for strength gains. It's harder to squat in a strict, upright manner, but doing so will provide more carryover to the competition lifts.

If you train using poor positions, you're not building the habits and strength you'll need to succeed in the snatch and the clean and jerk. Bad habits will need to be broken later, and that relearning process can stall your progress.

PROGRAMMING POSTERIOR-CHAIN EXERCISES

Many of the lifters I've coached prefer to supplement one or two heavy movements centered on the pulling muscles with one or two lighter movements. For example, you might do one set of five of the clean-grip deadlift, followed by two sets of 10 back or hip extensions. That's fine as long as it doesn't interfere with training heavy and hard on the snatch and the clean and jerk.

Keep exercises such as back and hip extensions, glute ham raises, pull-ups, death marches, single-arm deadlifts, Romanian deadlifts, and arch-back good mornings on the lighter side, so they simply complement your training. These exercises are supplemental; the focus should always be on the main strength exercises and competition lifts.

Keep your list of exercises short and simple.

PROGRAMMING THE COMPETITION LIFTS

Every weightlifter will eventually win or lose based on performance lifting for single repetitions. To be successful, lifters need to be skilled and strong at singles, both physically and psychologically. That's why we perform them in the initial training program. But there's still a place for doubles or even triples in training. These offer a change of pace while using the same motor patterns. Any performance gains from doubles or triples will transfer almost perfectly to a single in competition.

The amount of rest is always an issue when performing multiple reps from the floor. A few lifters are strict with rest times and only count it as a double if the bar spends a few seconds on the floor. That's hard to do, especially with challenging weights—most lifters let the rest period between reps extend as the weight increases.

Athletes and coaches are eventually forced to draw a line in the sand in terms of the amount of time the bar spends on the floor between reps. Every athlete is different, but I suggest 20 seconds as the maximum allowable rest before a double is counted as two singles.

For lifts from the hip or knee, it works best to never let the bar touch the floor. Just lower to the hip or knee, and go again. This can be accomplished by using straps for the snatch, but it's hard to do with the clean or clean and jerk. For clean and jerks or snatches from the hip or knee, if you're not wearing straps, you can adhere to a 20-second limit if the bar rests on the floor between reps.

Multiple reps per set of the competition lifts are a significant change of pace as opposed to only doing singles. Usually sets with multiple reps lead to a greater training volume with lower intensity. Multiple reps can also offer more time under tension in each set, which increases the stimulus for actual muscle growth.

Doubles and triples can also give an athlete more psychological motivation, especially on the last lift of a set. Think of it: No one wants to see the third rep hit the floor after having already performed two beautiful repetitions.

Athletes can also perform different numbers of reps from different positions. For athletes I coach, I often stick with singles from the floor, while moving to two or three reps per set for lifts done from the hip or knee.

I also often use a different number of repetitions for the snatch than the clean and jerk. For instance, we might do the snatch for doubles from the knee or hip, and use only singles on the clean and jerk for all positions.

When switching from singles to multiple reps, lower the weight enough to ensure successful lifts for at least the first week or two. Performing multiple reps per set is a skill, just as performing singles is a skill. Starting a notch below top capacity cuts down on pointless misses while you become accustomed to multiple reps per set.

A sample progression for a week of training on both the competition lifts and strength exercises might look like the tables on the following pages.

MONDAY		
Exercises	**Sets x Reps**	**Weight**
Snatch *(if necessary, from the knees)*	1 x 3 1 x 3 1 x 2 1 x 1 1 x 1 3 x 1	20 kg 40 kg 60 kg 70 kg 75 kg 85 kg
Clean and Jerk *(if necessary, from the knees)*	1 x 3 1 x 3 1 x 2 1 x 1 1 x 1 1 x 1 3 x 1	20 kg 50 kg 70 kg 80 kg 90 kg 100 kg 110 kg
Back Squat	1 x 5 1 x 3 1 x 3 1 x 1 1 x 1 3 x 5	50 kg 90 kg 110 kg 120 kg 130 kg 140 kg
Push Press	1 x 5 1 x 2 1 x 1 3 x 3	50 kg 60 kg 70 kg 75 kg

WEDNESDAY		
Exercises	**Sets x Reps**	**Weight**
Snatch *(if necessary, from the hips)*	1 x 3 1 x 3 1 x 2 1 x 1 1 x 1 3 x 1	20 kg 40 kg 60 kg 70 kg 80 kg 90 kg
Clean and Jerk *(if necessary, from the hips)*	1 x 3 1 x 3 1 x 2 1 x 1 1 x 1 1 x 1 1 x 1 3 x 1	20 kg 50 kg 70 kg 80 kg 90 kg 100 kg 110 kg 120 kg
Front Squat	1 x 3 1 x 3 1 x 2 1 x 1 1 x 1 3 x 3	50 kg 70 kg 90 kg 100 kg 110 kg 114 kg
Deadlift *(Snatch or Clean Grip)*	1 x 5 1 x 3 1 x 2 1 x 1 1 x 5	50 kg 90 kg 120 kg 140 kg 160 kg

FRIDAY		
Exercises	**Sets x Reps**	**Weight**
Snatch	1 x 3 1 x 3 1 x 2 1 x 1 1 x 1 3 x 3	20 kg 40 kg 60 kg 70 kg 75 kg 80 kg
Clean and Jerk	1 x 3 1 x 3 1 x 2 1 x 1 1 x 1 1 x 1 1 x 1 3 x 1	20 kg 50 kg 70 kg 80 kg 90 kg 100 kg 115 kg 125 kg
Back Squat	1 x 5 1 x 3 1 x 3 1 x 1 1 x 1 3 x 5	50 kg 90 kg 110 kg 120 kg 130 kg 142 kg

IMPORTANT PROGRAM NOTES

This simple, basic program is the foundation of what you'll be doing as a beginner; in fact, it should be the foundation of how to train your entire career. Continuity in training is underrated. Ideally, athletes would experience the same basic training structure from the time they first pick up a bar until they compete internationally. Wholesale changes should be kept to a minimum, or ideally, never happen. Constantly changing programs, coaches, and environments usually does more harm than good.

The following pages represent the general outline of the beginner program. Let's look at some of the finer points.

WEIGHT SELECTION

The weights for the snatch and the clean and jerk are different on Monday, Wednesday, and Friday. Lifts on each day are based on specific maxes from the position used that day. Your max snatch from the knees might be 80 kilos, your max snatch from the hips might be 70, and finally, your max snatch from the floor might be 65. Your work sets should be based on the specific numbers for each particular day.

"IF NECESSARY"

When learning the lifts, it's helpful for the vast majority of athletes to develop the three positions of the hips, knees, and floor learned and practiced in Chapter 1. Refining these positions is something you'll continually work on throughout your lifting career.

However, there are outliers for whom some positions come naturally, and not as much time needs to be spent from the hips, or the knees, or both. Everyone should learn the Three Step positions, and almost everyone should continue to practice them for the first few months at a minimum. But the need for continual practice from the hips and the knees will vary from lifter to lifter.

TRAINING VOLUME

The beginner program as written has three post–warm-up lifts per workout in the snatch and the clean and jerk. If you're a beginner just learning the lifts, that should be about right. It's always better to do too little than too much. Don't move from three to 12 singles or six doubles all in one step. Use moderation.

There's no rule that all of your work sets have to be done with the same weight. However, if you increase the weight during your work sets, make sure the jumps are small. Bigger jumps increase the likelihood of ending with a miss on your last lift. Always try to end each workout on a good note.

PROGRAMMING THE PRESS

The beginner program contains push presses, but no actual presses. Being a strong presser will lessen the likelihood of an elbow or shoulder injury. Lifters with extreme joint laxity are more susceptible to shoulder or elbow injuries; this includes more women than men. Lifters in this category might be well served to include pressing in the program.

To program the press, perform two or three sets of five reps on one or two training sessions per week with a similar linear progression to that used in the back squat. You can incorporate different variations on the press, such as the bench press, incline press, behind-the-neck snatch-grip press, and dumbbell press. However, focus only on one pressing exercise at a time. Remember, supplemental exercises shouldn't be your main training concentration.

WORKING ON MOBILITY

Any spare training time should be directed toward improving flexibility. If you're an American over the age of 12, chances are you have a mobility problem. This means range-of-motion restrictions might prevent you from achieving a solid overhead squat, front squat, or jerk position.

Although we covered specific stretches to improve these positions in their respective chapters, the simplest fix is to spend time in positions you're trying to improve. If your overhead squat is terrible, grab an empty bar or dowel and force your body into as deep a position as you can achieve for a few sets of 30 seconds each.

You could start adding one or two overhead squats after each snatch, which will significantly increase the amount of time spent in the bottom position. Similarly, extra front squats or jerks in training with the emphasis on full range of motion and improving mobility can also help to correct mobility issues in the clean and jerk.

For example, you could add another front squat to concentrate on improving the front-rack position. If you aren't good at a lift, practice it until you are. As a beginner, don't waste time tinkering with bands, chains, and fancy niche exercises. You need solid practice, not experimentation.

CHANGING THE PROGRAM

Most people realize that training has to change over time. For beginners, changes no bigger than a gradual increase in the weights is often adequate to stimulate continual adaptation. But, as people move beyond their natural ability and strength levels, further adaptations become more difficult to achieve.

Some people try to stick with a program they're comfortable with and are hesitant to change anything. But without changes, the program slowly loses its effectiveness. This often leads to frustration, then abrupt wholesale changes: changing the whole program—the volume, the intensity…everything at once. It's a vicious cycle, learning nothing from years of training experience, and only hitting upon a result-producing routine once in a while by dumb luck.

In a perfect world, you wouldn't make more than one change at a time in training. If you change two things at once and make five kilograms of progress on the snatch, how do you know which change was responsible? If you were doing five doubles on the snatch with 80% each workout, and you increased that to eight doubles with 85%, was it the increased volume or the increased intensity that was responsible for your new ability? You'd never know for sure.

There are far more variables in a training program than just intensity and volume. Training should be changed via an evolutionary process, not a revolutionary one—small changes, made one at a time.

Then, after each one, take stock of the effect the changes caused. The answer is often not just to work harder; it's to think harder and work smarter.

DEALING WITH MISSED LIFTS

Everyone misses lifts; that's part of lifting. Don't take it personally. I've seen people quit the sport because they couldn't mentally deal with misses. Don't beat yourself up every time you miss. If you do, this sport will make you miserable, and you'll eventually quit. You have to learn how to take misses in stride.

While you can't beat yourself up every time you miss, you also can't let yourself get too comfortable missing. Missing is something you have to hate but tolerate. There's an optimal frequency of misses, which I believe is between 10 and 15%, with almost all of these coming at near-maximal weights or when trying a new PR.

On average, you should probably miss about one or possibly two out of every 10 attempts in your work sets. Don't miss on your warm-up sets.

No one wants to miss, but if you never miss, it probably means you're not pushing yourself. On the other hand, missing too often can lead to bad habits. You'll almost certainly miss less often from some positions, and more from others, but over time, it should average out to about 15%.

Missing 10 to 15% of the time is a good goal that probably means you're pushing yourself. You're putting the correct emphasis on increasing the weight versus using consistent technique.

It also means you're doing far more correct reps than incorrect lifts, and your technique will likely get better and better over time.

Taking care not to let misses creep into your training is particularly important as you increase weight. When moving the weight up in your snatch and clean and jerk training, it's normal for your first lift with the increased weight to feel easy, and it's often tempting not just to increase one kilo at a time, but to throw on another five. After all, that first lift felt like you could do at least five kilos more.

That feeling can be deceptive.

And often, if you move up just two or three kilos, the lift feels 100% different...and you miss.

That first miss sets the stage for several more misses, and results in a bad workout. Don't let your enthusiasm run away with you; always take small jumps, especially in the snatch. The snatch can often feel like an entirely different lift with just two more kilos on the bar.

Small increases and consistency are what make a great training session, and eventually a great training week, month, and year.

ENJOY BEING A BEGINNER

I've mentioned it a few times already, but there's a stigma that goes along with being a beginner, as if a lack of experience is a badge of shame. It shouldn't be—it's actually a wonderful opportunity. Most of those who are past the beginner stage would pay good money to experience it again.

If there's anyone who should be ashamed, it's every athlete who managed to waste this phase of a career that's presented to everyone when they first begin this amazing sport. Each athlete begins with a clean slate with no bad habits and no conflicting movement patterns. Strength gains come like clockwork, and the lifts feel better every session.

You'll never have this opportunity again!

INSTANT GRATIFICATION

The pursuit of instant gratification is the biggest problem in modern American weightlifting. This has always been a temptation, but with the advent of the internet, the temptation has become overpowering for many.

And unfortunately, the training that leads to the most dramatic short-term gains often isn't what leads to long-term progress.

Case in point: Almost everyone understands that fatigue from a big squat workout is likely to lower the capability in the clean and jerk for at least a day or two. But the kind of strength program that leads to bigger numbers in the squat and deadlift, and potentially a vastly increased clean and jerk, is likely to leave the weightlifting numbers depressed for a while.

As a beginner, you should be completely

recovered—or close to it—before every workout. Every workout holds the potential for new records, not only in the snatch and clean and jerk, but also in the strength-building lifts like the squat, deadlift, and push press.

But as your career progresses, it takes more training stress to cause an adaptation. Soon, squatting hard enough to make continual progress in the squat means you won't be able to approach every workout in a completely recovered and fresh condition.

At some point, the start of a training cycle becomes the time to work on weak points and improving the squat and deadlift, and the end of the training cycle becomes the time to put it all together and use that strength to lift new numbers in the snatch and clean and jerk.

In fact, the more you advance as a lifter, the more you have to live with delayed gratification. Not being able to take the long view is the sign of an immature lifter. If it takes time to build a big total, you might be ready for a program that requires more than simply maxing out every day and hoping for the best.

For many lifters, sticking with the program is a difficult task. Beginners seem to have a particular problem with this, and it's understandable. Everything is changing quickly. One day, snatches feel natural; the next day, the bar goes everywhere except where it's supposed to go. On Monday, you may easily stand up with your clean on every rep. On Wednesday, you may be catching a bit forward and struggle to stand up, or even fail to stand up with weights that were easy two days earlier.

The temptation is to work extra hard on the snatch after a sub-par day of snatching, do extra front squatting after a day or two when the cleans are hard to stand up with, or to change your training plan or even your whole philosophy after a bad week or two.

Giving in to temptation like this is almost always wrong. Assuming you're following a well-balanced program to begin with, have some faith. The road to the top is always filled with curves, and this particular road will only get longer if you jump around from one thing to another in your training.

A solid belief in what you're doing, a willingness to stay the course and put in the required amount of work will get you to the finish line a lot quicker than changing your training program every time you hit a bump in the road.

SAMPLE BEGINNER PROGRAM ONE

In the sample program on the following page, the numbers are theoretical. They're only listed so you can see the progression of weight increases and decreases throughout the eight-week program.

The program shows the lifter moving up one kilo per week. Unfortunately, it will never happen like that. You might move the weight up one week and proceed to miss several times. Don't move up again until you make all your programmed weights.

Try to resist the temptation to make big jumps. You'll make faster progress in the long run if you make small jumps and …**MAKE YOUR LIFTS**.

This program was written with the expectation that the last week of the training cycle includes a short taper, and you'll be competing on the Saturday of the eighth and final week.

SAMPLE BEGINNER PROGRAM ONE

MONDAY

Exercises	Week 1	Week 2	Week 3	Week 4	Week 5	Week 6	Week 7	Week 8 Competition Week
Snatch (from knees)	85 kg 3 Singles	86 kg 3 Singles	87 kg 3 Singles	88 kg 3 Singles	89 kg 3 Singles	90 kg 3 Singles	91 kg 3 Singles	Snatch (from floor) 80 kg x 1 85 kg x 1 87 kg x 1
Clean (from knees) and Jerk	110 kg 3 Singles	111 kg 3 Singles	112 kg 3 Singles	113 kg 3 Singles	114 kg 3 Singles	115 kg 3 Singles	116 kg 3 Singles	Clean (from floor) and Jerk 120 kg x 1 125 kg x 1 130 kg x 1
Back Squat	140 kg 3 x 5	144 kg 3 x 5	148 kg 3 x 5	152 kg 3 x 5	156 kg 3 x 5	160 kg 3 x 5	164 kg 3 x 5	165 kg 1 x 5
Push Press	75 kg 3 x 5	76 kg 3 x 5	77 kg 3 x 5	78 kg 3 x 5	79 kg 3 x 5	80 kg 3 x 5	81 kg 3 x 5	77 kg 1 x 5

WEDNESDAY

Exercises	Week 1	Week 2	Week 3	Week 4	Week 5	Week 6	Week 7	Week 8 Competition Week
Snatch (from hips)	90 kg 3 Singles	91 kg 3 Singles	92 kg 3 Singles	93 kg 3 Singles	94 kg 3 Singles	95 kg 3 Singles	96 kg 3 Singles	Snatch (from floor) 67 kg for 3 Singles
Clean (from hips) and Jerk	120 kg 3 Singles	121 kg 3 Singles	122 kg 3 Singles	123 kg 3 Singles	124 kg 3 Singles	125 kg 3 Singles	126 kg 3 Singles	Clean (from floor) and Jerk 110 kg for 3 Singles
Front Squat	114 kg 3 x 3	116 kg 3 x 3	118 kg 3 x 3	120 kg 3 x 3	122 kg 3 x 3	124 kg 3 x 3	126 kg 3 x 3	Front Squat Your Clean and Jerk Opener 3 x 1
Snatch-Grip Deadlift	140 kg 1 x 5	142 kg 1 x 5	144 kg 1 x 5	146 kg 1 x 5	148 kg 1 x 5	150 kg 1 x 5	152 kg 1 x 5	None

FRIDAY

Exercises	Week 1	Week 2	Week 3	Week 4	Week 5	Week 6	Week 7	Week 8 Competition Week
Snatch	80 kg 3 Singles	81 kg 3 Singles	82 kg 3 Singles	83 kg 3 Singles	84 kg 3 Singles	85 kg 3 Singles	86 kg 3 Singles	Warm-Up Snatch and Clean and Jerk with an empty bar. Then go home and rest!
Clean and Jerk	125 kg 3 Singles	126 kg 3 Singles	127 kg 3 Singles	128 kg 3 Singles	129 kg 3 Singles	130 kg 3 Singles	131 kg 3 Singles	
Back Squat	142 kg 3 x 5	146 kg 3 x 5	150 kg 3 x 5	154 kg 3 x 5	158 kg 3 x 5	162 kg 3 x 5	166 kg 3 x 5	

YOUR FIRST MEET

At this stage, training for competition shouldn't be drastically different from any other week. You won't need to do much tapering or peaking for your first meet. You should already be improving almost every week in the lifts, and it would be harmful to interrupt that steady progress.

As you finish the initial eight-week program and sign up for a Saturday competition, you'll train as you normally would on Monday, six days before the meet. On Monday, determine your first lifts for the meet—what weightlifters call "openers."

All lifters receive three total attempts for the snatch and three for the clean and jerk, with the highest successful weight for each lift added together to make a total. You need to be somewhat cautious when choosing openers because you're not allowed to choose a lighter weight if you've already attempted a heavier one.

For example, if you attempt 60 kilos for your first snatch and miss horribly, you can't then try 55; you're only allowed to try 60 kilos again or increase the weight on the bar. Therefore, your openers for your first meet should be weights you can confidently make. Resist your ego and choose openers you could complete for a double or even triple.

You'll have a much better experience if you go six for six than if you bomb out and miss all your lifts because you opened too heavily. If you have any doubt, choose a lighter opener. You can always increase the weight on the second attempt, and if you've already made one lift prior to that, you'll be lifting with much more confidence.

On the Monday before the competition, make sure you can easily lift your openers. Then, do your regular back-squat progression and your flexibility work.

On Wednesday, I recommend doing three singles with a weight that's about 80% of your projected opening lift.

For the front squats, reduce the volume to just three singles with the weight you plan to open with for the clean and jerk.

To allow for extra recovery, there will be no deadlifts performed on Wednesday. This temporary reduction of intensity should allow your legs to recover enough for Saturday without interrupting the training progression.

On Friday, work with the bar for a while and then finish with your normal flexibility routine. Next, rest and relax!

Don't be that lifter who shows up Saturday morning tired and bleary-eyed after staying up too late or partying with friends.

When you arrive at the competition venue, introduce yourself to the meet director and the other competitors, and let them know this is your first meet. Most will be happy to help if you get confused. Camaraderie is one of the greatest attributes of our sport.

For additional information on the inner workings of a weightlifting competition, skip ahead to Chapter 11. That chapter goes more in depth than needed for your first meet, but it's helpful information.

It's also useful to have a coach or training partner at the meet to help you perform at your best.

SAMPLE BEGINNER PROGRAM TWO

The second program is meant for the athlete who's already spent eight weeks on the first beginner program, or is coming to weightlifting from another sport having previously built some level of strength or work capacity.

The competition lifts are performed three times per week, and the strength work is set up on a five-week cycle where the intensity increases each week.

The strength work is based on a 3RM for each exercise opposed to a 5RM to demonstrate an alternative way of programming strength workouts; you should establish a 3RM before starting the program.

We'll also utilize lighter supplemental exercises for the hips and back, such as glute ham raises, back extensions, and hip extensions for two sets of 10 each.

If you can handle more volume, by all means raise that number to four or more sets.

SAMPLE BEGINNER PROGRAM TWO

	Exercises	Week 1	Week 2	Week 3	Week 4	Week 5	Week 6	Week 7	Week 8 Competition Week
MONDAY	Snatch (from knees)	75% 1RM 5 Doubles	80% 1RM 5 Doubles	82% 1RM 5 Doubles	84% 1RM 5 Doubles	86% 1RM 5 Doubles	Build to PR Double	80% 1RM 3 Doubles	80% 1RM 2 Doubles
	Clean (from knees) and Jerk	75% 1RM 5 Doubles	80% 1RM 5 Doubles	82% 1RM 5 Doubles	84% 1RM 5 Doubles	86% 1RM 5 Doubles	Build to PR Double	80% 1RM 3 Doubles	80% 1RM 2 Doubles
	Snatch-Grip Push Press (from behind the neck)	90% 3RM 5 x 3	93% 3RM 4 x 3	96% 3RM 3 x 3	98% 3RM 2 x 3	101% 3RM Build to New PR	90% 3RM 3 x 3	85% 3RM 2 x 3	80% of 3RM 1 x 3
	Hip Extensions	Barbell 2 x 10	Barbell + Weight 2 x 10	Barbell + Weight 2 x 10	Barbell + Weight 2 x 10	Barbell + Weight 2 x 10	Barbell + Weight 2 x 10	Barbell + Weight 2 x 10	Barbell + Weight 2 x 10

	Exercises	Week 1	Week 2	Week 3	Week 4	Week 5	Week 6	Week 7	Week 8 Competition Week
WEDNESDAY	Snatch (from most-needed position)	Up to 80% 1RM Singles or Doubles	Up to 80% 1RM Singles or Doubles	Up to 80% 1RM Singles or Doubles	Up to 80% 1RM Singles or Doubles	Up to 80% 1RM Singles or Doubles	Up to 80% 1RM Singles or Doubles	85% 1RM 3 Singles from floor	85% 1RM 3 Singles from floor
	Clean (from most-needed position) and Jerk	Up to 80% 1RM Singles or Doubles	Up to 80% 1RM Singles or Doubles	Up to 80% 1RM Singles or Doubles	Up to 80% 1RM Singles or Doubles	Up to 80% 1RM Singles or Doubles	Up to 80% 1RM Singles or Doubles	Proposed Opener from floor	75% 1RM 3 Singles from floor
	Front Squat	90% 3RM 5 x 3	93% 3RM 4 x 3	96% 3RM 3 x 3	98% 3RM 2 x 3	101% 3RM Build to New PR	90% 3RM 3 x 3	85% 3RM 2 x 3	Front Squat Your Clean and Jerk Opener 3 x 1
	Snatch-Grip Deadlift	90% 3RM 5 x 3	93% 3RM 4 x 3	96% 3RM 3 x 3	98% 3RM 2 x 3	101% 3RM Build to New PR	90% 3RM 3 x 3	85% 3RM 2 x 3	None
	Glute Ham Raise	Barbell 2 x 10	Barbell + Weight 2 x 10	Barbell + Weight 2 x 10	Barbell + Weight 2 x 10	Barbell + Weight 2 x 10	Barbell + Weight 2 x 10	Barbell + Weight 2 x 10	Barbell + Weight 1 x 10

SAMPLE BEGINNER PROGRAM TWO

	Exercises	Week 1	Week 2	Week 3	Week 4	Week 5	Week 6	Week 7	Week 8 Competition Week
FRIDAY	Snatch	75% 1RM 5 Doubles	80% 1RM 5 Doubles	82% 1RM 5 Doubles	84% 1RM 5 Doubles	86% 1RM 5 Doubles	Build to PR Double	Proposed Opener from floor	Light Bar Work
	Clean and Jerk	75% 1RM 5 Doubles (2+1)	80% 1RM 5 Doubles (2+1)	82% 1RM 5 Doubles (2+1)	84% 1RM 5 Doubles (2+1)	86% 1RM 5 Doubles (2+1)	Build to PR Double (2+1)	80% 1RM 3 Singles from floor	Light Bar Work
	Push Press	90% 3RM 5 x 3	93% 3RM 4 x 3	96% 3RM 3 x 3	98% 3RM 2 x 3	101% 3RM Build to New PR	90% 3RM 3 x 3	85% 3RM 2 x 3	80% 3RM 1 x 3
	Back Squat	90% 3RM 5 x 3	93% 3RM 4 x 3	96% 3RM 3 x 3	98% 3RM 2 x 3	101% 3RM Build to New PR	90% 3RM 3 x 3	85% 3RM 2 x 3	80% 3RM 1 x 3
	Back Extensions	Barbell 2 x 10	Barbell + Weight 2 x 10	Barbell + Weight 2 x 10	Barbell + Weight 2 x 10	Barbell + Weight 2 x 10	Barbell + Weight 2 x 10	Barbell + Weight 2 x 10	None

CLOSING THOUGHTS

These training programs are a continuation of learning the lifts; there's no clear break between learning and training. Through the beginner program—and even the intermediate program—you're still learning.

o   The biggest mistake you can make is to increase the weight too quickly.

o   Sticking with the competition lifts is important for a beginner. Small changes in a starting position, such as starting from the hips or knees, are all the variety you need at this stage of your training.

o   Use this time to hone your technical abilities in the snatch and the clean and jerk, all while getting strong with squats, deadlifts, and push presses.

And finally, don't put off signing up for your first meet. We made a deal many pages ago that you would sign up for a competition or set a date on the calendar for a planned max-out day if a competition isn't available.

If you haven't done that yet, make a plan to because the weeks surrounding your first competition will be some of the most productive weeks in your weightlifting career.

CHAPTER 7
PROGRAMMING FOR INTERMEDIATE WEIGHTLIFTERS

When you first begin weightlifting, building good motor patterns in the snatch and clean and jerk is your first priority. Training should consist almost exclusively of the competition lifts and basic strength exercises like the back squat, deadlift, and push press. Beginners see rapid strength gains workout to workout by simply adding weight to the bar on the strength exercises each training session.

Technique also improves rapidly because for beginners, mistakes are usually big mistakes and are easy to see and correct. An intermediate lifter is one for whom the period of easy beginner gains is over. Strength increases no longer come easily and technique, while consistent, contains small errors that are more difficult to see and correct.

For a beginner, training won't change much week to week, except perhaps for the last week of a cycle leading into a competition. As a lifter progresses to the intermediate stage, training cycles will change both week to week within the cycle, and from one training cycle to the next.

Beginners should develop a foundation of strength and technical mastery. As an intermediate, you'll build on that foundation as you add a variety of exercises and methods of training, such as complexes, lifting from blocks, timed sets, and different rep schemes.

Many of these new exercises, training methods, and rep ranges will present opportunities to set and then break PRs. We've touched upon this subject here and there before, but it's worth looking a little deeper into the topic of breaking PRs before discussing the fine details of the intermediate programming.

BREAKING PRS

Going to maximum is a skill, and the only way to get good at maxing is through practice. You have to challenge and break your PRs again and again. This is a mental challenge as well as a physical one, and requires both mental and physical toughness.

Photo 7.1—Travis Cooper in deep thought before snatching

Snatching 101 kilos for a new PR is physically similar to snatching 100 kilos to tie a PR. Mentally, though, it's a different ball game.

Breaking into uncharted territory and lifting something you've never lifted requires more commitment. It requires you to fight and win a battle in your mind. Anyone who's ever had problems committing to a snatch knows what that feels like. But with practice, you can get better at winning this mental battle.

This is one of the reasons I advocate keeping track of PRs from the hip and from the knee, as well as from the floor. I also keep track of doubles from these positions, and even other combinations, such as one snatch from the hip plus one from the knee, or one from the knee plus one from the floor.

Keeping track of a variety of PRs and constantly challenging them ensures training at maximal intensity. It means you're getting enough variety so you don't get stale and are constantly practicing the mental skill of breaking into uncharted territory.

As you get physically stronger, you'll also be getting mentally stronger. A lifter who competes long enough is eventually in the situation of having to make a new PR to win a competition, qualify for a national meet, or beat a rival.

Who do you think is more likely to make the lift when it matters—someone who challenges PRs in training on a consistent basis, or someone who doesn't?

SETTING UP A TRAINING CYCLE FOR THE INTERMEDIATE LIFTER

Training cycles start at a lower intensity, and the intensity increases throughout the cycle. They also tend to start with a higher volume of work, and that volume decreases as the cycle progresses. As you near the end of the cycle, you'll be focusing primarily on preparing for a competition and attempting heavy singles in the snatch and the clean and jerk. Although there are endless ways to plan the early weeks of a training cycle, the last weeks should always focus on peaking for the competition lifts.

For beginner lifters starting to divide training into training cycles, most of the variation of volume and intensity during the cycle can be ignored and implemented in the intermediate or even advanced stages.

For the "new" intermediate athlete, the intensity and volume will be set by the training program and the style of training (complexes, lifting from blocks, timed sets, etc.). As your time in the sport of weightlifting increases, you'll find what works best for you in relation to volume, intensity, exercises, and methods.

Next, we'll discuss different methods of training to incorporate into your training cycles depending on your needs as a lifter. When progressing from beginner to intermediate, you may be tempted to immediately add all of these training tools into your programming. Let me be the voice of reason: Adding one method at a time per training cycle is more beneficial. That will allow you to better assess if each addition worked.

Hopefully, you'll have many training cycles to complete and many years of training to test and progressively add more variation and creativity.

COMPLEXES

Complexes are useful tools that often go underutilized. A complex is a combination of lifts or portions of a lift typically done without rest. For example, a complex for the clean and jerk may call for one clean, two front squats, and one jerk, all done in succession.

Many useful complexes combine strength movements with the competition lifts or portions of the competition lifts, which tends to build strength more applicable to the snatch and the clean and jerk. Strength built from front squats done in a complex is usually more applicable to the competition lift than strength built with front squats as a standalone exercise.

Complexes are also excellent tools to stimulate hypertrophy. Weightlifting doesn't usually lead to hypertrophy for several reasons. First, the time under tension is quite low with exercises like the snatch or clean and jerk. Second, the competitive lifts include a low amount of eccentric contraction. Finally, since the bar must move at speed and through a multipart movement pattern, it's more difficult to achieve maximal muscle tension than in a simpler exercise such as a deadlift or back squat.

When performing a snatch, the bar is briefly in hand and supported by the body. Even when doing multiple reps, the reps are usually separated by dropping the bar, which takes tension off the body.

In a complex, stringing together multiple reps of snatch-specific exercises like one snatch pull, one hang snatch, and two overhead squats requires four reps that work the muscles needed to snatch, without taking tension off the body. In most complexes, the bar is either in your hands, on your shoulders, or supported by your legs for extended periods each set. The cumulative time under tension throughout the set and over multiple sets stimulates weightlifting-specific muscle growth.

Complexes can also be used to correct technical deficiencies. Pulls are simpler and less technically demanding than a snatch or clean. This makes it easier to correct flaws like cutting the pull short or sticking with the pull too long.

Use the appropriate pulling assistance exercise in complexes based on the technical flaws that need to be corrected.

If an athlete sticks with the pull for too long, a pull ending with a shrug or panda pull might work better than a high pull. For athletes who have problems cutting the pull too soon, a high pull might work better. If speed under the bar needs work, a panda pull would help put emphasis on pulling under the bar. When programming pulls plus the lifts, I use reps of two pulls plus one lift, or one pull and one lift.

I've found these various types of pulling exercises are more useful as part of a complex than as standalone exercises. Programming the pull or high pull as part of a complex that also includes snatches or cleans ensures that the pulling exercises are treated as an important part of training instead of just throwaway exercises done after the "important" parts of training.

For example, placing high pulls in a complex such as two high pulls plus one snatch will help the lifter focus on correctly performing both the high pull and snatch. Thinking about where athletes put their focus is an important part of coaching and writing training programs.

Good coaches think about what parts of each workout the athletes will put the most emphasis on and devote the most mental and physical energy toward. Athletes should think about where the coach expects them to put the most effort, and then get to work.

Complexes can also help improve confidence and skill during the jerk after a heavy clean; in fact, this is one of Travis Cooper's favorite exercises. Travis has an unbelievably strong clean, and if he misses a lift during a competition, it's almost always the jerk.

These misses typically occur on a third attempt when he hasn't had enough rest between his first two clean and jerks.

It's a problem that frequently plagues him because he usually starts his clean and jerks after the other competitors have finished. Because of this, he often has to follow himself, meaning shorter rests periods between lifts. Doing complexes with multiple jerks after his cleans helped Travis overcome this weakness and strengthened his jerk in a fatigued state.

There are numerous complexes that can be created using different portions of the lifts. Coaches and athletes should assess the current deficits going into a training cycle, and build a complex to address those needs.

You can include snatches and cleans from the hip or knee positions as necessary. Clean and jerks with an extra front squat or snatches with an extra overhead squat are two basic complexes.

Other complexes include a clean or a snatch with an extra pull performed prior to the lift. Performing multiple jerks after cleans worked well for Travis. Multiple overhead squats or snatch balances done after a snatch would work in a similar way.

On the following page, you'll find an example of daily programming using complexes across an eight-week training cycle; weights are listed as percentages.

The table assumes the lifter has a maximum clean and jerk of 130 kilos.

CLEAN AND JERK			
TRAINING WEEK	**SETS**	**REPS**	**WEIGHT**
Week 1 1 Clean + 2 Front Squats + 1 Jerk	3	Full Complex	104 kg (80%)
Week 2 1 Clean + 2 Front Squats + 1 Jerk	3	Full Complex	109 kg (84%)
Week 3 1 Clean + 2 Front Squats + 1 Jerk	3	Full Complex	114 kg (88%)
Week 4 1 Clean + 2 Front Squats + 1 Jerk	3	Full Complex	118 kg (91%)
Week 5 1 Clean + 2 Front Squats + 1 Jerk	2	Full Complex	122 kg (94%)
Week 6 Clean and Jerk	2	Singles	126 kg (97%)
Week 7 Clean and Jerk	1	Single	101% Go for PRs!
Week 8 Clean and Jerk	3	Singles	80%
Competition	-	-	**Make lifts! Go for PRs!**

LIFTING FROM BLOCKS

Photos 7.2–7.4—Lifting from blocks at knee height

Donny Shankle introduced me to the idea of using blocks during our time at California Strength. He'd been to the Olympic Training Center and learned of their importance from Zygmunt Smalcerz.

When he arrived back in California, Donny and I discussed the use of blocks and decided to use them to lift heavier weights from the floor. Prior to this, Donny's clean had been stuck at 205 kilos. Lifting from the blocks helped him overcome and surpass that.

In fact, if you search for "pulls off the blocks with BIG weight" on the California Strength YouTube channel, you'll see many big lifts made by Donny and others on the team. In that "BIG weight" video, he cleaned 222 kilos with the bar starting just below the knees, and 220 with the bar starting above the knees.

Using lifting blocks starts a lift at a higher point than lifting from the floor. This makes them seem similar to lifts from the hang position, but there are differences and benefits to both.

Lifts from the hang place more stress on the body because of the increased time under tension. This time under tension tires out weaker muscles faster than lifting from the floor and stimulates hypertrophy in these lagging areas.

Lifting from the hang utilizes the stretch reflex to perform the lift. Unlike lifts from the hang, lifting from blocks starts from a dead stop; there's no stretch reflex. To lift from a dead stop, a lifter must go from no force output to maximal force output.

Many coaches think this makes lifts from blocks more similar to the actual lift from the floor, with greater carryover than lifts from the hang. One isn't better than the other—they're simply different skills that can be used to increase the weight lifted from the floor.

Photos 7.5–7.7—Lifting from blocks above knee height

SNATCH FROM BLOCKS			
TRAINING WEEK	**SETS**	**REPS**	**WEIGHT**
Week 1 **Snatch from Blocks, Knee Height**	3–5	Singles	80 kg (80%)
Week 2 **Snatch from Blocks, Knee Height**	3–5	Singles	84 kg (84%)
Week 3 **Snatch from Blocks, Knee Height**	3	Singles	88 kg (88%)
Week 4 **Snatch from Blocks, Knee Height**	3	Singles	91 kg (91%)
Week 5 **Snatch from Blocks, Knee Height**	2	Singles	94 kg (94%)
Week 6 **Snatch from Blocks, Knee Height**	2	Singles	97 kg (97%)
Week 7 **Snatch from Blocks, Knee Height**	1	Single	101 % Go for PRs!
Week 8 **Snatch from Floor**	3	Singles	80%
Competition	-	-	**Make lifts!** **Go for PRs!**

Correcting timing deficiencies in the snatch and clean is another benefit of using blocks that place the bar at varied heights. Blocks place the barbell at a specific point of the pull where you can execute the lift from that point, much like putting a ball on a tee. This way, we avoid the obstacles before that point in the pull.

For example, if a lifter has trouble navigating around the knees in the snatch, we might use blocks at a height that places the bar just below the kneecaps. The lifter can then snatch from this trouble spot without errors from the floor coming into play.

At California Strength, and later at MuscleDriver USA, we developed lifting from the blocks into a programming staple to improve weak points in the competition lifts. Over time, they even became a measure of efficiency for advanced lifters, the goal being to have the best lift from the hang match the best lift from the blocks.

For example, a lifter who can snatch 140 kilos from the hang, lowering the bar to the knees and a block height placing the bar at the knees has a high level of efficiency. A lifter who lacks in one lift has room for improvement.

Like any other method, lifting from blocks is a tool an athlete and coach need to discover how best to implement based on the individual needs. The correct block height is different for every lifter, and it can be difficult to find the correct spot.

The table on the previous page is an example of daily programming using snatches from blocks with the bar set at knee height across an eight-week training cycle. This would be a good change from snatches done from the knees on a Monday. Weights are listed as percentages; this example lifter has a maximum snatch from the blocks with the bar set at knee height of 100 kilos.

TIMED SETS

I got the idea for timed sets from Louie Simmons of Westside Barbell, who uses sets of one or two reps with a brief rest between sets for the powerlifters he coaches. As a former powerlifter, I used to talk to Louie often, and this was one of the ideas he suggested. I used it in the 1990s with the back squat, and had success improving my strength.

Later, when I converted to weightlifting, I tried it on the snatch and found the idea actually worked better for the Olympic lifts than it did for the power lifts.

After I used timed sets for several years, I discovered Joe Mills used something similar at the Central Falls Weightlifting Club in Rhode Island many decades prior.

Around 2005, when I first wrote blog posts explaining how they were done, several respected weightlifting coaches said it was a ridiculous idea to do another set before completely recovering from the prior set. Oddly, one of those people now uses them extensively in his online training programs.

In the current age of CrossFit, timed sets have gained popularity because they pair weightlifting with oxygen debt, two things CrossFitters love. But most CrossFit athletes don't know that a loose form of the idea was first used by Joe Mills in the 1960s, and an exact form of the Every Minute on the Minute workout (EMOM) was used in Texas in the 1990s—timed-set training predates CrossFit by decades.

This simple method can be used for both the snatch and the clean and jerk. The most basic example of a timed or EMOM set and what I originally used involves performing snatch singles EMOM for 10 minutes with 70% of a snatch 1RM. That will be a good starting point for many lifters. Most people can eventually use 75 or 80%, and some can go as high as 85%. With higher percentages, especially with clean and jerks, there's value in expanding the rest from 60 to 90 seconds.

THE BENEFITS OF TIMED SETS

Timed sets work because they allow fatigue to gradually accumulate. During a normal set with just a few seconds of rest between repetitions, the first rep will typically be the easiest, the smoothest, and done with the best technique.

As fatigue builds, subsequent reps will generally become sloppier, and usually the last rep of a set is both the most difficult and technically the worst.

But during a timed or EMOM set, the athlete has nearly a minute of rest between repetitions. It's not quite enough for full recovery, but enough to ensure that additional fatigue accumulates gradually.

This difference in the rate at which fatigue accumulates is why timed or EMOM sets work so well.

It's overwhelming when fatigue accumulates too quickly. When watching someone do a conventional set of three snatches, the buildup of fatigue and deterioration in technique over the three reps is usually very apparent.

But if it accumulates slowly enough, athletes adjust and find a way to make lifts in spite of it.

During an EMOM set, the changes happen gradually. Pulling strength fades throughout the set, but other aspects slowly improve. During a timed set, you'll find yourself moving a little faster, going under the bar a little deeper, and hesitating a little less as the set progresses. Timed or EMOM sets are a wonderful way to ingrain more efficient technique because they actually improve technique during the set and during the workout.

Every single rep is a first rep, and that's another benefit of this method. Each repetition requires that you approach the bar, lower yourself into position, grasp the bar, and lift—the elements of competition attempts. The first reps are always a little different from subsequent reps, even if just mentally.

Like anything else, you get good at what you practice: Timed sets provide a *lot* of practice on first reps.

PROGRAMMING TIMED SETS

Timed sets are a technique every lifter should experiment with at some point. My only caution is to gradually acclimate to the training style, as it can provide a deceptively intense training session.

No single lift ever feels maximal, but if this type of training is done with too high a percentage of maximum or too many lifts per session, you can burn out and go backward.

To avoid this, start with 70% once a week for both the snatch and the clean and jerk. You can do them both on the same day, but this makes for a very difficult training session. Make sure to use another method for the other training sessions during the week.

A repeating cycle is another idea I got from Louie Simmons. In this, a beginner might do 15 lifts with 70% the first week, then the next week 12 lifts with 75%, then nine lifts with 80% the third week.

I've had lifters with good work capacity work up to 24 lifts with 70%, then 18 lifts with 75%, and finally, 12 lifts with 80% on the third week.

I certainly wouldn't attempt that on your first cycle using timed sets; however, as your work capacity builds, you may be able to use 75, 80, and 85% intensities for a rotating cycle.

I've had the most success with timed sets when lifting from the floor, but it's worth trying from different positions.

Be creative and experiment with different ways of using timed sets, such as using them for one lift while using more conventional methods for another. Just remember that your goal is to increase the competition lifts at the end of each cycle.

With that goal in mind, timed sets have but one weakness—you usually can't approach maximal weights while doing them. That's primarily the reason to use this method at the start of a training cycle, and then switch to more conventional methods of training as the cycle progresses.

The table on the following page is an example of a training cycle starting with timed sets done once per week with the snatch. The lifter is assumed to have a max of 100 kilos. Week one will use 70% of the 1RM snatch. Week two will use 75% 1RM, and week three will use 80% 1RM.

Photo 7.8—Travis Cooper resting between lifts during training

SNATCH			
TRAINING WEEK	SETS	REPS	WEIGHT
Week 1	20	Singles	70 kg, EMOM
Week 2	15	Singles	75 kg, EMOM
Week 3	10	Singles	80 kg, EMOM
Week 4	2	Triples	82 kg, then 85 kg for PR Triple
Week 5	3	Doubles	88 kg
Week 6	2	Doubles	92 kg
Week 7	3	Singles	96 kg
Week 8	3	Singles	80 kg
Competition	-	-	**101 kg Competition PR!**

ASSISTANCE EXERCISES

As with the beginner programs, the strength work in the intermediate programs can be categorized as exercises related to pulling, squatting, or overhead strength. These exercises will aid in building strength and are complementary to the snatch, the clean, and the jerk.

Be careful not to get too carried away with assistance exercises. All assistance exercises, even the squat, are supplemental to the competition lifts. Two of the most common mistakes lifters make are either adding too many assistance movements, or putting too much emphasis on them.

For example, don't start with only the push press and bench press, and then add the snatch-grip push press. If the snatch-grip push press is what you really need, drop the bench press to make room for it. If an exercise isn't important enough to warrant excluding another from the program, it's probably not important enough to do.

It's possible to climb to a high level in weightlifting with only snatches, clean and jerks, and squatting. Assistance exercises do just what the name implies: They assist. Make sure to keep them in the proper place.

ASSISTANCE EXERCISES FOR THE PULL

DEADLIFTS VERSUS PULLS

Let's differentiate between snatch-grip and clean-grip deadlifts and their pull counterparts. In the beginner programs, there's no mention of snatch or clean pulls…only deadlifts. I call the lifts in that chapter "deadlifts" because of the way they're programmed based on capability in the deadlift motion, while exercises referred to as "pulls" are programmed based on the max snatch or clean.

As you will no doubt have learned over the weeks and months of practicing them, the weights used for deadlifts is often far in excess of what you're capable of in the competition lifts. That's normal; beginners usually aren't skilled enough to snatch and clean with weight that's representative of their actual strength, and is why we don't base the deadlift weights on the snatch or clean.

The weight used for deadlifts will always be heavy, and while it may seem impossible at times, put in the

effort to execute the double knee bend and shrug at the top—even a small effort will lead to more carry-over to the competition lifts.

My personal preference for pulling assistance even at the intermediate level remains snatch-grip and clean-grip deadlifts programmed as they were when initially learning them. The importance of increasing strength can't be overemphasized. But, as a lifter becomes more skilled, the snatch and clean will become more representative of the actual strength level. Hence, pulling assistance with weights based on the snatch or clean becomes a better choice.

Photo 7.9—Spencer Moorman training

Most athletes will have a long period as they move from the beginner stage to the intermediate stage when the deadlift is still important, but they'll need to modulate the intensity when they're near a competition so they aren't pulling weights too out of line with the competition lifts.

For a meet where it's important to make a big total, such as a qualifying meet or the state championships, I recommend not doing any pulling or deadlifting over 110% of your snatch or clean and jerk maxes for the last four weeks leading into the competition.

When performing pulls ending with a shrug, execute the double knee bend and start the second pull in the correct position, just as in the snatch or clean. The shrug on this exercise is performed as the bar is rising, and is used to pull the bar higher.

SNATCH AND CLEAN PULLS ENDING WITH A SHRUG

Photos 7.10–7.13—Snatch pull ending with a shrug

On the actual snatch or clean, it's the shrug that initializes the downward motion of the body. This exercise is a tool for training speed on the pull and developing strength by using weights heavier than you can currently snatch or clean.

Performance

Execute the movement just as you would the snatch or clean, but end the lift by shrugging the bar up instead of shrugging the body down. The arms should remain inactive other than simply holding the bar. Avoid purposely pulling the bar up with the arms.

Photo 7.14—Rob Blackwell snatching 120 kilos

Photos 7.15–7.18—Clean pull ending with a shrug

SNATCH AND CLEAN HIGH PULLS

Photos 7.19–7.22—Snatch high pull

Photos 7.23–7.27—Clean high pull

The high pull brings the traps, shoulders, and arms into play to continue pulling the bar upward after the influence of the hips and legs has ended. This places significant stress on these muscle groups and is one of the reasons to program this exercise.

The high pull can also have a straightening influence on the bar path for both competitive lifts. Many lifters allow the barbell to loop out away from the body during the pull. The high pull is a tool to correct this—especially for the snatch—by teaching lifters to keep the barbell close to the body and to actively use the arms in the later stages of the lift.

Performance

This exercise will build on the pulls ending with a shrug. Set up as you would when performing a snatch or clean, and begin to lift the bar. After the explosive second pull, instead of pulling your body down to the bar to catch it, you'll continue to pull the bar up with the traps, arms, and shoulders. As this happens, drive the elbows out to the side while pulling the bar. The bar path should remain as vertical as possible, and continue the upward movement of the bar.

SNATCH AND CLEAN PANDA PULLS

The panda pull has gained popularity—and its name—because of its use by Chinese weightlifters. It's a great exercise to develop timing and rhythm for the third pull of the snatch and the clean. It can be a tough exercise to master, but developing it will be a great asset to your lifting, especially when it's time to change direction to receive heavy snatches and cleans.

The contribution of the hips and legs are the same for the panda pull as they are for other types of pulls. But at the point in the high pull where the traps, shoulders, and arms are pulling the bar higher, the panda pull differs, as the athlete bends the hips and knees to lower the shoulders and hips and begin the motion of pulling the body down into the catch position. The athlete will stop short of turning the bar over to catch it in the receiving position—overhead on the snatch or on the shoulders for the clean.

You want to keep the torso upright when moving down, rather than let the shoulders be pulled forward.

Photos 7.28–7.32—Snatch panda pull

Photos 7.33–7.37—Clean panda pull

This pull is frequently used in complexes, along with the snatch or clean in a similar fashion as the pull or high pull. It's less often used for its effect on strength as for its effect on timing, and is the pull variation that most closely mimics the timing of the competition snatch and clean.

Performance

The panda pull is performed like a high pull, but instead of pulling the bar up with the shoulders, traps, and arms, you'll pull the body down at the end of the exercise. Keep the torso as close as possible to vertical. As you pull your body down to the bar, concentrate on pulling the hips down in a squatting motion, not leaning the shoulders forward. The elbows should travel straight out to the side as the torso moves down.

The bar path needs to be very straight as well. The torso is usually lowered four to six inches, and many lifters will move their feet into the receiving position as they pull the body down to the barbell.

POWER SNATCHES AND POWER CLEANS

As outlined in Chapter 1, the power snatch or power clean are best suited for athletes beyond the beginner stage, or at least beyond the first few months of lifting. The power versions of the lifts allow greater errors with the lift still successfully completed. This is bad for beginners. Missed lifts alert the athlete to mistakes. Masking that feedback with power variations makes it more difficult to learn efficient and consistent technique.

For example, we've all witnessed a lifter take steps forward or backward immediately upon completion of a lift when doing the power variations. It's likely the lift would have been missed if it had been received in a full squat, but there's more room for error catching the bar high rather than low. That may seem like a good thing, but it's not; missing sends a stronger message than simply taking a step. For beginners, the fact that the lift *has* to be in the right place to be successful is invaluable for learning.

"Powers" also encourage a slightly different movement pattern than their full counterparts. Lifters who first learn and develop the power variations almost inevitably have different pull mechanics in the full lifts. This pull is longer, slower, and just doesn't appear to have quite as much snap. These athletes frequently over-pull or stick with the pull too long instead of starting the descent under the bar. An athlete who over-pulls usually puts too much emphasis on the shrug, or uses the arms to pull the bar up.

Plenty of lifters can power snatch or clean more weight than they can use with the full lifts—it's no badge of honor. Continuing to pull the bar past the point where you should have started pulling your body down might give you success at first, but eventually you'll have to go back and learn to pull correctly, and this takes time…often a lot of time.

The correct time to introduce the power versions is after establishing proper motor patterns for the full lifts with a high level of consistency. This is usually somewhere after the third month through the first year of training.

Photo 7.38—Spencer Moorman walking the fine line between full and power snatch

Photos 7.39–7.45—The power snatch

BENEFITS OF THE POWER VARIATIONS

There's no doubt the initial learning of the snatch and the clean should be focused on cementing motor patterns that benefit the full lifts. However, once that's been accomplished, the power versions can be incorporated into training, and there's much to gain from using them.

The power variations are easier to recover from because they're done with a lighter weight and the bar is moving faster. You can do more lifts per session, train them more times per week, and use a higher percentage of max than with the full lifts.

However, if you're still at the point where you can power snatch or power clean more than you can snatch or clean, you shouldn't be doing them.

USING THE POWER VARIATIONS IN TRAINING

For the lifter who's ready, one way to program the power variations that's proven successful is to use them on alternate days from the full lifts. That's how I used them when coaching Donny, Jon, Travis, and many others. As a group, these lifters normally did at least as many total lifts to a power position as they did to the full position. They also averaged higher intensity in the power variations and went to max more often.

I've found over the years that challenging maximal lifts is the best way to employ the power snatch and power clean. The most valuable reps are where you really struggle to get your feet down and stop the bar before your thighs go below parallel.

As the weight becomes heavier and you catch it lower and lower, two things will happen. First, you have to put the bar in an increasingly perfect position. Second, you have to move faster and ready your body to receive the bar quicker.

The most useful reps for the power variations are those where you can stop with the thighs just above parallel for a good lift or where the thighs go just below parallel for a close miss. Those two or three repetitions where you're right around parallel with a maximal weight have more positive training effect than the entire rest of the workout.

I always encourage one more attempt at a power snatch or power clean PR if the last attempt was anywhere close, and this is why.

Photos 7.46–7.52—The power clean

OVERHEAD ASSISTANCE EXERCISES

Much like my feelings concerning the importance of the actual snatch and clean versus assistance exercises for the pull, the most important exercise you can do for overhead strength is the actual jerk (and snatch) as it's performed in competition. But, there are a couple of exercises that can both improve overhead strength and make it safer to hold weight overhead.

Weightlifting as a sport doesn't have a high injury rate, but some of the injuries that occur at the elbow and shoulder joints are difficult to come back from, if not career ending. You only have to witness one elbow dislocation to know you never want to put yourself at that risk. To ward off injury and ensure proper upper-body strength and muscular development, all weightlifters should do some amount of pressing.

Push presses can be performed multiple ways. In earlier chapters and in the beginner program, we used push presses from the front rack with a clean grip. As an intermediate, you can do the push press with a clean grip from the front rack or from behind the neck. Most athletes can lift a little more from behind the neck with a clean grip, but the exercises are largely the same. You can also do them with a snatch-width grip done from behind the neck.

All forms of push pressing are valuable, but most lifters find one version that works best for them and will stick with it for an extended time.

For one reason or another, an athlete will eventually find the need to add a second pressing or overhead assistance exercise. Some lifters have a unique need for more pressing. Many female lifters fall into this category because of joint laxity.

For these lifters, the bench press is a good addition. It's an excellent strength builder and is appropriate for any lifter who doesn't have a problem with tight shoulders or pecs. Saturday is a good day to do the bench press if you're already doing the push press on Tuesday or Wednesday.

You should be doing the jerk either by itself or as part of the clean and jerk two or three times per week, and that will continue to be the most important part of your jerk training. If you do pressing exercises on the same day as jerks, do the jerks first.

The same three sets of five reps used in the beginner program are still the right intensity and volume of work for the intermediate weightlifter. It's a little easier to overwork the shoulders than it is to overwork the hips and legs, so be careful not to unnecessarily increase the volume.

If you're a split jerker, adding the specific drills described in Chapter 3 to improve the split position makes a great training program for the jerk. Most athletes who split jerk can use more weight when they split, and will do that most of the time in training, but the power jerk is an excellent assistance exercise for the split jerk if needed.

Some lifters do more power jerks early in a training cycle, then progress to doing the majority of jerks with the split later in the cycle when the biggest weights are handled. This strategy works well for a lot of people.

ASSISTANCE EXERCISES FOR THE LEGS

Back squats are the best strength-building exercise for the entire body, as well as being a great leg developer. The front squat is also a valuable leg-strength builder, and has the advantage of being more specific than the back squat.

Every clean and jerk involves a front squat; how easily you stand is the key to successfully completing the lift. But, even with the front squat's specificity, I still program twice as many back squats as front squats for three reasons:

1. The back squat is a better strength developer than the front squat. It utilizes more muscle, and builds more muscle in the quads, hips, and hamstrings. It's a better overall leg developer.

2. A weightlifter will be front squatting two or three times per week as part of the clean or clean and jerk training. This lessens the need for as many front squat sessions.

3. Strength gained in the back squat carries over to the front squat to a large degree.

For these reasons, most athletes won't need to front squat as often as they back squat.

In the beginner program, we started with a simple three-day-a-week squat program, taking advantage of the linear progress that almost every beginner can utilize. For some, that lasts a couple of months; for others, it can last six months to a year. If you don't get enough sleep, have a poor diet, or are obsessed with keeping your abs sharp, the length of your beginner gains might be closer to a month or two.

On the other hand, if you get plenty of sleep, eat a great diet, and aren't afraid to eat enough, you have a good chance of making major progress on the squat and competition total during your first year of lifting. With a little effort, you can keep your beginner gains going longer.

But all good things eventually come to an end, and the days of automatically adding a couple of kilos to your squat bar every workout will be over. That doesn't mean your progress will grind to a halt; it just means it will slow down. At this point, you don't need more exercises, but instead will need an adjustment to the method.

THE TEXAS METHOD

The Texas Method is the first change an athlete should make when straight linear progression no longer works. I didn't come up with the name "The Texas Method;" someone else came up with the name and it stuck. It stemmed from my time in Texas when my lifters and I happened upon this method of progression by pure trial and error.

At the time, the lifters were back squatting on Mondays and Fridays for five sets of five reps, along with front squats on Wednesdays for three sets of three—not too different from what you previously experienced on the beginner program.

However, the volume was much greater, and a 5x5 program twice a week is particularly difficult. Because of that, a few lifters approached me with a bet to lessen their workload. They wanted to attempt a PR squat weight for just one set of five on Friday. If successful, they'd be excused from doing the remaining four sets of five that day. If they couldn't make the PR, they'd have to finish the other four sets.

A few lifters attempted a max set of back squats, and at least one of them made a five-rep PR. This challenge slowly caught on, and within a few weeks, about half the team was trying for a five-rep squat PR on Fridays with the incentive that they wouldn't have to endure the full squat workout.

It wasn't long before some of the athletes were trying to do as little as possible on Wednesdays (and going to great lengths to get away with doing as little as possible) to allow their bodies extra rest before attempting the PR sets on Friday.

I soon realized the athletes who were doing less on Wednesdays and attempting a PR every Friday were making better progress than those who were doing the whole program as written.

As a result, I adopted the "new" squat program, and it evolved into a hard squat session on Mondays, an easier session on Wednesdays, and then a PR attempt on Fridays—The Texas Method.

The Texas Method is probably one of the only training programs not designed by a coach, but instead coming from a group of lifters trying to get out of doing all the prescribed work. Even though this program was accidentally created largely by weightlifters, it works remarkably well—better than any other program I've used.

It's surprisingly adaptable, and as long as the basic premise is followed (a high-volume, medium-intensity session early in the week, a lower-volume, lower-intensity session in the middle of the week, and a lower-volume but high-intensity session at the end of the week), it can be adapted to many set-and-rep schemes and still retain its effectiveness. Over the years, I've used the Texas Method with hundreds of lifters—ranging from beginners to world team members—with equally great results.

As is typically the case, the program's effectiveness is due to its simplicity. Although any rep number can be used, the program is commonly done with sets of five.

On Monday, you'll perform three to five sets of five at a weight that's difficult but not impossible—for example, 90% of your best single set of five (5RM). Wednesday serves as a lighter day when you'll front squat for three sets of three. Although these front squats won't feel light, they'll place much less stress on the body than back squats, and will act as a form of recovery. Friday is the heaviest day, where you'll attempt a five-rep PR. Thus, Monday is the high-volume day, Wednesday is the "rest" day, and Friday or Saturday is the high-intensity day.

Additionally, the Texas Method can be utilized for many other exercises, such as pressing variations. Always start with three sets of five reps on Monday. With that as a base, many lifters can then work up to five sets of five on Monday, but there's no need to start with that much volume. Using this general principle of modulating intensity throughout the week, I've had success using sets of 10, sets of three, and even singles.

Moving from the beginner program using a linear progression to the Texas Method should be seamless. You can start your week as if you're continuing the linear progression with squats as usual on Monday. Simply use 10% less weight for three to five sets of five. Do your normal front squats on Wednesday, and then on Friday or Saturday, go for a PR set of five. After that, it's just a matter of gradually increasing the weight each week.

THE PENDLAY CYCLE

Should you reach a point using the Texas Method when consistent weekly progress has stalled on squats, deadlifts, and push presses, you might be ready for the more advanced approach of the Pendlay Cycle. This six-week cycle builds up to an attempt at a new rep max for the number of reps programmed on the sixth week of training. This cycle can be repeated indefinitely, and uses increasing intensity coupled with a decreasing number of sets each week.

I can't over-emphasize the importance of continuing to base all training on a rep max for the exercise and number of repetitions. Basing your strength training on a three- or five-rep max instead of a max single is a more precise method of programming because athletes differ in the ability to perform reps.

When basing squats or push presses on a maximum single, one athlete might easily be able to perform five repetitions with 90%. For this athlete, five reps at 90% might not be difficult enough to stimulate further adaptation. Yet for another athlete, five reps at 90% might be impossible.

You may look at this as one athlete being exceptionally good at singles, or as one athlete being exceptionally good at repetitions. No matter how you see it, athletes differ in the ability to perform reps at the same percentage of a single-rep maximum.

This difference can make it hard to precisely program sets of five, three or even two based on a single-rep maximum. Hence, in preparation for the cycle, you'll need to establish a best set of five, or whatever rep plan you intend to use.

Every athlete should go through at least one or two cycles based on the 5RM before trying another rep number. I use this method most often with sets of five, three, and two, but there's no reason you couldn't use it with other rep numbers as well.

The Pendlay cycle uses a repeating five-week plan of decreasing training volume by lowering the number of sets per session and increasing the intensity. The number of repetitions per set stays the same.

On the sixth week of training, I advise athletes to try for a one-kilo PR on the first set. Once a new PR has been set, try what you think you're capable of on the second set.

After finishing a complete cycle, go straight into another one, starting over at week one. Or take a rest week on whatever exercises you're using this cycle. I usually don't think a rest week is needed when doing squats, but when the exercise is the deadlift, one or two rest weeks might be necessary.

For a workout using sets of five reps, the cycle would look like the chart on the following page.

THE PENDLAY CYCLE		
Training Week	Intensity	Sets x Reps
Week 1	85 to 88% of 5RM	5 x 5
Week 2	90% of 5RM	5 x 5
Week 3	93% of 5RM	4 x 5
Week 4	96% of 5RM	3 x 5
Week 5	98% of 5RM	2 x 5
Week 6	101% of 5RM	2 x 5

INTERMEDIATE PROGRAMS

In the coming pages, you'll see examples of three intermediate training programs. They represent different approaches people take in training, and utilize different tools as outlined in this chapter.

The general intermediate programs presented consist of either four, five, or six training sessions per week. Four training sessions works well for those working a job or going to school full time. Five or six sessions per week are great for people who have more available time in their schedules. Having the time to train five or six days per week is the easy part, but you also need time to recover well with adequate amounts of rest, sleep, and a proper diet.

For intermediate athletes, training four days a week is a baseline that should work for almost everyone. A five- or six-day program is only achievable if weightlifting is the top priority. Everyone who loves lifting barbells would be thrilled to train six days per week, or even twice a day with the lifestyle of a professional weightlifter, but unfortunately, most of us aren't in that position. On the upside, you'll always make more progress doing too little than you will make doing too much.

As in the second beginner program, we base percentages on the actual lift, not on the full snatch or clean and jerk unless those are the exercises being performed. For example, a snatch from the knees at 75% is based on the one-rep max snatch done from the knees. A clean from the hips and jerk is based on the one-rep max clean from the hips and jerk.

The back squat and other strength exercise percentages are based on a rep maximum of the rep number. For example, five sets of three reps at 80% will be based on a 3RM for that particular exercise. By this point, every individual lift should have its own specific PR on which you'll base your training.

Throughout the programs, you'll see different representations of how sets and repetitions should be performed. For example, you might see a clean from the knees and jerk for five sets of two plus one. That "two plus one" indicates two cleans and one jerk.

On another day, you might see a snatch from the hips for five sets of two. On this day, you'd perform two consecutive snatches from the hip position without dropping the barbell between repetitions.

If you see "clean and jerk for five sets of two," perform five sets of one clean plus one jerk, immediately followed by one clean plus one jerk.

FOUR-DAY SAMPLE INTERMEDIATE PROGRAM

Each training session on the four-day plan should take two hours or less. Monday, Wednesday, and Friday start with the competition lifts. After following the three-day program for several months, you should know which positions work best for you, and you'll prioritize those positions based on your individual needs.

Most, but not all, lifters end up keeping the lifts from the knee in the program. The hip is the position most often eliminated in favor of two sessions from the knees or two sessions from the floor, or add one session lifting off the blocks with the bar starting at knee height. Regardless of the changes you make on Monday and Wednesday, I still recommend going from the floor on Friday.

All strength exercises are programmed with a training cycle that uses weekly increased intensity and a decreased number of sets. On Monday, you'll also train the push press for sets of five. At the end of training on both Monday and Friday, the program calls for posterior-chain assistance work, hopefully using the GHD to perform hip and back extensions for sets of 10 repetitions.

On Wednesday, after training the competition lifts, front squat for sets of three and snatch-grip deadlift for sets of five. By this point, you should have a feel for how heavy deadlifts affect your capacity in the competition lifts, and you can decrease the weight to something that won't negatively affect your snatch and clean and jerk prior to competition.

You should also be performing the deadlifts as close as possible to the performance of a snatch or snatch pull, or clean or clean pull. This includes starting with the hips in the same position as the competitive lifts, using the double knee bend, and ending with a shrug if possible.

On Saturday, you'll back squat, clean-grip deadlift, and bench press for sets of five on all three exercises. If you have a problem supporting snatches overhead, you could replace the bench press with snatch-grip push presses from behind the neck. Saturdays will conclude with sets of 10 glute ham raises.

A general program template for a four-day-a-week schedule is shown below.

MONDAY

Exercises	Sets x Reps	Weight
Snatch (from blocks at knee height)	3–5 Singles	80%
Clean (from blocks at knee height) and Jerk	3–5 Singles	80%
Overhead Assistance	5 x 5	85–88% 5RM
Posterior-Chain Assistance	2 x 10	Barbell

WEDNESDAY

Exercises	Sets x Reps	Weight
Snatch (from most needed position)	5 Doubles	80%
Clean (from most needed position) and Jerk	5 Doubles (2+1)	80%
Front Squat	5 x 3	85–88% 3RM
Pull Assistance	5 x 5	85–88% 5RM

FRIDAY

Exercises	Sets x Reps	Weight
Snatch	5 Doubles	80%
Clean and Jerk	5 Doubles (2+1)	80%
Posterior-Chain Assistance	2 x 10	Barbell

SATURDAY

Exercises	Sets x Reps	Weight
Back Squat	5 x 5	85–88% 5RM
Pull Assistance	5 x 5	85–88% 5RM
Overhead Assistance	5 x 5	85–88% 5RM
Posterior-Chain Assistance	2 x 10	Barbell

SAMPLE INTERMEDIATE 4-DAY PROGRAM

MONDAY

Exercises	Week 1	Week 2	Week 3	Week 4	Week 5	Week 6	Week 7	Week 8 Competition Week
Snatch from Blocks (from knee height)	80% 3–5 Singles	84% 3–5 Singles	88% 3 Singles	91% 3 Singles	94% 2 Singles	97% 2 Singles	101% Max Out	80% 3 Singles (from floor)
Clean from Blocks (from knee height) and Jerk	80% 3–5 Singles	84% 3–5 Singles	88% 3 Singles	91% 3 Singles	94% 2 Singles	97% 2 Singles	101% Max Out	80% 3 Singles (from floor)
Snatch-Grip Push Press (from behind the neck)	85–88% 5RM 5 x 5	90% 5RM 5 x 5	93% 5RM 4 x 5	96% 5RM 3 x 5	98% 5RM 2 x 5	101% 5RM 2 x 5	85% 5RM 1 x 5	80% 5RM 1 x 5
Hip Extensions	Barbell 2 x 10	Barbell + Weight 2 x 10	Barbell + Weight 2 x 10	Barbell + Weight 2 x 10	Barbell + Weight 2 x 10	Barbell + Weight 2 x 10	Barbell + Weight 2 x 10	Barbell + Weight 1 x 10

WEDNESDAY

Exercises	Week 1	Week 2	Week 3	Week 4	Week 5	Week 6	Week 7	Week 8 Competition Week
Snatch (from most needed position)	80% 5 Doubles	82% 5 Doubles	84% 4 Doubles	86% 3 Doubles	88% 3 Doubles	101% PR Doubles	80% 2 Doubles	80% 3 Singles (from floor)
Clean (from most needed position) and Jerk	80% 5 Doubles (2+1)	82% 5 Doubles (2+1)	84% 4 Doubles (2+1)	86% 3 Doubles (2+1)	88% 3 Doubles (2+1)	101% PR Doubles (2+1)	80% 2 Doubles (2+1)	80% 3 Singles (from floor)
Front Squat	85–88% 3RM 5 x 3	90% 3RM 5 x 3	93% 3RM 4 x 3	96% 3RM 3 x 3	98% 3RM 2 x 3	101% 3RM 2 x 3	85% 3RM 1 x 3	80% 3RM 1 x 3
Snatch-Grip Deadlift	85–88% 5RM 5 x 5	90% 5RM 5 x 5	93% 5RM 4 x 5	96% 5RM 3 x 5	98% 5RM 2 x 5	101% 5RM 2 x 5	85% 5RM 1 x 5	None

FRIDAY

Exercises	Week 1	Week 2	Week 3	Week 4	Week 5	Week 6	Week 7	Week 8 Competition Week
Snatch	80% 5 Doubles	82% 5 Doubles	84% 4 Doubles	86% 3 Doubles	88% 3 Doubles	101% PR Doubles	80% 2 Doubles	Barbell warm-up and stretching Go home
Clean and Jerk	80% 5 Doubles (2+1)	82% 5 Doubles (2+1)	84% 4 Doubles (2+1)	86% 3 Doubles (2+1)	88% 3 Doubles (2+1)	101% PR Doubles (2+1)	80% 2 Doubles (2+1)	
Back Extensions	Barbell 2 x 10	Barbell + Weight 2 x 10	Barbell + Weight 2 x 10	Barbell + Weight 2 x 10	Barbell + Weight 2 x 10	Barbell + Weight 2 x 10	Barbell + Weight 2 x 10	

SAMPLE INTERMEDIATE 4-DAY PROGRAM

	Exercises	Week 1	Week 2	Week 3	Week 4	Week 5	Week 6	Week 7	Week 8 Competition Week
SATURDAY	Back Squat	85–88% 5RM 5 x 5	90% 5RM 5 x 5	93% 5RM 4 x 5	96% 5RM 3 x 5	98% 5RM 2 x 5	101% 5RM 2 x 5	85% 5RM 1 x 5	**Competition Day!**
	Bench Press	85–88% 5RM 5 x 5	90% 5RM 5 x 5	93% 5RM 4 x 5	96% 5RM 3 x 5	98% 5RM 2 x 5	101% 5RM 2 x 5	85% 5RM 1 x 5	
	Clean-Grip Deadlift	85–88% 5RM 5 x 5	90% 5RM 5 x 5	93% 5RM 4 x 5	96% 5RM 3 x 5	98% 5RM 2 x 5	101% 5RM 2 x 5	85% 5RM 1 x 5	
	Glute Ham Raises	Barbell 2 x 10	Barbell + Weight 2 x 10	Barbell + Weight 2 x 10	Barbell + Weight 2 x 10	Barbell + Weight 2 x 10	Barbell + Weight 2 x 10	Barbell + Weight 2 x 10	

FIVE-DAY SAMPLE INTERMEDIATE PROGRAM

For most people, the Monday, Wednesday, and Friday workouts will take less than two hours. The Tuesday and Saturday workouts will take between 60 and 90 minutes, depending on training speed.

For the snatch and the clean and jerk, try to stick with the habit of pulling from the knees on Monday, from the hips on Wednesday, and from the floor on Friday. Keeping with that practice will help vary the stress placed on the body during this expanded training week.

Monday and especially Friday when doing the full lifts from the floor will be more difficult than Wednesday when working from the hips. Wednesday is also a little less intense because we separate the clean and the jerk. We do them together most of the time because they're done together in competition. However, not everyone cleans the same weights as they jerk, and some may need more work on one than the other.

The back squats on Mondays and Saturdays share a specific relationship. Back squats on Monday start at three to five sets of five reps at 85% 5RM. On Saturdays, the goal will always be to make a new PR.

When you set a new record on Saturday, the squats performed on the following Monday should then be adjusted to be a percentage of the new record from Saturday.

Squatting can be adjusted in several ways. You might try to do subsequent cycles with triples on the back squat. Or, if you have great work capacity and great recovery, you might opt to do Monday's squats with five or more sets with 90% of Saturday's weight, or even higher.

On the other end of the spectrum, you might find three sets of five at 80% of the Saturday weight works best for you. Athletes have to discover this for themselves.

The workouts don't contain the same volume because it seems to be helpful to have some variation in the difficulty of the training from day to day. Think of Monday, Wednesday, and Friday as the "hard" days and Tuesday and Saturday as the "easier" days. A general program template and sample program for a five-day-a week schedule is shown next.

MONDAY

Exercises	Sets x Reps	Weight
Snatch (from knees)	2 Triples	75%
Clean (from knees) and Jerk	2 Triples (3+1)	75%
Back Squat	5 x 5	85% 5RM

TUESDAY

Exercises	Sets x Reps	Weight
Pull Assistance	3 x 5	90% 5RM
Overhead Assistance	5 x 5	85%–88% 5RM

WEDNESDAY

Exercises	Sets x Reps	Weight
Snatch (from hips)	2 Triples	75%
Clean (from hips)	2 Triples	75%
Jerk	2 Triples	75%
Front Squat	5 x 3	85%–88% 3RM

FRIDAY

Exercises	Sets x Reps	Weight
Snatch	3–5 Singles	75%
Clean and Jerk	3–5 Singles	75%
Pull Assistance	3 x 5	90% 5RM

SATURDAY

EXERCISES	Sets x Reps	Weight
Back Squat	Build to a PR 3RM or 5RM	101+%
Overhead Assistance	5 x 5	85%–88% 5RM

SAMPLE FIVE-DAY CYCLE INTERMEDIATE PROGRAM

MONDAY

Exercises	Week 1	Week 2	Week 3	Week 4	Week 5	Week 6	Week 7	Week 8 Competition Week
Snatch (from knees)	75% 2 Triples	80% 2 Triples Then Go for PR Triple	82% 3 Doubles	84% 3 Doubles	86% 2 Triples Then Go for PR Triple	88% 3 Singles	80% 2 Doubles	Snatch (from floor) 80% 2 Doubles
Clean (from knees) and Jerk	75% 2 Triples (3+1)	80% 2 Triples (3+1) Then Go for PR Triple	82% 3 Doubles (2+1)	84% 3 Doubles (2+1)	86% 2 Doubles (2+1) Then Go for PR Double	88% 3 Singles	80% 2 Doubles	Clean (from floor) and Jerk 80% 2 Doubles
Back Squat	85% 5RM 3 x 5	90% New 5RM 5 x 5	90% New 5RM 5 x 5	90% New 5RM 5 x 5	90% New 5RM 5 x 5	90% New 5RM 5 x 5	90% New 5RM 5 x 5	80% 5RM 1 x 5

TUESDAY

Exercises	Week 1	Week 2	Week 3	Week 4	Week 5	Week 6	Week 7	Week 8 Competition Week
Weeks 1–5: Clean-Grip Deadlift **Weeks 6–8:** Clean Pulls	90% 5RM 3 x 5	93% 5RM 3 x 5	96% 5RM 3 x 5	98% 5RM 2 x 5	101% 5RM Build to New PR 1 x 5	100% Max Clean 3 x 3	100% Max Clean 2 x 3	100% Max Clean 1 x 3
Snatch-Grip Push Press (from behind the neck)	85–88% 5RM 5 x 5	90% 5RM 5 x 5	93% 5RM 4 x 5	96% 5RM 3 x 5	98% 5RM 2 x 5	101% 5RM Build to New PR 1 x 5	90% 5RM 1x 5	80% 5RM 1 x 5

WEDNESDAY

Exercises	Week 1	Week 2	Week 3	Week 4	Week 5	Week 6	Week 7	Week 8 Competition Week
Snatch (from hips)	75% 2 Triples	80% 2 Triples Then Go for PR Triple	82% 3 Doubles	84% 3 Doubles	86% 2 Doubles Then Go for PR Double	90% 2 Doubles	85% 2 Singles	Snatch (from floor) 85% 1 Single
Clean (from hips)	75% 2 Triples	80% 2 Triples Then Go for PR Triple	82% 3 Doubles	84% 3 Doubles	86% 2 Doubles Then Go for PR Double	90% 2 Doubles	Clean (from floor) and Jerk Opener	Clean (from floor) and Jerk 65% 1 Single
Jerk (from rack or blocks)	75% 2 Triples	80% 2 Triples Then Go for PR Triple	82% 3 Doubles	84% 3 Doubles	86% 2 Doubles Then Go for PR Double	90% 2 Doubles	-	-
Front Squat	85–88% 3RM 5 x 3	90% 3RM 5 x 3	93% 3RM 4 x 3	96% 3RM 3 x 3	98% 3RM 2 x 3	101% 3RM Build to New PR 1 x 3	90% 3RM 1x 3	Front Squat Your Clean and Jerk Opener 1 x 2

SAMPLE FIVE-DAY CYCLE INTERMEDIATE PROGRAM

FRIDAY

Exercises	Week 1	Week 2	Week 3	Week 4	Week 5	Week 6	Week 7	Week 8 Competition Week
Snatch	75% 3 to 5 Singles	80% 3 to 5 Singles	82% 3 to 5 Singles	84% 3 to 5 Singles	86% 3 to 5 Singles	Max Out Doubles	Opener	Warm-Up Snatch and Clean and Jerk with an empty bar Then go home and rest!
Clean and Jerk	75% 3 to 5 Singles	80% 3 to 5 Singles	82% 3 to 5 Singles	84% 3 to 5 Singles	86% 3 to 5 Singles	Max Out Doubles (2+1)	80% 2 Singles	
Weeks 1–5: Snatch-Grip Deadlift Weeks 6–8: Snatch Pulls	90% 5RM 3 x 5	93% 5RM 3 x 5	96% 5RM 3 x 5	98% 5RM 2 x 5	101% 5RM Build to New PR 1 x 5	100% Max Snatch 3 x 3	100% Max Snatch 2 x 3	

SATURDAY

Exercises	Week 1	Week 2	Week 3	Week 4	Week 5	Week 6	Week 7	Week 8 Competition Week
Back Squat	Go for PR 1 x 5	Go for PR 1 x 5	Go for PR 1 x 5	Go for PR 1 x 5	Go for PR 1 x 5	Go for PR 1 x 5	85% 5RM 1 x 5	Competition Day!
Push Press	85–88% 5RM 5 x 5	90% 5RM 5 x 5	93% 5RM 4 x 5	96% 5RM 3 x 5	98% 5RM 2 x 5	101% 5RM Build to New PR 1 x 5	90% 5RM 1 x 5	

SIX-DAY SAMPLE INTERMEDIATE PROGRAM USING TIMED SETS

Next, we'll discuss an example of an eight-week training cycle for an intermediate athlete using timed sets, every minute on the minute, which you already know as EMOMs.

Here, to show a different approach using prescribed percentages and previously calculated percentages, we'll use lifting maximums based on a theoretical lifter. This lifter's max lifts are as follows:

- o **Snatch:** 100 kg
- o **Clean and Jerk:** 120 kg
- o **Back Squat:** 150 kg x 5
- o **Front Squat:** 130 kg x 3
- o **Clean-Grip Deadlift:** 160 kg x 5
- o **Snatch-Grip Deadlift:** 140 kg x 5
- o **Push Press:** 90 kg x 5
- o **Snatch-Grip Push Press:** 95 kg x 5

If you begin this training cycle, base your own lifts in the training program similar to what's presented. It would be ideal before following this training cycle to have already gone through several cycles of the five-day or at a minimum, the four-day intermediate program.

I strongly recommend this because of the higher volumes of lifting on Mondays, the increasing intensities from maxing the snatch and the clean and jerk on Wednesdays and Fridays, and from the added intensity and volume gained from an extra day of training on Thursday. These additions to the program make it a much harder training schedule.

Every minute on the minute sets and maxing the competition lifts go hand in hand quite nicely. If you're using a cycle that maxes out often, the EMOMs provide a large volume of technical work at moderate intensities, which balances the technical errors that often occur with maximum lifts later in the week.

Take a look at the sample program on the next page.

SAMPLE INTERMEDIATE SIX-DAY TIMED-SET PROGRAM

MONDAY

Exercises	Week 1	Week 2	Week 3	Week 4	Week 5	Week 6	Week 7	Week 8 Competition Week
Snatch EMOM	70% 20 x 1	75% 15 x 1	80% 10 x 1	70% 20 x 1	75% 15 x 1	80% 10 x 1	70% 20 x 1	85% 6 to 8 x 1 (No EMOM)
Clean and Jerk EMOM	70% 20 x 1	75% 15 x 1	80% 10 x 1	70% 20 x 1	75% 15 x 1	80% 10 x 1	70% 20 x 1	85% 6 to 8 x 1 (No EMOM)

TUESDAY

Exercises	Week 1	Week 2	Week 3	Week 4	Week 5	Week 6	Week 7	Week 8 Competition Week
Back Squat	126 kg 5 x 5	132 kg 5 x 5	136 kg 5 x 5	138 kg 5 x 5	140 kg 5 x 5	142 kg 5 x 5	135 kg 2 x 5	130 kg 80–90% 1 x 5
Snatch-Grip Push Press (from behind the neck)	85 kg 3 x 5	91 kg 3 x 5	96 kg 1 x 5	97 kg 1 x 5	98 kg 1 x 5	99 kg 1 x 5	95 kg 1 x 5	80 kg 1 x 5

WEDNESDAY

Exercises	Week 1	Week 2	Week 3	Week 4	Week 5	Week 6	Week 7	Week 8 Competition Week
Power Snatch	Max Out (from hips)	Max Out (from knees)	Max Out (from floor)	Max Out (from knees)	Max Out (from hips)	Max Out (from floor)	Max Out (from floor)	75% 3 x 1 (from floor)
Power Clean and Jerk	Max Out (from hips)	Max Out (from knees)	Max Out (from floor)	Max Out (from knees)	Max Out (from hips)	Max Out (from floor)	Max Out (from floor)	75% 3 x 1 (from floor)

THURSDAY

Exercises	Week 1	Week 2	Week 3	Week 4	Week 5	Week 6	Week 7	Week 8 Competition Week
Front Squat	120 kg 3 x 3	126 kg 3 x 3	131 kg 3 x 3	133 kg 3 x 3	135 kg 3 x 3	137 kg 3 x 3	130 kg 1 x 3	REST DAY
Snatch-Grip Deadlift	130 kg 1 x 5	136 kg 1 x 5	141 kg 1 x 5	143 kg 1 x 5	145 kg 1 x 5	147 kg 1 x 5	140 kg 1 x 5	

FRIDAY

Exercises	Week 1	Week 2	Week 3	Week 4	Week 5	Week 6	Week 7	Week 8 Competition Week
Snatch	Max Out (from hips)	Max Out (from knees)	Max Out (from floor)	Max Out (from knees)	Max Out (from hips)	Max Out (from floor)	Max Out (from floor)	Warm-Up to 50 kg on both lifts
Clean and Jerk	Max Out (from hips)	Max Out (from knees)	Max Out (from floor)	Max Out (from knees)	Max Out (from hips)	Max Out (from floor)	Max Out (from floor)	

SATURDAY

Exercises	Week 1	Week 2	Week 3	Week 4	Week 5	Week 6	Week 7	Week 8 Competition Week
Back Squat	140 kg 1 x 5	146 kg 1 x 5	151 kg 1 x 5	153 kg 1 x 5	155 kg 1 x 5	157 kg 1 x 5	150 kg 1 x 5	
Push Press	80 kg 3 x 5	85 kg 3 x 5	91 kg 3 x 5	92 kg 3 x 5	93 kg 3 x 5	94 kg 1 x 5	90 kg 3 x 5	Competition Day!
Clean-Grip Deadlift	150 kg 1 x 5	156 kg 1 x 5	161 kg 1 x 5	163 kg 1 x 5	165 kg 1 x 5	167 kg 1 x 5	160 kg 1 x 5	

CLOSING THOUGHTS

The door to easy beginner gains may have closed, but that's not a bad thing. In fact, it demonstrates that the decisions you've made in training are paying off. Sure, strength gains are indeed coming at a slower rate, but technique is consistent and errors on the lifts are smaller. Progress can still be made and all it will take is continued patience and faith in the training process.

The biggest mistakes you could make now are to change too much too soon, and to discard what made you successful in the first place. Instead, when progress stalls, continue to build on the foundation of strength and technical mastery you've laid down by working on the basics. To do that, you'll start turning the knobs on new doors one by one to figure out which you can walk through and find even more success.

When the gains stop coming, ask yourself, "What do I need the most right now?" Then make one small change for a training cycle or two to see what happens. Remember, if you make too many changes at once, it will be near impossible to determine which change was the one that worked.

Maybe you've noticed that you frequently cut the pull short on your snatches. Great—a training cycle involving a complex of two high pulls plus one snatch could help. Or, it could be that you struggle on the pull when the bar is near your knees. Go ahead and program a training cycle of lifting from the blocks where the bar starts at the knees to see if that fixes your issue. It will involve trial and error…and that's a part of the training process. It's necessary if you're to be successful in weightlifting.

What you'll change to keep driving progress depends on your needs as an individual. So right now, keep opening doors to see what works. As your training progresses and you inch closer toward an advanced level, the need for further individualization of the programming will become even greater.

We'll discuss this at length in the next chapter.

CHAPTER 8
PROGRAMMING FOR ADVANCED WEIGHTLIFTERS

In the beginner chapter, I laid the foundation for training, and built upon that in the intermediate chapter. This advanced chapter will continue the development. The rate of progress is the difference between an intermediate and an advanced athlete. Intermediates are usually still able to make significant progress from one training cycle to the next, while advanced lifters are often past that point.

Advanced lifters are those who are near enough to their ultimate potential that monthly increases or gains from one training cycle to the next are no longer automatic. Advanced lifters have to look at how much the total has gone up year to year to see measurable progress.

Some of the athletes who would be called "advanced" are full-time weightlifters. They're people who aren't trying to hold down a full-time job in addition to a training schedule. That allows more time devoted to both training and recovery.

However, not every advanced lifter needs to train full time or with multiple sessions per day. The amount of training needed is individual, and the only rule is to do enough to allow the snatch and the clean and jerk to progress to the highest levels possible.

In this chapter, we'll cover the program I used for the full-time athletes at California Strength and MDUSA, and we'll look at other American lifters who progressed to the top of the rankings in the USA. I don't present these programs for you to copy, but simply to demonstrate how individualized programming is for advanced lifters. By the time athletes reach this level, they need to do their own programs geared specifically to their strengths and weaknesses.

Finally, we'll discuss advanced methods of training that can help advanced lifters make progress when progress stalls. Use the programs as a guide, but think for yourself. You can't copy your way to the top.

PROGRESSING TO FULL TIME

The advanced program I used at California Strength and MDUSA was geared toward full-time weightlifters who weren't holding down a job or going to school. It's comprised of nine training sessions per week. Nine sessions place an immense toll on the mind and body.

We've been discussing this all-too-important concept since the beginning: Doing too much training is *worse* than not doing enough. Don't jump straight from a four-, five-, or six-day-a-week intermediate program to a full nine-sessions-per-week plan.

I want to emphasize this: Don't schedule more sessions than you can recover from. The goal isn't to train as much as possible; it's to *lift* as much as possible. Lifting as much as possible and improving at a fast rate means limiting the training to what your body can adapt to and recover from. This may mean that for many, going to bed early is more important than squeezing in an extra training session.

If you suddenly find yourself without a job or with tons of free time, use that new-found time wisely. Ensure that your body can adapt to the new workload by adding only one new session per week. Otherwise, increasing the training volume too fast could set you up for an injury, or at least a downturn in performance.

If you decide to increase your training and work toward nine sessions per week, any increase in training volume is unlikely to help in the short term. Adapting to an increase in training volume is a long-term process, not a quick fix. Initially, there's often a *decrease* in performance, and you may struggle lifting weights that typically weren't challenging. That's normal. It might take weeks or months for your body to adapt to the increased training.

Weightlifting is an exercise in patience.

RECOVERY—GOING THE EXTRA MILE

Anything that helps your recovery becomes more vital as you get closer to your ultimate potential as a weightlifter. I'm always amazed at how many good athletes don't get enough sleep. Eating regular meals and getting plenty of sleep are no-brainers, yet many people want to talk about massage or cryotherapy or chiropractic care, rather than getting enough sleep.

If you're planning on training nine times per week or at least working toward it, you'll have to work on recovery. I've had many athletes tell me that trying to recover from training is harder than actually doing the work. It certainly takes more willpower. Training hard is a given. We all do that, and it's expected. But turning off the TV or computer and putting away your phone at a descent hour is hard. So is preparing your meals ahead of time so you have quality food available at the right time. These efforts have to be done. The body thrives on a consistent schedule, and this includes your diet, sleep, and rest schedule.

If you're used to eating breakfast at 8:30 a.m., training at 10:00 a.m., finishing training at noon, and having a snack as soon as you finish training, that's what you need to do every day.

That takes planning and attention to detail. Many athletes take one day on the weekends to do the food prep for the following week. It's worth it to have the right meals handy with exactly the right amount of protein, carbohydrates, and fat.

I guarantee you won't get exactly what you need if every meal is from a fast-food joint. This organized meal prep is the kind of thing most people aren't willing to do. But if you want to lift more than the average weightlifter, you'll have to do things the average weightlifter neglects.

THE CALIFORNIA STRENGTH AND MDUSA SCHEDULE

In this program, two sessions are performed on Monday, Wednesday, and Friday; Tuesday, Thursday, and Saturday have one session.

An athlete who can commit to being a full-time weightlifter ideally needs at least two hours between the sessions of a two-session day. One example of a day's schedule would have the morning session at 10:00 a.m. with the afternoon session beginning at 3:00 p.m. On single training session days, you can choose to train in the morning or afternoon.

The following is an example of a nine-session-per-week schedule. Of course, when it comes to specifics, the workouts change over time; but in general, this is what I've had athletes do during each of the individual training sessions.

DAY	SESSION TIME	TRAINING FOCUS
Monday (Session 1)	10 am to 12 pm	Power snatches and power cleans.
Monday (Session 2)	3 pm to 5 pm	Snatch from the low blocks or from the low hang; Clean from the low blocks and jerk; back squats.
Tuesday	10 am to 12 pm	Snatch with no hook grip; pulls or deadlifts; Snatch-grip overhead work.
Wednesday (Session 1)	10 am to 12 pm	Light snatches; power cleans.
Wednesday (Session 2)	3 pm to 5 pm	Snatch from the hips or high blocks; cleans from the hips or high blocks; Jerks from jerk stands; front squats.
Thursday	10 am to 12 pm	Snatch with no hook grip; Pulls or deadlifts; bench press.
Friday (Session 1)	10 am to 12 pm	Lighter snatch and clean and jerk movements.
Friday (Session 2)	3 pm to 5 pm	Heavy snatch and clean and jerk movements.
Saturday	10 am to 12 pm	Heavy overhead exercises; heavy back squats.

Doing the pulls or deadlifts on Monday, Wednesday, and Saturday, and the back and front squatting on Tuesday, Thursday, and Saturday is a change that seems to work better for some people. If you're going to do this, you'll double up on squats and pulls or deadlifts on Saturdays. In practice, that usually means moving heavy pulls to Friday and doing Romanian deadlifts or deadlifts on Saturday after squats.

Monday morning will usually be a lighter session. After having Sunday off, you'll need to do something light Monday morning to get back into the swing of training. A normal Monday morning might be power snatches and power cleans with something less than 80% for three or four work sets. Warm up extra slowly to work the kinks out on Mondays.

For my athletes, Monday afternoon is usually a fairly intense training session. We often do snatches from the low blocks or from the low hang. If we do them from the low hang, the athletes will often deadlift the weight up and lower it slowly to near the floor, reverse direction, and then snatch it. This serves as extra work for the pull and some work at less-than-full-speed pulling to pay extra attention to body positions.

This schedule worked for high-level American lifters at both MDUSA and California Strength. However, that only means it worked in those specific situations. Those were unique conditions with unique athletes; the same might not work in a different situation with a different group of lifters or a different coach.

Two things change as an athlete gets closer to his or her ultimate potential. First, there's less margin for error in terms of volume, intensity, and total workload. Training also has to be more specific to what each individual athlete needs.

With a beginner, three to five singles with the highest possible weight for a correctly performed lift causes positive adaptation in almost every weightlifter. For an intermediate lifter, weights in the 70 to 90% range for between six and 20 lifts work for almost every weightlifter. At the advanced level, some athletes still need to do a certain number of lifts with an intensity close to 70%. However, most won't need lifts near 70% for anything outside of warming up.

Some athletes need to lift very close to max to cause a positive adaptation either in strength levels or motor patterns. By the time they've trained for however many years it took to get to the advanced level, most lifters will, or should, have a good idea of what works for them and what's needed to make further improvements. This is certainly not going to be the same for everyone.

Photo 8.1—Spencer Moorman snatching

INDIVIDUALIZED TRAINING CYCLES

As noted, I prefer to limit training cycles to about eight weeks. This doesn't mean I never have a plan that ranges longer than eight weeks. However, instead of a yearlong plan, I use shorter cycles, and each cycle has a specific goal.

Right after the most important competition of the year, the first cycle for a lifter might be one where the emphasis is on pulling strength. This cycle will have more intensity, more volume, and more specific exercises geared toward developing a stronger pull. This cycle will be measured by pulling strength increasing in a significant way, as demonstrated by a bigger snatch-grip or clean-grip deadlift, or another strength exercise that demonstrates strength in the pull.

For another lifter—or perhaps the same lifter—the next cycle might be one geared toward increasing leg or squatting strength. In this case, the main goal would be to increase the front and back squat in a way that leads to easier recoveries from cleans.

A cycle focusing on leg or squatting strength will have the same increases in intensity, volume, and specific exercises—but of course, different—as one focusing on pulling strength. Many lifters need the same sort of cycle focusing on overhead strength for the jerk.

The main goal in these cycles is to maintain performance in the snatch and clean and jerk at either the present levels or higher, while bringing up a weak point. This is an important aspect of my coaching philosophy. Lifters should be able to make a competitive total year-round. Training with cycles focusing on pulling, squatting, or overhead strength is a great way to make progress, but it's a good indicator you're doing too much when you're unable to perform well on the competitive lifts.

For one lifter, the first training cycle might be one that focuses on pulling strength. The next might be one that focuses on leg or squatting strength. The third might focus on overhead strength. The next might be a pre-competition cycle leading into another important competition. Or, an athlete with a limiting weak point might have three or four training cycles with each having a focus on that.

These cycles may be followed by a pre-competition cycle leading up to an important competition. For this athlete, heavier pulling movements such as deadlifts are important, but so are faster movements like power snatches or power cleans. This athlete's first cycle might involve heavy snatch-grip deadlifts, and a subsequent cycle will focus on power snatches. In either of these situations, the athlete should aim to maintain the ability to put up 90% of the best total at any point throughout the training. Ninety-five percent might even be better.

ADVANCED STRENGTH TRAINING METHODS

The back squat is the most important strength exercise when starting to train for the sport of weightlifting. It's not specific; it effectively builds whole-body strength, and as a beginner, that's exactly what you need.

The front squat, push press, and snatch-grip and clean-grip deadlifts are more specific, and when added to the back squat, these exercises form the basis of the strength program you'll be using and should continue to use. The squatting, pulling, and pressing are supplemental to training the competition lifts.

In previous chapters, we discussed the basic strength exercises. In this chapter, we'll cover several alternatives, including methods such as isometrics and supplemental strength exercises. However, many strength athletes in weightlifting, track and field, and even powerlifting have gone through entire careers and built astronomical levels of strength with multiple sets of three to five reps using basic exercises like squats and deadlifts. The basics might be unimaginative and boring, but they work.

ISOMETRICS

In the 1960s, weightlifters at York Barbell began to experiment with steroids, gained significant strength and muscle, and made huge improvements on their competition lifts in a short period of time. The York Barbell® founder, Bob Hoffman, had to explain these dramatic changes in performance; he couldn't tell the public the improvements were due to a little pill called Dianabol and instead "blamed" it on isometrics.

"Isometric" means exerting muscle tension without producing an actual movement or a change in muscle length. Isometrics are typically done by holding a weight motionless at specific joint angles.

Claiming this isometric win helped Hoffman by setting York Barbell up to sell a ton of power racks designed for the isometric training lifters were doing at the time. Eventually, the genie got out of the bottle and the average lifter probably felt taken advantage of after discovering the York Barbell power rack wasn't the secret the York lifters utilized to make fantastic progress. Isometrics quickly fell out of favor.

The power rack stuck around, but in a version almost unrecognizable to the original from York Barbell. Disregarding the unfortunate and unearned association with drug use, isometrics are very effective—maybe not as effective as Dianabol, but certainly a most effective means of increasing strength, even when not paired with anabolics.

Today, many lifters haven't heard of isometrics, let alone used them. The type of rack designed for this form of training is a forgotten relic in the strength training world, particularly among weightlifters. That's regrettable because training with isometrics is an extremely effective tool.

WHY ISOMETRICS ARE IMPORTANT

Research done in the 1950s and '60s indicates that isometrics led to faster strength gains than any other method. Holding an isometric contraction at a precise joint angle will increase strength from 15 degrees below to 15 degrees above the training angle. Strength gains are greatest at the joint angle trained, and decrease farther from that angle.

In a sport like football, where movement can occur in three dimensions, isometrics are less useful. It's difficult to pinpoint a specific joint or joint angle where greater strength is especially beneficial. In weightlifting, however, athletes do the same movements again, again, and again. There are specific joint angles within a snatch pull or a clean pull that limit the amount of weight that can be used for the movement as a whole.

The most common weak points are right off the floor and just below the kneecaps. If a lifter can keep the back arched while moving more weight faster off the floor, and produce greater acceleration near the knee joint, more weight can be lifted in the snatch or clean. With isometrics, training can be concentrated on the specific points in the pull that need to be stronger.

The lifters at York believed progress with isometrics was dependent on making continual weight increases week to week, and I've found that to be true. Ideally, the position of the hold is precisely the one in which you want to gain strength.

Once you dial that in, the load *has* to increase each workout, or you're just wasting time.

I recommend training with isometrics no more than one or two times per week because this is a concentrated form of training and the recovery is difficult.

ISOMETRICS FOR THE SNATCH AND CLEAN

To use an isometric hold that would benefit the start of the snatch or clean pull, set up the rack with low pins to stop the barbell just as it comes off the floor.

The specificity of the height is important. You want the bar to be stopped by the pins as the bar breaks off the floor, not six or more inches above that spot—the closer to the floor, the greater the strength carryover.

After warming up, load the bar in the proper position with the maximum weight you can hold for 10 seconds. This weight will eventually be greater than your max snatch or clean. Be just as meticulous and precise in the pin placement when performing this exercise from just below the kneecaps.

A good rack isn't absolutely necessary for isometrics. In fact, neither Donny Shankle nor Jared Fleming had access to a rack when they used this method. They broke the bar enough off the floor to slide a piece of paper under the plates and held that position. For the hold below the kneecaps, they'd pull the bar to a position slightly below the knees and hold there for 10 seconds.

For many athletes, it's easier to first pull the bar to the waist, slowly lower the bar to the correct position just below the kneecaps or just off the floor, and then perform the 10-second hold.

Photos 8.2 and 8.3—Snatch isometric hold just off the floor

Photos 8.4 and 8.5—Snatch isometric hold at the knees

Photos 8.6 and 8.7—Snatch isometric hold above the knees

Photos 8.8 and 8.9—Snatch isometric hold at the hips

Photo 8.10—Snatch deadlift isometric hold one inch off the floor

Photo 8.11—Snatch deadlift isometric hold at the knees

Photo 8.12—Snatch deadlift isometric hold at the hips

The top of the pull right at or slightly below the hips—about two-thirds of the way up the thigh—is another position to use isometric holds to improve either the snatch pull or clean pull.

Here, the objective is to lean your shoulders over the bar as far as you can, while pushing back on the bar with your triceps and lats to hold it against the thighs. This position is more difficult to get right. It's also more difficult to choose the right weight since you'll often have to use far more weight than you can snatch or clean.

The position near the hip was Donny Shankle's favorite position, and he felt that holds there were effective in helping him keep his shoulders over the bar in the snatch and clean. For the hold at the hip, it's almost always better to first deadlift the weight to full extension, then lower it slightly and lean forward to the position of the hold.

Donny used isometrics while training on a normal weightlifting platform. He'd start his workout by setting up in his snatch start position. The bar would be loaded to about 60% of his best snatch-grip deadlift, and he'd pull to a point where the plates were just barely off the floor.

He held the weight for 10 seconds, keeping the weight and his body motionless. He'd then repeat the 10-second hold with the bar lifted to two more positions: just below the knees and just below the hips while leaning over the bar.

Jared Fleming used the same strategy to break the American record in the snatch with a 170-kilo lift. He also used three positions with a 10-second hold in each position.

With Jared doing no other deadlift training, he was also able to increase his deadlift personal record by about 30 kilos.

Photo 8.13—Clean deadlift isometric hold one inch off the floor

Photo 8.14—Clean deadlift isometric hold at the knees

Photo 8.15—Clean deadlift isometric hold at the hips

These holds would have worked even better if they had access to a rack where they could lift off a bottom pin and hold the bar against a higher pin. Their ability to successfully use this method without the right equipment proved that it's usable by anyone in almost any situation.

Donny and Jared both did the isometric training after their normal snatch and clean and jerk training. If you use this method, within a few months you'll work up to extremely heavy weights at the positions of the holds, certainly weights far in excess of what you can snatch or clean—maybe even weights in excess of what you can lift in the snatch-grip or clean-grip deadlifts.

The correct volume is one or two 10-second holds at each position—off the floor, below the knees, and at the hips—one or two times per week, increasing the weights week to week.

ISOMETRICS FOR THE SQUAT

The squat is another movement for which isometrics are tailor-made. My first introduction to using them with squats came from Jim Moser. Jim was a lifter in the 1980s, one of the last to train at York Barbell. He's also the father of the immensely talented James Moser. Jim sent James to live with me in Texas during his senior year in high school. When James started having trouble increasing his front squat, Jim sent some isometric workouts for him. They were modeled on what Jim had seen at York Barbell, or perhaps, something he'd been given by Bill Starr or Tommy Suggs.

We were fortunate enough to find a gym with a power rack suitable for isometrics. The programming called for James to complete several six-second holds at his weakest position. He performed these similarly to how they're performed with pulls, with a bottom pin to lift the bar from, and another pin to hold the bar against at the top. James wedged himself under the bar as it rested on the bottom pins, and lifted the bar until it was stopped by the top pins, holding it there for the required six seconds.

You can get away without a rack for pull isometrics, but for the squat, you'll absolutely need one.

Photos 8.16 and 8.17—Isometric squat hold low pins

Photo 8.18—Isometric squat hold against high pins

These holds are effective, but also incredibly taxing. In fact, isometrics are so taxing, I don't recommend them for both squats and the pull in the same training cycle, at least not until you have experience using them. To start, pick the variation you need the most, and progress from there.

SNATCHES AND CLEANS WITH A PAUSE

Using a short isometric pause in the snatch pull or clean pull is a less-intense but still effective way to utilize isometrics. Pulls or lifts with a pause are done with a lot less weight and are easier to recover from, but they're also not as powerful a strength stimulus.

They have the advantage of reinforcing good habits during the lift, and they apply stress in a way that's different enough from the normal snatch or clean to stimulate adaptation.

In every movement, there are parts in the range of motion where the bar slows. These are the positions where your body isn't producing enough force to overcome gravity, and are where you will need to build strength. Not every lifter needs a pause in the same place. The ability to insert a pause precisely where you need it is one of the benefits of using pauses during the snatch pull, clean pull, or during the actual lift.

A short pause at the most difficult point in the pull produces adaptation in two ways. The pause itself is a stimulus for strength adaptation. Pausing also promotes adaptation by requiring more force to accelerate the bar from motionless after the pause.

When pausing in the snatch or clean, try a two-second pause just off the floor or right below the knees. The pause needs to be long enough for the bar to come to a definite stop before it begins moving again to complete the lift. When using pauses on the snatch or clean, use about 10% less than your max weight, but much heavier weights with pauses on pulls. The added difficulty is both because of the pause itself, and the difficulty of accelerating the bar from motionless after the pause.

During the pause, hold the bar absolutely still for two seconds; it'll be hard to keep it from either inching up or slowly drifting downward. It may take a few attempts to get this right.

Various scenarios might warrant pauses at different positions. Pause or isometric holds off the floor are useful if a lifter has a hard time holding the back tight at the start of the lift. Pausing just below the knees is beneficial for lifters who have trouble with a slowing bar speed in the middle of the pull or who aren't accelerating through that portion of the lift. The bar should never slow down; instead, it continues accelerating through the entire pull.

Think back to Chapter 1 where we covered the rhythm of the lifts and how they should progressively accelerate from fast to faster to fastest. Purposefully pausing where you're weak and making the lift even more difficult at that point will help you build enough strength to pull harder and not allow the bar to decelerate in the middle of a pull.

From a coaching standpoint, isometric hold variations give us a chance to watch a lifter in the positions. The lifter can also mentally check where the balance is on the feet, and provide feedback on positions. For example, when pulling at full speed, it's hard to pinpoint exactly when your weight has transferred to your heels; however, holding a troublesome position for two seconds should make this clear.

LIFTS WITH A SLOW ECCENTRIC

Performing lifts with a slow eccentric portion is another strategy similar to isometric holds and pauses. When teaching the lifts, I use this method quite liberally, along with pauses so beginner lifters can learn how to find positions and feel the correct working muscles. For the advanced lifter who already possesses a sound foundation of technique, we utilize slow eccentrics with challenging weights for strength development.

To perform the pull or actual lift, quickly lower the bar back to the hips, then lower it back to the floor notably slower than you normally would. Aim for a 10-second eccentric. Try to lower it in the mirror image of the way it was raised—flex at the hip until the bar passes the knee, then squat until the plates touch the floor—to exponentially increase the difficulty. This is extremely difficult with weights over 80% of the max snatch or clean, but it's productive

for building strength and reinforcing the proper positions of the pull.

Usually, the portion of the lift where the bar is between the knees and the floor is the most difficult part, possibly because of fatigue when the bar arrives at that position. You'll be tempted to allow the bar to speed up just to bring the rep to an end, but don't do it. I encourage lifters to pretend they're setting the bar down on a carton of eggs while trying to make sure none of the eggs are broken.

Slow eccentrics are very effective for lifters who have problems breaking the bar off the floor and losing proper back position when pulling. A word of caution: You don't need a ton of volume for slow eccentrics to work. Four or five slow reps per workout are enough for most people. It can be easy to overdo it, and if done correctly, a little work goes a long way.

ADVANCED TRAINING PROGRAM EXAMPLES

The standard three-day-a-week program works well for nearly all beginners who pick up the sport of weightlifting. The four- or five-day-a-week programs with a few minor tweaks depending on training age, skill level, and the individual needs of each athlete will be excellent for intermediate lifters. Once a lifter is at the advanced stage of development, he or she will have unique strong and weak points, and training programs must be individualized.

This is the reason there are no standard advanced programs in this chapter, like there were in the beginner and intermediate chapters. Even more than beginner or intermediate lifters, advanced-level lifters must have a training program tailored to their individual needs. Generic just won't do it.

Lifters like Donny Shankle, Jon North, Caleb Ward, Travis Cooper, James Tatum, and Jared Fleming all have individual needs, and all use slightly different programs. We—I and the lifters I coached—built the foundation of the program together as a team to climb to high levels in the sport, and it took quite a bit of trial and error.

When you reach an advanced level in the sport, you won't need a template for programming. Your template will have been created by the trial-and-error efforts you'll have put in as a beginner and intermediate lifter.

Instead of providing you with a general advanced version of my program, I'll instead present examples of training programs used by Team USA lifters who are advanced by anyone's standard. In the weeks leading up to the 2015 World Championships, I interviewed each of these athletes to gain a brief history of their weightlifting careers. The following thoughts will allow you to see firsthand how athletes from all over the country developed over the course of years.

It's my intent to provide you with perspective not only on how a few athletes trained, but also on the uniqueness of their individual programs. These aren't my programs; they're only snippets of the training some of our country's best lifters used at one point in time—you certainly shouldn't follow the programs. Instead, use them to learn just how individualized programming can and should be.

The programs in this section haven't been edited or altered in any way. I want to present them in the manner they were given to me by the athletes. This allows us to see a truer representation of different styles of programming from various coaches around the country. It's simply not my place to edit them or attempt to dissect their logic.

You'll see exercises, labeling, wording, and writing styles that are unique to the coaches who wrote these programs. You may not understand what's written, and that's okay because the programming represents an opportunity to look into the communication between these amazing American athletes and their coaches as they work together to accomplish a shared goal: success in the sport of weightlifting.

Stylized tables that fit the aesthetic of this book have been added for organizational purposes and continuity in the text.

We'll begin the advanced program reviews on the following page.

DONOVAN FORD'S PROGRAM

Photo 8.19—Donovan Ford

Donovan Ford is a lifter I've admired since my Cal Strength days; in fact, I tried to convince him to train at Cal Strength, but instead, he ended up at the Olympic Training Center when it was still a part of the USA Weightlifting development program. That was probably for the best because he did extremely well and became one of the top-ranked lifters in the USA.

Donovan had been lifting for over 10 years, having started as a sophomore in high school. At the beginning of his career, he competed for the Hassle Free Barbell Club with Paul Doherty as his coach. Being a high school club, many of the Hassle Free lifters also compete in other high school sports. Donovan was no exception, having played football for three years, as well as competing in the shot put and discus.

Donovan had the chance to play football in college, but chose to pursue weightlifting instead. One reason he made that decision was that he felt he could control his own destiny in weightlifting, which isn't a possibility with football.

A sense of self-control is important to Donovan; he grew up in the foster care system, and during his childhood had very little control over his life.

In high school, Donovan trained five days a week. The program looked "normal," consisting of three days a week of snatching, three days a week of clean and jerks, and squats and pulls. According to Donovan, he trained particularly hard on the squat because Coach Doherty was determined that none of his lifters would miss lifts because of a lack of leg strength.

Looking back on his early training at Hassle Free, Donovan felt the strong points of the program were that he had a well-rounded training program with a minimum of pressure. He said weightlifting was always fun at Hassle Free, and that's a big reason he fell in love with the sport. Donovan credits Paul Doherty for keeping him and the other kids motivated.

When he eventually left Hassle Free and moved to the OTC, Donovan encountered new coaches who contributed to his training. Paul Fleschler was his coach during the first few months at the facility. Then, Bob Morris took over the OTC program, and coached Donovan for about nine months. Finally, the OTC hired Zygmunt Smalcerz, who went on to coach Donovan for the next five years until the closing of the program.

The training program at the OTC was similar to the program I've used. They trained nine sessions per week—two sessions per day on Monday, Wednesday, and Friday, and one session on Tuesday, Thursday, and Saturday. Squatting was performed on Tuesday, Thursday, and Saturday.

The weights and intensities provided in the sample program from Donovan's training changed from week to week and evolved over time. The following sample week should give you an idea on how he trained while at the OTC.

MONDAY

Exercises	Workload Prescription
Push Snatch	70/6, 90/5, 110/4, 130/3, 145/2, 155/1
Snatch Hip / Knee	50/1/1, 70/1/1, 90/1/1, 110/1/1, 120/1/1
Pull Snatch / Snatch Box Below Knee	70/2/2, 90/2/2, 135/2/2, 4/145/2/2, 120/2/2
Pull Snatch / Knee	2/160/1/1, 2/170/1/1, 2/180/1/1
Split Squat Forward	120/3, 150/3, 180/3, 200/3, 210/3

TUESDAY

Exercises	Workload Prescription
Press in Split	40/6, 50/5, 60/4, 70/3, 75/2
Jump to Split	70/2, 100/2, 130/2, 150/2, 170/2
Jerk Back Collars	70/2, 90/2, 110/2, 140/2, 160/2, 175/2
Dip	185/2, 195/2, 205/2, 215/2
Back Squat	3/235/3

WEDNESDAY

Exercises	Workload Prescription
Clean Knee / Squat Jerk	60/1/2, 80/1/2, 100/1/2, 120/1/2, 140/1/2
Pull Clean / Clean Below Knee / Squat Dip	70/1/1/1/1, 100/1/1/1/1, 130/1/1/1/1, 160/1/1/1/1, 4/175/1/1/1/1
Pull Clean Down	2/190/2, 4/200/2
Press in Seating Snatch Grip	60/6, 70/5, 80/4, 90/3, 100/2, 105/1, 3/90/4
Rowing	60/6, 80/5, 100/4, 115/3, 130/2, 140/1

THURSDAY

Exercises	Workload Prescription
Drop Bar / Squat	70/6/1, 90/5/1, 110/4/1, 130/2/1, 140/1/1
Snatch Without Moving Feet	60/2, 80/2, 95/2, 105/2, 115/2, 125/2
Snatch Pull Bench	150/6, 160/6, 4/170/6
Front Squat	140/2, 170/2, 190/2, 3/210/2

FRIDAY

Exercises	Workload Prescription
Press in Snatch	40/6, 50/5, 60/5, 65/3, 70/2
Pull Snatch / Snatch	70/2/2, 100/2/2, 120/2/2, 135/2/2, 6/145/22
Press in Seating	60/6, 75/5, 85/4, 3/95/3
Pull Clean / Clean / Dip	70/2/2/1, 100/2/2/1, 130/2/2/1, 160/2/2/1, 6/175/2/2/1
Rowing	70/6, 90/5, 110/4, 130/2, 140/1, 120/6

SATURDAY

Exercises	Workload Prescription
Press in Split	50/6, 60/5, 70/4, 75/3, 80/2
Jerk in Split	80/2, 100/2, 120/2, 135/2, 145/2
Jerk Back / Jerk	90/1/1, 110/1/1, 130/1/1, 150/1/1, 170/1/1, 155/1/1, 175/1/1, 160/1/1, 180/1/1
Jerk Position	200/2, 210/2, 220/2, 230/2
Back Squat	200/2, 230/2, 245/2, 260/2

JENNY ARTHUR VARDANIAN'S PROGRAM

Photo 8.20—Jenny Arthur Vardanian

Jenny Arthur Vardanian is from Gainesville, Georgia, and was introduced to weightlifting while in high school, where she also ran track and played softball. Stan Luttrell, who was the school's football coach, was her first coach, but Matt Mays also assisted with her early training, which she performed at 6:30 a.m. with the football team.

Jenny recalls her early training was most often performed with multiple sets of three and multiple sets of five at around 60 to 70% intensity.

Jenny believes mental strength is her best quality as a lifter, and she credits her parents for that. Her parents were strong-willed people, and they passed that determination on to her.

One of Jenny's biggest goals as a young lifter was to get to the OTC—she never considered any other college program. Jenny was accepted to the OTC immediately out of high school, and started taking college courses at UCCS when she got to Colorado Springs.

When Jenny arrived at the training center, there was a huge increase in training intensity, as well as an increased focus on technique. When she started at the OTC, she experienced a few injuries. She learned to sometimes hold back in training, and that she doesn't always have to make PRs. She learned to pick her battles.

Jenny felt at this point in her career, she still needed a lot of technical work. She was still getting stronger, but not nearly as fast as when she first got to the OTC. While I was at the 2015 World Team Camp, I watched her break a squat PR she'd originally set nearly two years prior with a back squat of 126 kilos.

The following is an excerpt from her training log that will give you an idea of what she did in training.

Photo 8.21—Jenny Arthur Vardanian preparing to lift

MONDAY	
Exercises	**Workload Prescription**
Snatch Balance + Squat	35 2/1, 50 5/1, 65 4/1, 75 5/1, 85 3/1, 90 2/1, 75 2/1
Snatch	35/2, 45/2, 55/2, 60/2, 65/1
Snatch Pulls	45, 55, 65, 75 2 for 2, 3 / 85 1 for 1
Front Squat	3 95/1 (3 Singles with 95)
Sots Press in Snatch	15/6, 25/4, 35/4, 40/4
Snatch	40/2, 50/2, 60/2, 65/2, 65/2, 70/2, 75/2, 80/2, 3 83/1
Press in Split	30/4, 35/4, 40/4, 45/4
Jerks	55 2/2, 65 2/2, 85 2/2, 95 2/2, 103 1/1, 3 109 1/1
Pulls Clean	115 3 for 2, 102 2 for 2, 125 1 for 1

TUESDAY	
Exercises	**Workload Prescription**
Back Squat	55/6, 75/5, 84/5, 110/3, 125/3, 140/2, 155/1, 165/2, 169/1
Power Clean	45/3, 60/3, 70/3, 80/2, 90/2, 100/1
Power Jerk	45/2, 60/2, 70/2, 80/2, 90/2, 100/1, 105/1, 110/1
Jump Up	10 x 3

WEDNESDAY	
Exercises	**Workload Prescription**
Push Snatch + Squat	35 4+1, 45 3+1, 55 2+1, 65 2+1
Snatch	40/2, 50/2, 60/2, 65/2, 70/2, 3/75/2, 78/1
Snatch Pulls	45 2/2, 60 2/2, 70 2/2, 80 2/2, 90 2/2, 3/97 2/2, 102 1/1
Clean Pulls	110/2, 117/2, 122/2, 125/2

THURSDAY	
Exercises	**Workload Prescription**
Front Squat	55/3, 70/3, 85/3, 100/3, 115/3, 125/3, 136/1, 143/1, 148/1
Push Press	35/6, 45/6, 55/4, 65/2, 70/1
Jump Up	10 x 3

FRIDAY	
Exercises	**Workload Prescription**
Drops + OHS	30, 40, 50, 60, 54 all 2 + 1
Snatch	30/2, 40/2, 50/2, 60/2, 64/1
Clean Pulls	45, 60, 70, 80 2 for 2, 84 1 for 1
Front Squat	3/95/1

SATURDAY	
Exercises	**Workload Prescription**
Front Squat	65/6, 80/5, 95/4, 110/3, 122/3, 132/2, 142/1
Power Clean	45/2, 55/2, 65/2, 75/2, 85/2
Power Jerk	45/2, 55/2, 65/2, 75/2, 85/2
Pulls	50/2, 60/2, 70/2, 80/2, 90/2, 95/2, 100/2
Jump Up	10 x 3

JARED FLEMING'S PROGRAM

Photo 8.22—Jared Fleming

Jared Fleming did what every weightlifter wishes they could do: go back in time and start at age 10. He didn't start his career in a haphazard way; his dad took him to upstate New York native Jim Storch to learn how to lift weights. Storch became his first coach, and continued with him until he was 12 years old. Jared has a great deal of respect for Storch and still mentions him frequently. When he was 12, Jared's dad, David Fleming, took over coaching duties and continued to coach him until he graduated from high school.

Starting and receiving great coaching early in his career certainly paid off for Jared, as he won Youth Nationals at age 12. He took second the next year, and reeled off a long string of first place finishes that lasted until he ended his career as a youth athlete. He also broke the Youth American records in the snatch and the total. During this time, Jared was also playing soccer with an elite traveling squad, and he also wrestled for a year.

Throughout that period, Jared never trained more than three times a week. It's hard to believe in an age when every CrossFit athlete with six month's experience is training twice per day, Jared managed to win five School-Age National titles, three Junior National Titles, an American Open title, and was on two Junior World teams while training three days per week.

Jared attended Louisiana State University Shreveport (LSUS), training under Kyle Pierce—and he continued to win. He made another Junior World team, won another Junior National title, another American Open title, won three University National titles, made the senior World Team twice, won his first national title, and broke two junior records and one University National record. While at LSUS, Jared increased his training to five times per week, and got significantly stronger.

Jared eventually moved on to train at MDUSA, where he was coached by yours truly with his dad still offering advice and helping at competitions. Training at MDUSA seemed to agree with him, as he increased his total 16 kilos in his first year in South Carolina.

While at MDUSA, Jared increased his training to nine sessions per week. He won yet another American Open and National title, qualified for another World Team, and broke his first senior American record with a 170-kilo snatch.

Photo 8.23—Jared Fleming holding the American record overhead

The following is a look at Jared's workout log. This was about four weeks prior to the 2015 World Championships in Houston.

MONDAY

Exercises	Workload Prescription
Snatch Sots Press	50 2 x 3
Snatch	110 2 x 1, 130 2 x 1, 140 2 x 1, 150 x 1, 160 x 1 (94%), 150 x 1
Clean and Jerk	170 x 1, 180 x 1, 190 x 1 (96.4%)
Clean Pull	200 x 3, 210 x 3, 215 x 3

Typically two training sessions on Monday with snatch and snatch accessories in the morning and clean and jerk accessories in the afternoon.

Accessories for Back Health

One Leg RDL	30 2 x 8 per side
Suitcase Deadlift	60 2 x 8 per side

TUESDAY

Exercises	Workload Prescription
Snatch Balance + OHS	150 x 1, 160 x 1, 170 x 1 *(100% of Snatch)*
Front Squat	200 x 3, 215 x 3
RDL	150 x 3, 170 x 3, 190 x 3

Accessories for Back Health

Lunges	70 x 5, 90 x 5, 100 x 5 *(Opposite leg than I jerk with forward)*
One-Arm Walking Deads	20 lb. 2 x 13 Steps per side

WEDNESDAY

Exercises	Workload Prescription
Snatch	130 x 1, 140 x 1, 150 3 x 1

Normally there are two sessions on Wednesday, typically snatch and snatch pull in the morning and clean and jerk and clean pull in the afternoon.

THURSDAY

Exercises	Workload Prescription
Back Squat	210 x 3, 230 x 3, 240 x 3* *(Heaviest squatted since 2013 back injury)*
Jerk Recoveries	200 x 1, 220 x 1
Good Mornings	80 3 x 5

Accessories for Back Health

Lunges	80 x 5, 100 x 5, 110 x 5 *(Opposite leg than I jerk with forward)*

Long stretch session in the sports medicine facility.

FRIDAY

Exercises	Workload Prescription
Morning Training	
Snatch Sots Press	50 2 x 3
No Hook Snatch	120 x 1, 130 x 1, 135 x 1, 141 x 1, 142 x 1 *(PR No Hook Snatch)*
Afternoon Training	
Snatch	124 x 1, 134 x 1, 144 x 1, 154 x 1, 164 x 1, 167 x 1, 160 x 1

Normally clean and jerk and clean pull after snatching

KATHLEEN WINTERS HARRIS'S PROGRAM

Photo 8.24—Kathleen Winters Harris

Kathleen Winters Harris began weightlifting when she was 19. She rose quickly in the sport; in fact, she might have had the least training experience of anyone on the 2015 World Team. Kathleen is coached by Steve Gough, who has been her first and, as of this writing, only coach. She resides in Montana, where she resurrected Steve's old team, Team Montana.

Kathleen was formerly a high-level gymnast, although she's quick to point out that she never made it to the elite level in that sport. She competed in gymnastics from age two to 14; after she gave up gymnastics, she quickly found a new activity: CrossFit.

Initially, her only interest in weightlifting was as something to help her get better at CrossFit, but Kathleen's interest in the sport increased when her mother decided to enter the World Masters Games. To qualify, she needed a total in a weightlifting meet. Kathleen's mother trained for the meet, but broke her foot the week prior. Since travel plans had already

been made and the entry fee paid, Kathleen decided to take her mother's place at the meet. Kathleen did well enough at the competition to qualify for the Junior Nationals, the American Open, and the Senior Nationals. She then started training seriously for the next national meet on the calendar, the 2012 American Open. Kathleen did well at the Open, totaling 147 kilos, which was good enough to earn a bronze medal in the 53-kilo weight class.

While she was training for CrossFit, Steve had been coaching weightlifting classes at the gym where Kathleen frequently trained, so picking him as her coach was natural. Having discovered that weightlifting was something she was good at and could compete in at a high level, she continued to train with Steve a couple times a week. He drove down to her gym to watch her biggest training sessions on Wednesdays and Saturdays, and on the other days she trained alone.

Kathleen competed in the next Junior Nationals as a 53-kilo lifter. She earned a silver medal at Juniors, and did well enough to qualify for the Junior World team. She totaled 159 kilos at Junior Worlds, earning 12th place. She then made the Junior Pan American team, where she earned second place with a 160-kilo total.

Kathleen competed in the 2013 American Open, but unfortunately bombed out. She took some time off after that setback, and came back strong for the 2014 National Championships, totaling 165 kilos and placing second.

After Nationals, Kathleen became extremely sick, which caused her to lose a lot of weight and forced her into the 48-kilo class. The new weight class worked well: She won the National Championship in 2015 and made the Senior World Team, where she went on to represent the United States in the first Weightlifting World Championships held in our country in 40 years.

Here's an outline of Kathleen's training program.

MONDAY	
Exercises	**Workload Prescription**
Front Squat	Work up to a max double *(she makes a new PR about once a week)*
Snatch	Built to a max for the day *(if she feels good this might be a PR; if not it will always be at least 90%)*
Clean and Jerk	80% for 5 singles

TUESDAY	
Exercises	**Workload Prescription**
Snatch	At least 90%
Clean and Jerk	10 singles around 70%

WEDNESDAY	
Exercises	**Workload Prescription**
Front Squat	90 to 95% for 2 doubles
Snatch	Max Effort
Clean and Jerk	Max Effort
Snatch	Max Snatch (again) *(she sometimes snatches more the second time than the first)*

If she is feeling really good, Kathleen might take 10 to 15 minute rest and then snatch for a third time.

THURSDAY	
Exercises	**Workload Prescription**
This is usually a rest day. She may do a CrossFit workout from time to time, but nothing heavy.	

FRIDAY	
Exercises	**Workload Prescription**
Front Squat	Max Double
Snatch	Up to 90%
Clean and Jerk	Up to roughly 85%

SATURDAY	
Exercises	**Workload Prescription**
Snatch	To Max
Clean and Jerk	To Max
Clean and Jerk	Reduce weight to 85% for 8 Singles
Snatch	To Max (again)

LEO HERNANDEZ'S PROGRAM

Photo 8.25—Leo Hernandez

Leo Hernandez was born in Cuba, and began his weightlifting career in the Cuban sports system at the age of nine. He attended school for the first half of the day, and for the second, he and the other weightlifters were picked up by the coach and driven to the training center where they trained for two to three hours. The training in Cuba for lifters that young didn't emphasize heavy weights; instead, they were "graded" on their technique.

Leo says the program was well rounded and emphasized general physical preparedness and lots of basic physical skills designed to prepare them for the heavy specialized training they'd do as teenagers. There were lots of sprints, jumping, and a lot of variations of the snatch and the clean and jerk. Leo entered a sports school at age 12, where his training increased to six days a week. At the sports school, the athletes went to school for half a day, from 8:00 a.m. to noon with the afternoons reserved for training.

While at the training camp, the athletes followed the Russian school of lifting, using a periodized approach, lots of volume, and a large variety of exercises. Leo says he made good progress every year

until he was 16, at which point he spent two years in the Cuban military. Once out of the military, he opted to go to college instead of returning to his weightlifting training.

At age 22, Leo immigrated to the United States, where he worked for a couple of years without resuming his training. People kept asking him about lifting, and why he had given it up, and eventually, Leo decided to resurrect his lifting career. He says that restarting his training was the hardest thing he'd ever done.

In his first US competition, he snatched 130 kilos and clean and jerked 156. At the 2013 Arnold Classic, he lifted 135 and 165 kilos, respectively, and the next year at the Arnold, he increased that to 141 in the snatch and 170 in the clean and jerk. At the 2015 Arnold, he did 148 kilos in the snatch and 184 in the clean and jerk, but bombed out at the 2015 National Championships. The bomb-out at Nationals forced him to go to a Grand Prix in China to earn a spot on the world team, which he did.

Photo 8.26—Leo Hernandez, calm and intense

The following table is a quick peek at how Leo trained for the 2015 Worlds.

MONDAY	
Exercises	**Workload Prescription**
Morning Training	
Muscle Snatch	70/4, 80/3, 90 4/2
Push Press (:2 Pause in Dip)	100/3, 110/2, 125 3/2
Romanian Pull	120 4/6
Afternoon Training	
Snatch + OHS	70/3, 90/3, 100/2, 110/2, 120 2/2
Clean and Power Jerk	100/3, 120/3, 140/2, 147 2/2
Back Squat	140/4, 160/3, 185/3, 200/2, 220 3/2
20 minutes of accessory work	

TUESDAY	
Exercises	**Workload Prescription**
Power Snatch	70/3, 90/3, 100/2, 110/2, 115 3/2
Power Clean and Jerk	100/3, 120/3, 130/2, 140 2/2
Clean Pull	170/3, 195 3/3
20 minutes of accessory work	

WEDNESDAY	
Exercises	**Workload Prescription**
Morning Training	
Snatch Balance	90/3, 110/3, 130/3, 145 3/2
Hyper Snatch Pull	155 3/3
Military Press	100 5/3
Afternoon Training	
Hang Snatch	70/3, 90/3, 110/3, 120/2, 130 2/2
Clean and Jerk	100/3, 120/3, 130/2, 145/2, 155 2/2
Front Squat	140/3, 165/3, 180 4/2
20 minutes of accessory work	

THURSDAY	
Rest Day	

FRIDAY	
Exercises	**Workload Prescription**
Morning Training	
Power Snatch	70/3, 90/3, 100/2, 110 3/1
Snatch Pull	150 3/2
Push Press	100/4, 120/3, 130 3/3
20 minutes of accessory work	
Afternoon Training	
Snatch	70/3, 90/3, 100/2, 110/2, 120/2, 130 3/1
Clean and Jerk	100/3, 120/3, 140/2, 155/2, 165 3/1
Back Squat	160/3, 180/3, 200/3, 215 3/3
20 minutes of accessory work	

SATURDAY	
Exercises	**Workload Prescription**
Power Snatch off Blocks	70/4, 90/3, 100/2, 110/2, 115 3/1
Power Clean and Push Press	90/3, 110/3, 120/2, 135 2/2
Clean Pull	185 3/3
20 minutes of accessory work	

CLOSING THOUGHTS

Many pages ago, I spoke of the stigma surrounding being a beginner and how many people mistakenly don't embrace that phase of their lifting careers. After a short time in the sport, they begin to yearn for the day they can call themselves "advanced," and even take steps to rush the process to get there.

I've seen it many times: That path eventually leads to burn out, and finally quitting the sport altogether.

One could argue this is all facilitated in many ways by social media. Today you can follow and witness firsthand the lifestyle of countless advanced athletes. You can watch them setting new personal records daily, winning medals, and receiving sponsorship deals. It looks like a glamorous way to live, and may tempt you to skip steps to try to get there.

What you need to consider is that the person you're following spent years climbing to the upper echelons of the sport. Countless hours were spent pursuing technical mastery in the snatch, building the courage to go under heavy cleans, and overcoming the heartache followed by missing jerks that meant the difference between winning and losing.

There were most likely many days in the beginning when this hero of the sport seemingly forgot how to snatch. There were moments of throwing a lifting belt in anger after pulling the bar to the belly button on a clean, and then failing to go under. No doubt there were tears shed and threats of quitting the sport after bombing out at local meets.

Rising through the rankings and earning their way to the top was difficult and tedious…and this is what you don't see on social media. You don't see the hours of meal prep, going the extra mile on recovery, or skipping social occasions to get a good night's sleep. Sacrifice is rarely featured on social media, but instead lived privately, which presents a false representation of what it takes to be successful.

It's okay to have idols in the sport. But you'll have to weather your own storms to get where they are. The sport will test you and your will to win session after session and meet after meet. Do yourself a favor and practice patience.

Don't try to be like someone else. You can't copy your way to the top, so don't follow the training programs of the best in the world and expect their results.

Instead, work on yourself as an individual and tailor all aspects of your training to your own needs. That might mean the training doesn't look as flashy as some you see on the internet. You don't need training to be flashy; you need it to be effective.

If you're suddenly afforded extra time in your schedule, then by all means train and train hard, but be smart about it.

The amount of training needed is individual, and the only rule is to do enough to allow the snatch and the clean and jerk to progress to the highest possible levels. Focus on your own needs, and be patient as the training process runs its course.

CHAPTER 9

WESTSIDE FOR WEIGHTLIFTERS
with appreciation of Louie Simmons' efforts and his generosity in sharing this with me

MY HISTORY WITH WESTSIDE

I began my training as a powerlifter, and eventually adopted Louie Simmons' Westside system. When I switched sports from powerlifting to weightlifting in the 1990s, I saw no reason I couldn't adapt the system to my new sport and continue to use it.

Trying to adapt Louie's system to weightlifting is kind of a strange concept because weightlifting is where he originally got most of his ideas and knowledge of training methods. He's always been up front about this, but everyone who interprets an idea does it a little differently. Louie definitely put his own twist on many of the concepts he got from Russian books published in the 1970s and '80s. He's been developing his system for more than 30 years, and has come up with plenty of his own ideas. Some relate best to powerlifting, but many of his concepts relate to weightlifting as well.

I have a working knowledge of the Russian training methods from that timeframe, much of it gathered when I was working on my master's degree. But aside from Bud Charniga, I've never met anyone with as much knowledge of the Russian methods as Louie.

My initial attempts at trying to use Louie's ideas in weightlifting centered around the use of limited rest periods on a speed day for the squat, and making some changes on the max-effort day for the lower body and back. The limited rest periods for the squat, which I called timed sets, continued to work like they did in powerlifting, and all the good mornings and box squats made me stronger.

But my snatch and clean and jerk weren't moving up as I thought they should.

I started using the timed sets—what we now call EMOM, which you remember as every minute on the minute sets—back in the 1990s for the snatch and clean and jerk. And get this: They work even better for weightlifting than for powerlifting. Review the intermediate chapter of this book for a refresher on the technique, but to paraphrase, EMOMs cause the fatigue to build slowly over 20 or more minutes.

There isn't as big a change from one rep to the next as there is with a conventional set of three or five. This slow buildup of fatigue allows the body to deal with the gradual loss of strength and power by moving faster or deeper under the bar, pulling in a more efficient manner, and allowing a lifter to lift more with whatever strength and power can be retained.

In spite of having visited Louie a couple of times and having talked to him at length about how to best implement his ideas in the sport of weightlifting, I continued to feel I was missing something important.

Let's fast forward to my time at California Strength when I met Ivan Abadjiev and a couple of his lifters. I'd already tried the Bulgarian system for weightlifting with the same mixed results many others had. I had initial success, followed by a gradual drop-off, and eventually, burnout. In spite of not being sold on the Bulgarian style of training, it was still the most intellectually consistent training program I'd found at the time. It's much like the Ayn Rand of weightlifting systems. It's brutally honest, unforgiving, and makes you feel like you're the problem if you don't get it or can't do it.

During my time at California Strength, it was even more valuable to have Ivan coach Donny Shankle. That led to a better understanding of the Bulgarian method, training to maximum, and how the body responds. My association with Abadjiev convinced me there was something about the way I was implementing the Bulgarian system that was missing, and it could and would work if I could just find the missing ingredient.

Oddly, that was exactly how I felt about Westside.

At California Strength and then at MuscleDriver, I steadily moved toward using more max-effort training during the week. It started in California with the adoption of "Max-Out Friday." I gradually started adopting the practice of training to maximum with power snatches and power cleans on Tuesdays and Thursdays. As everyone who's done these exercises knows, the power versions are much less stressful to the body than the full versions, and can be done consistently at a higher percentage of maximum. A 100% power snatch is about as stressful on the body as an 80% or 90% snatch, so the power version could be done heavier more often.

By then, I'd experimented with all the major components I'd need to successfully implement the Westside program for weightlifting, but hadn't yet brought them together at one time, nor had I used them correctly. We'd used EMOM sets for snatches and cleans, limited rest periods and a dynamic-effort day for squats, max effort on hip and back exercises, and max effort on the snatch and clean and jerk. However, the system wasn't working like it should have, and I couldn't figure out why.

The reason for this should have been obvious, and it's a little embarrassing that it took years to figure out. The exercises used for max-effort day utilized the same muscles as the snatch and clean and jerk, but were different in every other way. The movement speed was slower, the bar speed was much slower, the power output was lower, but the force generated and the time under tension were both higher. They couldn't have been more different.

If I chose a variety of max-effort exercises similar to the competition lifts and rotated to a new and different one every max-effort workout, I could continue indefinitely without ill effects on the central nervous system. Even better, because the bar velocity is so high in the weightlifting movements and there's no negative portion, a lifter can do many more max-effort exercises in a workout or even more max-effort workouts per week than would be possible with powerlifting movements.

Finally, a lifter who used the Westside powerlifting system explained it to me. I consider myself fairly educated when it comes to human physiology, and still have the student loan payments to prove it. But I felt stupid because I'd just made the kind of mistake I'd have expected a freshman to make when I was teaching exercise physiology at Midwestern State.

I wasn't getting the results I wanted because I'd misunderstood and misapplied some basic physiology principles, not because the system didn't work. All I had to do to make it work was combine the parts that did work with a constant diet of heavy max weightlifting movements like the Bulgarians use.

EMOM sets for technical practice on the competitive weightlifting movements work amazingly well for building and reinforcing efficient motor patterns.

Multiple max-effort training sessions per week or even per day on the snatch and clean and jerk works extremely well for building strength in those lifts, as demonstrated by the Bulgarians. Combining these two methods is an idea that's time has come.

Louie Simmons built a phenomenal powerlifting system by taking many ideas from the Russian weightlifting system. He added unique twists to dominate the world of powerlifting over the last few decades. Mix in things learned from the Bulgarian weightlifting team of the 1970s and 1980s, and we're left with a whole new system—maybe a way to produce athletes who are fast, strong, and powerful in less time than ever before.

Over the past few years, I've developed a plan to use this system for weightlifting, and have actually been using it with great results. But there are many parts of this plan I've used longer that will be easily recognizable if you watch the California Strength or MDUSA videos. Some of my lifters from even as far back as Wichita Falls will recognize certain parts of this system.

I'd been trying to adapt the Westside powerlifting system to the sport of weightlifting for two decades. This should have been easy, because Louie got many of the ideas that eventually became the Westside system from Olympic weightlifting. But over the last 30 years, Louie's training system morphed into something few Russian weightlifters would recognize.

Louie likes to experiment with new ideas—in particular, new training equipment—and the Westside system has always been in a constant state of change and improvement. This is basically the definition of "conjugate," as Westside is known.

THE CONJUGATE SYSTEM

In the Westside system for powerlifting, Louie uses one dynamic-method day for the bench press, with another dynamic-method day for the squat and deadlift training. There's a max-effort day for the bench press, and a max-effort day for the squat and deadlift. Louie and his lifters round out the training week with a lot of "smaller" workouts utilizing the repetition method. These workouts make up a large part of the weekly training volume of the Westside method.

In my interpretation of this method, I put the dynamic method for the snatch and clean and jerk on Monday with every minute on the minute sets for each lift. I schedule this on Mondays for a symbolic reason: The snatch and clean and jerk are what weightlifting is all about, and the dynamic-method day is when we're performing the competition movements as they're done in competition.

Monday also works best as a dynamic day on the lifts for a practical reason. The snatch and clean and jerk done with moderate weights as they are on the dynamic day produce very little soreness, and if done correctly, lead only to an overall physical tiredness. In fact, Joe Mills used to say you could tell what you were doing wrong by the muscle that was unduly sore or tired because when done correctly, there should be no especially tired or sore body part. That the dynamic day for the lifts doesn't interfere with subsequent training days makes it a natural for the first day of the week.

We use the dynamic method for the squat on Tuesday, and many lifters think this is the most demanding training day of the week. It's also my personal favorite. Squatting—in particular, front squatting—is a cornerstone of weightlifting. You have to be able to front squat a weight to clean and jerk it. And the ease in which you stand with it is one of the main determinants of whether you'll succeed with the jerk. Making sure your front squat is strong is vitally important, but learning how to bounce using the myotatic reflex—the stretch reflex—is also essential to get out of the hole quickly with as little effort as possible.

In this plan, the rest of the week is devoted to max-effort training. Wednesday, Thursday, and Friday are max-effort training days with variations of the snatch and clean and jerk. Saturday's max-effort training includes variations of the squat, good morning, and deadlift. These are slower, heavier lifts that stress the same muscles as the weightlifting movements.

Depending on whether you're a beginner, an intermediate, or an advanced athlete, you'll complete between one or two training sessions on Wednesday, Thursday, and Friday for a total of three to six sessions across all three days. The bulk of the weekly training is done at high intensity with exercises similar to the competitive lifts in bar velocity, movement speed, and coordination.

USING BANDS AND CHAINS

Photos 9.1–9.3—Using bands

A lot of weightlifters—and even more weightlifting coaches—hate bands and chains. This is probably one of the main reasons they react negatively to

Louie Simmons' work. However, neither bands nor chains are necessary to use this system. If you have such an emotional response to bands that you simply won't or can't use them, then don't. They aren't necessary to make this system work…not necessary, but helpful.

Louie first started using chains years ago to make the bar heavier as it neared lockout on the squat. When squatting with compensatory acceleration, you have to modulate the force as the bar nears lockout or you'll come off the ground.

Chains served the same purpose as did the cam of a Nautilus machine: They provide variable resistance… in this case, more resistance when more of the chain is off the ground, with the most resistance nearing lockout. For squats, bands are a cheaper and less clunky way of achieving this goal. A weightlifter or coach who refuses to use chains or bands is just being obstinate.

Using bands or chains on the lifts is murkier. I don't believe chains have a place in training the snatch or clean and jerk; the difficulties and disadvantages are too numerous. Bands, on the other hand, are a different story.

What makes bands unique is what they do to the bar while you're moving under it. During the unweighted portions of the lift, bands make the bar return to the earth faster. In effect, they speed up gravity. It's like instead of gravity accelerating the bar at 9.8 meters per second every second, gravity suddenly accelerates the bar at 15 meters per second every second. You simply have less time to move under the bar and prepare to catch it.

Photos 9.4 and 9.5—Using bands in a squat rack

This can be a positive in that it teaches lifters to move faster under the bar. But it can also be a negative because the snatch and clean and jerk require finely honed timing to succeed. Bands have the potential to alter that timing. I think they can alter it in a helpful way, but I understand the argument against this method as well.

Most people who give bands a fair chance will see their value. If you're still uneasy with bands on the lifts or with bands or chains in general, I encourage you to give the system a try. There's much more in this system than just chains or bands.

THE REPETITION METHOD

There's a third aspect of the Westside system I haven't talked about yet: On Saturdays, we employ the maximum-effort method. This is the method an athlete uses when doing a max back squat or deadlift. It's also what a weightlifter uses when executing a max snatch or clean and jerk. Tuesdays, we use the dynamic method for squats, executing them with moderate intensity, but completing the concentric portion of the movement as fast as possible.

Mondays—and every other day we do the weight-lifting movements—we're also using the dynamic method. After all, this is what the Olympic lifts are, moving a weight fast enough that there's time to squat under and catch it. The weightlifting movements practically define the dynamic method.

The third method of gaining strength is one many weightlifters ignore. The repetition method—lifting a submaximal weight many times in a row—is the method bodybuilders almost exclusively use. Power-lifters also use it for a large part of their training. However, many weightlifters ignore it.

This is an important part of training for injury prevention, for building good technique, and also for strength and power. Lifters I coach do a number of movements using this method, normally at the end of the workout, and usually for multiple sets of 10. Beginners start with two exercises for two or three total sets; intermediate athletes can usually use up to six total sets, and advanced athletes use two or three exercises for up to 10 total sets.

REPETITION METHOD EXERCISES

For increasing strength and power, my favorite exercises in this class are hip extension movements such as the hip extension and glute ham raise. The back extension is another exercise I frequently program. We touched upon all three of these exercises earlier in the book.

In addition to performing them with a bar behind the neck, you can also attach a band to the machine to hold onto or loop it around the body. If you're doing more than one set, add weight from set to set, and try to set a PR on your last set.

SEATED GOOD MORNING

The seated good morning is another exercise I'm fond of that's unique to this chapter. Seated good mornings are one of the only seated exercises I've found useful. To perform them, straddle a bench; then, while holding a bar on your back, bend forward until your face is as close as possible to the bench.

I love these for erector strength when done for sets of three to five heavy reps, but they're also great when done with submaximal weights at the end of a workout for sets of 10.

Jerk steps, split-stance good mornings, Romanian deadlifts, arch-back good mornings, and death marches are other useful exercises in this programming.

Photos 9.6–9.8—Seated good morning

JERK STEPS

Because of the speed of the split jerk, practicing correct foot movement is difficult. Slowing the movement makes the precise split geometry easier to practice.

Jerk steps slow down the movement and allow heavier weight than can be used in an actual jerk with the bar overhead.

Jerk steps won't help the lockout, but they will build strength and confidence in the split position. The jerk step also helps correct the common technical error of overreaching with the back leg. The jerk occurs with lightning speed, and you can't think your way through it. The jerk step is slow enough to allow you to think, and emphasizes stepping forward with the front foot, something many lifters need.

Jerk steps can improve balance of the muscular development of both hips and legs, because an equal number of steps are performed with both the right and left leg stepping forward. At one point, James Tatum had uneven development between his right and left hip and leg musculature. This led to one hip being higher than the other, causing lower-back pain. Jerk steps provided symmetry and relieved the back pain by strengthening the musculature of his non-dominant hip and leg, and by bringing the hip position into balance. By achieving balance in both limbs, one might even find the squat numbers increase dramatically, in addition to staving off potential injury.

A jerk step is performed by holding a heavy weight on your back, a weight at or above your maximum jerk. Take 20 steps into your split stance, 10 with the left leg leading, and 10 with the right leg leading. Make sure your leg geometry is correct with every step, with your front shin vertical, your back knee down, and both feet slightly toed in.

Adjust the length of each step to achieve the correct leg geometry.

Every step, you'll have to fight for your posture, engage the muscles of your upper back and core, maintain balance while stepping into the split, and stop your forward momentum. You'll also have to recover properly out of each split by first bringing the front foot back, followed by bringing the back foot forward. That's an incredibly demanding task, and will force the body to move precisely under high fatigue.

Most training in weightlifting is geared toward building more strength and better motor patterns that allow an athlete to efficiently perform lifts in competition. However, overcoming fatigue is also important, especially when a jerk is required after a hard-fought clean. If an athlete rarely experiences the fatigue that might cause a missed jerk, there's more difficulty overcoming that situation. Performing precise movement patterns in a fatigued state is trainable, and the jerk step is a great way to train it.

Photos 9.9–9.13—Jerk steps

Performance

Starting with the feet in line, take a step forward into a split stance. Make sure the front shin is vertical, the back knee is down, and both feet are in a slightly toed-in position. Recover as you would from a jerk by first bringing the front foot back, covering half the distance needed to bring the feet back in line. Finish the recovery by bringing the back foot forward so both feet are again in line. Perform half of the repetitions with one leg stepping forward, then perform the other half with the second leg stepping forward. For example, step across the room with the right leg leading, then turn around and step back with the left leg leading.

Don't rush when performing this exercise. Take a step, and when the leading foot lands on the floor, engage the muscles in the hips and legs to stop the forward momentum. Make adjustments where necessary; take the time to ensure the back knee is down and the front shin is vertical by adjusting your stride each step. Jerk steps can be done with the bar in a front- or back-squat position.

ROUND-BACK GOOD MORNING

Photos 9.14–9.17—Round-back good morning

Round-back good mornings are in essence back extensions performed from a standing position. They supply the same eccentric and concentric loading that makes the back extension such an important exercise. Regardless of how strong or large your spinal erectors, they can be bigger and stronger from the back extension and the round-back good morning.

Performance

During this exercise, you'll flex and extend the spine just as you would on a back extension done on a GHD. Start with a bar in the back-squat position.

Relax the spinal erector muscles as you lean forward, allowing the spine to slowly flex and bend. When your spine is as flexed as possible, extend it as you would a back extension. The goal is to move from an extended and arched position at the top, to a bent-over position at the bottom, to finally back up in an extended position. The movement should be fluid.

This is an exercise that should be done with light weights, usually much lighter than your arch-back good morning.

ROMANIAN DEADLIFTS

Photos 9.18–9.22—Romanian deadlift

The Romanian deadlift, commonly referred to simply as an RDL, is another great exercise to strengthen the muscles of the back, hips, and hamstrings. It can be done with a snatch-grip or clean-grip. This is a unique exercise that when done correctly challenges the flexibility of the hamstrings, as well as the strength of the entire posterior chain.

For beginners, there's no substitute for heavy snatch-grip or clean-grip deadlifts. On those exercises, there's the benefit of lifting a heavy weight while attempting to perform the correct movement pattern of the snatch or clean pull. One could argue that's all a lifter would ever need. But, exercises such as RDLs and arch-back good mornings are reasonable options for increasing pulling strength for lifters who need a break from heavy deadlifts.

A case can be made for using the RDL in preference to the deadlift in much the same way one could reasonably argue for using the dip as an alternative to bench presses. One could never argue that the dumbbell fly is an alternative to the bench press, but since the dip is so similar in the way it affects and strengthens the body, an argument can be made for using it in preference to the bench press. This is how I feel about the RDL. I prefer deadlifts, but another person might prefer the RDL.

Performance

Stand with your feet hip width apart while holding a barbell with a double-overhand grip. Keeping the knees relatively straight (about the same flexion as in step one of the Three Step Method), bend at the hips and allow the barbell to slide down the thighs as low as your flexibility allows.

During this exercise, progressively push your hips behind you to stretch the hamstrings. For most athletes, the barbell will reach a position somewhere below the knees, but many won't be flexible enough to let the plates touch the floor. If your plates touch the floor, make sure you're performing the RDL with the back locked in the correct position and that the knees have the correct amount of flexion.

If your position is as it should be and you're blessed with greater flexibility than most, try standing on a sturdy box or stacked plates to allow the bar to travel farther. When you've reached the limit of your flexibility, stand up by extending the hips. Make sure the knees maintain the same amount of flexion during the eccentric and concentric portions of the lift.

THE PENDLAY ROW

Photos 9.23–9.27—Pendlay row

The "Pendlay" row gained its name because of a post I made on a weight training forum back in the dark ages of the internet. I was explaining the correct performance of a strict barbell row, one done with the back remaining parallel to the floor throughout the execution of the lift.

In response to that post, lifters coined the name "Pendlay row" and many still call it that today. I've always referred to the way I coach this movement as a "strict row," but the name became so ubiquitous that at some point I stopped fighting it.

173

Performing a row in this fashion is valuable for several reasons. First, it works the whole back better than any other exercise—and I mean the whole back, including the traps, lats, and spinal erectors. And second, it helps teach the lifter how to use the lats to arch the spine to put the body in the correct posture necessary to snatch and clean. Finally, it's *explosive*—and we're training for weightlifting where we perform explosive movements.

There are a great many exercises that work the back in a similar fashion to the strict or Pendlay row. Pull-ups, dumbbell rows, and chest-supported rows are all great and have a place in training, but the Pendlay row trains the back in a more complete fashion than any other back movement.

Performance

Set up with the mid-back slightly rounded and the plates touching the floor. Begin the lift by explosively arching the back and pulling the bar toward the upper abdominals. Many athletes dip the torso just a hair as the bar contacts the body. The torso should stay close to parallel to the floor, and the plates should rest on the floor between each repetition.

This is different from a traditional bodybuilding-style barbell row. With that exercise, the plates don't touch the floor between reps, taking advantage of the stretch reflex in the working muscles. With the Pendlay row, the barbell is pulled from a dead stop every repetition. The aim is for a "stricter" rowing motion, opposed to using "body English" by swinging the torso to move the weight.

DEATH MARCH

The death march is a hip, hamstring, and lower-back exercise with a name that makes you think twice. It's performed by walking—putting one foot in front of the other—while holding dumbbells or kettlebells in your hands, touching the weights to the floor with each footstep. The first couple of steps will feel easy, but if you march a long enough distance, the difficulty will rise with each progressive stride.

Keeping your balance will become an issue, and you might start to weave a little with each step. When this happens, congratulations! You're now feeling like a weightlifter on a third attempt clean and jerk right after a particularly tough clean—your body has become fatigued to the point where you must now concentrate on more precise movement.

This is the beauty of the death march as it combines a unique posterior-chain movement, a metabolic conditioning effect, and something else: a real test of mental toughness.

It's a trainable ability to fight through the fatigue and move precisely on your last clean and jerk attempt or on the death march after you've stepped 100 feet with 100-pound dumbbells. The more you've been to that dark place in training, the better you'll be at moving correctly and precisely when in competition.

Performance

Grab either a dumbbell or kettlebell in each hand. Start light. Begin walking while lowering the weights and touching them to the floor with every step. Take medium steps, and keep an unbroken stride as much as possible. Don't wait until the next foot touch before lowering the weight.

Try doing these on a track or a place you can walk in a straight line between 20 to 100 yards. If you pick the weight correctly, by the time you get 10 or 15 yards out, you'll begin to see why the death march can help in any sport or activity that requires you to perform precise movements when fatigued.

Photos 9.28–9.36—Death march

SUITCASE DEADLIFT

Photos 9.37–9.41—Suitcase deadlift

The suitcase deadlift, which we got from strength coach Dan John, targets the muscles of the posterior chain the same as other deadlift variations. But here, the load is asymmetrical, which adds major stress to the abdominals and the rest of the core muscles. This stimulus is unusual in weightlifting, as everything in the sport is usually done in a symmetrical manner.

Asymmetrical lifting allows the lifter to work both the hip extensor muscles and the muscles used to stabilize the core. The exercise can expose imbalances a lifter may possess but hide in normal movements. Travis Cooper used the suitcase deadlift to help rehab and strengthen his core after a lower-back injury.

While it may never be a major part of training, exercises such as this certainly provide benefits when incorporated as an accessory exercise.

Performance

This exercise can be performed with a barbell, kettlebell, dumbbell, or farmer's handle. You can also stand on a box to increase the range of motion.

To start, stand with the implement at your side so the spot where you grip is directly in line with the outside of your shin. Bend at the waist and grip the object, and keep a flat back as you perform the deadlift. Return the implement back to the floor to complete the repetition.

Because the load is asymmetrical, you'll have to work hard not to lean excessively when raising or lowering the weight.

ONE-ARM KETTLEBELL SWINGS

The kettlebell swing performed with both hands gripping a single kettlebell is a great exercise for the whole posterior chain, but doing them with one arm adds a unique element of torso stabilization to resist rotating at the spine.

I prefer to do these in the Russian style, where you swing the bell to shoulder height with the arm parallel to the floor instead of swinging all the way overhead. I also have my athletes go *heavy;* I've had a few lifters who were strong enough to use the 203-pound kettlebell I keep on my front porch in Kansas. (I'm not too concerned with anyone walking off with it.)

The first time you do these, you'll be sore in unusual places where you may not normally experience soreness. Muscles such as the obliques will often be noticeably sore, along with other abdominal and torso muscles. You might also notice the muscles of the hip and hamstring in one leg are more affected than those of the other leg.

Performing exercises where you use both arms in a symmetrical manner actually doesn't always work muscles symmetrically—you can easily get away by cheating with your stronger or dominant side. Doing the swings with one arm ensures that both sides of the body are used to the same degree.

Photos 9.42–9.45—One-arm kettlebell swing

Swings also develop a feel for using your hips. This is something many lifters have trouble with—using the hips and not the arms to accelerate the bar overhead. I've had great success teaching hip acceleration to young kids and beginners by using this exercise.

One last benefit: Swings work the grip in a major way, especially when pushing the weight. If you don't have a strong grip, this exercise will develop it quickly.

Performance

To perform the one-arm kettlebell swing, stand in front of a kettlebell with the feet hip width apart. From there, while keeping a flat back, bend at the hips and knees, and place one hand on the middle of the handle. Swing the kettlebell back between the legs, and extend the hips and knees forcefully to swing the bell.

Allow the bell to swing back between the thighs, and as it does, push the hips back as far as possible. Keep a flat back and use as much hip and leg musculature as possible when performing this movement. Don't allow the kettlebell to swing down at or below knee

level; it should always be kept up near the crotch and high inner thighs. After performing the desired number of repetitions—typically a set of 10—switch hands and repeat on the other side.

PULL-UPS

Photos 9.46 and 9.47—Pull-up

When weightlifters discuss back training, they're often talking about the spinal erectors. But it takes more than just erectors to hold the body in the correct and most efficient position to perform the snatch and the clean and jerk—and exercises such as pull-ups and chin-ups are great back developing movements.

Most rowing and chinning exercises require equipment not normally seen in a weightlifting gym. The advent of CrossFit has changed this somewhat, yet many lifters still don't have access to the same equipment you might find in a gym catering to bodybuilders. One of the great things about the pull-up is that the equipment needed is simple: Only a chinning bar is required.

Some weightlifters are oddly resistant to doing things like pull-ups, and this is unfortunate. There's no room for weakness anywhere for a weightlifter, and not being able to do a reasonable number of pull-ups is a weakness. The pull-up also develops the forearms and biceps, and having bigger arms and a stronger grip is a good thing.

One of the most important details of pull-ups is to start from the dead hang, meaning the body hangs in

a totally relaxed position. Getting these two or three extra inches of range of motion involves many of the smaller muscles around the scapula. These muscles might not move large amounts of weight, but they're important for overall shoulder health and stability in the overhead position of the snatch or the jerk.

MAX-EFFORT EXERCISES

Max-effort days are a major component to the programming. For the snatch and clean and jerk, going to maximum is a skill only improved through practice. You'll do plenty of technique work, but technique work must be balanced with the technique of going heavy. This will be done on Wednesdays and Fridays in the programming.

See pages 187–189 to see a list of snatch, clean, and jerk variations to choose from when planning your future programming. When choosing a variation to max on, pick one that ends with receiving the weight overhead or on the shoulders. Different styles of pulls should rarely replace the lift you'd be doing that day; rather they should be used to supplement it. There are no medals given to the person with the best high pull.

Saturday's max-effort training will be comprised of squat, good morning, and jerk variations. This is also a good day to incorporate maximal snatch-grip or clean-grip deadlifts if overall pulling strength is something you need to work on.

Back squats and front squats should both be a mainstay of max-effort days. Regular back squats will always have a huge value, partly because they teach an athlete how to get in and out of the bottom position while expending the least effort possible.

Catching the bounce out of the bottom of the squat can be learned with enough practice, and immeasurably increases the chances of making a jerk. We've all seen lifters perform a clean that took 10 seconds to stand up from…and have nothing left for the jerk. Both the front squat and the back squat can be put to use in perfecting the ability to finish the clean portion of the clean and jerk with the most energy left over.

Box squats are also a useful tool for max-effort day. I like to do these to a box as low as I can touch, and also to a medium box that puts the thighs at about parallel, or exactly where they'd be at the bottom position of a legal powerlifting squat. I do these with a wider stance than my normal squat stance.

No matter the height of the box, you should descend slowly until your hips touch the box, relax on the box for an instant, and finally explode up, rising as fast as possible.

Front squats can be done to a box as well. All lifters have done a clean where they almost didn't get under it, then had to struggle for several seconds to secure it on their shoulders before starting to rise. Front squats to a box are one of the best exercises you can do to simulate this situation. Sometimes to simulate this, I have lifters pause for three to five seconds on the box instead of just for a second or two. Try varying your stance too. My favorite stance for these is the same as for box squats with the bar on my back, slightly wider than my normal squat stance.

Overhead squats can be useful, but usually not as useful as the front or back squat. This is because the weak point in an overhead squat is less likely to be leg strength and more likely to be either the inability to balance the weight or the arms' inability to hold it overhead. CrossFitters probably do more training on the overhead squat and get more from it than weightlifters. It can still be useful in some instances, and you certainly need to be able to overhead squat at least near the weight you can pull overhead. If not, this exercise will be vital for you.

Photos 9.48 and 9.49—Chad Muehler demonstrating a clean-grip overhead squat

Clean-grip overhead squats can be done normally or from the bottom up with the bar and plates starting on lifting blocks. These might be more useful than the snatch-grip version that's more widely used.

There's definitely a carryover from the clean-grip to the snatch-grip version, and the clean-grip version will help immensely when an athlete has to go just a little deeper than planned to catch and stabilize a jerk.

Whether you're a power jerker or a split jerker, it wouldn't hurt to have at least some experience deeper than usual under a heavy jerk. And you may be so good at clean-grip overhead squats that you become the next great squat jerker.

Other exercises you can do on max-effort day include snatch-grip and clean-grip deadlifts, muscle snatches, arch-back good mornings, split-stance good mornings, Romanian deadlifts, jerk recoveries, step-ups, yoke carries, and push presses.

MUSCLE SNATCHES

Many people use the muscle snatch as a beginner exercise, but I also use them for their strength- and muscle-building qualities. The muscle snatch especially excels as a builder of all the muscles in the shoulder girdle and upper back.

I had great success using the muscle snatch with Caleb Ward. When he first began training, he didn't have a lot of upper-body strength. This exercise was one he used frequently throughout his career, and he built up to very heavy weights. Muscle snatches also gave Caleb confidence, and when he was strong at them, he snatched his best.

According to Caleb, *"The muscle snatch was my favorite assistance exercise. It taught me to keep the bar close, and helped me build upper-body strength. I typically incorporated this movement into my daily warm-up routine (up to about 50 or 60% of my snatch 1RM) and would max this movement about twice a month. Since I heavily relied on speed and technique in my career, I enjoyed these because they challenged my strength outside the traditional snatch movement. My best muscle snatch was 105 kilos, and that was when my best training snatch was about 155."*

There are two ways to perform a muscle snatch: with and without bar body contact. Both variations can be prescribed depending on the needs and preferences of the lifter. Caleb usually used bar body contact, aside from light warm-up sets when he might have skipped the hips.

Photos 9.50–9.54—Muscle snatch

When doing the movement with bar body contact, you'll have the benefit of more carryover to the full snatch. Typically, less weight can be lifted if the bar doesn't come into the hips.

Because this exercise can be performed with much less weight than the competition lift, we go heavy on them fairly often. Weights over 90% of maximum can be handled regularly.

Performance

To perform a muscle snatch, pull exactly as you would a snatch until you execute the second pull, then instead of pulling under the bar, use your upper back and shoulder strength to drive the bar upward and over your head with no dip or re-bend in the knees or hips.

JERK RECOVERIES

Photos 9.55–9.59—Jerk recovery

Jerk recoveries allow a lifter to overload the muscles used in supporting heavy weight overhead in the jerk, and build confidence in the receiving position. This exercise can be done with at least 110% of your maximum jerk, and many have gone far beyond that. Jerk recoveries are an example of a portion of the jerk that normally occurs quickly, but has been isolated, slowed down, and overloaded to build strength and awareness of correct movement patterns.

Here's where you can practice using the correct sequence for the jerk recovery, namely pushing back with the front foot, then bringing the back foot forward. This sequence is important, as it leads to the least possible horizontal bar motion.

Beginners can continually practice front foot back first, then back foot forward second with light weights. Intermediate athletes are reminded to bring their feet back together correctly after every lift. Advanced athletes have the mechanics down, and with this exercise can now challenge the sequence with heavy weight.

Performance

The setup for this exercise may be difficult if you don't have a squat rack that allows you to set spotting pins at heights that place the bar at eye level. Utilizing adjustable lifting blocks could potentially work. The barbell will need to be set to eye level with weights close to your max jerk.

When you have the proper equipment set up, position your grip to where you'd have it for the jerk. Split under the barbell, and then pause. Make sure your legs are in the correct geometry for your split position. Tighten your torso, brace your arms, and drive up with the legs, lifting the bar off the rack pins or blocks. From there, push back with the front foot, then bring the back foot forward, bringing both feet back together as you would when finishing a heavy jerk. After a successful recovery, lower the bar back to the pins or blocks.

SPLIT-STANCE GOOD MORNING

The split-stance good morning is an excellent exercise to help develop symmetry in the hips, thighs, and legs. The exercise places you in the same split position as in the jerk, and then requires that you perform a good morning in that position.

In addition to muscle and strength development, you also gain the added benefit of it working as a teaching tool to reinforce the split. Much like jerk steps, this exercise requires the same number of repetitions using the same weight with each leg in both the front and back positions.

Performance

Place a barbell on your back as you would for a back squat. Move your feet into your jerk split stance—start with your normal front split leg first. Once in the split stance, perform a good morning by pushing your hips back as far as possible, and allow the torso to lean forward. The back should be arched as much as possible, and the knees shouldn't excessively bend or extend; your split stance should remain intact.

Perform the desired repetitions on that leg, then switch and repeat the movement with your non-dominant leg.

Photos 9.60–9.64—Split-stance good morning

ARCH-BACK GOOD MORNING

Some people think of the arch-back good morning as a dangerous exercise—a judgment I disagree with. A better description would be that it's a taxing exercise and one that can cause extreme, even debilitating soreness. The range of motion takes you right to the edge of your hamstring flexibility, which means it's prudent to work into this exercise more slowly than you would with most others.

As anyone who has done arch-back good mornings with challenging weights has discovered, it's essential to tighten your core as much as possible. It's helpful to wear a belt and push the abs out against the belt as a brace. There's some controversy about whether this actually works, but I don't think you'll find anyone who has performed this exercise with 400 or 500 pounds debating it. In fact, many people—including me—rank this exercise right up there with heavy squats when it comes to building a bulletproof core.

Photos 9.65–9.67—Arch-back good morning

Performance

The arch-back good morning is similar to a Romanian deadlift, but instead of having the bar in your hands, it's on your back. When performing a repetition, the knees are slightly flexed, similar to how they would be in step one of the Three Step Method of learning a snatch or the bottom of the dip and drive for the jerk. The spine is braced in an extremely arched position, and the hips are flexed until reaching the limit of hamstring flexibility. You then extend the hips to finish the repetition.

STEP-UPS

Lifters and coaches have tried to find a replacement for the back squat, but so far, no one has found one. In many situations, the front squat is a great substitute, but at some point, those trying to find a replacement for the back squat must ask, "Why bother?" The back squat works so well, and is such a perfect strength developer for weightlifting, why would you struggle to find something different?

The thing that sets the back squat apart from other exercises is the act of holding a heavy weight on your back for an extended time. The torso strength developed by simply holding the weight is indispensable to a weightlifter. Thus, the step-up can never replace the back squat because it doesn't require holding as heavy a weight on the back for as long, so it won't develop torso strength like the back squat. However, when it comes to developing the hips and legs, the step-up is a great exercise, and may even be superior in some ways.

I've run into a few situations over the years where something made the back squat impossible, and in that situation, the step-up is a great temporary replacement. There's also the consideration of advanced lifters who have pushed the back squat so hard for so long that it's become mentally difficult to keep pushing. Sometimes switching to another exercise is needed for a while.

The step-up is a single-leg exercise that can also be used to equalize development of a lagging limb if one leg becomes significantly stronger than the other. I recommend stepping to a height that places the stepping thigh at or slightly above parallel with the floor. Stepping to a higher box throws more stress to the hips and hamstrings, and balance will also be more of a potential challenge. Stepping to a lower box will place more stress on the quads.

Performance

For a weightlifter, the step-up can be done at slightly higher repetitions than the back or front squat simply because it's done with less than half the weight. For the same reason, it can also be performed more frequently. In this respect, it's much like the front squat, but even more so.

Most athletes can do the step-up with max weights several times a week, if not several times a day. For advanced lifters, a combination of arch-back good mornings and step-ups represents a major change of pace in movement patterns, intensity, and volume from heavy back squats.

The fact that it's so completely different in every way makes it a great temporary change for a lifter who either can't physically back squat or who needs a mental break from them.

Photos 9.68–9.75—Step-up

YOKE CARRIES

The yoke carry is a popular test of strength in the strongman community, but isn't widely used by weightlifters in regular training. The exercise consists of supporting a heavy loaded bar on the back while walking a predetermined distance. Yoke and other forms of weighted carries are excellent tools for stimulating stability in the torso and new strength gains.

Lifters who have plateaued on traditional strength exercises like the squat might substitute heavy yoke carries for a training cycle or two for a break. Those unable to back squat because of an injury could potentially use this exercise to reap the benefits of the heavy spinal loading that it and the back squat provide. The spinal loading also makes yoke carries and step-ups a good combination in training since the step-up lacks heavy spinal loading.

Photos 9.76 and 9.77—Yoke grip one demonstrated by Louis Vidal

Photos 9.78 and 9.79—Yoke grip two demonstrated by Louis Vidal

Performance

While yoke carries can be a good option when temporarily unable to back squat, you'll need a yoke to do it right. If you're lucky enough to have one, adjust the middle bar of the yoke so it's roughly chest height. If the bar height is set incorrectly, you risk the bottom of the yoke dragging or bumping along the floor.

To perform the movement, set up under the yoke bar as you would a back squat. Those with good shoulder flexibility might find it more comfortable to use a similar hand placement as used when back squatting. Others will have to take their hands wider or potentially hold the yoke uprights. Both set-ups are shown in the demonstration photos.

Brace your abdominals and upper back, and then stand tall, lifting the yoke off the floor. Pause for a second before starting the carry. If you begin the walk too quickly, the yoke may begin to swing excessively.

The carry distance will depend on what's available to you, but 50 to 100 feet is a good goal. When you walk, do so with quick, short, and precise steps. To avoid lumbering from side to side with the weight loaded on your back, keep your feet under you as you walk as opposed to taking long strides.

EXERCISE VARIATIONS

All training in weightlifting should be based on the snatch and clean and jerk as they're done in competition. Variation from the competition lifts can be useful, but only if they increase the competition total. There's a fine line between variation for its own sake and variation that actually increases the lifts. Make sure you have a reason for each variation you use.

There are many reasons to add variations, including the following:

1. To emphasize parts of the lift where you're lacking—for example, by adding a pause at a weak point in the pull

2. To exaggerate a part of a movement pattern to help overcome technical flaws, such as using muscle snatches to help straighten the pull

3. To keep training interesting—variations can give an athlete more chances to go after PRs on a regular basis

The following pages show breakdowns of the different variations you can program to help work on the snatch, the clean, and the jerk.

These are not exhaustive lists, but lists of exercises I have found to work well for my athletes.

SNATCH VARIATIONS

Muscle Snatch

Muscle Snatch (No contact*)
Muscle Snatch Pausing at the Knees (No contact)
Hang Muscle Snatch from the Knees (No contact)
Hang Muscle Snatch from the Hips (No contact)
Muscle Snatch (Contact*)
Muscle Snatch Pausing at the Knees (Contact)
Hang Muscle Snatch from the Knees (Contact)
Hang Muscle Snatch from the Hips (Contact)
Muscle Snatch from the Low Blocks
Muscle Snatch from the Mid Blocks
Muscle Snatch from the High Blocks

Power Snatch

Power Snatch
Power Snatch, Pausing at the Knees
Hang Power Snatch from the Knees
Hang Power Snatch from the Hips
Power Snatch from the Low Blocks
Power Snatch from the Mid Blocks
Power Snatch from the High Blocks

Snatch

Snatch
Snatch, Pausing at the Knees
Hang Snatch from the Knees
Hang Snatch from the Hips
Snatch from the Low Blocks
Snatch from the Mid Blocks
Snatch from the High Blocks

Snatch Accessory Exercises

Snatch Deadlift
Snatch Pull
Snatch Pull from the Low Blocks
Snatch Pull from the Mid Blocks
Snatch Pull from the High Blocks
Snatch High Pull
Snatch High Pull from the Low Blocks
Snatch High Pull from the Mid Blocks
Snatch High Pull from the High Blocks
Snatch Panda Pull
Snatch Panda Pull from the Low Blocks
Snatch Panda Pull from the Mid Blocks
Snatch Panda Pull from the High Blocks
Snatch Isometric Holds (1-inch, Knees, Hips)

*"No contact" means the barbell doesn't make contact with the hips or body during the extension of the pull. While the bar won't touch the body, you'll still work to keep it as close as possible to the body when performing this variation of the muscle snatch. "Contact" means the bar touches the hips as you move into and through the power position. This is true for muscle clean variations, although the bar may make contact with the hips for "hip cleaners" or the upper thigh as is traditionally done by most lifters.

CLEAN VARIATIONS

Muscle Clean

Muscle Clean (No contact)
Muscle Clean, Pausing at the Knees (No contact)
Hang Muscle Clean from the Knees (No contact)
Hang Muscle Clean from the Hips (No contact)
Muscle Clean (Contact)
Muscle Clean, Pausing at the Knees (Contact)
Hang Muscle Clean from the Knees (Contact)
Hang Muscle Clean from the Hips (Contact)
Muscle Clean from the Low Blocks
Muscle Clean from the Mid Blocks
Muscle Clean from the High Blocks

Power Clean

Power Clean
Power Clean, Pausing at the Knees
Hang Power Clean from the Knees
Hang Power Clean from the Hips
Power Clean from the Low Blocks
Power Clean from the Mid Blocks
Power Clean from the High Blocks

Clean

Clean
Clean, Pausing at the Knees
Hang Clean from the Knees
Hang Clean from the Hips
Clean from the Low Blocks
Clean from the Mid Blocks
Clean from the High Blocks

Clean Accessory Exercises

Clean Deadlift
Clean Pull
Clean Pull from the Low Blocks
Clean Pull from the Mid Blocks
Clean Pull from the High Blocks
Clean High Pull
Clean High Pull from the Low Blocks
Clean High Pull from the Mid Blocks
Clean High Pull from the High Blocks
Clean Panda Pull
Clean Panda Pull from the Low Blocks
Clean Panda Pull from the Mid Blocks
Clean Panda Pull from the High Blocks
Clean Isometric Holds (1-inch, Knees, Hips)

JERK VARIATIONS

Presses

Press
(also known as the military, overhead, or strict press)
Press (Behind the Neck, Clean Grip)
Press (Behind the Neck, Snatch Grip)
Press in Split

Push Presses

Push Press
Push Press (Behind the Neck, Clean Grip)
Push Press (Behind the Neck, Snatch Grip)
Push Press from the Split

Push Jerks

Push Jerk (from the Blocks or Rack)
Push Jerk (Behind the Neck, Clean Grip)
Push Jerk (Behind the Neck, Snatch Grip)

Jerks

Split Jerk (from the Blocks or Rack)
Split Jerk (Behind the Neck, Clean Grip)
Split Jerk (Behind the Neck, Snatch Grip)
Jerk from the Split

Jerk Accessory Exercises

Jerk Steps (Back Rack)
Jerk Steps (Front Rack)
Jerk Steps (Overhead)
Split-Stance Good Morning

WESTSIDE FOR WEIGHTLIFTERS PROGRAMMING OVERVIEW

Use movements you think will help you. The program is meant to be individualized and will work much better that way.

If snatches from a riser help and your competition snatch goes up every time you make a record from a two-inch riser, include more of those. Do them for up to six weeks if you want. Research shows that accommodation, which causes your performance to stagnate or decrease, occurs after six weeks, so you probably shouldn't stick with one exercise longer than that. But I expect everyone to keep coming back to the things that work, and if you want to stick with something that works particularly well for four or five weeks, go for it.

I don't specifically program isometrics for beginning lifters, but a lot of beginner lifters will benefit from using isometric holds in the snatch or clean, pausing more than two seconds. If using pauses in a snatch or clean, after the pause, go straight into the lift without setting the bar down. This is hard, but it works. I've used pauses as long as five or 10 seconds with the bar just off the floor or at the knee.

You can and should individualize the assistance exercises using the repetition method for sets of 10. This is something most American lifters don't do often enough. Push the weight up in those sets of 10 over time.

In the beginning, you might only be able to do hip and back extensions using your bodyweight. When you're strong enough, add a barbell. Then, add weight to that barbell every workout.

You don't have to make big jumps when progressing the weight on accessory exercises. For example, maybe you end up using just bodyweight for hip extensions for a few weeks. Then, progress to holding a 10-kilo plate for a few more weeks. Eventually, you'll build up enough strength to hold a 20-kilo barbell on your back.

That's fantastic progress. From that point, you can make as small of increases as you desire, maybe even one kilo per week. Regardless of the increase, the goal is to complete all sets of 10 reps. If you have to stop, the weight progression should be restarted on the next workout.

For example, if you maxed out at 50 kilos, take 10% off that and perform two sets of 10 at 45 kilos the next workout. The next week, do 46…and so on.

You should be making progress on the back extension, hip extension, glute ham raise, pull-ups, chest-supported rows…and everything else. If you aren't, something is wrong. You should be making progress, pushing the weights as far as possible every week with exercises done with the dynamic method, max-effort method, and the repetition method.

In the program, you'll consistently "build to a 1RM" or some other rep maximum. It's expected that you take the lift to maximum for the day. Some days you might set a new PR and others you might just go as heavy as possible. When going for a PR, try to break the old record by just a kilo or two. Get a score on the board and then go for another attempt after that first successful one.

You won't always be successful when maxing out. Some days your upper limit will be much lower than what you've done in previous weeks. Days like this would be a good time to utilize drop sets for additional practice and volume on the competition lifts.

For example, if your upper limit on a max out day is 100 kilos and you've missed several attempts at 105, reduce the weight 10 to 15% and perform two or three singles or doubles with that weight. Being able to connect with lifts again after a string of misses is a positive way to end your snatch or clean and jerk session. After a couple makes at 90 kilos, you may even be motivated to build back up and try 103 or even 105 again, something I'm not opposed of lifters doing.

SAMPLE BEGINNER PROGRAM

MONDAY

The training week will start on Monday when we do technical practice using EMOM sets. I like to use a perpetually repeating cycle of 70% the first week, 75% the second week, and 80% intensity the third. Beginners will start with 12 lifts at 70%, eight lifts at 75%, and then six lifts at 80%.

You have to do this in the snatch and the clean and jerk. Most athletes should be able to go straight from the snatch to clean and jerk with only a short break, with the clean and jerk warm-up in between.

TUESDAY

Tuesday is high-volume dynamic-effort squat day. I consider this the most difficult day of the week. You'll do both front squats and back squats. Doing the front squats first works best.

We use a perpetually repeating cycle for the intensity. This time, the numbers are 70%, 75%, 80%, and finally 85% for successive weeks of your 3RM front squat and 5RM back squat. Do front squats for four sets of three reps, and back squats for four sets of five reps.

When my lifters do this, they normally only warm up for the front squats, then the work sets on front squats serve as adequate warm-up for the back squats. Later in the intermediate and advanced programs, you'll use a 3RM for both the front and back squat, although other rep maximums can be used as well.

When switching from front to back, just add the weight increase and get straight to it. Do the concentric part of the reps as fast as possible on all sets.

This sounds difficult, but I saved the best for last: We aim to stick to a two-minute rest period for all eight sets. This is hard on the 70% week…and gets downright brutal by the 85% week. Without extending the rest periods, many lifters won't make all the back squat reps during the 85% week. At least, not the first time through.

This type of repeating cycle is another thing I picked up from Louie. It gives the athlete a variation every week, but keeps the intensity in the most productive range for the entire length of the cycle.

WEDNESDAY

This is our first workout of the week at maximum intensity. Useful variations include snatches and cleans from the hips, snatches and cleans from the knees, and snatches and cleans standing on a riser. These variations can also be performed as power movements. The idea is to only do a movement for one to three weeks, then switch.

THURSDAY

Thursday will be a rest day for most trainees.

FRIDAY

Pick another variation of the snatch, then one for the clean. Choose something different than what you did on Wednesday. A power variation on Wednesday, then the same variation but done as a full lift on Friday has worked well for my athletes. For instance, power snatch from the knees on Wednesday, then snatch from the knees on Friday.

SATURDAY

Saturday is usually the heaviest day of the week. Pick variations of the squat, the deadlift or the good morning. Then choose a heavy movement that simulates the jerk—I love jerk steps, jerk recoveries, and death marches for Saturday's jerk movement.

SUNDAY

This should be a rest day for all athletes. Spend time prepping meals for the week, going for walks, or even dragging a sled. At the end of the day, eat a big steak and go to bed early to be ready for Monday's training.

The sample program begins on the following page.

WEEK 1

Monday

Exercises	Sets x Reps	Weight
Snatch EMOM	16 x 1	70% of 1RM
Clean and Jerk EMOM	16 x 1	70% of 1RM
Hip Extensions	2 x 10	Barbell or Bodyweight

Tuesday

Exercises	Sets x Reps	Weight
Front Squats	4 x 3 Rest 2 minutes between work sets	70% of 3RM
Back Squats	4 x 5 Rest 2 minutes between work sets	70% of 5RM
Press from the Split	2 x 10	Barbell

Wednesday

Exercises	Sets x Reps	Weight
Power Snatch	-	Build to a 1RM
Power Clean	-	Build to a 1RM
Power Jerk	-	Build to a 1RM
Clean High Pulls	3 x 5	80% of 1RM Clean
Back Extensions	2 x 10	Barbell or Bodyweight

Friday

Exercises	Sets x Reps	Weight
Snatch	-	Build to a 1RM
Clean	-	Build to a 1RM
Behind-the-Neck Jerk	-	Build to a 1RM
Snatch High Pulls	3 x 5	80% of 1RM Snatch
Hip Extensions	2 x 10	Barbell or Bodyweight

Saturday

Exercises	Sets x Reps	Weight
Back Squats	-	Build to a 3RM
Seated Good Mornings	-	Build to a 5RM
Jerk Steps	3 x 10 steps each leg	100% 1RM Jerk

WEEK 2

Monday

Exercises	Sets x Reps	Weight
Snatch EMOM	12 x 1	75% of 1RM
Clean and Jerk EMOM	12 x 1	75% of 1RM
Hip Extensions	2 x 10	Barbell + Weight (or continue with bodyweight)

Tuesday

Exercises	Sets x Reps	Weight
Front Squats	4 x 3 Rest 2 minutes between work sets	75% of 3RM
Back Squats	4 x 5 Rest 2 minutes between work sets	75% of 5RM
Press from the Split	2 x 10	Barbell + Weight

Wednesday

Exercises	Sets x Reps	Weight
Power Snatch (from a 2-inch riser)	-	Build to a 1RM
Power Clean (from a 2-inch riser)	-	Build to a 1RM
Behind the Neck Power Jerk	-	Build to a 3RM
Clean High Pulls	3 x 5	85% of 1RM Clean
Back Extensions	2 x 10	Barbell + Weight (or continue with bodyweight)

Friday

Exercises	Sets x Reps	Weight
Snatch (from a two-inch riser)	-	Build to a 1RM
Clean (from a two-inch riser)	-	Build to a 1RM
Block or Rack Jerk	-	Build to a 3RM
Snatch High Pulls	3 x 5	85% of 1RM Snatch
Hip Extensions	2 x 10	Barbell + Weight (same weight as Monday or continue with bodyweight)

Saturday

Exercises	Sets x Reps	Weight
Front Squats	-	Build to a 3RM
Arch-Back Good Mornings	-	Build to a 5RM
Jerk Recoveries	-	Build to a 1RM

WEEK 3

Monday

Exercises	Sets x Reps	Weight
Snatch EMOM	8 x 1	80% of 1RM
Clean and Jerk EMOM	8 x 1	80% of 1RM
Hip Extensions	2 x 10	Barbell + Weight (heavier than last week or continue with bodyweight)

Tuesday

Exercises	Sets x Reps	Weight
Front Squats	4 x 3 Rest 2 minutes between work sets	80% of 3RM
Back Squats	4 x 5 Rest 2 minutes between work sets	80% of 5RM
Press from the Split	2 x 10	Barbell + Weight (heavier than last week)

Wednesday

Exercises	Sets x Reps	Weight
Power Snatch (from a 2-inch riser)	-	Build to a 1RM
Power Clean (from a 2-inch riser)	-	Build to a 1RM
Behind the Neck Power Jerk	-	Build to a 1RM
Clean High Pulls	3 x 5	90% of 1RM Clean
Back Extensions	2 x 10	Barbell + Weight (heavier than last week or continue with bodyweight)

Friday

Exercises	Sets x Reps	Weight
Snatch (from a 2-inch riser)	-	Build to a 1RM
Clean (from a 2-inch riser)	-	Build to a 1RM
Snatch High Pulls	3 x 5	90% of 1RM Snatch
Hip Extensions	2 x 10	Barbell + Weight (same weight as Monday or continue with bodyweight)

Saturday

Exercises	Sets x Reps	Weight
Step Ups	-	Build to a 5RM (with each leg)
Split-Stance Good Mornings	-	Build to a 5RM (with each leg)
Death March	1 x 40 Yards	Use as heavy a pair of dumbbell or kettlebells as possible

WEEK 4

Monday

Exercises	Sets x Reps	Weight
Snatch EMOM	16 x 1	70% of 1RM
Clean and Jerk EMOM	16 x 1	70% of 1RM
Hip Extensions	2 x 10	Barbell + Weight (heavier than last week or continue with bodyweight)

Tuesday

Exercises	Sets x Reps	Weight
Front Squats	4 x 3 Rest 2 minutes between work sets	85% of 3RM
Back Squats	4 x 5 Rest 2 minutes between work sets	85% of 5RM
Press from the Split	2 x 10	Barbell + Weight (heavier than last week or continue with bodyweight)

Wednesday

Exercises	Sets x Reps	Weight
Power Snatch (from hips)	-	Build to a 1RM
Power Clean (from hips)	-	Build to a 1RM
Behind the Neck Push Press	-	Build to a 3RM
Clean High Pulls	4 x 5	80% of 1RM Clean
Back Extensions	2 x 10	Barbell + Weight (heavier than last week or continue with bodyweight)

Friday

Exercises	Sets x Reps	Weight
Snatch (from hips)	-	Build to a 1RM
Clean (from hips)	-	Build to a 1RM
Snatch High Pulls	4 x 5	80% of 1RM Snatch
Hip Extensions	2 x 10	Barbell + Weight (same weight as Monday or continue with bodyweight)

Saturday

Exercises	Sets x Reps	Weight
Box Squats (to as low a box as possible)	-	Build to a 3RM
Front Squats	-	Build to a 1RM
Power Jerk	-	Build to a 1RM

WEEK 5

Monday

Exercises	Sets x Reps	Weight
Snatch EMOM	12 x 1	75% of 1RM
Clean and Jerk EMOM	12 x 1	75% of 1RM
Hip Extensions	2 x 10	Barbell + Weight (heavier than last week or continue with bodyweight)

Tuesday

Exercises	Sets x Reps	Weight
Front Squats	4 x 3 Rest 2 minutes between work sets	70% of 3RM
Back Squats	4 x 5 Rest 2 minutes between work sets	70% of 5RM
Press from the Split	2 x 10	Barbell + Weight (heavier than last week)

Wednesday

Exercises	Sets x Reps	Weight
Power Snatch (from knees)	-	Build to a 1RM
Power Clean (from knees)	-	Build to a 1RM
Behind the Neck Push Press	-	Build to a 1RM
Clean High Pulls	4 x 5	85% of 1RM Clean
Back Extensions	2 x 10	Barbell + Weight (heavier than last week or continue with bodyweight)

Friday

Exercises	Sets x Reps	Weight
Snatch (from knees)	-	Build to a 1RM
Clean (from knees)	-	Build to a 1RM
Block or Rack Jerk	-	Build to a 3RM
Snatch High Pulls	4 x 5	85% of 1RM Snatch
Hip Extensions	2 x 10	Barbell + Weight (same weight as Monday or continue with bodyweight)

Saturday

Exercises	Sets x Reps	Weight
Back Squats	-	Build to a 5RM
Seated Good Mornings	-	Build to a 3RM
Jerk Steps	3 x 10 steps each leg	105% 1RM Jerk

WEEK 6

Monday

Exercises	Sets x Reps	Weight
Snatch EMOM	8 x 1	80% of 1RM
Clean and Jerk EMOM	8 x 1	80% of 1RM
Hip Extensions	2 x 10	Barbell + Weight (heavier than last week or continue with bodyweight)

Tuesday

Exercises	Sets x Reps	Weight
Front Squats	4 x 3 Rest 2 minutes between work sets	75% of 3RM
Back Squats	4 x 5 Rest 2 minutes between work sets	75% of 5RM
Press from the Split	2 x 10	Barbell + Weight (heavier than last week)

Wednesday

Exercises	Sets x Reps	Weight
Power Snatch (from below the knee)	-	Build to a 1RM
Power Clean (from below the knee)	-	Build to a 1RM
Power Jerk	-	Build to a 3RM
Clean High Pulls	4 x 5	90% of 1RM Clean
Back Extensions	2 x 10	Barbell + Weight (heavier than last week or continue with bodyweight)

Friday

Exercises	Sets x Reps	Weight
Snatch (from below the knee)	-	Build to a 1RM
Clean (from below the knee)	-	Build to a 1RM
Behind-the-Neck Jerk	-	Build to a 1RM
Snatch High Pulls	4 x 5	90% of 1RM Snatch
Hip Extensions	2 x 10	Barbell + Weight (same weight as Monday or continue with bodyweight)

Saturday

Exercises	Sets x Reps	Weight
Back Squats	-	Build to a 1RM
Arch-Back Good Mornings	-	Build to a 5RM
Push Press	-	Build to a 3RM

WEEK 7

Monday

Exercises	Sets x Reps	Weight
Snatch EMOM	16 x 1	70% of 1RM
Clean and Jerk EMOM	16 x 1	70% of 1RM
Hip Extensions	2 x 10	Barbell + Weight (heavier than last week or continue with bodyweight)

Tuesday

Exercises	Sets x Reps	Weight
Front Squats	4 x 3 Rest 2 minutes between work sets	80% of 3RM
Back Squats	4 x 5 Rest 2 minutes between work sets	80% of 5RM
Press from the Split	2 x 10	Barbell + Weight (heavier than last week)

Wednesday

Exercises	Sets x Reps	Weight
Power Snatch (from knee-height blocks)	-	Build to a 1RM
Power Clean (from knee-height blocks)	-	Build to a 1RM
Behind-the-Neck Jerk	-	Build to a 3RM
Clean High Pulls	5 x 5	80% of 1RM Clean
Back Extensions	2 x 10	Barbell + Weight (heavier than last week or continue with bodyweight)

Friday

Exercises	Sets x Reps	Weight
Snatch (from knee-height blocks)	-	Build to a 1RM
Clean (from knee-height blocks)	-	Build to a 1RM
Snatch High Pulls	5 x 5	80% of 1RM Snatch
Hip Extensions	2 x 10	Barbell + Weight (same weight as Monday or continue with bodyweight)

Saturday

Exercises	Sets x Reps	Weight
Step Ups	-	Build to a 5RM (with each leg)
Arch-Back Good Mornings	-	Build to a 3RM
Death March	1 x 40 Yards	Use as heavy a pair of dumbbell or kettlebells as possible

WEEK 8

Monday

Exercises	Sets x Reps	Weight
Snatch EMOM	12 x 1	75% of 1RM
Clean and Jerk EMOM	12 x 1	75% of 1RM
Hip Extensions	2 x 10	Barbell + Weight (Heavier than last week or continue with bodyweight)

Tuesday

Exercises	Sets x Reps	Weight
Front Squats	4 x 3 Rest 2 minutes between work sets	85% of 3RM
Back Squats	4 x 5 Rest 2 minutes between work sets	85% of 5RM
Press from the Split	2 x 10	Barbell + Weight (heavier than last week)

Wednesday

Exercises	Sets x Reps	Weight
Power Snatch	-	Build to a 1RM
Power Clean	-	Build to a 1RM
Power Jerk	-	Build to a 1RM
Clean High Pulls	3 x 5	80% of 1RM Clean
Back Extensions	2 x 10	Barbell + Weight (heavier than last week or continue with bodyweight)

Friday

Exercises	Sets x Reps	Weight
Snatch	-	Build to a 1RM
Clean and Jerk	-	Build to a 1RM
Snatch High Pulls	3 x 5	80% of 1RM Snatch
Hip Extensions	2 x 10	Barbell + Weight (same weight as Monday or continue with bodyweight)

Saturday

Exercises	Sets x Reps	Weight
Front Squats	-	Build to a 3RM
Back Squats	-	Build to a 5RM
Jerk Recoveries	-	Build to a 1RM

SAMPLE INTERMEDIATE PROGRAM

Much of the progression from the beginner program to the intermediate program is based on what an individual lifter needs. For example, if a lifter needs more posterior-chain development, increases can be made in the number of sets done on hip extensions, back extensions, and glute ham raises. Instead of doing two sets of 10, you'd increase to four sets of 10. If more work is needed in the split position, spend more time there by adding additional sets of presses in the split or by doing jerks from the split. I've provided examples of this in the sample programming.

Exercises are interchangeable; the decision of which need to be done should be based on current performance. If bar path or cutting the pull short on the snatch or clean is an issue, more sets of high pulls can certainly help. Panda pulls or pulls ending with a shrug might be a better choice for lifters who tend to over-pull. Think to yourself "what do I need?" Then, make a decision.

Finally, see if it works. This is an unending process you'll do over your entire career.

MONDAY

The intermediate programming will increase the number of sets and reps done on EMOM sets. Lifters will now do 20 lifts at 70%, 15 lifts at 75%, and then 10 lifts at 80%. We'll also increase the number of sets done on hip extensions from two up to four sets of 10 repetitions.

TUESDAY

Tuesday's squat workout will remain largely unchanged in the intermediate program. The one exception is to base your back squat numbers on a 3RM opposed to a 5RM. This should allow for even heavier weights to be used in the session.

Another change to the day involves the inclusion of the jerk from the split exercise. You'll perform two sets of 10 reps for additional work and more time spent in the split position.

WEDNESDAY

Wednesday will continue to be a day when you'll do maximal lifts on power variations of the snatch and clean. You'll also continue to work on variations of the jerk separately from the clean. The volume on high pulls will increase to five sets of five reps weekly at various percentages of your best clean. The number of sets done on back extensions will increase from two up to four sets of 10 repetitions.

THURSDAY

Thursday will remain a rest or active recovery day.

FRIDAY

Fridays continue the trend of mimicking the movements done on Wednesday for the snatch and clean, except these will be full lifts. More training will be done on the jerk independent of the clean. The volume on high pulls will increase to five sets of five reps weekly at various percentages of your best snatch. The number of sets done on glute ham raises will increase from two up to four sets of 10 repetitions.

SATURDAY

On Saturdays, you'll continue to pursue maximal squat and good morning variations. Those exercises will be accompanied by heavy training on jerk assistance exercises. Week to week, you'll rotate between jerk steps, jerk recoveries, and death marches.

SUNDAY

Sunday will remain a rest day.

WEEK 1

Monday

Exercises	Sets x Reps	Weight
Snatch EMOM	20 x 1	70% of 1RM
Clean and Jerk EMOM	20 x 1	70% of 1RM
Hip Extensions	4 x 10	Barbell + Weight

Tuesday

Exercises	Sets x Reps	Weight
Front Squats	4 x 3 Rest 2 minutes between work sets	70% of 3RM
Back Squats	4 x 3 Rest 2 minutes between work sets	70% of 3RM
Press from the Split	2 x 10	Barbell + Weight
Jerk from the Split	2 x 10	Barbell + Weight

Wednesday

Exercises	Sets x Reps	Weight
Power Snatch	-	Build to a 1RM
Power Clean	-	Build to a 1RM
Power Jerk	-	Build to a 1RM
Clean High Pulls	5 x 5	80% of 1RM Clean
Back Extensions	4 x 10	Barbell + Weight

Friday

Exercises	Sets x Reps	Weight
Snatch	-	Build to a 1RM
Clean	-	Build to a 1RM
Behind-the-Neck Jerk	-	Build to a 1RM
Snatch High Pulls	5 x 5	80% of 1RM Snatch
Glute Ham Raises	4 x 10	Barbell + Weight

Saturday

Exercises	Sets x Reps	Weight
Back Squats	-	Build to a 3RM
Seated Good Mornings	-	Build to a 5RM
Jerk Steps	3 x 10 steps each leg	100% 1RM Jerk

WEEK 2

Monday

Exercises	Sets x Reps	Weight
Snatch EMOM	15 x 1	75% of 1RM
Clean and Jerk EMOM	15 x 1	75% of 1RM
Hip Extensions	4 x 10	Barbell + Weight (heavier than last week)

Tuesday

Exercises	Sets x Reps	Weight
Front Squats	4 x 3 Rest 2 minutes between work sets	75% of 3RM
Back Squats	4 x 3 Rest 2 minutes between work sets	75% of 3RM
Press from the Split	2 x 10	Barbell + Weight (heavier than last week)
Jerk from the Split	2 x 10	Barbell + Weight (heavier than last week)

Wednesday

Exercises	Sets x Reps	Weight
Power Snatch (from 2-inch riser)	-	Build to a 1RM
Power Clean (from 2-inch riser)	-	Build to a 1RM
Behind the Neck Power Jerk	-	Build to a 3RM
Clean High Pulls	5 x 5	85% of 1RM Clean
Back Extensions	4 x 10	Barbell + Weight (heavier than last week)

Friday

Exercises	Sets x Reps	Weight
Snatch (from 2-inch riser)	-	Build to a 1RM
Clean (from 2-inch riser)	-	Build to a 1RM
Block or Rack Jerk	-	Build to a 3RM
Snatch High Pulls	5 x 5	85% of 1RM Snatch
Glute Ham Raises	4 x 10	Barbell + Weight (heavier than last week)

Saturday

Exercises	Sets x Reps	Weight
Front Squats	-	Build to a 3RM
Arch-Back Good Mornings	-	Build to a 5RM
Jerk Recoveries	-	Build to a 1RM

WEEK 3

Monday

Exercises	Sets x Reps	Weight
Snatch EMOM	10 x 1	80% of 1RM
Clean and Jerk EMOM	10 x 1	80% of 1RM
Hip Extensions	4 x 10	Barbell + Weight (heavier than last week)

Tuesday

Exercises	Sets x Reps	Weight
Front Squats	4 x 3 Rest 2 minutes between work sets	80% of 3RM
Back Squats	4 x 3 Rest 2 minutes between work sets	80% of 3RM
Press from the Split	2 x 10	Barbell + Weight (Heavier than last week)
Jerk from the Split	2 x 10	Barbell + Weight (Heavier than last week)

Wednesday

Exercises	Sets x Reps	Weight
Power Snatch (from 2-inch riser)	-	Build to a 1RM
Power Clean (from 2-inch riser)	-	Build to a 1RM
Behind the Neck Power Jerk	-	Build to a 1RM
Clean High Pulls	5 x 5	90% of 1RM Clean
Back Extensions	4 x 10	Barbell + Weight (heavier than last week)

Friday

Exercises	Sets x Reps	Weight
Snatch (from 2-inch riser)	-	Build to a 1RM
Clean (from 2-inch riser)	-	Build to a 1RM
Snatch High Pulls	5 x 5	90% of 1RM Snatch
Glute Ham Raises	4 x 10	Barbell + Weight (heavier than last week)

Saturday

Exercises	Sets x Reps	Weight
Step Ups	-	Build to a 5RM (with each leg)
Split-Stance Good Mornings	-	Build to a 5RM (with each leg)
Death March	1 x 40 Yards	Use as heavy a pair of dumbbell or kettlebells as possible

WEEK 4

Monday

Exercises	Sets x Reps	Weight
Snatch EMOM	20 x 1	70% of 1RM
Clean and Jerk EMOM	20 x 1	70% of 1RM
Hip Extensions	4 x 10	Barbell + Weight (heavier than last week)

Tuesday

Exercises	Sets x Reps	Weight
Front Squats	4 x 3 Rest 2 minutes between work sets	85% of 3RM
Back Squats	4 x 3 Rest 2 minutes between work sets	85% of 3RM
Press from the Split	2 x 10	Barbell + Weight (heavier than last week)
Jerk from the Split	2 x 10	Barbell + Weight (heavier than last week)

Wednesday

Exercises	Sets x Reps	Weight
Power Snatch (from hips)	-	Build to a 1RM
Power Clean (from hips)	-	Build to a 1RM
Behind the Neck Push Press	-	Build to a 3RM
Clean High Pulls	5 x 5	80% of 1RM Clean
Back Extensions	4 x 10	Barbell + Weight (heavier than last week)

Friday

Exercises	Sets x Reps	Weight
Snatch (from hips)	-	Build to a 1RM
Clean (from hips)	-	Build to a 1RM
Snatch High Pulls	5 x 5	80% of 1RM Snatch
Glute Ham Raises	4 x 10	Barbell + Weight (heavier than last week)

Saturday

Exercises	Sets x Reps	Weight
Box Squats (to as low a box as possible)	-	Build to a 3RM
Front Squats	-	Build to a 1RM
Power Jerk	-	Build to a 1RM

WEEK 5

Monday

Exercises	Sets x Reps	Weight
Snatch EMOM	15 x 1	75% of 1RM
Clean and Jerk EMOM	15 x 1	75% of 1RM
Hip Extensions	4 x 10	Barbell + Weight (heavier than last week)

Tuesday

Exercises	Sets x Reps	Weight
Front Squats	4 x 3 Rest 2 minutes between work sets	70% of 3RM
Back Squats	4 x 3 Rest 2 minutes between work sets	70% of 3RM
Press from the Split	2 x 10	Barbell + Weight (heavier than last week)
Jerk from the Split	2 x 10	Barbell + Weight (heavier than last week)

Wednesday

Exercises	Sets x Reps	Weight
Power Snatch (from knees)	-	Build to a 1RM
Power Clean (from knees)	-	Build to a 1RM
Behind the Neck Push Press	-	Build to a 1RM
Clean High Pulls	5 x 5	85% of 1RM Clean
Back Extensions	4 x 10	Barbell + Weight (heavier than last week)

Friday

Exercises	Sets x Reps	Weight
Snatch (from knees)	-	Build to a 1RM
Clean (from knees)	-	Build to a 1RM
Block or Rack Jerk	-	Build to a 3RM
Snatch High Pulls	5 x 5	85% of 1RM Snatch
Glute Ham Raises	4 x 10	Barbell + Weight (heavier than last week)

Saturday

Exercises	Sets x Reps	Weight
Back Squats	-	Build to a 5RM
Seated Good Mornings	-	Build to a 3RM
Jerk Steps	3 x 10 steps each leg	105% 1RM Jerk

WEEK 6

Monday

Exercises	Sets x Reps	Weight
Snatch EMOM	10 x 1	80% of 1RM
Clean and Jerk EMOM	10 x 1	80% of 1RM
Hip Extensions	4 x 10	Barbell + Weight (heavier than last week)

Tuesday

Exercises	Sets x Reps	Weight
Front Squats	4 x 3 Rest 2 minutes between work sets	75% of 3RM
Back Squats	4 x 3 Rest 2 minutes between work sets	75% of 3RM
Press from the Split	2 x 10	Barbell + Weight (heavier than last week)
Jerk from the Split	2 x 10	Barbell + Weight (heavier than last week)

Wednesday

Exercises	Sets x Reps	Weight
Power Snatch (from below the knee)	-	Build to a 1RM
Power Clean (from below the knee)	-	Build to a 1RM
Power Jerk	-	Build to a 3RM
Clean High Pulls	5 x 5	90% of 1RM Clean
Back Extensions	4 x 10	Barbell + Weight (heavier than last week)

Friday

Exercises	Sets x Reps	Weight
Snatch (from below the knee)	-	Build to a 1RM
Clean (from below the knee)	-	Build to a 1RM
Behind-the-Neck Jerk	-	Build to a 1RM
Snatch High Pulls	5 x 5	90% of 1RM Snatch
Glute Ham Raises	4 x 10	Barbell + Weight (heavier than last week)

Saturday

Exercises	Sets x Reps	Weight
Back Squats	-	Build to a 1RM
Arch-Back Good Mornings	-	Build to a 5RM
Push Press	-	Build to a 3RM

WEEK 7

Monday

Exercises	Sets x Reps	Weight
Snatch EMOM	20 x 1	70% of 1RM
Clean and Jerk EMOM	20 x 1	70% of 1RM
Hip Extensions	4 x 10	Barbell + Weight (heavier than last week)

Tuesday

Exercises	Sets x Reps	Weight
Front Squats	4 x 3 Rest 2 minutes between work sets	80% of 3RM
Back Squats	4 x 3 Rest 2 minutes between work sets	80% of 3RM
Press from the Split	2 x 10	Barbell + Weight (heavier than last week)
Jerk from the Split	2 x 10	Barbell + Weight (heavier than last week)

Wednesday

Exercises	Sets x Reps	Weight
Power Snatch (from knee-height blocks)	-	Build to a 1RM
Power Clean (from knee-height blocks)	-	Build to a 1RM
Behind-the-Neck Jerk	-	Build to a 3RM
Clean High Pulls	5 x 5	80% of 1RM Clean
Back Extensions	4 x 10	Barbell + Weight (heavier than last week)

Friday

Exercises	Sets x Reps	Weight
Snatch (from knee-height blocks)	-	Build to a 1RM
Clean (from knee-height blocks)	-	Build to a 1RM
Snatch High Pulls	5 x 5	80% of 1RM Snatch
Glute Ham Raises	4 x 10	Barbell + Weight (heavier than last week)

Saturday

Exercises	Sets x Reps	Weight
Step Ups	-	Build to a 5RM (with each leg)
Arch-Back Good Mornings	-	Build to a 3RM
Death March	1 x 40 Yards	Use as heavy a pair of dumbbell or kettlebells as possible

WEEK 8

Monday

Exercises	Sets x Reps	Weight
Snatch EMOM	15 x 1	75% of 1RM
Clean and Jerk EMOM	15 x 1	75% of 1RM
Hip Extensions	4 x 10	Barbell + Weight (heavier than last week)

Tuesday

Exercises	Sets x Reps	Weight
Front Squats	4 x 3 Rest 2 minutes between work sets	85% of 3RM
Back Squats	4 x 3 Rest 2 minutes between work sets	85% of 3RM
Press from the Split	2 x 10	Barbell + Weight (heavier than last week)
Jerk from the Split	2 x 10	Barbell + Weight (heavier than last week)

Wednesday

Exercises	Sets x Reps	Weight
Power Snatch	-	Build to a 1RM
Power Clean	-	Build to a 1RM
Power Jerk	-	Build to a 1RM
Clean High Pulls	5 x 5	80% of 1RM Clean
Back Extensions	4 x 10	Barbell + Weight (heavier than last week)

Friday

Exercises	Sets x Reps	Weight
Snatch	-	Build to a 1RM
Clean and Jerk	-	Build to a 1RM
Snatch High Pulls	5 x 5	80% of 1RM Snatch
Glute Ham Raises	4 x 10	Barbell + Weight (heavier than last week)

Saturday

Exercises	Sets x Reps	Weight
Front Squats	-	Build to a 3RM
Back Squats	-	Build to a 5RM
Jerk Recoveries	-	Build to a 1RM

SAMPLE ADVANCED PROGRAM

For most lifters, doing both the snatch and clean and jerk together is best. However, advanced lifters can split them into two workouts, doing a snatch variation early and a clean variation later in the day.

In both the beginner and intermediate sample programs, only one workout was done across five training days. This advanced sample program will demonstrate nine training sessions across six days of training. Monday, Wednesday, and Friday will be organized into morning and afternoon or evening sessions where the focus in the morning is on the snatch, and the focus of the later session is on the clean.

Those able to lift full time can individualize the number of workouts done per week to include more training sessions. This doesn't have to be done in one shot. If you suddenly have a lot of extra time to train, add sessions gradually to see how your body adapts. Adding training also means you need to include more time for recovery to get the full benefit of that extra training. If you're not willing to eat more food and go to bed at a reasonable time each night, don't even bother increasing the number of sessions per week.

Another change to the programming at this stage will occur with the accessory exercises. First, you'll notice high pulls for both the snatch and clean are now done three days per week on Monday, Wednesday, and Friday. Snatch high pulls are coupled with the snatch in the early training session, and clean high pulls in the later session. This extra practice will serve to iron out deficiencies in the bar path, and develop the muscles used in the pulling motion—especially in the upper body.

The work done on posterior-chain exercises will also be split across the two sessions. Doing two sets of 10 in the morning and the remaining two sets in a later session will allow for the appropriate amount of volume for the day without overly fatiguing lifters for the evening session.

The one exception to this occurs on Wednesday's evening session, where lifters do four sets of 10 on the hip extension. The program calls for two extra sets here because other exercises will be the focus during the morning session, and Thursday will be a less stressful day of training.

The weight performed on these accessory exercises will be the same for both training sessions. However, you'll notice that some accessory movements, such as the press from the split, back extension, and hip extension, are repeated later in the week. For those, attempt to increase the weight from what you used earlier in the week. The increase doesn't need to be a large one, but you want to always be progressing the weights as much as possible.

For example, if you used 60 kilos for two sets of 10 on the press from the split on Tuesday, increase that to 62 kilos on Friday. The following Tuesday, increase the weight to 64. As was practiced in the earlier training programs, decrease the weight by 10% and start the progression again when you're no longer able to increase the weight to complete all sets and reps of an accessory exercise.

MONDAY

For Monday's training, continue using EMOM sets for the snatch and clean and jerk. At this level, lifters can progress the number of sets to 24 lifts at 70%, 18 lifts at 75%, then 12 lifts at 80%.

TUESDAY

Tuesday's session will remain largely the same as the previous two programming samples. The squat workout is meant to be done with the back squat following the front squat, so I don't recommend splitting this day into multiple sessions.

WEDNESDAY

On Wednesday's training sessions, power variations of the lifts will continue to be the focus. Cycle to a different variation of a power snatch and power clean week to week, lifting off risers, from different hang positions, and blocks. Add the split-stance good morning to the early session to provide posterior-chain training specific to the jerk.

THURSDAY

Thursday has typically been a rest day in the beginner and intermediate programs. Here in the advanced program, we'll make use of isometric holds on this day. The specific positions will be one inch off the floor, at the knee, and at the hip. Review the advanced training methods on pages 147–150 for specific instruction on how to perform these holds.

The load will be based on percentages of your 1RM snatch-grip and clean-grip deadlifts. These holds are all that's programmed for the day. Take the time to warm them up properly instead of just loading the bar and doing the holds. Perform full snatch-grip and clean-grip deadlifts up to the working weight with the holds.

To aid in recovery, it could be beneficial to add other accessory exercises that don't have an eccentric portion, such as sled drags.

FRIDAY

Friday is the last day of the week that will feature two training sessions. Week to week, cycle between different variations of the full snatch and clean. It's helpful to have the variation match Wednesday's variation. For example, if you did power snatches and power cleans from a two-inch riser earlier in the week, do full snatches and cleans off the riser on Friday.

SATURDAY

Each training week ends on Saturday, when you'll continue to work to maximums on variations of the squat, good morning, and exercises for the jerk. Unlike the previous programming samples, here we'll make weekly use of jerk steps.

Follow the progression, increasing the weight each week. When you periodically PR your split jerk 1RM throughout the training cycle, the percentages used on jerk steps will also need to be adjusted.

SUNDAY

Sunday remains a rest day. Spend time with friends or family, watch a good movie, and prepare mentally for the following week of training. Oh, and don't forget, if you consider yourself an advanced lifter, you better be prepping your food for the week in substantial quantities.

WEEK 1

Monday AM

Exercises	Sets x Reps	Weight
Snatch EMOM	24 x 1	70% of 1RM
Snatch High Pulls	5 x 5	80% of 1RM Snatch
Hip Extensions	2 x 10	Barbell + Weight

Monday PM

Exercises	Sets x Reps	Weight
Clean and Jerk EMOM	24 x 1	70% of 1RM
Clean High Pulls	5 x 5	80% of 1RM Clean
Hip Extensions	2 x 10	Barbell + Weight (same weight as the morning session)

Tuesday

Exercises	Sets x Reps	Weight
Front Squats	4 x 3 Rest 2 minutes between work sets	70% of 3RM
Back Squats	4 x 3 Rest 2 minutes between work sets	70% of 3RM
Press from the Split	2 x 10	Barbell + Weight
Jerk from the Split	2 x 10	Barbell + Weight

Wednesday AM

Exercises	Sets x Reps	Weight
Power Snatch	-	Build to a 1RM
Snatch High Pulls	5 x 5	80% of 1RM Snatch
Split-Stance Good Mornings	2 x 10 each leg	Barbell + Weight
Back Extensions	2 x 10	Barbell + Weight

WEEK 1

Wednesday PM

Exercises	Sets x Reps	Weight
Power Clean	-	Build to a 1RM
Clean High Pulls	5 x 5	80% of 1RM Clean
Power Jerk	-	Build to a 5RM
Hip Extensions	4 x 10	Barbell + Weight (heavier than Monday's session)

Thursday

Exercises	Sets x Reps	Weight
Snatch-Grip Isometric	2 x 10 Seconds (1 inch off floor) 2 x 10 Seconds (at knees) 2 x 10 Seconds (at hips)	70% 1RM Snatch-Grip Deadlift
Clean-Grip Isometric	2 x 10 Seconds (1 inch off floor) 2 x 10 Seconds (at knees) 2 x 10 Seconds (at hips)	70% 1RM Clean-Grip Deadlift

Friday AM

Exercises	Sets x Reps	Weight
Snatch	-	Build to a 1RM
Snatch High Pulls	5 x 5	80% of 1RM Snatch
Press from the Split	2 x 10	Barbell + Weight (heavier than Tuesday's session)
Back Extensions	2 x 10	Barbell + Weight (heavier than Wednesday's session)

Friday PM

Exercises	Sets x Reps	Weight
Clean	-	Build to a 1RM
Block or Rack Jerk	-	Build to a 5RM
Clean High Pulls	5 x 5	80% of 1RM Clean
Press from the Split	2 x 10	Barbell + Weight (same weight as the morning session)
Back Extensions	2 x 10	Barbell + Weight (same weight as the morning session)

Saturday

Exercises	Sets x Reps	Weight
Back Squat	-	Build to a 5RM
Seated Good Mornings	-	Build to a 5RM
Jerk Recoveries	-	Build to a 1RM
Jerk Steps	3 x 10 steps each leg	100% 1RM Jerk

WEEK 2

Monday AM

Exercises	Sets x Reps	Weight
Snatch EMOM	18 x 1	75% of 1RM
Snatch High Pulls	4 x 4	85% of 1RM Snatch
Hip Extensions	2 x 10	Barbell + Weight (heavier than last week)

Monday PM

Exercises	Sets x Reps	Weight
Clean and Jerk EMOM	18 x 1	75% of 1RM
Clean High Pulls	4 x 4	85% of 1RM Clean
Hip Extensions	2 x 10	Barbell + Weight (same weight as the morning session)

Tuesday

Exercises	Sets x Reps	Weight
Front Squats	4 x 3 Rest 2 minutes between work sets	75% of 3RM
Back Squats	4 x 3 Rest 2 minutes between work sets	75% of 3RM
Press from the Split	2 x 10	Barbell + Weight (heavier than last week)
Jerk from the Split	2 x 10	Barbell + Weight (heavier than last week)

Wednesday AM

Exercises	Sets x Reps	Weight
Power Snatch (from 2-inch riser)	-	Build to a 1RM
Snatch High Pulls	4 x 4	85% of 1RM Snatch
Split-Stance Good Mornings	2 x 10 each leg	Barbell + Weight (heavier than last week)
Back Extensions	2 x 10	Barbell + Weight (heavier than last week)

Wednesday PM

Exercises	Sets x Reps	Weight
Power Clean (from 2-inch riser)	-	Build to a 1RM
Clean High Pulls	4 x 4	85% of 1RM Clean
Power Jerk	-	Build to a 3RM
Hip Extensions	4 x 10	Barbell + Weight (heavier than Monday's session)

WEEK 2

Thursday

Exercises	Sets x Reps	Weight
Snatch-Grip Isometric	2 x 10 Seconds (1 inch off floor) 2 x 10 Seconds (at knees) 2 x 10 Seconds (at hips)	75% 1RM Snatch-Grip Deadlift
Clean-Grip Isometric	2 x 10 Seconds (1 inch off floor) 2 x 10 Seconds (at knees) 2 x 10 Seconds (at hips)	75% 1RM Clean-Grip Deadlift

Friday AM

Exercises	Sets x Reps	Weight
Snatch (from 2-inch riser)	-	Build to a 1RM
Snatch High Pulls	4 x 4	85% of 1RM Snatch
Press from the Split	2 x 10	Barbell + Weight (heavier than Tuesday's session)
Back Extensions	2 x 10	Barbell + Weight (heavier than Wednesday's session)

Friday PM

Exercises	Sets x Reps	Weight
Clean (from 2-inch riser)	-	Build to a 1RM
Block or Rack Jerk	-	Build to a 3RM
Clean High Pulls	4 x 4	85% of 1RM Clean
Press from the Split	2 x 10	Barbell + Weight (same weight as the morning session)
Back Extensions	2 x 10	Barbell + Weight (same weight as the morning session)

Saturday

Exercises	Sets x Reps	Weight
Back Squat	-	Build to a 3RM
Seated Good Mornings	-	Build to a 3RM
Jerk Recoveries	-	Build to a 1RM
Jerk Steps	3 x 10 steps each leg	105% 1RM Jerk

WEEK 3

Monday AM

Exercises	Sets x Reps	Weight
Snatch EMOM	12 x 1	80% of 1RM
Snatch High Pulls	3 x 3	90% of 1RM Snatch
Hip Extensions	2 x 10	Barbell + Weight (heavier than last week)

Monday PM

Exercises	Sets x Reps	Weight
Clean and Jerk EMOM	12 x 1	80% of 1RM
Clean High Pulls	3 x 3	90% of 1RM Clean
Hip Extensions	2 x 10	Barbell + Weight (same weight as the morning session)

Tuesday

Exercises	Sets x Reps	Weight
Front Squats	4 x 3 Rest 2 minutes between work sets	80% of 3RM
Back Squats	4 x 3 Rest 2 minutes between work sets	80% of 3RM
Press from the Split	2 x 10	Barbell + Weight (heavier than last week)
Jerk from the Split	2 x 10	Barbell + Weight (heavier than last week)

Wednesday AM

Exercises	Sets x Reps	Weight
Power Snatch (from 2-inch riser)	-	Build to a 1RM
Snatch High Pulls	3 x 3	90% of 1RM Snatch
Split-Stance Good Mornings	2 x 10 each leg	Barbell + Weight (heavier than last week)
Back Extensions	2 x 10	Barbell + Weight (heavier than last week)

Wednesday PM

Exercises	Sets x Reps	Weight
Power Clean (from 2-inch riser)	-	Build to a 1RM
Clean High Pulls	3 x 3	90% of 1RM Clean
Behind the Neck Power Jerk	-	Build to a 3RM
Hip Extensions	4 x 10	Barbell + Weight (heavier than Monday's session)

WEEK 3

Thursday

Exercises	Sets x Reps	Weight
Snatch-Grip Isometric	2 x 10 Seconds (1 inch off floor) 2 x 10 Seconds (at knees) 2 x 10 Seconds (at hips)	80% 1RM Snatch-Grip Deadlift
Clean-Grip Isometric	2 x 10 Seconds (1 inch off floor) 2 x 10 Seconds (at knees) 2 x 10 Seconds (at hips)	80% 1RM Clean-Grip Deadlift

Friday AM

Exercises	Sets x Reps	Weight
Snatch (from 2-inch riser)	-	Build to a 1RM
Snatch High Pulls	3 x 3	90% of 1RM Snatch
Press from the Split	2 x 10	Barbell + Weight (heavier than Tuesday's session)
Back Extensions	2 x 10	Barbell + Weight (heavier than Wednesday's session)

Friday PM

Exercises	Sets x Reps	Weight
Clean (from 2-inch riser)	-	Build to a 1RM
Behind-the-Neck Jerk	-	Build to a 3RM
Clean High Pulls	3 x 3	90% of 1RM Clean
Press from the Split	2 x 10	Barbell + Weight (same weight as the morning session)
Back Extensions	2 x 10	Barbell + Weight (same weight as the morning session)

Saturday

Exercises	Sets x Reps	Weight
Back Squat	-	Build to a 1RM
Arch-Back Good Mornings	-	Build to a 5RM
Jerk Recoveries	-	Build to a 1RM
Jerk Steps	3 x 10 steps each leg	110% 1RM Jerk

WEEK 4

Monday AM

Exercises	Sets x Reps	Weight
Snatch EMOM	24 x 1	70% of 1RM
Snatch High Pulls	5 x 5	80% of 1RM Snatch
Hip Extensions	2 x 10	Barbell + Weight (heavier than last week)

Monday PM

Exercises	Sets x Reps	Weight
Clean and Jerk EMOM	24 x 1	70% of 1RM
Clean High Pulls	5 x 5	80% of 1RM Clean
Hip Extensions	2 x 10	Barbell + Weight (same weight as the morning session)

Tuesday

Exercises	Sets x Reps	Weight
Front Squats	4 x 3 Rest 2 minutes between work sets	85% of 3RM
Back Squats	4 x 3 Rest 2 minutes between work sets	85% of 3RM
Press from the Split	2 x 10	Barbell + Weight (heavier than last week)
Jerk from the Split	2 x 10	Barbell + Weight (heavier than last week)

Wednesday AM

Exercises	Sets x Reps	Weight
Power Snatch (from knees)	-	Build to a 1RM
Snatch High Pulls	5 x 5	80% of 1RM Snatch
Split-Stance Good Mornings	2 x 10 each leg	Barbell + Weight (heavier than last week)
Back Extensions	2 x 10	Barbell + Weight (heavier than last week)

Wednesday PM

Exercises	Sets x Reps	Weight
Power Clean (from knees)	-	Build to a 1RM
Clean High Pulls	5 x 5	80% of 1RM Clean
Behind the Neck Power Jerk	-	Build to a 5RM
Hip Extensions	4 x 10	Barbell + Weight (heavier than Monday's session)

WEEK 4

Thursday

Exercises	Sets x Reps	Weight
Snatch-Grip Isometric	2 x 10 Seconds (1 inch off floor) 2 x 10 Seconds (at knees) 2 x 10 Seconds (at hips)	85% 1RM Snatch-Grip Deadlift
Clean-Grip Isometric	2 x 10 Seconds (1 inch off floor) 2 x 10 Seconds (at knees) 2 x 10 Seconds (at hips)	85% 1RM Clean-Grip Deadlift

Friday AM

Exercises	Sets x Reps	Weight
Snatch (from knees)	-	Build to a 1RM
Snatch High Pulls	5 x 5	80% of 1RM Snatch
Press from the Split	2 x 10	Barbell + Weight (heavier than Tuesday's session)
Back Extensions	2 x 10	Barbell + Weight (heavier than Wednesday's session)

Friday PM

Exercises	Sets x Reps	Weight
Clean (from knees)	-	Build to a 1RM
Behind-the-Neck Jerk	-	Build to a 5RM
Clean High Pulls	5 x 5	80% of 1RM Clean
Press from the Split	2 x 10	Barbell + Weight (same weight as the morning session)
Back Extensions	2 x 10	Barbell + Weight (same weight as the morning session)

Saturday

Exercises	Sets x Reps	Weight
Front Squat	-	Build to a 3RM
Arch-Back Good Mornings	-	Build to a 3RM
Jerk Recoveries	-	Build to a 1RM
Jerk Steps	3 x 10 steps each leg	115% 1RM Jerk

WEEK 5

Monday AM

Exercises	Sets x Reps	Weight
Snatch EMOM	18 x 1	75% of 1RM
Snatch High Pulls	4 x 4	85% of 1RM Snatch
Hip Extensions	2 x 10	Barbell + Weight (heavier than last week)

Monday PM

Exercises	Sets x Reps	Weight
Clean and Jerk EMOM	18 x 1	75% of 1RM
Clean High Pulls	4 x 4	85% of 1RM Clean
Hip Extensions	2 x 10	Barbell + Weight (same weight as the morning session)

Tuesday

Exercises	Sets x Reps	Weight
Front Squats	4 x 3 Rest 2 minutes between work sets	70% of 3RM
Back Squats	4 x 3 Rest 2 minutes between work sets	70% of 3RM
Press from the Split	2 x 10	Barbell + Weight (heavier than last week)
Jerk from the Split	2 x 10	Barbell + Weight (heavier than last week)

Wednesday AM

Exercises	Sets x Reps	Weight
Power Snatch (from knees)	-	Build to a 1RM
Snatch High Pulls	4 x 4	85% of 1RM Snatch
Split-Stance Good Mornings	2 x 10 each leg	Barbell + Weight (heavier than last week)
Back Extensions	2 x 10	Barbell + Weight (heavier than last week)

Wednesday PM

Exercises	Sets x Reps	Weight
Power Clean (from knees)	-	Build to a 1RM
Clean High Pulls	4 x 4	85% of 1RM Clean
Power Jerk	-	Build to a 1RM
Hip Extensions	4 x 10	Barbell + Weight (heavier than Monday's session)

WEEK 5

Thursday

Exercises	Sets x Reps	Weight
Snatch-Grip Isometric	2 x 10 Seconds (1 inch off floor) 2 x 10 Seconds (at knees) 2 x 10 Seconds (at hips)	90% 1RM Snatch-Grip Deadlift
Clean-Grip Isometric	2 x 10 Seconds (1 inch off floor) 2 x 10 Seconds (at knees) 2 x 10 Seconds (at hips)	90% 1RM Clean-Grip Deadlift

Friday AM

Exercises	Sets x Reps	Weight
Snatch (from 2-inch riser)	-	Build to a 1RM
Snatch High Pulls	4 x 4	85% of 1RM Snatch
Press from the Split	2 x 10	Barbell + Weight (heavier than Tuesday's session)
Back Extensions	2 x 10	Barbell + Weight (heavier than Wednesday's session)

Friday PM

Exercises	Sets x Reps	Weight
Clean (from 2-inch riser)	-	Build to a 1RM
Power Jerk	-	Build to a 1RM
Clean High Pulls	4 x 4	85% of 1RM Clean
Press from the Split	2 x 10	Barbell + Weight (same weight as the morning session)
Back Extensions	2 x 10	Barbell + Weight (same weight as the morning session)

Saturday

Exercises	Sets x Reps	Weight
Front Squat	-	Build to a 2RM
Seated Good Mornings	-	Build to a 5RM
Jerk Recoveries	-	Build to a 1RM
Jerk Steps	3 x 10 steps each leg	100% 1RM Jerk

WEEK 6

Monday AM

Exercises	Sets x Reps	Weight
Snatch EMOM	12 x 1	80% of 1RM
Snatch High Pulls	3 x 3	90% of 1RM Snatch
Hip Extensions	2 x 10	Barbell + Weight (heavier than last week)

Monday PM

Exercises	Sets x Reps	Weight
Clean and Jerk EMOM	12 x 1	80% of 1RM
Clean High Pulls	3 x 3	90% of 1RM Clean
Hip Extensions	2 x 10	Barbell + Weight (same weight as the morning session)

Tuesday

Exercises	Sets x Reps	Weight
Front Squats	4 x 3 Rest 2 minutes between work sets	75% of 3RM
Back Squats	4 x 3 Rest 2 minutes between work sets	75% of 3RM
Press from the Split	2 x 10	Barbell + Weight (heavier than last week)
Jerk from the Split	2 x 10	Barbell + Weight (heavier than last week)

Wednesday AM

Exercises	Sets x Reps	Weight
Power Snatch (from hips)	-	Build to a 1RM
Snatch High Pulls	3 x 3	90% of 1RM Snatch
Split-Stance Good Mornings	2 x 10 each leg	Barbell + Weight (heavier than last week)
Back Extensions	2 x 10	Barbell + Weight (heavier than last week)

Wednesday PM

Exercises	Sets x Reps	Weight
Power Clean (from hips)	-	Build to a 1RM
Clean High Pulls	3 x 3	90% of 1RM Clean
Power Jerk	-	Build to a 3RM
Hip Extensions	4 x 10	Barbell + Weight (heavier than Monday's session)

WEEK 6

Thursday

Exercises	Sets x Reps	Weight
Snatch-Grip Isometric	2 x 10 Seconds (1 inch off floor) 2 x 10 Seconds (at knees) 2 x 10 Seconds (at hips)	95% 1RM Snatch-Grip Deadlift
Clean-Grip Isometric	2 x 10 Seconds (1 inch off floor) 2 x 10 Seconds (at knees) 2 x 10 Seconds (at hips)	95% 1RM Clean-Grip Deadlift

Friday AM

Exercises	Sets x Reps	Weight
Snatch (from hips)	-	Build to a 1RM
Snatch High Pulls	3 x 3	90% of 1RM Snatch
Press from the Split	2 x 10	Barbell + Weight (heavier than Tuesday's session)
Back Extensions	2 x 10	Barbell + Weight (heavier than Wednesday's session)

Friday PM

Exercises	Sets x Reps	Weight
Clean (from hips)	-	Build to a 1RM
Block or Rack Jerk	-	Build to a 3RM
Clean High Pulls	3 x 3	90% of 1RM Clean
Press from the Split	2 x 10	Barbell + Weight (same weight as the morning session)
Back Extensions	2 x 10	Barbell + Weight (same weight as the morning session)

Saturday

Exercises	Sets x Reps	Weight
Front Squat	-	Build to a 1RM
Seated Good Mornings	-	Build to a 3RM
Jerk Recoveries	-	Build to a 1RM
Jerk Steps	3 x 10 steps each leg	105% 1RM Jerk

WEEK 7

Monday AM

Exercises	Sets x Reps	Weight
Snatch EMOM	24 x 1	70% of 1RM
Snatch High Pulls	5 x 5	80% of 1RM Snatch
Hip Extensions	2 x 10	Barbell + Weight (heavier than last week)

Monday PM

Exercises	Sets x Reps	Weight
Clean and Jerk EMOM	24 x 1	70% of 1RM
Clean High Pulls	5 x 5	80% of 1RM Clean
Hip Extensions	2 x 10	Barbell + Weight (same weight as the morning session)

Tuesday

Exercises	Sets x Reps	Weight
Front Squats	4 x 3 Rest 2 minutes between work sets	80% of 3RM
Back Squats	4 x 3 Rest 2 minutes between work sets	80% of 3RM
Press from the Split	2 x 10	Barbell + Weight (heavier than last week)
Jerk from the Split	2 x 10	Barbell + Weight (heavier than last week)

Wednesday AM

Exercises	Sets x Reps	Weight
Power Snatch (from hips)	-	Build to a 1RM
Snatch High Pulls	5 x 5	80% of 1RM Snatch
Split-Stance Good Mornings	2 x 10 each leg	Barbell + Weight (heavier than last week)
Back Extensions	2 x 10	Barbell + Weight (heavier than last week)

Wednesday PM

Exercises	Sets x Reps	Weight
Power Clean (from hips)	-	Build to a 1RM
Clean High Pulls	5 x 5	80% of 1RM Clean
Behind the Neck Power Jerk	-	Build to a 3RM
Hip Extensions	4 x 10	Barbell + Weight (heavier than Monday's session)

WEEK 7

Thursday

Exercises	Sets x Reps	Weight
Snatch-Grip Isometric	2 x 10 Seconds (1 inch off floor) 2 x 10 Seconds (at knees) 2 x 10 Seconds (at hips)	100% 1RM Snatch-Grip Deadlift
Clean-Grip Isometric	2 x 10 Seconds (1 inch off floor) 2 x 10 Seconds (at knees) 2 x 10 Seconds (at hips)	100% 1RM Clean-Grip Deadlift

Friday AM

Exercises	Sets x Reps	Weight
Snatch (from Hips)	-	Build to a 1RM
Snatch High Pulls	5 x 5	80% of 1RM Snatch
Press from the Split	2 x 10	Barbell + Weight (heavier than Tuesday's session)
Back Extensions	2 x 10	Barbell + Weight (heavier than Wednesday's session)

Friday PM

Exercises	Sets x Reps	Weight
Clean (from hips)	-	Build to a 1RM
Behind-the-Neck Jerk	-	Build to a 3RM
Clean High Pulls	5 x 5	80% of 1RM Clean
Press from the Split	2 x 10	Barbell + Weight (same weight as the morning session)
Back Extensions	2 x 10	Barbell + Weight (same weight as the morning session)

Saturday

Exercises	Sets x Reps	Weight
Back Squat	-	Build to a 5RM
Arch-Back Good Mornings	-	Build to a 5RM
Jerk Recoveries	-	Build to a 1RM
Jerk Steps	3 x 10 steps each leg	110% 1RM Jerk

WEEK 8

Monday AM

Exercises	Sets x Reps	Weight
Snatch EMOM	18 x 1	75% of 1RM
Snatch High Pulls	4 x 4	85% of 1RM Snatch
Hip Extensions	2 x 10	Barbell + Weight (heavier than last week)

Monday PM

Exercises	Sets x Reps	Weight
Clean and Jerk EMOM	18 x 1	75% of 1RM
Clean High Pulls	4 x 4	85% of 1RM Clean
Hip Extensions	2 x 10	Barbell + Weight (same weight as the morning session)

Tuesday

Exercises	Sets x Reps	Weight
Front Squats	4 x 3 Rest 2 minutes between work sets	85% of 3RM
Back Squats	4 x 3 Rest 2 minutes between work sets	85% of 3RM
Press from the Split	2 x 10	Barbell + Weight (heavier than last week)
Jerk from the Split	2 x 10	Barbell + Weight (heavier than last week)

Wednesday AM

Exercises	Sets x Reps	Weight
Power Snatch	-	Build to a 1RM
Snatch High Pulls	4 x 4	85% of 1RM Snatch
Split-Stance Good Mornings	2 x 10 each leg	Barbell + Weight (heavier than last week)
Back Extensions	2 x 10	Barbell + Weight (heavier than last week)

Wednesday PM

Exercises	Sets x Reps	Weight
Power Clean	-	Build to a 1RM
Clean High Pulls	4 x 4	85% of 1RM Clean
Power Jerk	-	Build to a 1RM
Hip Extensions	4 x 10	Barbell + Weight (heavier than Monday's session)

WEEK 8

Thursday

Exercises	Sets x Reps	Weight
Snatch-Grip Isometric	2 x 10 Seconds (1 inch off floor) 2 x 10 Seconds (at knees) 2 x 10 Seconds (at hips)	105% 1RM Snatch-Grip Deadlift
Clean-Grip Isometric	2 x 10 Seconds (1 inch off floor) 2 x 10 Seconds (at knees) 2 x 10 Seconds (at hips)	105% 1RM Clean-Grip Deadlift

Friday AM

Exercises	Sets x Reps	Weight
Snatch	-	Build to a 1RM
Snatch High Pulls	4 x 4	85% of 1RM Snatch
Press from the Split	2 x 10	Barbell + Weight (heavier than Tuesday's session)
Back Extensions	2 x 10	Barbell + Weight (heavier than Wednesday's session)

Friday PM

Exercises	Sets x Reps	Weight
Clean and Jerk	-	Build to a 1RM
Clean High Pulls	4 x 4	85% of 1RM Clean
Press from the Split	2 x 10	Barbell + Weight (same weight as the morning session)
Back Extensions	2 x 10	Barbell + Weight (same weight as the morning session)

Saturday

Exercises	Sets x Reps	Weight
Back Squat	-	Build to a 3RM
Arch-Back Good Mornings	-	Build to a 3RM
Jerk Recoveries	-	Build to a 1RM
Jerk Steps	3 x 10 steps each leg	115% 1RM Jerk

CLOSING THOUGHTS

I've been a USAW coach since 1995 and at the top level of international coaching for more than 10 years. I've been the head coach of the World Team several times, the coach of the Pan Am team a couple of times, the head coach of the Junior World team twice. I've also coached numerous junior Pan Am teams and a few other Junior and Youth teams. In short, I've put my time into this sport. I believe Louie has something worthwhile to say, and it's ridiculous not to listen.

Some American lifters and coaches haven't reacted well to Louie talking about the training of American weightlifters—some have been downright derogatory. The material in this section is for people who want to try applying Louie's ideas to test the results firsthand. The system makes sense to me. I ask you keep an open mind, and give it an honest shot before passing judgment.

Everyone who interprets an idea does it a little differently. Louie has been constantly developing his system for 30 years, and in that time, he came up with plenty of his own ideas. Louie has taken the time to push the envelope on what can be done when developing strength. He actually has new ideas that are worth exploring. How many naysayers can say the same?

Not many.

CHAPTER 10
PROGRAMMING FOR YOUTH, JUNIOR, AND MASTERS WEIGHTLIFTERS

Weightlifting is a lifetime sport with athletes ranging from ages four years old all the way up to 80 and older. In recent years, there's been an influx of new athletes picking up a barbell for the first time, and they come from a variety of athletic backgrounds.

There are also more barbell clubs and gyms catering specifically to weightlifting than ever—and a large part of that growth is due to CrossFit. Due to the organization's contribution, we now have kids being raised in gyms performing the competitive movements, and older people who have found a new athletic outlet in weightlifting. It's truly a wonderful time to be involved in the sport.

Youth, junior, senior, and masters weightlifters all need to work on the snatch and the clean and jerk. However, there are special considerations coaches must take into account when training members of each age group.

So far, most of what we've discussed pertains to senior athletes, but you'll often find that all roads lead back to the three-days-per-week basic template outlined in Chapter 6. It may seem simplistic, but I can't adequately stress the effectiveness of this program for the majority of weightlifters.

You'll find specific competition information on age categories and weight classes for youth, junior, and masters athletes in Chapter 11.

YOUTH WEIGHTLIFTERS— GENERALLY AGES 4 TO 9

EARLY ATHLETIC DEVELOPMENT

Prior to the use of the internet and cell phones becoming widespread, training kids was vastly different.

Photo 10.1—Coaching Caleb Muehler

Our youth were considerably more active with less time spent online, who instead were playing sports or otherwise being active outside. With the advancements of the internet and other technologies, our youth are now encouraged to spend more time indoors with their eyes glued to a screen. As a result, athletic development and movement competency is on the decline.

Learning how to move one's body and developing athleticism needs to begin at an early age. Those years between four and nine years old are crucial, and if wasted, it's time a person can never get back. We need to teach young kids the value of physical activity and how to move early in life. That's where programs such as CrossFit Kids can have a tremendous impact. CrossFit Kids teaches kids of all ages movement skills such as climbing, crawling, jumping, running, and problem solving. Those skills help kids be successful in sports…and life.

Learning to move one's body is like learning a language. If you begin learning a language at the age of four, you'll speak like a native when you're older. But if you learn a language when you're 20, you'll never truly be as fluent as native speakers, and you'll lack the nuances.

The same analogy can be used for human movement. When you learn the snatch and clean and jerk at the ages of five, seven, or nine, you'll be able to attain a higher level of skill later in life than would have been possible if you began learning at age 25…or even 17. It's as hard to perfect new movement patterns later in life as it is to perfect language skills as we get older.

WEIGHTLIFTING IS A SAFE SPORT

At first glance, people often assume weightlifting is an unsafe sport for young athletes. That thought couldn't be further from the truth.

In fact, weightlifting by comparison is a much safer activity than sports like football, gymnastics, soccer, or wrestling. In weightlifting, the weight is adjustable as appropriate for the person, whereas in other sports, the forces placed on the athletes are coming from their own bodyweight, gravity, speed, or another athlete—none of which are adjustable.

It's much safer to lift an adjustable weight within a child's current capabilities than to have a young body subject to the kind of uncontrolled and unexpected forces, impacts, and collisions that occur in many sports. That's why other sports have such higher instances of injury.

Many people think weightlifting is unsafe because the main objective is to lift the most weight. When learning to snatch, people learn how to use the biggest muscle and joint groups to complete the lift. That helps make the sport safe; it ensures that force is placed on the larger muscles and joints that can handle it.

Proper technique ensures that the smaller muscles and joints are not overly stressed. To lift the most weight, athletes have to lift correctly with technique developed over years of practice.

In weightlifting, the forces come from a barbell that can be loaded with light weight, or none.

Photo 10.2—Correcting Landon Thompson's bench press technique

There are training bars of various weights, and if necessary, the weightlifting movements can also be done with wooden dowels—essentially no weight. There's never a need for people to lift a weight they aren't ready for or can't safely lift.

Unlike sports such as soccer and football, the movements in weightlifting are the same every time you do them. By the time you're ready to lift a challenging weight, you've already practiced the exercise for countless repetitions—hopefully under the supervision of a knowledgeable coach—and are able to do so safely with good technique.

Growth-plate injury is another common concern in youth weightlifting, but there's never been a verified instance of weightlifting harming a child's growth plates. Growth-plate damage is more likely to come from a sport like cross country because repetitive stress is usually the cause of growth-plate injury, not traumatic stress. The volume of work done in weightlifting isn't high enough to cause the repetitive stress that would lead to growth-plate damage.

WILLIAM PENDLAY'S TRAINING

Photo 10.3—William Pendlay snatching

My son William is a perfect example of a kid who started weightlifting early in life with no ill effects. As soon as he could walk, he was in the gym with me, trying to pick up bars. At about age three, I constructed a bar for him out of wood. It had a thin wooden shaft and larger collars just like a real Olympic bar. I painted it gray and made multicolored discs to simulate weights. The bar and all the "weights" together weighed one or two pounds. This was William's first bar, and he lifted it constantly. He did about 10 workouts a day with that bar. He literally lifted all day, mimicking what he saw the lifters on the weightlifting team doing.

It wasn't long before he was adding small metal weights to the bar on the outside of the wooden plates, usually just two-and-a-half-pound plates or the green one-kilo plates. Eventually, his wooden bar broke in half, which prompted me to create something new. Since I was manufacturing bars at the time, I made him an aluminum bar with the same shaft length and diameter as the women's weightlifting bar, but with shorter collars. This bar weighed five kilos, light enough for him to snatch and clean and jerk at ages four and five.

I made the first one with no intent to sell it, but eventually, people who came to the gym in Wichita Falls saw the bar and convinced me to make a few more. I ended up selling hundreds of those bars, advertising them as "The William Bar" on my website.

William did his first competition at the age of five, where he snatched seven kilos and clean and jerked 12 kilos. At the age of seven, he won the YMCA Nationals. At eight, he snatched 23 kilos and clean and jerked 32. I felt safer having him participate in weightlifting that allowed for adjustable weights and forces placed upon his body than I would have felt about him participating in football, gymnastics, soccer, or wrestling.

At one point, people were worried William would stunt his growth by lifting so young. He was 6′ 2″ at age 15—which is taller than I am—so I don't think his growth was stunted by weightlifting.

Photo 10.4—William Pendlay cleaning

A SIMPLE PROGRAM—PRACTICE THE LIFTS

There are a few qualities kids should possess before training for weightlifting. First, they should have the body awareness necessary to go into a deep squat, hold their arms straight overhead, and to arch their back and hold the proper posture necessary to snatch or clean.

The second quality needed is the maturity to pay attention and follow directions. For the very young, training sessions have to be short because they won't have a long attention span. Those training session times can increase as they develop the ability to pay attention. When William trained 10 times a day at age three, he could only pay attention for a few minutes at a time. He'd do a few lifts, and then run off to do something else after losing interest.

Whether they're four, five, or eight, if they have those qualities, they're ready to train in weightlifting.

Training for this age group should be kept simple. A knowledgeable coach just needs to have kids practice the full snatch, clean, and jerk with the intent on building solid technical skills in those movements. We don't worry about making nine-year-olds stronger because they haven't yet developed the nervous systems and motor patterns to do so.

The snatch, clean, and jerk are complex movements; that complexity makes them self-limiting and is another reason they're inherently safe for young athletes. For example, a kid can't snatch too much weight when first starting training because the snatch is a difficult movement to perform correctly. The type of efficient movement required to lift heavy weights in the snatch, clean, and jerk takes time to master, and during the time that takes, the body also adapts to the stresses the weight places on the body.

Training and practicing the lifts are required before anyone can lift challenging weights. That's why this age is a perfect time to practice and focus on the lifts. If we teach kids to train with the intent and concentration of doing the lifts correctly every repetition, we'll set them up for success as they mature into young adults.

There's no set program for this age group. Coaches should drill technique, make sure the kids develop the ability to hold correct positions, and to keep training fun because…well, they're kids. Kids want to have fun; if weightlifting is boring, they won't want to do it very long.

YOUTH WEIGHTLIFTERS— GENERALLY AGES 10 TO 14

Youth lifters ages 10 to 14 are entering a transitional phase in life as they develop from kids into young adults. As they mature, they begin to share more similarities with their senior counterparts. They can begin training for strength, may have reasonable levels of technique (not perfect, but in the ball park), and possess the maturity to extend their focus on tasks.

The differences between a 12-year-old weightlifter and an adult weightlifter mostly concern the rate at which things happen. Younger athletes adapt faster, gain skill faster, and recover from training faster. But they also get bored faster and can burn out if not paced.

Photo 10.5—Enjoying time with Landon Thompson and Cory Muehler

As adult lifters, we like excitement in training. But youth lifters need consistent, constant change, along with the excitement of challenges. For youth athletes, training always needs to be fun and exciting.

Photo 10.6—Landon Thompson training weighted pull-ups

THE GROUP ATMOSPHERE

Making training a social event is the easiest way to keep it fun and engaging for kids. Kids and teenagers want to be around their friends or others their age. Whether it's football or weightlifting, they love to be part of a team and are far more likely to stick to the sport long enough to accomplish something if they're a part of group.

School-age lifters love to compete…with each other or themselves. When you have five teenagers training together, motivation will rarely be a problem. If one kid hits a milestone, it will raise the standard and encourage the rest of them to do the same. Lifting in a group setting will motivate these young athletes far better than a coach training individual athletes.

Photo 10.8—Discussing the game plan with Landon Thompson

Photo 10.7—Cory Muehler lifting under the watchful eyes of Landon Thompson, Donny Shankle, and me

PROGRAMMING FOR AGES 10 TO 14

There's no single program or way to coach this age group. Every kid is different, a unique snowflake (in this one instance), and much of the training will be determined by the current level of maturity. In addition, these youth athletes don't yet have the attention span as do senior lifters. As adults, we sometimes forget how quickly boredom can kick in with 12-year-olds.

A predetermined intensity and amount of work are the programs kids are the least excited about. When you tell 12-year-olds the day's workout is three sets of five with 80%, they get bored. I've never met a kid who thought a workout like three sets of five was exciting or fun.

A program that's engaging and exciting will have two main characteristics. It will allow them to exert some control over their own destiny, and will have a lot of variety. Whenever possible, no two workouts should be the same.

VARIETY WITH COMPLEXES

Youth athletes from four to nine years old start training by simply learning and practicing the snatch and clean and jerk. Ten- to 14-year-olds can start to incorporate complexes into their training that consist of the lifts, in addition to pulls and squats. The use of complexes adds more variety to training, keeps the training emphasis on the competition lifts, and keeps the absolute intensity lower.

We build most complexes with four to six total repetitions. This limits the weights lifted to around 75 or 80% of an athlete's maximal snatch and clean and jerk. Complexes are self-limiting because of the number of reps performed…a good thing for this age group. Two snatch pulls plus one snatch plus two overhead squats, or one clean plus three front squats plus one jerk are examples of complexes I regularly use.

There's no way kids can lift weights approaching their personal best snatch or clean and jerk, regardless of how hard or how many times they try. Telling a group of 13-year-olds they can go as heavy as they want satisfies the need for control of their training, and makes training more fun and exciting. You just have to be creative to make the complex hard enough that the weight is inherently limited. There are an infinite number of complexes you can think up if you use your imagination.

SETTING NEW PRS

Everyone loves the challenge of going after and setting new personal records, but this is especially important for youth lifters to keep their enthusiasm for weightlifting high. I found using one complex on Monday, then a slightly different one on Wednesday, and finally another variation on Friday to work best. That way, a kid can try to PR the Monday complex every subsequent Monday, and the same on Wednesday and Friday.

Every two or three weeks, usually on Friday, try to PR the actual snatch or clean and jerk either for a single, double, or even a triple.

PRs are the lifeblood of a training program. When coaching young athletes, take yourself back to a 10-year-old's head. To truly understand them, reflect on how big of a deal it is to make new PRs in training, or place first in a local competition. Putting yourself in their shoes is best thing you can do as a coach.

That will help you be as excited as they are when these events happen, and to understand what they're going through when things falter.

PROGRAMMING FRONT AND BACK SQUATS

Use your head when progressing a young athlete into squatting for strength. That experience will be different for each individual kid. Once they show they're capable of keeping the core and back tight and positioned correctly, you can start using squats in their training. For youth or school-age lifters who meet those requirements, do some form of squatting three days a week.

This has worked extremely well for me: five sets of five on the back squat on the first training day of the week, then doing front squats in the middle of the week, then finally doing a single, heavier set of five on the last training day of the week.

Stick to five reps. It becomes tempting to increase the weight too much with lower reps, and with higher reps, it's too easy for fatigue to cause a technical breakdown. This is essentially the Texas Method we discussed in Chapter 7.

Photo 10.9—Landon Thompson back squatting 60 kilos

I don't like to use percentages for these squats. Starting with one set of three on the front squat with the same weight they can lift for the clean and jerk is the best way to calculate the optimal weight.

Once you have this starting point, pick the same weight for Monday's five sets of five back squats. If they're successful with that, try increasing the weight by 10% for the set of five on Friday.

Keeping good records of the weight on the bar is important at this age, as with any age, and allows you to accurately increase by small, steady increments. It's tempting for kids (and their parents) to push for bigger weights, but it's the coach who should be the voice of reason.

EXAMPLE WEEK OF YOUTH PROGRAMMING

The tables on the next page show three examples of complexes that limit kids to 80% or less of their maximums. You can build your own complexes based on what your young athletes need. Do the same complexes for several weeks because that's one of the draws. Every two or three weeks, go up to max on Friday on the competition lifts. Kids *love* to make PRs, and this program gives them a chance to try for a PR every workout.

MONDAY

Exercise	Load
2 Snatch Pull + 1 Snatch + 2 Overhead Squat	4 to 5 sets to build to a max weight
1 Clean Pull + 1 Clean + 3 Jerk	4 to 5 sets to build to a max weight
Back Squat 5 x 5	Week 1: Start with clean and jerk 1RM

WEDNESDAY

Exercise	Load
2 Snatch + 3 Overhead Squat	4 to 5 sets to build to a max weight
1 Clean + 3 Front Squat + 1 Jerk	4 to 5 sets to build to a max weight
Front Squat 3 x 3	Week 1: Start with clean and jerk 1RM

FRIDAY

Exercise	Load
3 Snatch Pull + 1 Snatch + 1 Overhead Squat	4 to 5 sets to build to a max weight
3 Clean Pull + 1 Clean + 1 Jerk	4 to 5 sets to build to a max weight
Back Squat 1 x 5	Week 1: Add 10% to clean and jerk 1RM

For the squats, make sure they're able to complete all sets and reps at a given weight before making a small increase the following week. Keep the focus on lifting weights they're capable of lifting. There's no reason to push young athletes too hard on squats—they have a whole career ahead of them for that sort of thing. Keep everything fun.

TRAINING FREQUENCY

Two or three days per week is the ideal training frequency for kids 10 years old all the way up to 17. That age group doesn't need to train more than that, but some athletes will occasionally have the desire to do so. If you have an athlete asking to do more, go with it. There needs to be balance between managing their enthusiasm without squashing their ideas, and keeping them on track with what's beneficial in the long run. You can't always give in, but as they get older, they'll demand some level of control.

If you have a teenager who's bored and impatient with training three days a week, increase the days. As coaches and parents, we know it's unlikely their enthusiasm for more training will last too long. Increasing the training frequency a month or so before a big competition is the best strategy I've come up with to validate what they want and still avoid burnout. Let them train four or five days a week; be excited with them about this change in their weightlifting schedule and the prospects of setting a big PR at the meet.

Change the training volume and intensities to spread across the additional days. After all the training for and excitement of the meet passes, they'll be fine with going back to less training.

COMPETITION

Lifters in this age group should be encouraged to compete in local meets as often as possible. Most don't require any sort of pre-competition training or peaking cycle. As they're learning the sport, treat meets as fun events, and give clear, simple directions when it's their turn to lift.

In many ways, coaching young athletes at meets is much easier than adults. Kids don't carry preconceived notions of how they should be doing; they don't have a fear of failure, or compare themselves in a negative way to other lifters. Instead, they're supportive of one another and enjoy cheering others as much as lifting. In the warm-up room, just tell them when to take a lift and when to sit down. As long as they don't have a history of behavioral problems—which definitely happens from time to time—they listen well, and event day will go smoothly.

To help keep meets fun, set your young lifters up for success. Make sure the weights loaded on the bar are weights they can make. Having a 12-year-old bomb out because the opener was too heavy is a great way to kill the enthusiasm for lifting and competing. Missed lifts will eventually happen, and you should have a discussion about that with your young athletes. But do what you can to put them in a situation where making the lifts is the norm.

YOUTH WEIGHTLIFTERS— GENERALLY AGES 15 TO 17

PROGRAMMING FOR AGES 15 TO 17

Every youth athlete will eventually need to transition to the same programming used by senior athletes. For many, this transition can begin around the ages of 14 or 15. There's no doubt some will be ready earlier, while for others the transition will be later. At 12 years old, use complexes to limit intensity to around 80% of maximums. As they move away from complexes and focus on the snatch, clean and jerk, squats, deadlifts, and presses, you'll begin to use greater intensities. The three-day-a-week program from Chapter 6 is a good starting point.

These kids have an incredible capacity to recover from training and can handle higher training frequencies. Many of them can go from three days a week to four or five days a week in minimal time; however, try to increase training days gradually over time. This age group is incredibly enthusiastic and will want to do more before they're ready.

Many youth athletes and young adults underestimate the effectiveness of a three-day-a-week program. People of all age groups often forget that senior lifters have made the Olympic team, and youth and junior lifters have made the World team while training only three days a week.

PROGRAMMING FOR MULTI-SPORT ATHLETES

Many youth athletes want to play other sports while weightlifting. It's possible to do both, and often, playing another sport will actually help in weightlifting. Many sports have a symboitic relationship with weightlifting. Weightlifting training and being stronger in general will help almost every sport, and participation in most other sports will also help with overall athleticism and eventual achievements in weightlifting.

Some sports, such as wrestling and track, are wonderful when combined with weightlifting. The training for those sports is great for an athlete's conditioning and general physical preparedness. Cross country keeps kids active, and helps to build stamina for training. I've found that many kids use cross country as additional training for other sports, and they can still train in the weightroom while doing it.

Wrestling shares some similarities with weightlifting in that it's an individual sport. There may be a team on the sidelines, but it's up to the athlete on the mat or platform to perform well. In that regard, wrestling helps sharpen the mental toughness for a future high-level weightlifter. They're also both weight-class sports that require weigh-ins and making weight. That helps keep focus on proper diet; managing bodyweight is a part of training.

I've coached a lot of weightlifters who also wrestled. Wrestling is a tough sport, and weightlifting performance usually decreases about 10% when wrestling season starts. After a few weeks of weightlifting, performance rebounds. At the end of the wrestling season, after eliminating the two-hour nightly wrestling practices, young athletes will see a substantial increase in weightlifting performance. If an athlete trained one or two days per week during the sporting season, you can quickly move into a normal weightlifting schedule. However, if an athlete has taken a few weeks off, you'll have to come back gradually.

Most sports kids participate in are seasonal. During other sports seasons, weightlifting training will have to be cut back to one or two days per week. Normally, this initially results in a big decrease in weightlifting performance. However, I'm always surprised by how quickly performance comes back, even while the other sport's season is still in progress.

Kids, especially talented athletes, have many different sporting careers to pursue. Eventually, the kid you've been training since age six might need to stop weightlifting and take advantage of other opportunities…and that's okay. Yes, it'll be difficult as the coach because you love weightlifting and are trying to produce weightlifters. But coaches can't be one-dimensional—it's the kid's life, not yours.

Be supportive of your athletes' decisions, and leave the door open to come back to weightlifting. This provides a long-term vision for athletic development. Instead of trying to build the best 15-year-old star athlete now, plan to develop an individual who's capable of great feats when at age 20 or 30, playing at the collegiate level, professional level, or at the Olympic Games for weightlifting…or another sport.

AUTONOMOUS TEENS

Coaches and parents should never lose sight of the social demands placed upon athletes as they progress into their teenage years. It's a tricky time in life, filled with learning to drive, boyfriends, girlfriends, part-time jobs, school work, family obligations, and of course, sports.

In addition to devoting time to all these important elements of their lives, teens are also beginning to move away from accepting adult supervision and control—and that's ultimately a good thing.

We want responsible young adults capable of critical thinking as they enter society, and we need to foster their growth as individuals. However, they still need parental guidance and coaching in sports. In weightlifting, you'll have to maintain a delicate balance as your teen athletes ask for increased levels of autonomy over their training.

Most teens aren't mentally or emotionally able to make adult decisions. For the kids' benefit, a good coach needs to have lines that can't be crossed, but at the same time remember that training is a small part of their lives, and it should be fun.

Weightlifting will have a lot of competition for this age group. But if you foster a positive and fun environment, kids will look forward to coming to the gym. If the training is well planned, they'll leave always wanting more. Forcing the issue and making them train too much is one way to kill a kid's enthusiasm for lifting. To be successful, let them be kids and live their lives.

Using the first program from the beginner's chapter as a base makes it easy for them to fit weightlifting into their schedules. If they can only train two or three days per week, that's perfect! Never suggest or mandate that they skip other social events. That's a battle weightlifting won't win.

Photo 10.10—Neiman Melton performing a clean and jerk demo during a seminar

JUNIOR WEIGHTLIFTERS— AGES 17 TO 20

Junior athletes can be categorized into two groups with unique needs: early and late starters.

EARLY STARTERS

The first group is comprised of the kids who entered the sport as school-age lifters prior to the age of 13 to 15. These athletes have learned efficient motor patters prior to puberty. This is important, since prior to puberty, they're incapable of significant strength increases, and this leaves increases in skill and lifting efficiency as the only avenue for increasing the competition totals.

I encourage those who coach early starters to focus on technique, not because heavy lifting is dangerous—I don't believe it is—but because they don't yet have the ability to gain significant strength. Yet, they do have the ability to perfect motor patterns and gain skill that will make later strength increases pay off exponentially.

These early starters are the athletes who will be high performers as juniors, and for all practical purposes, their training will be the same as adults and senior lifters. These will be the kids who will go after Junior American records and make teams such as the Junior Pan Am or Junior World team.

Juniors who start early have several advantages over adult lifters. The recovery ability of an 18- or 19-year-old is normally better than the 28- or 30-year-old, so the junior will probably be able to train harder and more often.

Mindset and belief in outrageous possibilities is an often-overlooked advantage of juniors. For an athlete who struggled for months to snatch 100 kilos, the thought of a 200-kilo snatch or gold at the Olympics or World Championships is outrageous. But the next American who does it will first have had to believe it was possible. This belief is more likely to have started in a young mind than later in life after learning to "be sensible." Belief is a powerful thing.

For quite some time, too many American lifters and coaches have lacked this kind of belief, but we're slowly gaining it back. Thankfully, there are more junior lifters these days who have a similar belief system James Moser had in his training. If there are any lifters from this group reading this book, my message to you is this: Don't let anyone tell you what you *can't* do. You can be one of the next generations of American lifters to reestablish America's rightful place in the sport of weightlifting.

LATE STARTERS

The late-starters group is the second category of junior lifters and is comprised of those who began weightlifting in high school or college. When I started coaching in 1995 and then up to about 2007, it was possible to start the sport as a junior or senior in high school or even as a freshman or sophomore in college…and still do quite well at competitions within a year or two. I've coached several who started late and won both the Junior and Collegiate Nationals.

I also coached the Midwestern State University team during the time when we were almost perpetual Collegiate National Champions winning consecutive men's titles. Many of the kids who contributed to those team titles and even those who won individual titles were lifters who started in the sport only a year or two earlier.

This wouldn't be possible today; the landscape of the sport has changed. The growth of CrossFit is one reason—CrossFit introduced countless individuals to weightlifting. More people are participating in the sport, and the level of competition has risen considerably. Today, unless you're truly a freak athlete, you won't be winning major weightlifting meets your first or second year in the sport.

This rise in the level of competition is good for USA Weightlifting. We needed the level of competition to rise in the USA to better prepare our lifters for success in international competition. USA Weightlifting needs not only the best junior lifters in each weight class to raise their performances; we need the fifth and tenth place athletes to improve as well.

At national and international competitions, lifters are grouped into sessions depending on their ranking and qualifying total. Lifters in the "A" session are most likely to medal or win the competition outright. Lifters in the "B" session could possibly medal if they put up a big enough total and someone from the "A" session slips up. Lifters in the "C" session are least likely to earn a medal or to podium. "C" sessions and lower are a backlog of up-and-coming weightlifters who hope to someday make it to the upper tiers of competition.

When lower-ranked lifters improve, it puts pressure on those ranked ahead of them. Eventually a "C" session lifter might be pushed to the medal stand at Nationals by those coming up through the ranks. Those already on the medal stand will be pushed to World teams, the "A" session, and perhaps someday, the podium at international meets because of the pressure to improve placed on them by other up-and-coming lifters.

This is why USA Weightlifting needs everyone to participate and succeed. It's not only the star performers who are responsible for the resurgence of USA Weightlifting in the world ranking. It's also those silver medalists who made the gold-medal performance possible…and also those in the top 10 who pushed the medalists.

That's one reason to coach kids from this second group. Encourage them to keep lifting! They'll be behind the eight-ball when it comes to winning big meets, but that doesn't mean it's impossible. Donny Shankle didn't enter the sport until a little after his 21st birthday, and he's become practically a legend in American weightlifting.

Great things can be accomplished by those who start late. It will be hard, but it can be done. Most lifters need the motivation provided by competition to bring the best out of them. It's the several lifters who place second, third and fourth at Junior Nationals and push the national champion to lift a big total to make the Junior World team who are the real heroes of the American resurgence in the sport. They won't get a lot of glory, but they made it possible.

PROGRAMMING FOR EARLY STARTERS

If you're a junior lifter who started early or you're coaching such a lifter, the task is straightforward. Usually, training will be four or five days a week. The four- and five- and even six-day programs in Chapter 7 are representative of what a high-performing junior lifter should be doing.

Training will be essentially identical to a senior lifter. These lifters will have learned efficient technique years ago, or should have, and by now it'll have become so firmly ingrained that they rarely deviate from it with anything but the heaviest attempts.

Building strength will be the main challenge for a junior lifter in this category. At this point, a high-performing junior athlete will be carrying a high training workload, and sometimes sacrificing many other areas of life. At the highest levels, coaches need to maintain a delicate balance when athletes are often training twice a day. Without good time management, this can interfere with school and social life. It will be a challenge for both athlete and coach, but if it was easy, everyone would be champions.

PROGRAMMING FOR LATE STARTERS

A late starter will need to put in a lot of work on the competitive lifts in the first two or three years if they're going to have a chance to catch up. This is one place where timed sets (EMOMs) can shine. It takes a long time to build the musculoskeletal system to a point where it can withstand high-intensity training, such as a lot of maximal attempts.

I usually come down on the opposite side of caution when it comes to training practices, but in this case, I believe it's risky to use something like the Bulgarian system for lifters with less than two years of experience. On the other hand, timed sets can build exceptional technique with weights as low as 70%. They also allow a lifter to accumulate reps in a short amount of time, which is what late starters need.

If you're a late starter, or are coaching one, a couple of days of EMOM work might be just what the doctor ordered. That and building the squat from zero to as high as possible in as little time as possible should be the main training goals.

If you're talented, you only need to be able to make up for lost time. Don't be discouraged, but instead, take the difficulty of your task as a challenge and work hard to overcome the obstacle.

MASTERS WEIGHTLIFTERS—
AGES 35 TO 80 AND ABOVE

The masters age group encompasses a wide variety of athletes ranging from 35 to 80 years old and older. The range presents potential challenges for coaches, as there will be a lot of variation in physical abilities between athletes. Someone who is 40 years old may still have much of the strength and physical capabilities as those in their 20s and 30s. Another masters lifter—either the same age or older—might have fewer capabilities.

Different people age at different rates because of both genetics and lifestyle.

Because of these varying capabilities in strength, flexibility, athleticism, and recovery ability, group programming is nearly impossible; masters athletes need to be approached as individuals. Some athletes start weightlifting in their 50s, while others may be coming back to it after participating in their teens or 20s. A masters athlete needs an individualized program based on specific capabilities and a partnership with a knowledgeable coach or training partner.

Masters lifters can have plenty of advantages over their younger peers. Having the funds to participate in the sport is a big advantage. Being adults who've had careers, many masters athletes are able to plan in advance the meets they want to participate in and are able to afford the expenses of a trip.

Mental and psychological maturity is another masters advantage. Progress in weightlifting happens slowly and requires patience many youth, junior, and even senior lifters lack. Having maturity, patience, and the ability to stick to a long-term plan is a huge advantage.

Some masters lifters in their 40s can even produce better athletic performances than they achieved in their 20s when at the peak of their athletic careers. Diran Lancaster, as a chiropractor and masters athlete in his 40s, clean and jerked more than he could clean when he was a starting safety at Texas Tech at the peak of his athletic abilities. A masters lifter like Diran might not have the absolute athletic ability, recovery ability, or time to train as he did in his 20s, but maturity, patience, and the ability to stick to a long-term plan often make up for the missing elements.

Some masters may be retired and able to devote more time and energy to a sport and recovery than they could at any other stage in life. A lifter who's retired will have more flexibility in the training and competition schedule.

PROGRAMMING FOR MASTERS ATHLETES

The three-day-a-week program as outlined in Chapter 6 is a good place to start for any weightlifter, including masters. Masters athletes have a wide diversity, wider in their physical abilities than any other group. A 60-year-old masters athlete learning the snatch and clean and jerk for the first time might require the majority of training to be focused on learning the lifts and developing the flexibility needed for the sport. A 40-year-old masters athlete who learned the lifts as a school-age or junior lifter with a long career as a senior lifter might have capabilities on par with most senior athletes.

The three-day-a-week program offers flexibility to cater to the individual needs of almost any lifter. The training schedule can be adjusted to two days if needed, and an emphasis can be placed on strength development or technical ability. Anyone coaching a masters athlete has to gear the programming toward getting the most out of that individual athlete.

MAINTAIN A HEALTHY LIFESTYLE

As people age, their deficiencies magnify, causing weak legs to be weaker or flexibility issues to become more troublesome. When we're older, everything from athletic development to injury recovery takes longer. An ache or pain that used to go away in a week now takes a month. That's why an athlete needs to have patience when starting or continuing the sport at an advanced age.

Older athletes need to listen to their bodies. If something hurts or is injured, older lifters should take the time to heal before rushing back into training. Going back to training too soon will likely make the problem worse, or create a new one, and then training will be sidelined longer.

To stay injury-free, a masters weightlifter should place a greater emphasis on general health. Eating a healthy, low-inflammatory, Paleo-ish style of diet as outlined in Chapter 13 will greatly aid this athlete. Staying active outside of weightlifting is also a good idea, especially if training only one or two times per week. Walking and swimming are excellent low-impact activities. Both are easy on the joints, and just 10 minutes spent with them will have a great benefit on conditioning and recovery from training.

I also recommend training with dumbbells and kettlebells, at a commercial gym if appropriate. A scheme of three sets of 10 reps on exercises such as rows, presses, and sit-ups will go a long way to ensure muscular symmetry and joint health.

Most masters lifters will have a challenge controlling bodyweight. If this is you, it's great if you want to make a specific weight class to place better in competition, but I advise against drastically cutting weight.

The weight-cutting practices outlined in Chapter 12 can be stressful and hard to recover from for a masters athlete. It's not worth cutting weight if performance or health are negatively affected longer term.

The goal in general should be to live a healthy lifestyle. If losing weight enhances overall health, take the logical steps to accomplish that goal. In addition to good dietary practices, adding one or two weekly conditioning or CrossFit workouts could also be beneficial. Performing functional movements such as pull-ups, push-ups, squats, and breaking a sweat on a Concept 2 rower will do wonders for muscular development, weight loss, and maintaining general health. If you lead a healthy lifestyle and eat a balanced diet in addition to the weightlifting training, bodyweight might never be an issue.

MARY MCGREGOR

Mary McGregor is the most successful masters weightlifter I've coached. Mary never pursued sports at a younger age, and didn't consider herself an athlete. She was unique in that not many people at the time started a weightlifting career at the age of 58. Mary initially wanted to get her granddaughter, Neiman, involved in weightlifting, and that turned into her picking up the sport as well.

Photo 10.11—Mary McGregor, 2009

Mary and I hit it off immediately, and she's a close friend to this day. If there's one word I'd use to describe Mary, it would be "perseverance." Initially, she didn't stand out as someone who had talent for the sport and didn't make particularly fast progress. She did possess a decent amount of strength for someone her age, and didn't have any physical limitations that would make snatching or clean and jerking impossible.

Mary started with a blank slate, and weathered all the frustrations that come with learning the lifts for the first time at an advanced age. The thing that made Mary remarkable is this: She stuck it out. No matter how long it took to get a lift right, she just kept working.

My goal with her was the same as it is for any lifter: to develop exceptional technique. A masters lifter should strive to have such good technique that younger lifters will envy their lifting. And to that end, Caleb Ward once commented, "I wish I had technique as good as Mary."

Sure, along the way, Mary experienced the normal aches and pains that come with training when you're almost 60 years old. None of that really affected her work ethic though. In fact, possibly the biggest challenge was the psychological aspect of going out on stage wearing a weightlifting singlet. This often brings out a certain amount of stress for most women, but is probably more stressful for a 60-year-old woman than a 20-year-old. In the end, like always, Mary persevered.

Mary McGregor's Training

Mary and I worked as a team to ensure her success. We placed an emphasis on her general health and weightlifting technique. In her late 50s, it took Mary more time to recover from her training sessions, and a three-day-a-week schedule worked well for her. She followed the same three-day-a-week program found in Chapter 6. Based on her feedback, I made adjustments to accommodate her schedule and how she was feeling. When she could train three days a week, she did, and when she couldn't, there were no qualms about switching to two days a week.

The keys to her success were listening to her body, backing off weightlifting when needed, and working hard outside the gym. Mary often walked at night to maintain general and cardiovascular health. She'd also frequent a commercial gym to work on exercises that had nothing to do with weightlifting. That work provided her with safe joint movement, muscle development, and activity that wasn't as stressful as her weightlifting training.

I've had several junior lifters who placed fifth or sixth at Nationals eventually win Junior Nationals. When I asked one kid how he improved from fifth to first, he said, "All the guys who used to beat me quit." The same thing happened to Mary. When she first started lifting, she'd look at the totals for the Pan American or World Championships, and see she had a ways to go. But, as the years went by, her total edged up, and many of the people who were beating her quit competing, or their totals started going down as Mary's kept climbing.

Mary had exceptional dedication to the craft of training and competing in weightlifting. She dotted her Is and crossed her Ts, which led to becoming a true technician in the snatch and the clean and jerk. During her career, Mary won the 2004 Pan American Masters Championships, and won gold at the 2008 Masters World Championships in Athens, Greece, where she also set world records in the 75-plus kilo category with a 43-kilo snatch, 63-kilo clean and jerk, and 106-kilo total. She also won best lifter for her age group.

Mary's progress can be measured in years, not months. Being patient, maintaining her health, and having the maturity to stick to a long-term plan paid off with a gold medal and best lifter award at the Masters World Championships.

CLOSING THOUGHTS

Weightlifting is a safe and inclusive sport. Anyone and everyone is welcome in the community that surrounds it, and it's up to the members of that community to continue to help the sport grow.

If you're a coach, you need to be knowledgeable enough to relay that safety message to concerned parents. Yes, know the science behind weightlifting being safer than other sports, but also realize much of this is about trust. You need to earn the trust of parents, which you can do by being as transparent as possible. Demystify weightlifting by showing them the training program and what you plan to have the kids practice.

Explain the emphasis on building technical mastery, as opposed to only focusing on heavy weights—which is probably what they think is the singular focus until you show them otherwise.

Don't forget to highlight other attributes of weightlifting, such as building self-confidence, encouraging a high work ethic, setting and accomplishing goals, and the social element. As with everything, building trust takes time, but it will happen sooner if you're honest and show people you care.

Athletes in the sport have a role to play as well. You know how great weightlifting is, so share it with the people you love. Your younger siblings, parents, co-workers, and even grandparents can all benefit from lifting a barbell. People can be intimidated by going to the gym, but one of the best ways I've seen to get loved ones training is to simply invite them to watch you lift. Bring them along, introduce them to your coach or training partner, and explain what you're doing while you do it. Share your goals with them, and tell them how you've had to work to get to your current level.

Avoid being pushy about it. Simply show them how much you love the gym and plant the idea that they might too. With any luck, they'll be on the platform next to you in no time, and we will have all gained another member of our great community.

SECTION C
ESSENTIALS FOR AMERICAN WEIGHTLIFTERS

Regardless of the level of the lifter—beginner, intermediate, or advanced—they all require the same thing: the continual learning of the lifts. It always comes down to that all-important end goal for weightlifters, from the first time they pick up an empty barbell, all the way to the point at which they break a record. If you can keep that premise alive in your training, you can indeed find success in this sport.

Outside of that and the hard training you'll do every day, there are plenty of other ins and outs of being a weightlifter, which we'll cover in this section.

But before you go deeper into these pages, here's how to best apply the following information. You first need to take an audit of your training age and current strength and skill levels. Be honest with yourself based on what you've learned so far. Are you a beginner, intermediate, or advanced lifter? A true understanding of where you are will lead you to a more accurate representation of what you need right now to be better for tomorrow.

Photo C1—Pendlay change plates

Chapter 11—Competition Guide

In Chapter 6, we made a pact that you'd sign up for a meet, and I hope you kept your end of the bargain. Both beginner and intermediate athletes should know the subtle nuances of how a weightlifting meet unfolds. You should be fully aware of the rules of the sport, the process of warming up and making attempts. This information is valuable to review before competitions for both athletes and newer coaches.

For newer athletes, I highly recommend finding a coach to help you. Advanced athletes will more than likely either have a coach or are capable of taking care of themselves after years of experience and countless meets.

Chapter 12—Making Weight

This chapter isn't intended to be a weight-loss program. If you're a beginner, cutting weight for a competition should be the last thing on your mind. Lift at your natural bodyweight.

At a weightlifting meet, beginners should be having fun and making lifts—cutting weight is not a fun process, and could lead to being so depleted and exhausted that you'll find making your lifts difficult. For some intermediate and advanced athletes looking to qualify for major competitions, cutting weight might be a reality. This chapter will be useful information for those athletes.

Chapter 13—The Weightlifter's Kitchen

Properly fueling your body for performance in weightlifting is an important subject for all levels of lifters in the sport.

Your eating habits will be a cornerstone of your training, so treat every meal as important. Proper nutrition and proper training go hand in hand toward building high-performance bodies.

Chapter 14—The Razor's Edge

Do you have what it takes to make it in the sport of weightlifting? I can tell you from personal experience that to be successful in this sport requires a lot of special qualities.

The successful athletes have courage to pull under weights the average lifter is afraid of touching. They have to be willing to endure the pain of training day after day. They have to accept that pursuing technical mastery and ultimate strength gains will be done by navigating through countless "bad" days at the gym.

As a beginner, bouncing back from missteps is easy and one can literally fall into success. But when lifters continue to advance in ability, the fine line they walk between success and failure narrows. This is when the sport will test them more and more physically and mentally...many won't make it and will quit. I've seen it time and time again.

I've also seen a few beautifully navigate this part of their careers and it led them to gold medals, American records, and World Teams. That's why I want to help you avoid quitting. I encourage you to keep going because I know the value of weightlifting in a person's life even when weathering the storms of training and competition feel impossible. This chapter contains my closing thoughts about weightlifting. I hope it helps.

CHAPTER 11
COMPETITION GUIDE

COMPETITION FOR THE ATHLETE AND COACH

As an athlete or coach, time spent in the gym should be focused on more than just training. Competing is a lot of fun, and competition is the place where confidence and long-lasting relationships are built. As an athlete, compete as soon as possible; as a coach, have your athletes compete before they feel ready.

Photo 11.1—Spencer Moorman in the warm-up room at a competition

BECOMING A MEMBER OF USA WEIGHTLIFTING

To compete in local and national competitions in the United States, a lifter must join our country's governing body of weightlifting, USA Weightlifting (USAW). Being a USA Weightlifting Certified Coach and having all your athletes become members of the USAW has a lot of benefits, including incidental insurance. For that reason and many others, I highly recommend competing in USAW-sanctioned competitions, so if an injury does occur, coverage will be available.

Athletes can register online for a membership with USA Weightlifting, and you'll also find local competitions on the USA Weightlifting website. Registering for five or six competitions per year will better guide a training schedule, and will help maintain motivation, focus, and continued progress.

AGE CATEGORIES

Weightlifting is a sport for all ages. One of the best things about weightlifting is that a competitor can compete against other athletes who are both the same weight and similar age.

Below is a table of the age categories for weightlifting, regardless of gender.

Youth	Up to 17 years of age
Junior	15 to 20 years of age
Senior	15 and up
Masters	35 and up*

*There are numerous age categories at the master's level. The first is from 35 to 39 years old. The second is from 40 to 44. The categories advance like that all the way up to the final age group of 80 years old and above. Each age category abides by the standard weight classes within the sport.

WEIGHT CATEGORIES

On July 5, 2018, the International Weightlifting Federation's (IWF) executive board voted on new bodyweight categories for the sport. These new categories are listed next, but throughout the majority of this text and in the coming chapters, you'll see the older categories. That's because lifters such as Donny Shankle, Caleb Ward, and Jon North all competed in those now-outdated weight classes.

To avoid confusion for future competition, I'll only list the new categories in this chapter, and we'll refer to the older classes as they occur in the story of my coaching and my athletes' careers.

At the time of printing this text, there are currently 10 weight categories for junior, senior, and masters women and men that are used for national or IWF competitions, and seven that are contested for the Olympics. The categories will differ slightly for youth-level competitions. The sport is constantly changing and it's possible these weight classes will change on a future date.

JUNIOR, SENIOR, AND MASTERS WEIGHT CLASSES

Men		Women	
IWF Categories	Olympic	IWF Categories	Olympic
55 kg	61 kg	45 kg	49 kg
61 kg	67 kg	49 kg	55 kg
67 kg	73 kg	55 kg	59 kg
73 kg	81 kg	59 kg	64 kg
81 kg	96 kg	64 kg	76 kg
89 kg	109 kg	71 kg	87 kg
96 kg	109+ kg	76 kg	87+ kg
102 kg		81 kg	
109 kg		87 kg	
109+ kg		87+ kg	

YOUTH WEIGHT CLASSES

Men	Women
49 kg	40 kg
55 kg	45 kg
61 kg	49 kg
67 kg	55 kg
73 kg	59 kg
81 kg	64 kg
89 kg	71 kg
96 kg	76 kg
102 kg	81 kg
102+ kg	81+ kg

YOUTH (14–15) WEIGHT CLASSES

Boys	Girls
39 kg	36 kg
44 kg	40 kg
49 kg	45 kg
55 kg	49 kg
61 kg	55 kg
67 kg	59 kg
73 kg	64 kg
81 kg	71 kg
89 kg	76 kg
89+ kg	76+ kg

YOUTH (13 AND UNDER) WEIGHT CLASSES	
Boys	**Girls**
32 kg	30 kg
36 kg	33 kg
39 kg	36 kg
44 kg	40 kg
49 kg	45 kg
55 kg	49 kg
61 kg	55 kg
67 kg	59 kg
73 kg	64 kg
73+ kg	64+ kg

PREPARING FOR A COMPETITION

Local competitions tend to be easier to prepare for, typically being within driving distance of an athlete's home or training location. Most of the time, local competitions are more relaxed than national or international events. Since many athletes will hopefully have the opportunity to compete nationally, the content in this section will explain how to prepare for a national competition that requires travel. Much of this information will also apply to beginners lifting at a local competition.

A national competition requires online preregistration by a designated deadline. National competitions also require minimum qualifying totals to be met and confirmed at a USA Weightlifting-sanctioned competition. You can find current qualifying totals on the USAW website.

Once an athlete is registered for a competition and travel plans have been finalized, the lifter must be prepared to pack appropriately. Below is a list of must-haves for athletes and coaches.

FOR THE LIFTER

Scales

With an influx of competitors at national meets, it might not always be possible to access a scale. It's beneficial to bring a personal scale that can be kept nearby. The first step at a weightlifting meet is to weigh in prior to the session. You should be prepared with a scale and check your weight often if it's borderline for a weight class. Once you know what you weigh, you can adapt your plans accordingly—you'll

cut weight, use a sauna, sleep, or for the lucky ones, enjoy breakfast.

When you compete in a national competition, you're required to lift in the weight category you qualified in unless you've met the qualifying numbers for another weight class. Regardless, this must be declared at the verification meeting before the competition begins.

Photo 11.2—James Tatum and Travis Cooper

Sauna Suit

Every meet has unique conditions for cutting weight. You often won't know the status of a local sauna until you arrive. If you have to cut down to a weight class, it's best to be prepared, and expect the unexpected. Having a sauna suit is a good back-up plan if the venue doesn't have a sauna on site or if it's malfunctioning.

Pedialyte

After weigh-ins, lifters should replenish with electrolytes, especially if they had to dehydrate to make weight. Pedialyte is the best way to do this quickly.

Driver's License or Passport

At weigh-ins, lifters will need an official ID for identification. Athletes usually have one of these on hand since most people will be flying or driving long distances. But you'd be surprised how many people forget these back in the hotel room! You won't be allowed to weigh in without proper identification, so this should be one of the most important things to pack and keep on you on lift day.

USAW Membership Card

At weigh-ins, you'll need your USAW membership card. Bring a hard copy for weigh-ins since technology has a tendency to fail when you need it most.

Pack Competition Gear in Your Carry-On Bag

Pack your singlet, shoes, knee sleeves, wrist wraps, belt, tape, and of course, that important identification in your carry-on bag. I can't tell you how many times I've seen lifters pack their lifting shoes and knee sleeves in their checked baggage…and the bags end up five states away. Many things can be replaced easily, but a lifter will have a hard time competing in a new pair of lifting shoes, or lifting without knee sleeves after being used to training with them.

FOR THE COACH

Copies of Your Lifters' IDs

Lifters all need IDs at weigh-ins. It pays to have a copy of their licenses, passports, and USAW membership cards, just in case.

Medications

You should pack all medications the team might need on the trip. Since you never know what will be readily available at the venue, items such as ice packs, band aids, Advil, athletic tape, and any special medications athletes need should be kept in a safe place. This includes those sent by parents for youth lifters.

Credit Cards and Cash

Most places take credit cards, but places that only accept cash still exist. Keep some cash separately in case your credit cards are misplaced or stolen.

Small Notebook and a Pen

A notebook can help a coach keep track of counting attempts, notes, or contact information you might collect over the weekend.

Photo 11.3—Coaching in China

Copy of the Schedule and Start List

The schedule and start list are subject to change up to the technical and verification meetings, but going in, it helps to have a full schedule planned and a start list showing which lifters are in each session.

Copies of All Lifters' Insurance Information

As one of the least-thought-of essentials, be prepared in case any of your lifters get extremely sick or injured during the competition. National-level competitions see athletes lifting at a high level and pushing themselves to the limits of their capabilities. Accidents are rare, but certainly can happen. Be prepared!

Pack Essentials in Your Carry-On

Pack all of those important documents in your carry-on baggage, as well as coaching clothes, shoes, and any of your athletes' items you'll be responsible for transporting.

Team Competition Kit

Packing a team competition kit may come in handy when least expected. Be sure to include tape, shoelaces, elastic, scissors, ammonia, an extra singlet, socks, and bandages.

AFTER ARRIVAL AT THE COMPETITION

Check In

When athletes and coaches arrive at a national competition, they'll first check in to receive their credentials. The credentials will provide access to watch the competition, use the training hall, and entry to the warm-up room during the competition.

Technical Meeting

The technical meeting takes place the night before a national competition begins. Technical details such as recent rule changes and any final schedule changes are discussed in this meeting.

The predetermined lifting date for the athletes can't change. However, the time of their session is subject to change until the technical meeting is held and the schedule is finalized.

Verification Meeting

The verification meeting begins right after the technical meeting, and is an important meeting for coaches to attend to finalize their rosters for team points, as well as make sure their individual lifters are in the right weight category with the correct entry totals.

An entry total represents a lifter's best performance and is an important part of the placement in the competition as it allows officials to group athletes with comparable abilities in the same session. This grouping helps reduce the instances of athletes "following themselves," and if done right, will yield a more exciting and competitive competition.

When registering for a competition and declaring an entry total, the number shouldn't be higher than something you've done before in competition, or in training if it's your first time at a meet. When finalizing entry totals, keep the 20-kilo rule in mind.

The 20-kilo Rule

In national and international competitions, an athlete's opening attempts must total within 20 kilos of their entry total. For instance, if the entry total for a female lifter is 150 kilos, the openers must add up to or above 130. Example openers might be (snatch/clean and jerk): 60/70 kilos, 55/75 kilos, 57/73 kilos, or any opener combinations that add up to or above 130. For a male lifter with an entry total of 275 kilos, the openers must add up to or above 255. Example openers for this lifter might be 110/145 kilos, 115/140 kilos, 120/135 kilos, or any openers that add up to or above 255.

COMPETITION DAY

AT WEIGH-INS

At least one day before the competition, familiarize yourself with the venue and know the location of the official scale. Often, lifters can check their weight on the official scale prior to the session to make sure their personal travel scales or the check scales are in alignment with the official scale. A check scale is a scale provided by those running the meet for lifters to use when the official scale is in use by competition officials. It's typically in a room or area not far from where weigh-ins are being conducted.

At the official weigh-in, lifters need to be prepared with an official ID. At a local or national competition, this can be a passport or driver's license, but at an international competition, a passport is required. The USA Weightlifting membership card is also mandatory at local or national-level competitions.

When lifters enter the weigh-in, they must be prepared with a declaration of their opening attempts in kilograms. I recommend lifters declare five kilos less than their planned opener in both lifts if they can still fulfill the 20-kilo rule with those declarations. This provides room to make adjustments if the timing of warm-ups goes off schedule.

After weigh-ins and making your declarations, double-check the weight on the card to make sure it matches the lifter's actual weight, and verify that the declarations are what was actually stated. At this point, the lifters will be asked to sign the competition cards to give approval that these numbers match their intentions.

Each weight class has an upper and lower limit that a lifter's bodyweight must fall within in order to compete. For example, a 96-kilo male lifter's bodyweight must be heavier than 89 kilos and at or below the weight class limit of 96. A lifter weighing in at 89.1 kilos qualifies for the 96-kilo weight class. A lifter weighing 96.1 kilos has failed to make weight and must lose that .1 kilo before the weigh-in time period expires.

Photo 11.4—The Cal Strength Team

WARM-UP PROGRESSION FOR THE SNATCH

Document your plan to prepare for the opening attempt on the competition platform. To warm-up properly, most lifters have a schedule of eight snatch attempts in the warm-up room prior to the opening attempt on the platform. This can vary from lifter to lifter, but the goal is for the lifter to warm up in the same manner used in training. You must plan the warm-up schedule, doing enough to be ready for an opening attempt without doing too many lifts and tiring the athlete.

The lifter should make bigger jumps at the beginning of the warm-up, and smaller jumps the closer the bar weight builds to the opener. That sequence should be continued throughout the snatch portion of the event. The lifter should never make a bigger increase than the previous one during the warm-up and competition progression. If the lifter made a 10-kilo increase for the second warm-up lift, the next lift should be increased by 10 kilos or less.

Always work *backward* when planning the warm-up progression. For example, if the opener is 100 kilos, think ahead to what the last warm-up attempt should be to be successful. Typically, there should be no more than a five-kilo jump from the last warm-up attempt and opening attempt for any lifter with less than a 150-kilo opening attempt and a three or four-kilo jump into the competition for women under the 71-kilo weight class. The most common last warm-up for a 100-kilo opener, for example, is 95.

Continue this process until the lifter completes a schedule of eight warm-up sets.

A lifter who is opening with 100 kilos might plan eight warm-up sets as follows:

100 kg—Opening Attempt
95 kg—**Last Warm-Up**
90 kg
83 kg
75 kg
65 kg
55 kg
40 kg x 2
Bar Warm-Up

Start the warm-up with the empty bar to get the blood flowing. Then, this lifter takes a 20-kilo increase to 40 kilos, a 15-kilo increase to 55, a 10-kilo increase to 65, a 10-kilo increase to 75, an 8-kilo increase to 83, a 7-kilo increase to 90, a 5-kilo increase to 95, and a 5-kilo increase into the competition opener at 100 kilos.

Plan for all situations. The plan should be adjustable, but thought out in advance. Consider different situations when a lifter's first attempt looks strong or weak. If the opening attempt is strong, the lifter would usually choose to take a generally standard jump—for example, 105 kilos after taking a strong 100-kilo opening attempt. However, if the opener was a mediocre lift, consider taking a more conservative jump to 103 kilos or 104 rather than 105.

Stay consistent with increments when you increase weights between attempts. In the earlier warm-up example, since the last attempts were five kilos apart, the competition attempts should also be no more than five kilos apart. Do the same between the second and third attempts.

If the lifter took 105 kilos for a second attempt, there's another decision to make: How did the lift look? Did the lifter miss, barely make, or solidly make the second attempt? Each situation will require quick thinking, so consider all situations in advance.

In the event the lifter made a solid 105 kilos, it would be typical to consistently increase by five kilos to 110. If the athlete barely made the lift, 107 or 108 is a more reasonably conservative choice. If the athlete took 103 or 104 kilos on the second attempt, a descending jump would be smart. It would then make sense to take 105 to 107 kilos for the third attempt.

Remember, the goal is to optimize the competition total and to *make lifts*. A missed lift, no matter how close, doesn't count toward the total, so a slightly conservative approach in the snatch is usually beneficial.

I make a table like the following for reference during the competition. This enables me to make quick decisions based on each situation.

Current Attempt	Missed Lift	Made Strong	Made Weak
100 kg	100 kg	105 kg	103 kg
103 kg	103 kg	106 kg	105 kg
105 kg	105 kg	110 kg	107 kg

If the lifter misses 100 kilos, we'll keep it on the bar for the second attempt. If the athlete makes the lift and it was strong, we bump up to 105, but if it looked weak, we take a smaller increase to 103 kilos for the second attempt.

Once you finalize the plan for the warm-up attempts, fill out the table. In competition, you'll determine how many attempts "out" you are from the first or next attempt on the competition platform.

Determining the "count" will be explained later in this chapter.

Generally, a lifter will take one warm-up lift for every three attempts other athletes take on the platform. This allows a warm-up attempt approximately every two-and-a-half to three-and-a-half minutes. This is a good tempo to keep warm, but also not too fast to tire anyone out.

Continuing with our example of a lifter opening with 100 kilos, the athlete's full competition warm-up schedule might look like this:

100 kg—**Opening Attempt**
95 kg—**Last Warm-Up—3 Lifts Out**
90 kg—**6 Lifts Out**
83 kg—**9 Lifts Out**
75 kg—**12 Lifts Out**
65 kg—**15 Lifts Out**
55 kg—**18 Lifts Out**
40 kg x 2 kg—**21 Lifts Out**
Bar Warm-Up—**24 Lifts Out**

As you can see, approximately 24 attempts or 24 minutes before the opening attempt in the snatch, the lifter will start with a bar warm-up. Approximately every three minutes from that point, the lifter will take the next warm-up on the schedule. This will provide a steady flow of warm-ups. If the count gets off track at any time, the lifter can repeat a warm-up, skip a warm-up, or backtrack to a specific point as necessary.

Coaches always aim to perfect the count, but in actuality, a lot of jockeying occurs among other coaches and athletes that keeps warm-up situations from being ideal. Plan in advance for adjustments so you can adapt to any situation.

WARM-UP PROGRESSION FOR THE CLEAN AND JERK

The snatch and the clean and jerk progression for warm-ups and attempts is similar, but with a few notable differences.

Once warm-ups start for the clean and jerk, the lifter will have already completed the entire snatch portion of the event. This means the athlete's body should be warmed up for clean and jerks.

Given that the clean and jerk is a more taxing movement at heavier weights, the aim should be for six warm-up sets. A bigger jump into the competition is common.

For a male lifter opening at 120 kilos, the following schedule of warm-ups would be appropriate:

120 kg—**Opening Attempt**
113 kg—**Last Warm-Up**
105 kg
95 kg
85 kg
75 kg
50 kg

The schedule should allow for more rest in the clean and jerk between attempts, especially toward the end of the warm-up. The complete schedule might look something like this:

120 kg—**Opening Attempt**
113 kg—**Last Warm-Up—3/4 Lifts Out**
105 kg—**6/8 Lifts Out**
95 kg—**9/11 Lifts Out**
85 kg—**12/14 Lifts Out**
75 kg—**15/17 Lifts Out**
50 kg—**18/20 Lifts Out**

Eighteen to 20 minutes before the planned opening attempt, the lifter should be taking the first warm-up lift.

From there, the athlete will continue to take warm-up attempts at a reasonable pace every three or four minutes to have a steady flow to keep warm, but not tired. Follow the same concept of making larger jumps at the beginning of the warm-up attempts,

and smaller jumps toward the end of the progression and into the competition.

Once the athlete has made a total, there might be situations when considering attempts for placement. In this case, it might be advantageous to take a bigger jump than the previous one if there's potential to medal, make a team, or win the overall competition.

Photo 11.5—James Tatum lifting in the training hall in China

COMPETITION COACHING

Before arriving at the competition, plan your warm-up schedules and theoretical scenarios. By not having to focus on those things, the coach is free to focus the timing of those warm-ups to make sure they happen properly.

CURRENT COUNT

As soon as the competition cards or scoreboard are available to athletes and coaches, the current count will be established. The "current count" shows how many attempts out the lifter is from the first declared attempt.

For example, if the first athlete in the lifting order is opening with a 90-kg snatch, and your athlete is the second lifter opening with 120 kilos, it's safe to assume the first lifter will make all three attempts before you take the first. The current count would be three lifts or attempts.

The math becomes more complicated the deeper into the lifting order. Luckily, there are strategies you can employ to help figure out the current count.

FOR MEN

Men can assume two- to five-kilo increases between lifts. Typically, between the first and second attempt, you can expect five kilos, and between the second and third attempt, you can expect two- to five-kilo increases.

However, if another athlete is set to open 10 kilos or more below your athlete's declared opener, it's safe to assume the lifter will attempt all three lifts before yours first takes the platform. If the athlete declares between six to 10 kilos lower than your declared opener, you can assume there will be two attempts before your lifter's opener. If the athlete declares an opener that's five kilos or less from your declared opener, there will probably be one lift before your athlete's opening attempt.

For example, if there are three athletes opening more than 10 kilos below your athlete, two opening between six to 10 kilos below, and three opening five kilos or less below, 16 lifts out would be a good starting schedule, assuming all lifts are made.

$$(3x3) + (2x2) + (3x1) = 16 \text{ total lifts}$$

More than 10 kilos below	3 attempts added to the current count
6–10 kilos below	2 attempts added to the current count
Less than or equal to 5 kilos below	1 attempt added to the current count
Opening higher	0 attempts added to the current count

FOR WOMEN

Women can assume two- to five-kilo increases between lifts. Typically, between the first and second attempt, you can expect three or four kilos, and between the second and third attempts, probably two- or three-kilo increases.

If another athlete is set to open more than seven kilos below your athlete's declared opener, it's safe to assume she will take all three attempts before your lifter takes the platform for the first time. If another athlete declares between four to six kilos lower than your declared opener, she'll probably attempt two lifts before yours.

If the athlete declares an opener three kilos or less from your athlete's declared opener, you can assume

there will probably be one lift before your lifter's opening attempt.

More than 7 kilos below	3 attempts added to the current count
4–6 kilos below	2 attempts added to the current count
Less than or equal to 3 kilos below	1 attempt added to the current count
Opening higher	0 attempts added to the current count

For example, if there are five athletes opening more than seven kilos below your athlete, two opening between four and six kilos below, and two opening three kilos or less below, planning 21 lifts out is a good starting schedule, assuming all lifts are made.

$$(5x3) + (2x2) + (2x1) = 21 \text{ total lifts}$$

This number is dynamic because each lifter has two change declarations after the declared attempt, and misses do occur. Change declarations are opportunities to update the weight they'll be attempting higher or even lower as long as it's not below the weight already loaded on the competition barbell.

As a generalized guide, a male lifter is 16 attempts out once the competition starts, but warm-ups are set to start at 24 attempts out. This is often the case when there aren't as many attempts before the lifter is planned on the schedule and you have to simulate additional attempts to have the correct warm-up timing.

The introduction clock—which monitors the time period 10 minutes before the competition officially starts—and time before the introduction clock must be used to properly time your warm-ups.

Each attempt is approximately one minute, meaning you would start the warm-ups with eight minutes left on the introduction clock. It looks like this:

16 actual attempts plus 8 minutes = 24 out

The second warm-up will be at five minutes; the third lift will be at two, and the fourth lift will be right after the first lift drops on the platform.

From there, the competition will have begun, and you must reevaluate the current count after every couple of lifts to make sure you're still on time with the warm-ups.

Throughout the competition, there will be misses and changes that alter the expected count. A coach must evaluate the probabilities of misses and changes to make educated guesses at the count. Only experience will give you the ability to accurately guess the count. New coaches will do best to shadow an experienced coach to understand counting in competition for proper warm-up flow.

The following competition rules are complicated, but will make more sense once you've been through the process. You'll learn a lot during your first competition, and that's one reason I want you to compete early in your lifting career.

THE AUTOMATIC INCREASE

After a successful attempt in a competition, an automatic one-kilo increase is applied. Aside from the automatic increase, there's a declaration, and two changes are allowed.

A declaration doesn't have to be announced immediately, but *must* be made, and the competition card *must* be signed by 1:30 on a two-minute clock if a lifter is to follow him- or herself, or by the :30 mark on a one-minute clock.

All changes must be made by the 30-second mark.

THE DECLARATION

Make the declaration meaningful. Many coaches just declare the automatic increase so they can attain their two changes, but most of the time, this isn't a meaningful declaration.

Sometimes it's best to wait to make the declaration. You might want to wait to make a declaration to attempt to "freeze" a lifter who's ahead on the warm-ups or the potential to force a one-minute clock on a lifter who missed the last attempt.

THE FORCED ONE-MINUTE CLOCK

Typically, if a lifter doesn't have another lifter following, there will be two minutes between lifts. This gives the lifter more time between attempts to be properly rested for the next lift.

There's a way to keep the lifter from receiving the two-minute clock after a missed lift in a close competition. In the clean and jerk, if you don't get a two-minute clock after a miss, it's extremely taxing to attempt a max after less than a minute rest. Still, a good coach will be able to help the lifter by making meaningful declarations and keeping competitors from having a two-minute clock after a miss.

If a lifter misses an attempt but another person is called to make the same attempt, that person might choose to declare a higher attempt, which will again bring up the person who just missed the lift. Now, instead of having two minutes, the person who missed only has a one-minute clock.

This tactic is much more effective in the clean and jerk, but it certainly can catch a lifter off guard in the snatch event as well.

Photo 11.6—With Ethan Harak

MAXIMIZE REST WITH A TWO-MINUTE CLOCK

In the situation where lifters follow themselves—they miss a lift or there's no one else taking an attempt between the declaration—there will be a two-minute clock. This means there's an automatic increase, a declaration, and two changes a coach may use. Immediately declaring the next attempt is the biggest mistake coaches make at this point.

The automatic increases act as another change if used properly.

Allow the loaders to put the automatic increase on the bar, and let the clock run a few seconds before making a declaration.

After the declaration, let the clock run a few seconds, and then make the first change.

Let the clock run a few more seconds, and then make the second change.

Be sure the declaration is made by the 1:30 mark, and both changes are made by the :30 mark.

If possible, make all changes by the 1:00 mark, so you have plenty of time to go through the pre-lift routine. Changes take about the same amount of time regardless of time between changes, so let the clock run a few seconds with the loaders off the platform.

The idea is to utilize every possible second to rest.

EXAMPLE WARM-UP PROGRESSIONS

Earlier in the chapter, I discussed general guidelines for warm-up progressions. In real life, warm-up progressions are individualized with some similarities.

The following pages cover real warm-up progressions from three National Champion weightlifters, Travis Cooper, James Tatum, and Jared Fleming.

The weight classes in the sport have changed since these events. Those represented here were the weight classes in which these lifters competed when I coached them.

TRAVIS COOPER (77 KILOS)

Travis typically opened between 140 and 145 kilos on the snatch, and 180 and 185 kilos on the clean and jerk.

This is actual warm-up progressions I used for Travis in national and international competitions.

Snatch Warm-Up Progressions for 140 kg, 142 kg, 145 kg			
Opening Weight	140 kg	142 kg	145 kg
3 Lifts Out	135 kg	137 kg	140 kg
6 Lifts Out	130 kg	130 kg	130 kg
9 Lifts Out	120 kg	120 kg	120 kg
12 Lifts Out	110 kg	110 kg	110 kg
15 Lifts Out	90 kg	90 kg	90 kg
18 Lifts Out	70 kg	70 kg	70 kg
21 Lifts Out	50 kg x 2	50 kg x 2	50 kg x 2
24 Lifts Out	Bar Warm-Up	Bar Warm-Up	Bar Warm-Up

*As you can see, only the last warm-up and opening attempts typically change.

Clean and Jerk Warm-Up Progressions for 180 kg	
Opening Weight	180 kg
4 Lifts Out	170 kg
8 Lifts Out	150 kg
12 Lifts Out	130 kg
15 Lifts Out	100 kg
18 Lifts Out	70 kg
21 Lifts Out	Bar Warm-Up

JAMES TATUM (85 KILOS)

James usually opened between 145 and 150 kilos on the snatch, and 170 and 180 kilos on the clean and jerk.

Snatch Warm-Up Progressions for 145 kg, 150 kg		
Opening Weight	145 kg	150 kg
3 Lifts Out	140 kg	145 kg
6 Lifts Out	135 kg	140 kg
9 Lifts Out	130 kg	130 kg
12 Lifts Out	120 kg	120 kg
15 Lifts Out	100 kg	100 kg
18 Lifts Out	80 kg	80 kg
21 Lifts Out	60 kg x 2	60 kg x 2
24 Lifts Out	40 kg x 2	40 kg x 2
27 Lifts Out	Bar Warm-Up	Bar Warm-Up

Clean and Jerk Warm-Up Progressions for 170 kg, 180 kg		
Opening Weight	170 kg	180 kg
3 Lifts Out	165 kg	173 kg
6 Lifts Out	155 kg	165 kg
9 Lifts Out	140 kg	150 kg
12 Lifts Out	120 kg	130 kg
15 Lifts Out	100 kg	100 kg
18 Lifts Out	70 kg	90 kg
21 Lifts Out	Bar Warm-Up	70 kg
24 Lifts Out	-	Bar Warm-Up

JARED FLEMING (94 KILOS)

Photo 11.7—Jared Fleming snatch pull

Jared usually opened between 160 and 163 kilos on the snatch, and 185 and 193 kilos on the clean and jerk.

Snatch Warm-Up Progressions for 160 kg, 163 kg		
Opening Weight	**160 kg**	**163 kg**
3 Lifts Out	150 kg	155 kg
6 Lifts Out	140 kg	145 kg
9 Lifts Out	130 kg	135 kg
12 Lifts Out	120 kg	125 kg
15 Lifts Out	100 kg	105 kg
18 Lifts Out	80 kg	80 kg
21 Lifts Out	50 kg x 2	50 kg x 2
24 Lifts Out	Bar Warm-Up	Bar Warm-Up

Clean and Jerk Warm-Up Progressions for 185 kg, 193 kg		
Opening Weight	185 kg	193 kg
3 Lifts Out	175 kg	183 kg
6 Lifts Out	155 kg	173 kg
9 Lifts Out	140 kg	153 kg
12 Lifts Out	120 kg	130 kg
15 Lifts Out	100 kg	100 kg
18 Lifts Out	70 kg x 2	70 kg x 2
21 Lifts Out	Bar Warm-Up	Bar Warm-Up

CLOSING THOUGHTS

Competing in the sport is essential for weightlifters of all skill levels and age groups. Not only does it help weightlifting grow in our country, but putting training to the test is invaluable for the development of a lifter.

There's no other scenario where your lifts will be judged under such scrutiny or where you'll be required to perform under pressure. We can simulate the environment all we want in training, but nothing can top the real deal…and all the steps leading up to that point when your name is called and you step onto the competition platform.

Different considerations need to be taken depending on the level of the lifter.

Fun is the name of the game for youth lifters. It should have already been the goal of a coach to make the gym a place a youth lifter looks forward to going to, but a meet—that should be the ultimate party on the calendar.

After the first meet is in the books, the prospects of seeing new friends and making a new PR should be enough motivation to plan another one.

Just as in training, set your young athlete up for success and go for one-kilo PRs when you can. Celebrate like you just won the lottery after making the lift, and don't forget to tell the lifter "good job" after good efforts.

Teen and junior lifters are a similar story. Going to a meet should be an enjoyable experience and the pressure they feel to perform shouldn't come from their coach. Meet with your lifters before the event to explain the expectations of the day. Don't hide difficult aspects of the meet, such as bombing out. Teens want to be taken seriously and treated like the young adults they are, so don't hide things from them. Instead, teach them about the highs and lows of the sport, how to react to them, and that you will always be proud of their efforts.

With new lifters, set a goal of making all the lifts and starting with opening weights you're confident of. Explain the jumps from attempt to attempt and ask for their input. If an athlete has already done multiple meets and the goal is to win or qualify for another meet, have that conversation.

The more communication between athlete and coach covering the expectations, the better.

Many adult beginners struggle with the prospect of pulling on a singlet and doing their first weightlifting meet. Countless times, I've heard, "I'll do a meet when I'm lifting enough weight." I'm always honest and tell them they will never be lifting "enough weight" and instead need to participate in the sport to begin laying the foundation of a competitive career.

People doing a first meet don't need to change much leading up to a competition. These athletes don't need to do much tapering or peaking, and it would be harmful to their progress to interrupt training to even try.

The goal of a first meet should be to go six for six, making all of their lifts. That will be a much better experience than bombing out by going too heavy on the opener.

The story changes slightly for intermediate lifters. These lifters have most likely been active in the local meet scene. They've pushed to increase their totals, bombed out here and there, and are looking to win medals and qualify for bigger meets. These lifters are fun to coach at meets because they're mentally ready to take a risk in competition and engage in battles against other lifters. The goal with intermediates is to consistently push the total and do what needs to be done to continue to rise up the rankings.

Advanced lifters fit this model too, but there's much more on the line. In most cases, weightlifting is the full-time job of the advanced weightlifter. They're already at the top of the sport in their country and have the ability to earn money by competition placements and sponsorships.

Different meets will have different goals. Local meets are more than likely just practice and will be trained through. At national-level competitions, the top spot of the podium is the goal.

International competitions are a whole different story. Depending on the rest of the field, you and your athlete could be vying for a podium spot or trying to help Team USA earn points. Lifters and coaches at this level need to have the highest levels of communication and make smart decisions with the coming years in mind.

Competing in a weightlifting meet is a prerequisite to calling yourself a weightlifter. So, do yourself a favor and sign up for one.

For the beginner, it can be nerve-racking, but that's okay. Even world champions get nervous at weight-lifting meets. It comes down to how you use those nerves to drive your performance.

Photo 11.8—Champions

CHAPTER 12
MAKING WEIGHT

Weightlifting is a weight-class sport. As the weight classes increase, so do the weights required to win. All athletes have a class where their bodies are most efficient, mostly determined by height. Obviously, an athlete who is 6′ 0″ tall will usually be in a higher weight class than one who is 5′ 2″. Regardless of height, we want the most *usable* weight possible—the most muscle mass. It's always better to be leaner than fatter.

In addition to being as lean as possible, most lifters find the body is the most efficient in a certain weight class. This is dependent upon individual leverages and the idiosyncrasies of each body. Athletes often cut a little weight to get into the next lower weight class because typically, the lower the weight class, the lower the total needed to win.

However, being as light as possible in a lower weight class isn't always advantageous. Szymon Kolecki is over 6′ 0″ tall and was a 94-kilo world champion and world record holder. He performed quite well in that weight class.

Donny Shankle, while shorter than Kolecki, was able to make multiple world teams as a 105-kilo lifter, but wasn't able to perform well weighing 94 kilos. Donny reduced weight to 94 or near 94 kilos a couple of times in his career. We found the weight reduction cost him so much strength, it made him significantly less competitive.

Travis Cooper made his best lifts at 85 kilos, but when he reduced to 77, he was able to retain enough strength that it made him more competitive in the lower class.

James Tatum, while being tall, was very competitive as a 77, winning several national championships and making World and Pan Am teams. After moving up to the 85-kilo weight class, he lifted more, but the extra bodyweight never increased his total enough to make him as competitive. I believe James could have eventually been a better 85 than a 77, but it would

have been a multi-year process to build the muscle mass and strength to achieve the same efficiency at 85 as he had as a 77.

There are guidelines, but the process of finding the right weight class for each lifter is individual. I've never met an athlete who enjoys making weight, but unless you compete in the super heavyweight class, this process will be unavoidable throughout your weightlifting career. However, many athletes make the process much harder and more painful than it needs to be. This chapter will present a simple and effective way to make weight with a minimal performance loss.

When I coached him, Travis Cooper typically competed in what was then the 77-kilo class. Like most athletes in that class, Travis usually trained at a weight above 77 kilos. Most athletes in that class weigh between 78 and 81 during training, then employ a weight cut to step on the scale at the weigh-in two hours before the competition session weighing at or below the required 77 kilos.

Some lifters prefer to use a long, slow cut, dropping the weight gradually over a period of several weeks, and others use a quick cut losing several kilos immediately before the weigh-in. I use a combination of both methods, which I found leads to the easiest and best results.

To do that, you'll use a long, slow cut to gradually reduce to three to five percent over your weight class a week prior to competition. Then, through a process of hyperhydration, which I'll explain shortly, and perhaps using a sauna if needed, you'll arrive at the competition weight immediately prior to weigh-in. This will result in the least possible loss of strength.

PRACTICE CUTTING WEIGHT FIRST

The first point to emphasize is to not stress about this process. Many lifters experience so much stress and anxiety when making weight that the resulting performance loss is more a function of psychological factors than it is about the actual loss of bodyweight. *Relax,* try not to stress out. Practice the weight cut so you know what to expect, and that will help you relax and make the whole process less stressful.

Try to do a trial weight cut at least once before you actually do it for a competition. Plan your trial run at least five weeks prior to the competition; go through the whole process, including the hyperhydration and at least the initial 12 to 24 hours of carbohydrate deprivation, which we'll discuss shortly.

Don't actually go through the full process by sitting in the sauna and then hitting your weight class because that's stressful to your body, and will probably interfere with your training and recovery. But if you're planning for a morning weigh-in, do the trial run, including everything you'd do prior to the weigh-in except getting in the sauna.

For the trial run, sit down for breakfast instead of getting in the sauna on the morning of the competition. This will tell you how much weight you should lose in the carb depletion and hyperhydration process. This will lead to less stress as the competition nears because you'll know the method works.

THE FOUR-STEP PROCESS

The method I advocate for involves four major steps:

- A mild amount of carbohydrate depletion
- Hyperhydration
- Low-intensity walking
- Sauna sessions

Using this process, you should be able to cut two to three percent of bodyweight quite easily in a short time without much strength loss, if any. In fact, there's published data in exercise physiology journals showing that as much as a five-percent drop in bodyweight is possible without any strength or performance loss. However, in my experience, two or three percent is a more realistic cutting goal, especially if you're relatively inexperienced in making weight for a competition.

For the purposes of this chapter, let's assume the weigh-in for the upcoming meet is 8:00 a.m. on a Saturday morning.

While we know the target bodyweight needed at the weigh-in, it helps to set benchmarks along the way to ensure the rate of weight loss is on track. For this to work, you need an accurate scale you can frequently use in the days leading up to the meet. For example, five days out from competition (Monday in our example), you should be three to five percent over the target bodyweight, which for a 77-kilo lifter represents 2.3 to 3.9 kilos.

At 24 hours prior to weigh-in, you should be only two percent over…for a 77-kilo lifter this would be 1.5 kilos. The night before—about 12 hours out—you should ideally be only one-and-a-half percent over, and by morning should be one percent or closer to the target weight.

That last half to one percent of bodyweight can easily be shed in water weight by spending 30 to 60 minutes in a sauna before weighing in. Time in the sauna should be broken into short 10-minute intervals. Staying in the sauna for too long can be uncomfortable for some people, and longer periods of time spent in the sauna can lead to dehydration. For optimal results, spend 10 minutes in, then 10 minutes out, and repeat.

STEP ONE—CARBOHYDRATE DEPLETION

In the weeks leading up to the meet, you should be eating a consistent and healthy diet at a slight caloric deficit, which should make the weight-cutting process easier as you get closer to the meet. Your body will already be closer to the target weight, and the last few kilograms will come off much easier than if you wait until a week before the meet to begin cutting calories.

As far as specific dietary recommendations, there are countless ways to achieve a healthy caloric deficit that depend on a variety of individually determined characteristics, such as age, gender, food preferences, and lifestyle. I'll give specific recommendations for only the final few days of the weight cut when the content of what you eat and drink is most critical. We'll discuss health and balanced nutrition in Chapter 13.

On the third day before the weigh-in (Wednesday in our example), eliminate all processed foods. From this day until the meet, you'll live on chicken breasts, steamed or raw vegetables, pasta without sauce, boiled eggs, and bread.

This diet is admittedly boring and excruciatingly bland, but it's a tested method to make weight without hassle or stress. Experienced lifters typically prepare all of this food at once and refrigerate it in microwave-safe containers for the final days before the weigh-in. This process will go a long way toward eliminating temptations to cheat because the food is already prepared and easy to reheat.

In general, keep your food intake calorically consistent until the second day prior to weigh-in, in this case Thursday. Even though you've been eating a bland diet for only a day or so, you should have already lost a little weight from Wednesday to Thursday simply because you're consuming less sodium, which tends to cause water retention. From about Thursday at noon—36 hours out from the weigh-in—stop eating carbohydrates altogether, but keep your caloric intake steady by substituting additional chicken breasts and boiled eggs.

With about 24 hours until weigh-in, you should be about two percent over your target bodyweight. If you're more than two percent over the target, you can fast during the last 24 hours, but only do this as a last resort. You need fuel to perform during the meet, so cutting out all food is not ideal.

These guidelines should help you lose that last two percent without signifcant issues in the hours leading up to the weigh-in.

STEP TWO—THE HYPERHYDRATION PROCESS

Although diet is important for a proper weight cut, water consumption will make or break your weigh-in. On the fifth and fourth day before weigh-in (Monday and Tuesday in our example), you should begin the process of hyperhydration, which simply means consuming more water than your norm.

Now, this may seem a little counterintuitive because all that excess liquid will cause a short-term increase in water weight. However, soon after beginning this process, the body will work overtime to remove this excess water by increasing the frequency and volume of urination.

As your body becomes accustomed to these more frequent and voluminous urination episodes, you'll cut back on the water intake, taking advantage of the lag time between hydration and urination.

In the final days before the competition, your body will be expelling more fluid than you're consuming, resulting in a net decrease in bodyweight.

On Monday and Tuesday, you'll drink two gallons of water each day. This will be much more than you normally drink, and you'll begin urinating more frequently than usual.

On the third day before the competition (Wednesday), switch to distilled water, but still consume two gallons throughout the day. Depending on its source, tap and bottled water may contain a small amount of sodium, which causes the body to retain water. Distilled water will ensure that the process of hyperhydration will be as effective as possible, and no excess water weight will be retained.

Two days out (Thursday), cut your water intake to one gallon of distilled water. This would be the period between 48 and 24 hours before weigh-in. During the 24 hours prior to the weigh-in, don't drink any other fluids. Since your body should now be accustomed to consuming excess levels of water, your body will continue to eliminate water at a higher-than-normal rate during this last day before the meet. This may cause an uncomfortably dry mouth, which you can address by chewing gum or using dry-mouth lozenges.

STEP THREE—LOW-INTENSITY WALKING

During the final 24 hours, go on several low-intensity walks to burn muscle and liver glycogen. The human body stores two grams of water for every gram of glycogen, so burning up even a little of this stored glycogen can lead to a sizable weight loss. However, don't walk or exercise at too high an intensity. A slow walk for one to two miles at a pace that won't leave you winded is enough.

Right before bed on the night before your morning weigh-in is another good time to walk. Alternatively, if your weigh-in is in the afternoon or evening, stop drinking water the evening prior to the weigh-in, and take a walk in the morning before the weigh-in.

STEP FOUR—SAUNA SESSIONS

If the weigh-in is in the morning, get up early enough to allow for last-minute sauna sessions as needed. It's advantageous for weightlifters to be at competition bodyweight for as little time as possible because that low bodyweight represents a higher-than-normal state of stress.

If you wake up and find yourself still half a kilo over your competition weight, an hour in the sauna is more than enough time to close that gap to get to the required bodyweight.

Fifteen to 30 minutes in a sauna is enough for most people to lose that much bodyweight, but you should still allow yourself an hour prior to weigh-in just to be sure. Do your sauna sessions in 10-minute intervals.

Since there are often last-minute surprises or emergencies, make sure you're out of bed at 6:00 a.m. for an 8:00 a.m. weigh-in, and check your weight soon after waking. If you still have weight to lose, you can be in the sauna at 7:00 a.m. with plenty of time to sweat away the last few grams.

This process can be stressful if you've never done it before.

Go through a trial run before doing it for a meet.

TIMELINE TO THE WEIGH-IN

Days or Time Out from Competition	Percent Overweight	Action
5 days	3 to 5%	Start drinking two gallons of water per day
3 days	2 to 3%	Eliminate processed foods and switch to distilled water
2 days	2 to 3%	Cut to one gallon of water
36 hours	2 to 3%	Stop eating carbohydrates Go for low-intensity walks
24 hours	2%	Stop all liquid consumption
12 hours	1.5%	Sleep
2 hours	<1%	Sauna

REGAINING THE LOST WEIGHT

The only thing more important than cutting weight is how you gain the weight back after weighing in. Unless the meet is running behind, you'll typically have one to two hours after the weigh-in before your session starts. I've seen a two- to four-hour break, depending on how late the competition is running. If that happens, just thank the weightlifting gods that you have extra time to rehydrate and eat. Don't depend on that happening because as soon as you do, it will be the one meet that year that runs on time.

But even with no extra time, two hours is more than enough time to rehydrate and refuel.

Notice I wrote *rehydrate before* refuel. You'll be extremely hungry after the weigh-in, but hold off on food until you consume some fluids. For performance on the platform, being rehydrated is far more important than eating. I recommend drinking Gatorade or Pedialyte instead of water because they contain sugar and electrolytes, both of which your body will desperately need given the low-caloric intake over the previous days.

Make sure you have at least a liter of Pedialyte, Gatorade, or other drink with you in the weigh-in area so you can start rehydrating as soon as you step off the scale.

Don't wait to buy a drink and food at the nearest store. Have your food and drink with you at the weigh-in and start drinking immediately.

Most people should aim to consume one liter of fluid, but that figure can be adjusted up or down depending on body size and hydration status.

Try to wait for 20 to 30 minutes before eating anything because food may slow down the absorption of fluid, which is what you need the most.

Additionally, be smart about your food choices; you'll probably be exceptionally hungry, but avoid the temptation to stuff your face with all the unhealthy food you've been craving.

Every lifter will have a slightly different choice of pre-meet food, but a simple sandwich works well for almost everybody.

For example, a sandwich with sliced turkey breast, cheese, and some light condiments has a reasonable composition of carbohydrates, protein, and fat, and is easily digestible. While somewhat boring, a sandwich is a gastronomically safe and effective food to refuel when nervousness and stress are high.

Because you've been eating less food over the past few weeks, your stomach may not be accustomed to digesting large quantities of fat-laden foods. Stay away from the fast food joints. You're safer being conservative with your food choices than eating everything in sight. Eating an extra sandwich may not significantly impact your performance, but being nauseous from overeating will destroy your meet.

Even if you adequately rehydrated and refueled, you should still keep food and drink on hand to consume in the break between the snatch and the clean and jerk sessions.

I wish I had a dollar for every time a lifter refused to eat or drink anything after snatching, and then hit a wall during the clean and jerk. What would be even better than all those dollar bills would be seeing lifters listen, and then perform up to their capabilities.

It's understandable that you may not want to eat something right after finishing the snatches. Do it anyway! You'll thank me later.

TIMELINE FOR REFUELING AFTER THE WEIGH-IN

Time (after weigh-in and between events)	Action
0 to 30 minutes	Drink up to one liter of Gatorade or Pedialyte.
20 minutes	Eat a small snack *(sandwich)* and continue drinking.
After the last snatch	Eat another sandwich or snack. Continue to drink.

CRUSH THE CLEAN AND JERK AND PR YOUR TOTAL!

CLOSING THOUGHTS

There will come a time in your lifting career when cutting weight before a big competition is necessary. Here are some important considerations for future weight cuts:

o   You shouldn't cut weight before your first weightlifting meet. There will already be stress during the day and there's no need to have a weight-class goal add even more. Register for the class your bodyweight will comfortably place you in and focus on making your lifts.

o   Cutting weight is a skill that needs to be practiced. The worst possible time to practice is when you have a meet on next week's calendar. If cutting is something you need to do to be competitive, practice making weight during training at least five weeks before your competition.

o   Put just as much emphasis on refueling as you did cutting. You're not out of the woods once you make weight; you still have to perform well and that's where refueling comes into play. Practice this aspect of the cut as well in your training so you know what food items help you perform your best.

One of the best ways to make sure your bodyweight is not an issue for competition is developing skills in the kitchen. In the next chapter, we'll discuss what weightlifters need to do to be successful in that often-daunting room of your house.

CHAPTER 13
THE WEIGHTLIFTER'S KITCHEN

This is a book about weightlifting, and I'm not going to turn it into a diet manual. Having said that, I know what has worked for the people I've coached over the years, and I want to pass that on to you.

Growing up outside the city limits of McPherson, Kansas, we had enough land to raise animals like chickens, goats, and sometimes cows or pigs. Our diet, when looking back, was pretty unusual for today. My family ate wild game, like rabbits and squirrels, and always butchered several deer each year. We also milked our own cows and goats. Much of our meat was venison or other wild game, and most of our dairy was farm raised. We had a large garden with an assortment of vegetables such as cabbage, carrots, peppers, and tomatoes my mother canned for the winter. Between butchering several deer, milking our own animals, and the vegetable garden, we were much more self-sufficient than is the norm today.

We ate home-cooked meals—and rarely fast foods. My mother believed it was her job to prepare home-cooked meals instead of relying on what sounded good on a restaurant's menu. This practice of eating at home is vastly different from the way Americans live today, often eating fast food one or two times daily. I didn't know many families during my childhood who would have been able to afford spending so much money eating out.

I appreciate and have adopted a diet I'd call "paleo-ish." I say "ish" because I still consume and see a lot of value in food items like milk, which classic versions of the diet restrict. I don't see a reason to eat 100% paleo, but that's the foundation of the diet I advocate. This diet works great for any athlete looking to be healthy and perform at a high level.

If you're healthy, you recover better, and if you recover better, you perform better…simple as that.

Unfortunately, many people—including athletes—want to fuel their bodies with crap. Fast food is crap. Everyone knows it's crap, but many still eat too much

of it, including weightlifters. It's hard to build an athletic body that performs at a high level and wins gold medals on Big Macs. In weightlifting, you can't control everything, but one thing you do have control over is what you put in your mouth.

Photo 13.1—Jared Fleming and me, showing off our premade paleo meals

As an athlete, managing your nutrition and bodyweight is 100% your responsibility. Yes, a coach can give guidance, but at the end of the day, you're the one eating the food—you need to make decisions in line with your goals.

SIMPLE GUIDELINES

It makes sense to eat in a way that gives your body actual food instead of relying on protein powders and shakes. This is why the paleo diet is such a perfect fit for athletes: It puts emphasis on eating nutrient-dense foods instead of relying on supplements.

RECOMMENDATIONS FOR MACRONUTRIENTS

Protein

I'm not a big proponent of consuming protein bars and shakes. By utilizing artificial macronutrient and micronutrient sources, you lose an important part of the nutrition you'd gain from natural foods. I'd much rather see my athletes eat more meat and fewer protein bars. At the annual Pendlay weightlifting camps, we usually have stews made with venison, which is a wonderful lean protein source. I realize many people don't have access to venison, but if you do, you should utilize it.

Carbohydrates

Carbohydrates are an important energy source, but the amount needed is dependent upon how much you can eat and still maintain your competition weight. I've coached plenty of lifters who needed lots of starchy carbohydrates like rice or potatoes to keep their weight up and still stay within a certain competition category. If you're one of those people, more power to you. If not, you'll have to limit the amount of starchy foods. Concentrate on eating non-starchy vegetables such as broccoli, spinach, kale, zucchini, cauliflower, peppers, cabbage, and squashes because they contain higher nutritional value. Use fruits sparingly to keep the natural sugar intake down.

Fat

Fat is underappreciated; strength athletes need fat in their diets. Fat sources that are nutrient dense and healthy are preferable.

In some countries, fat consumption for athletes is considered more important than protein. When speaking with Eastern European coaches, I was surprised at the importance they place on the consumption of fat and cholesterol. The first time I heard the Russian emphasis on fat consumption was from Alexander Medvedev in Moscow when he encouraged me to put more butter on my bread. The language barrier prevented a more detailed conversation, but it was easy to understand he believed adequate fat consumption was important for a weightlifter.

There's actually some science behind this idea. Cholesterol is used by the body to produce testosterone. This must be one of the reasons Medvedev frowned upon a low-fat diet.

MEAL FREQUENCY AND SUPPLEMENTS

A lifter should plan to eat three full meals per day in addition to pre- and post-workout meals strategically placed around training sessions. Ideally, the pre- and post-workout meals combined should roughly equate to the calories of one regular meal. When you split that meal in half, eat the carbohydrates pre-workout and the protein post-workout. For example, a sweet potato before training fuels activity, while a post-workout steak helps the body recover.

If you're looking for "easy" and don't have time for food prep, an apple, orange, or banana pre-workout, and chocolate milk post-workout is quick, easy, and cheap. You can purchase the most expensive post-workout protein shake, but it's not going to be much better than chocolate milk, which is a good balance of protein, carbohydrates, and fat.

To speak further on supplements: Do yourself a favor and stay away from whatever is currently advertised as the latest, greatest, muscle-building product ever discovered. These products come and go, and then return a few years later. Millions of dollars are spent on advertising to convince athletes that the last 799 new and revolutionary products were all scams, but the new product is somehow different. Be smart.

There are great options of actual foods, not prepackaged supplements for athletes looking to perform at the highest levels. There are better options in the food realm as well. You want to eat foods with a lot of bang for your buck, those that have great nutrient density. Eat sweet potatoes over white potatoes… choose spinach over lettuce for your salad.

I do recommend fish oil, purely from a cost consideration. Fish oil helps fight inflammation, but it's difficult and expensive to eat enough salmon and other fatty fish to gain that benefit. Capsulated fish oil is a cost-effective way of gaining the anti-inflammatory benefits that come with consuming large amounts of fish.

EVERY LIFTER IS DIFFERENT

Each individual athlete will have strengths and weaknesses when it comes to nutrition. Donny Shankle liked to eat, ate a lot, and ate pretty healthily. No one had to convince Donny to eat. I completely agree with his "Ya gotta eat" philosophy. There's a huge energy cost for an athlete who trains two or more times per day like he did. Foods Donny liked to eat were healthy and good for an athlete.

Jon North was the polar opposite of Donny. Jon has incredible talent with a barbell, but eating the amount of food I'd have liked him to eat—especially high amounts of protein—was difficult for him. At dinner, when Donny had a steak, Jon had pasta with Alfredo sauce. He was never concerned with food or eating, and always had trouble keeping up his bodyweight. I'm so glad he turned around this aspect of his training later in his career.

Photo 13.2—Travis Cooper approves of putting in the reps while in the kitchen

Travis Cooper is one of those unlucky people who holds onto extra bodyweight and has to work hard to cut weight before a competition. Fortunately, he's a by-the-numbers type of guy, which makes monitoring his nutrition an easy task, so the situation suits him.

In my experience, lifters who start to count calories will become overly concerned with hitting a specific daily macronutrient number, and will eventually start to rely on prepackaged foods and protein powders. I don't think itemizing everything eaten is necessary for most weightlifters, but Travis is the exception to the rule. He kept a detailed record of his food intake, and because of good planning, was still able to eat whole foods like steak, chicken, and vegetables.

James Tatum, on the other hand, has the perfect nutritional situation. He's self-regulating, and his metabolism works in such a way that he doesn't need to make a great deal of effort to cut weight. He eats in moderation when the time calls for it. For him, not having second helpings equates to making weight on competition day.

CLOSING THOUGHTS

When it comes to nutrition, chances are you have something in common with one of these lifters. It comes down to making the right decisions in line with your goals as a weightlifter. Take ownership of how you fuel your body. When you do that, you'll recover more efficiently and the work you put in during training sessions will be more effective. Find what works for you, and just as with the barbell, put in the reps every day that will lead to success.

CHAPTER 14
THE RAZOR'S EDGE

Sometimes in training, things just go your way. Everything is working. The rhythm is steady; you're working hard, you're feeling good…the weights are moving up. You're consistent. Tired, but not too tired. Sore, but it's a good sore that doesn't quite hurt. And because you're consistently making the planned weights, you get confident—maybe a bit cocky.

You are on the razor's edge.

When you're a beginner, that edge is wide—a damn four-lane highway. You can veer right or left and still stay on the road. It's easy to train a bit too much, or not near enough, and still make progress. Do the wrong exercises? No matter, you're training and will make progress. Don't sleep or eat right? Don't worry; your snatch will still go up.

When you're more toward intermediate, it's a bit different. Go out drinking one night? Your training is likely to suck tomorrow. Do too much? Progress will most likely stop, and you'll be hurting. Do the wrong exercise? Your technique will get less efficient, and your lifts will slowly become harder to make.

When you get to the elite level, you aren't walking on a balance beam; you're walking on a rope. You are really on the razor's edge. And with one little push either direction, you'll fall. If someone pushes you to one side, you'll get hurt. If someone pushes you the other way, progress will cease.

The longer you train, the thinner the edge becomes, and the sharper it gets. And eventually, it's very hard to balance and very easy to cut yourself. At the highest levels, all athletes seek to balance on that sharp edge. They know the risk, but it's where they want to be. The person who does it for the longest time is the one who will be the greatest weightlifter.

I've seen three people balance on the razor's edge in 25 years of coaching—the thin edge, the one that can cut you. Caleb Ward, Jon North, and Donny Shankle have all done it.

Caleb came back from his first semester at Northern Michigan University on a mission. He'd put almost seven years of work into the sport of weightlifting, and badly wanted the Junior American records. He quit school and came back to Texas and trained full time. Things went well.

Caleb was always consistent, but he was getting *really* consistent with weights very close to his maximums. He was training heavy, but was still showing up fresh and feeling good almost every day. His morning workouts, which were supposed to be working up to 90% weights, were feeling light and easier than normal. Things were going well, but not quite magical yet.

We made one small adjustment that brought everything together. Instead of two workouts a day—lighter in the morning, then heavy snatch, clean and jerk and squatting in the afternoon—we split up the afternoon workout to do snatching and squats. Then he rested a couple of hours and came back a third time in the evening for heavy clean and jerks and more squats.

What was it about that change that made everything come together, that really put him on the razor's edge and led to maybe the best period of training in his life? That one little change did it for him. It didn't last forever, but it was fun to watch a good athlete doing everything right and becoming great. He clean and jerked 203 kilos for a new American record a short time later.

Jon North had a run like that in the snatch not long after I moved to California. He made a major change in his snatching technique as I began to coach him. At first, it didn't seem to make much of a difference. And then we could see things start to click.

I couldn't quite see the kid hiding in there who'd be snatching over 160 kilos and cleaning over 200 kilos a year later. But something special was going on, and even with weights in the 135 to 170 range on the snatch and clean, we could see the wheels turning in his head when he started to hit a lift here or there that was way too easy for the weight on the bar.

Jon ended up going even further with the technical changes I advised for his pull, creating his own personal style. He snatched 166 and cleaned 205 using his unique style of pulling, and those lifts were over 70 and 90 percent of his best back squat. This is unreal efficiency, truly one of the most efficient lifters in the world.

It was fun watching it happen, watching him evolve as a lifter—watching ordinary become extraordinary, normal become great. The razor's edge for Jon was mental, not physical. It was him becoming more confident going under weights that were more unreal compared to his actual strength. Nurturing that confidence along, that apple cart could have easily been upset. But somehow he prevented that, and did something very special.

Donny Shankle also balanced on the edge of a very sharp razor. After nine years of training, we stumbled upon a training template that allowed him the kind of progress that isn't normal after that many years of training. Whatever it was, the training, the mental outlook, the lifestyle, the rest, the food… whatever it was, it was working.

One misstep and failure was on one side, injury on the other. Chad Vaughn gave Donny some of the best advice he ever received when he simply said, "Take it one lift at a time."

Take things one step at a time to move forward just a little more along the razor's edge.

A COMPLICATED
RELATIONSHIP WITH WEIGHTLIFTING

We've covered quite a bit of material in this book. Where do we go from here?

Coach Joe Mills said it best in one of my favorite quotes: "I can tell you everything I know about weightlifting in 15 minutes. But it will take you 15 years to understand what I'm talking about."

I couldn't agree more. Weightlifting is not a sport you can understand in just a few months, or without doing it at all.

I can explain the snatch or clean and jerk for hours. I can go over everything that happens in the pull in detail, but until you experience it yourself, you have no idea what it really means. This is a mistake often made by new coaches and lifters. Over-explaining and over-analyzing the lifts actually interferes with learning the lifts.

Donny Shankle has a rule in his club that lifters aren't allowed to ask him questions on the lifts until they've trained for a year. I think that's a good rule. It allows for the training process to take place uninterrupted. It drives adaptation through completing the snatch and clean and jerk. Most importantly, it requires a person to actually become a weightlifter instead of *thinking about* being one.

Make no mistake, weightlifting is an intellectual pursuit. You can't just show up and put in your time— of course, you have to think about what you're doing. But paradoxically, you can't think at all during the snatch or clean and jerk. Those movements happen too quickly. You have to form and rely on instincts. Constantly changing your technique because of all the social media posts you read stunts that development.

You know what's better than the internet? Training partners. Developing the ability to critique and improve your training partner's lifting is an important part of becoming a better lifter yourself.

I know this is a difficult concept. However, having people explain the lifts to you can make you think you understand something you actually don't. What you have instead is a false sense of comprehension without experience. You know what? There's a big difference between knowing the definition of heartbreak as outlined in the dictionary, and actually having your heart broken.

DO YOU HAVE WHAT IT TAKES?

I love weightlifting the way Howard Roark loved architecture. For the uninitiated, Roark is the heroic protagonist in Ayn Rand's classic, *The Fountainhead*. In the story, Roark is fiercely independent, innovative, and possesses great courage to overcome naysayers and pursue his dreams.

There's no doubt that if he were a real person, Howard would be a great weightlifter, because courage is the most important quality for a weightlifter. It takes raw courage to catch a PR snatch or to pull under a heavy clean and attack the jerk…then to put one more kilo on the bar and do it again. That's courage.

It takes a special type of person to endure the discomfort of the training process. There's no way around it: Training hurts. Effective training hurts even worse. All aspiring weightlifters will have their bravery tested by the barbell on the platform.

There will be many rough days in training and competition. In spite of that, you have to keep putting more weight on the bar. You have to keep pushing your strength levels higher and higher. If you truly consider yourself a weightlifter, there's no other choice.

While training will be difficult at times, there are no real "bad" days. The ability to perform at 95% of your maximum even on a "bad" day is more important than the ability to perform at 101% on that day you're rested up and everything is perfect.

Ninety-five percent completed when tired and grinding through the lift builds character. It helps you learn to overcome adversity. One-hundred-and-one percent when training is filled with sunshine and rainbows doesn't.

Expect weightlifting to be hard. Hard is normal. Hard makes us stronger. Hard produces champions on the platform, the sports field, and in life.

THE OTHER SIDE OF TECHNICAL MASTERY AND GAINING STRENGTH

Building a big total requires maximizing two things: strength and the ability to use strength efficiently. These two qualities are sometimes independent of one another, or build on one another, or at times interfere with one another. The relationship is complicated, but one thing is certain: No one accidentally gets stronger.

Beginners need to learn the lifts and learn how to train. They should enjoy this period of a career because after this is when they'll truly be tested by the sport. Pursuing strength and technical mastery will help them overcome the challenges they'll experience down the road.

As they develop into intermediate and eventually advanced weightlifters, the training will become more individualized. The need for pursuing maximums, to push the limits of the body, and to display courage on the platform will be necessary to drive progress.

Going to maximum is a skill. Like any skill, the only way to get good at it is through practice. Maxing out is a legitimate part of the training process. Making a new snatch or clean and jerk PR is the best possible training for making a new snatch and clean and jerk PR.

We're not weight training; we're *weightlifting*. The only thing that matters in weightlifting is lifting more today than you lifted yesterday. PRs are the lifeblood of training and programming. Everything else is just noise. Learn technique, then push the limits of that technique.

Can you get strong only lifting with picture-perfect technique? Yes, to a point. Can you break American records, make world teams, and win championships if your form never breaks down? No.

As a weightlifter, never forget the whole point of weightlifting is to lift the most weight. If you're going to err, err on the side of *going for it!*

Don't fail for lack of trying.

CLOSING THOUGHTS

Over the last 25 years, I've spent countless hours in the gym coaching athletes and testing training methods. I concluded that the process of coaching weightlifting is one of encouraging athletes to do things that will result in them learning weightlifting for themselves. Sure, a coach can give pointers and advice to make the journey easier, but the athlete is still the one who has to pick up the bar and put it overhead.

For a beginner, discovering what weightlifting is starts when picking up an empty barbell for the first time to learn how to snatch and clean and jerk. Those early, awkward reps moving the bar in the first training session are the beginning of a career-long pursuit of technical mastery.

Through much trial and error, beginners learn how to use their hips and legs to move the bar. They slowly smooth out the bar path, making each lift a little better than the one that came before.

Along with learning the lifts, they grind through many heavy squats, fight for that extra half-inch on the lockout when pressing overhead, and endure endless sets of deadlifts.

Eventually, they earn the title of "weightlifter" after lifting in their first meet.

Over time, the beginner develops into an intermediate, and for some, an advanced weightlifter. They start to understand what they individually need from weightlifting programming to continue making progress. But that still won't be enough to understand what weightlifting means in their lives. I won't give some generic definition, because it means something different from one person to the next.

It certainly takes time. It takes enough time, training, and meets to have found success, but also to have felt the sting of defeat, to miss lift after lift, but to keep trying; to want to quit the sport badly when training is hard, only to return the next day; to do all the sets and reps they don't want to do.

These are situations where a coach comes into play to help facilitate an understanding of the sport. A coach is either pushing athletes to do things they didn't think they could, or holding them back—there's no middle ground. I never considered myself married to one way of coaching during my career. There were always new methods to learn and experiments to be tested in the laboratory that's the gym. Most importantly, there's always feedback from athletes to be implemented into the training program. It really is all about them.

What is weightlifting? It's a difficult question, one I've pondered for a long time. These are my closing thoughts on the subject after all these years. I hope they help you find deeper understanding so you can continue to make progress and reach your ultimate potential as a weightlifter.

AND FINALLY...

Before we move into the Pendlay System for athletic development, let me ask you a few important questions.

Can you now make the snatch look as breath-takingly easy as Caleb Ward? Do you possess the brutal strength levels of guys like Travis Cooper and Jared Fleming? Are you as fearless as James Moser when you approach PR lifts? Do you bring emotion to your performance on the competition platform or training as Jon North does? Do you attack every lift with the ferocity of Donny Shankle?

I would guess the answer is no. And, you know what? It's completely okay that you haven't yet mastered weightlifting. It's okay if you haven't figured out the sport. No one ever really does. Even those lifters I just mentioned are still searching for unobtainable levels of technical mastery and strength.

What can you do if perfection is something no one achieves? You can keep lifting. You can keep showing up because you love the challenge and you love weightlifting. You can put another kilo on the bar because of what it does for you as a person.

I've long thought that success in weightlifting isn't measured by the size of the mark we left on the sport, but by the size of the mark the sport left on us. If you have the right circumstances in your life and you work hard enough, you can indeed win gold medals, break American records, and become a champion. I've seen it time and time again.

But if you play your cards right, the sport can make you a better person and give you direction in life as well—it certainly did that for me.

This is just the beginning for you.

SECTION D
THE PENDLAY SYSTEM
FOR ATHLETIC DEVELOPMENT

I've spent my entire career coaching and developing athletes in the sport of weightlifting. Sections A, B, and C of this book have expanded on my personal coaching methods and philosophies pertaining to training weightlifters. While I love weightlifting, I also amassed a great deal of experience over the last 25 years training athletes for sports such as football, track and field, wrestling, and many others.

Section D will house chapters outlining my thoughts and experiences training and programming for athletes in those sports. It's important to note upfront that the beginner, intermediate, and advanced

programs discussed in the coming chapters are not intended for weightlifters, although the weightlifting skills and other familiar exercises such as squats and deadlifts will certainly make an appearance. When I refer to "athletes" in these chapters, I'm talking about football players or those participating in other ball sports, sprinters, throwers, and wrestlers, to name a few—sports outside of Olympic weightlifting.

It's my hope that this information will help strength and conditioning coaches make better decisions for their athletes in the weightroom, which will in turn help them excel even more on the field of play.

Photo D1—A loaded bar often yields good results

A BRIEF SYNOPSIS OF EACH CHAPTER

CHAPTER 15
THE CLOCK IS TICKING

No time should be wasted during the early developmental years of an aspiring athlete. Young athletes need to develop a solid foundation of movement competency and conditioning that will bleed into building adult levels of strength in their mid-teens. From there, they can channel their abilities, forged through several years of practice and training, into high levels of performance that for some will lead to even bigger opportunities in the sporting world.

Unfortunately, it doesn't always happen like this and too much time passes before young athletes and their parents begin taking training into serious consideration. In this chapter, I'll discuss my experiences working in the weightroom with young athletes, my thoughts on the nuances of coaching, and the ideal time for athletes to begin training.

CHAPTER 16
THE PENDLAY TOTAL

Testing athletic performance is an important but sometimes overlooked aspect of athletic development. In weightlifting, we test maximums on the competition lifts either in training or competition. The results allow for course correction in the overall training program. This is relatively easy because the training of the sport and the sport itself are so closely interconnected.

Testing becomes harder the more dynamic the sport and the further removed it is from training in the weightroom—think back squats versus the intricacies of movement occurring in all positions of an individual play during a football game. How do we determine if the training program works? The Pendlay Total. In this chapter, I'll break down the Pendlay Total testing protocol step by step and compare it to other totals. You'll learn why each specific movement is included in the test and how to effectively use it to evaluate training and athletic performance.

CHAPTER 17
BEGINNER AND INTERMEDIATE ATHLETIC PROGRAMMING

Aspiring athletes who hope to have successful athletic careers should start their training early in life. Most kids starting in their early teens are already behind their peers who have been building a foundation of athleticism and strength in earlier years. In this section, I outline a simple program to use for preadolescents. The sample programming can be used as a template for coaches to build upon, depending on the needs of their athletes. These are simply examples of what I've found success with when working with young athletes.

CHAPTER 18
ADVANCED ATHLETIC PROGRAMMING

This chapter will progress the information covered in Chapter 17. Here, I discuss how to progress young athletes who are typically 12 years of age or slightly older to the next level of training. This rate of progress is entirely based on the individuals, and coaches need to make a judgment call determining the readiness of their athletes for advanced training. Again, I'll provide a programming template and information on how to implement methods previously discussed in the text, such as The Texas Method.

CHAPTER 19
IMPLEMENTING ATHLETIC PROGRAMS

Chapters 17 and 18 outline the beginner, intermediate, and advanced training program templates for athletes. They also serve to help categorize young athletes. The beginner program provides guidance on how to program for preadolescent kids. The intermediate-level programming describes how to progress young kids who are entering adolescence. Finally, the advanced program advises how to progress teenage athletes. This chapter goes into further detail about how to properly implement these programs with special considerations for each age group.

CHAPTER 15
THE CLOCK IS TICKING

Twenty years ago, a high school athlete could gain a real edge by engaging in some type of strength training program. It didn't need to be a great program; the fact that the athlete trained with weights at all was enough to provide an edge. The strength and conditioning profession was in its infancy. Lifting year-round in the 1990s was almost unheard of, so even engaging in the three-month summer program that most high schools offered for athletes was enough to provide an advantage to the few who participated.

Ten years ago, strength and conditioning programs were offered over summer break at most high schools, and lifting weights over the summer became standard, especially for football players. Almost all sports started to incorporate some strength and conditioning by then; to have an edge and stand out among their peers, athletes had to train year-round.

Today, the bar is even higher. If athletes want to stand out, not only do they need to train year-round, they need a well-planned program…and they need to start early. An athlete who wants to play at a higher level needs to start serious strength training in the freshman year at the very latest, and soon even this will be considered to be too late.

Starting in seventh or eighth grade is becoming more common. Many of my best athletes started even earlier—some as early as seven or eight years old! Those who start very early have an advantage over those who wait until high school. I have 12-year-old kids squatting 200 pounds. Those kids will have adult-level strength by the time they're freshmen in high school.

If a high school athlete wants to play at a high level, the time to start training seriously is the seventh or eighth grade. At the Division 1 level, 300-pound bench presses and cleans aren't considered exceptional. That level of strength is common, even for quarterbacks. It takes time—years—to develop that level of strength and power.

Many athletes finally decide to get serious about strength training in their junior year in high school, because that's when the scouts start to look at them. But by that time, they've missed years of strength development…it's too late. The clock is ticking and an athlete who wants to play at the higher level cannot afford to waste any time. The time to start is yesterday. The right year to start is last year.

During a sport season, the rigorous practice and game schedule make strength and power gains less likely. Preseason conditioning also slows the rate of strength and power gains.

The same is true for spring ball. This leaves less than half the year to focus on gaining strength and power. As a result, if a serious strength program is not initiated immediately post-season, athletes will likely make very little progress during the year simply because there's so little time.

Many athletes believe that because their bench press or squat went up from their freshman to sophomore year, they're making progress. They fail to realize that all their peers are also maturing and getting bigger and stronger. Every young athlete is in a race; they don't just have to get stronger, they have to improve faster than their peers to get ahead. Anything that delays the start of training or slows progress once it starts is not just a delay, it's a step backward.

Despite these challenges, much can be accomplished with well-planned year-round training. For example, I was asked to work with a high school football team in Texas, where I taught the coaches how to teach the lifts in the Pendlay Total, which I'll describe in the next chapter, and helped them establish a strength program based on those lifts.

When I was brought in, they had only a few athletes able to clean over 200 pounds. The coaches did a great job of implementing the program and establishing a culture of excellence in the weightroom. The juniors and seniors were expected to lead and teach the lifts to the incoming freshmen. The athletes pushed one another and held each other accountable for missed workouts or poor effort.

Four years later, they had their first players who were able to clean over 400 pounds and *every single* starting player could clean more than 300.

In a medium-sized high school in Wichita Falls, I saw three athletes on the same team cleaning in excess of 400 pounds. Two of them were quarterbacks! Though they were good athletes, they weren't genetic freaks. They simply started early (sixth and seventh grade), worked hard, and started their off-season training as soon as the season was over.

As I write this, one of my sixth-graders got his first back squat with 200 pounds at a bodyweight of about 140. I fully expect him to clean over 400 pounds as a senior. In fact, I'd be disappointed if he doesn't clean significantly more than that.

Those results may sound remarkable, but that kind of progress should be expected with a year-round, well-planned program when an athlete starts early and sticks with the program for the entire high school career. We need to raise the bar.

TRAINING THE YOUNGER ATHLETE

A lot of high school football players want to get bigger and stronger, and they're the athletes any strength coach would love to work with. They're kids who are already big, strong, fast, and have the genetic talent to get much bigger and stronger with the application of a good training plan. They're also motivated, and will work hard.

The most typical situation involves a kid who started as a junior and got some "attention." Often the kid has been told by a coach—or his father—that with another 20 or 30 pounds of muscle, he'd be playing in college on a scholarship. At some point, between the junior season and the summer prior to his senior year, he decides to get serious about weight training, hits the gym hard and tries to lock in that college scholarship.

There's one unfortunate fact here: Rome was not built in a day. While a person can easily make solid progress in the two to three months these football players give themselves to get stronger, they can't do in two months what they should have had six or more years to do.

Preparation to do your best in any sport as a young adult should begin at the age of five or six years old. When I was young, I didn't have a computer or any electronic games—and our TV was black and white with two channels. Kids' shows were limited to Saturday morning cartoons. This set of conditions meant we played outside. We built forts, raced bikes and jumped ramps with them. We played various games, and got into fights.

Once, when I was maybe nine, we decided to dig as big a hole as we could at the edge of the wheat field that separated my parent's small farm from the town. We dug for a whole weekend, got it deep enough that we could all get in it and stand up with our heads below ground. We had dreams of covering it with boards, then with dirt over that for camouflage. We'd have a secret entrance and make it our fort, but my dad found out what we were doing and made us fill it in because he was afraid it would fall in and bury us.

We don't see kids playing like that much anymore. Digging and sweating outside all day would be punishment for them, and not at all fun. This lack of an active childhood with lots of physical play hurts ultimate athletic development. And the effect lasts beyond childhood. If you grew up in a rural area, weren't the farm kids the ones who excelled in gym class and on the athletic field?

How do you replace what many of us experienced as children with our own children today? Coach Don McCauley told me that the CrossFit Kids program is excellent. Promoting the participation in various sports is also great. Between the age of four and 10, my son William did martial arts, wrestling, soccer, boxing, and weightlifting. I didn't make him do anything he didn't want to do, and he was always participating in at least one sport year-round.

It's important to make exercise the norm from a young age. Walks to the park and spending time on the climbing walls was normal for William, as was a short session of kettlebells before bedtime. This was fun for us; he used an eight-kilo kettlebell and I used a 24 and we were quite competitive with how many snatches we could complete in five or 10 minutes. And oh, how William loved to beat Dad.

Can these make up for hours of physical play every day? Probably not, but it's better than lying on the couch watching TV or playing video games.

If plenty of general preparedness is just what the doctor ordered during the grade school years, strength comes next. Twelve or 13 years old is a great time to start a year-round strength training program.

If we start them at this age, they'll already have great technique firmly ingrained and the body toughened enough that when they reach the age that allows serious strength gains—14 or 15 for most—we don't have to waste time teaching technique or adapting to a workload. Traveling this path will have kids reach a high percentage of their ultimate strength potential by age 18…that senior year in football.

If this path were followed, 400-pound cleans among high school football players would be fairly common. But more importantly, if this were more common, I wouldn't have had to remind so many kids and their parents that Rome wasn't built in a day.

THE ART AND SCIENCE OF COACHING

Strength coaching is both an art and a science. I earned my master's degree in exercise physiology because I believe it's important to understand the science behind the methods. But I rely mostly on my experience under the bar and my years of experience when I coach.

When it comes to building great athletes, the *art* is even more important than the science. There's no course or degree that can teach you how to coach. Time under the bar and time on the field is much more important. Coaching can't be taught in a classroom. It certainly can't replace time under the bar.

My time spent under the bar as a weightlifter and powerlifter, and as a coach training athletes, is what I have found to be most valuable. Experience is what shapes the "art" side of coaching.

The art involves a kind of intuition about what's needed, based on thousands of hours of "doing." This doing provides the kind of knowledge that can't be gained in the classroom.

TRAINING MEN AND WOMEN

Before we go further, I want to be clear that I'm talking about both men and women. There's essentially no difference in how I train either sex. In previous generations, it was dogma that serious strength training was not suitable for women. My mother remembers being told by her doctor when she was in seventh grade that if she worked too hard in gym class, she could ruin her ability to have children. But we now know that in several ways, women might actually be physically superior to men, even in strength sports.

In the sport of Olympic weightlifting, it's an advantage to have a higher percentage of muscle mass in the hips and legs, as is their better flexibility and ability to withstand higher training volumes. In China, female athletes are actually trained with a higher training volume than the men because of this. The difference between the male and female world records in similar weight classes is getting closer and closer to equal. Who knows, in 50 years, there might be no difference at all. Already the world record snatch in at least one female weight class is over double bodyweight. That's something no male football player can do.

Currently, the biggest limitation for women in the USA is sociological, not physical. This is changing, though. I give a lot of the credit to CrossFit for bringing more girls and women into the strength sports. There's no difference in suitability for training between boys and girls. Before puberty, there's almost no difference in physical ability.

If you look at weightlifting records, the gap between male and female numbers is closing.

THE RIGHT TOOL FOR THE JOB

Using the right tool for the job is a major part of my coaching philosophy. People have often asked me, "What about bodyweight training?" or "How about TRX or kettlebells?" Those tools are okay, but this book and this program is a roadmap to better athletes, and the primary tool is the barbell.

In the past 25 years, I've tried every conceivable method to improve performance. A lot of things work, but none can achieve the complete transformation of an athlete the way a barbell can. We tried improving sprinting speed with sprint work, and jumping ability with plyometrics and jump training, but in the end, improving strength and power was the one thing that had the biggest impact on running and jumping. In order to run faster and jump higher, athletes have to get strong. And the best way to do that is with a barbell.

Progressive resistance and the ability to make small progressive changes in the load is the key to barbell training. The human body can only gain strength at a certain rate. That rate varies depending on the experience of the lifter and the lift itself. Strength improves faster for novices and big lifts involving a lot of muscle mass like the squat. It improves more slowly for more experienced lifters and for lifts involving less muscle mass like the military press. A barbell is effective because it allows athletes to change the load in small but progressive increments.

A 200-pound clean doesn't become a 300-pound clean in one step or in response to one training session. A 200-pound clean can become a 205-pound clean in response to one training session. And it can become a 300-pound clean over years of small steps, each with progressively greater load. A 200-pound load can change the 200-pound clean to a 205-pound clean, then a 205-pound load can change the clean to a 210-pound clean, and so on for months and years. It's a slow process, but it works.

And neither I nor anyone else has found a way that works faster. A realistic rate of strength gain for a novice athlete on a "big" exercise like the clean might be five pounds per workout or per week. For an athlete past the novice stage or training an exercise that uses a smaller muscle mass, the rate of progress might be a pound per week. Every athlete has a period of novice gains that lasts from a month to as long as a year, depending on the genetic ability of the body to adapt to training.

Because the human body adapts slowly, we have to start early. You can't cram five years of strength training into one season simply by working harder!

The key to gaining strength is to use the correct exercises, the correct load, and the correct volume of work, and time. The barbell is the right tool for this job because of the ability to make small progressive changes in the load.

CLOSING THOUGHTS

Decades ago, a young athlete could be successful training minimally in the weightroom during summer break. That has changed significantly, and today the bar is simply too high for that strategy to work. Unfortunately, many fail to realize the competitiveness of modern-day athletics before it's too late. Aspiring athletes need to start early and do more if they hope to stand out to coaches and earn starting positions. They have to do more to channel their talents into starting positions and college scholarships and beyond. To do that, they need to do well-planned year-round training programs written by coaches who have the experience to produce results.

Not only has the bar been raised for athletes, but for strength coaches as well. Coaches have a tremendous responsibility to set their young athletes up to be in contention for those starting positions, scholarships, and future careers. They must know how to write a well-thought-out year-round training plan, but also have the experience to know when to make a judgment call and adjust the program based on the ebbs and flows of the sporting season or in a young athlete's life.

How do you get experience? By doing.

It certainly helps to have spent time under the bar yourself and on the field of play. From there, you need time working with youth athletes, traveling with teams, and seeing how training systems work. In the following pages, I'll outline what I've come to find to be the best testing method for athletes. Then I'll discuss programming for beginner, intermediate, and advanced athletes.

What I present was built through time under the bar, on the field of play, and endless hours in the gym working with young athletes. I hope it helps.

CHAPTER 16
THE PENDLAY TOTAL

As a strength coach, I need to answer the question, "Is it working?" Measuring strength is how I do this. But what lifts do I measure? Coach Dan John has said, "Knowing what to measure simplifies life." I agree. I've spent a lot of time testing athletes and thinking about this. My answer to the question is the Pendlay Total. Before we get to the specifics, let's discuss why we test.

Why not just look in an athlete's training log instead of testing? There are lots of reasons, and the first is that there are standards. Three-time world champion shot putter and coach John Godina once told me that when a thrower could bench press 400 pounds, additional bench press strength doesn't correlate as strongly with shot put performance.

Once the bench press exceeds 400 pounds, bench press strength and shot-put throw distance doesn't correlate the way it does from say, 300 to 400 pounds. It's always better to be stronger, but at some point, the added strength doesn't add as much as you'd think it would. That's a standard.

The same is true for a 500-pound squat. When an athlete benches less than 400 and squats less than 500, added strength is extremely important. Past those marks, it starts to matter less. At some point, you're better off training using other modalities than heavy squats and bench presses.

Standards are easy for the track and field sports. Either the discus went farther, or it didn't. Either the athlete ran faster or jumped higher, or didn't. Measuring performance in track and field is as simple as looking at a clock or measuring distance.

This simplicity has provided thousands of data points for coaches and athletes. That's how standards get established. The fact that track and field sports have measurable standards that are directly correlated to performance is, I believe, the most important reason sprinters and throwers have the best-planned training of all strength-power athletes.

The situation is a bit muddier with ball sports like football. Although it's almost universally accepted that getting stronger and more powerful will help a football player, it's harder to directly observe. A football player's "performance" is not as simple as a discus thrower or sprinter. That performance is impacted by who the athlete is lined up against. Line up against Reggie White, and you're likely to have a bad day.

Performance is also impacted by teammates, play calling, skills, experience, and the ability to recognize the opponent's strategy. In short, lots of extraneous variables affect performance. As a result, standards are not as well developed or as universally applied as in the track and field sports, and training methods for football have lagged behind the track and field sports.

For this reason, it's even more important that ball sport athletes test strength and power. As we accept that strength and power are important variables in performance along with the other extraneous variables, we should establish standards and measure them. Because of what it measures, the Pendlay Total is perfect for establishing standards that are relevant for ball sports that require speed, agility, powerful motion, and strength.

Put a single athlete in a weightroom with a plan, and it's called training. Put two athletes in a weightroom with the same plan, and it becomes a competition. Is it too obvious to state that athletes are competitive? This highlights the other reason to test. It leverages the competitive drive of the athletes.

Testing is like a legal steroid. If you believe that what you are testing is important for that athlete's performance, and the athlete is motivated to improve the test scores due to competition, you have a winning formula. Testing also tells you where an athlete stacks up compared with athletes who've been successful in the sport. It often gives specific information on what we need to work on.

The real key is to ensure that you're testing what's important. That's the purpose of the Pendlay Total.

WHY NOT USE THE OLYMPIC LIFTING TOTAL?

Some people use the Olympic lifts as a test of athletic strength and power. There's no question that Olympic lifting is an impressive sport and is perhaps the pinnacle of athletic strength and power. The problem with using the Olympic lifts is that they're so technique intensive. As a strength coach, the goal is to produce a better athlete, not just a better weightlifter.

Remember our track and field discussion: Did the discus go farther? For Olympic lifts like the snatch, an athlete's technique may not be good enough to challenge basic physical abilities of strength and power. This is an important point and is worth pondering for a moment. If we want to use lifts with a high skill component to test strength and power, the athlete has to have a high level of competency with those lifts. Otherwise, we're testing lifting skill, not strength and power that transfer to the field of play.

It can take six months to 10 years to reach the point where an athlete's snatch technique can fully exploit strength and power. Until that point, small changes in technique can dramatically impact an athlete's ability to *access* their existing strength and power. Therefore, a large part of what you're measuring with the snatch is the ability to access available strength and power, rather than just measuring strength and power itself.

To be clear, many athletes won't have good enough snatch technique to challenge their basic physical ability. The technique changes that improve the ability to access strength and power in the snatch may have little to do with the athlete's ability to access strength and power for a sport. A lot of what we're measuring is snatch technique, which doesn't transfer to a different sport, not basic physical ability, which does.

If an athlete's snatch has improved, we don't know if the basic strength and power has improved, or if the ability to access that strength and power in the snatch has improved. Basic strength and power will transfer directly to a wide variety of sports skills. Snatch technique will improve the snatch. In fact, the snatch will continue to improve due to better motor patterns for as long as 10 years.

Let me give you an example. After multiple national title wins, Travis Cooper came to live with me for a month to work on his lifts. His snatch was too low compared to his clean and jerk. His squat was over 600 pounds—more than three times his bodyweight, so his strength was good, and he should have been able to snatch more. I saw that his second pull was way too low, starting from too low a position somewhere near mid-thigh rather than at the hip, which would be ideal for utilizing his available strength and power on the snatch. This was preventing him from accessing all of his strength.

This was a significant problem because at the World Team level, a one-percent difference in the total can make the difference between making the team or not. For four weeks, we worked on correcting his second pull, and he refined it during the next year. His snatch really improved and became more balanced with his clean and jerk, showing that he was now able to access more of his available strength. This is an example of how sensitive to technique the snatch is, and illustrates how long it can take for snatch technique to develop to the point to be able to fully stress an athlete's basic speed-strength ability.

For sport athletes, we want to measure not snatch technique, but basic strength and power transferable to sport. Athletes typically don't simultaneously have the time necessary to master the snatch or clean and jerk and train their sports. The fact that lift-specific skill can impact an Olympic lifting total to a large degree, and that the Olympic lifts can take so long to get to the point to fully access the available strength and power makes them less than ideal for measuring athletic strength and power.

WHY NOT USE THE POWERLIFTING TOTAL?

Powerlifters compete in the squat, bench press, and deadlift. All of these lifts are great tests of strength, but there are two problems with using this total as a measure of athletic strength and power: redundancy and bar speed.

The powerlifting low-bar squat and the deadlift are similar lifts. They both involve hip and knee extension. The squat involves a bit more quadriceps activation than the deadlift, but there's considerable overlap between the two lifts. They're generally testing the same thing and are therefore redundant.

Bar speed is the other issue. The power lifts, which should more correctly be called "strength lifts," are done at a slow bar speed. The bar speed is too low to maximally develop power. The slow lifts develop lots of strength, but that strength doesn't transfer well to faster movements like sprinting, jumping, or changing direction.

The sweet spot of bar speed for developing athletic power is one-and-a-half to two meters per second. The power lifts are done at a much slower bar speed. This makes using the three power lifts less than ideal for testing and developing athletic strength and power.

WHY NOT USE THE CROSSFIT TOTAL?

The CrossFit Total consists of the press (what some people call the "military press" or "standing overhead press"), the deadlift, and the squat. Again, the squat and deadlift are largely redundant. The press is also not ideal for testing.

First, it tests relatively small muscle groups—mainly the deltoids and triceps, although there's a bit of pectoral involvement. Also, the sticking point is the first 10 degrees of the movement, from the chest to the nose. Athletes are rarely applying max strength or power in that range of motion. Athletes are more likely to be applying maximal strength or power in the last 10 degrees of the pressing motion from the nose to overhead. Think about throwing a punch or pushing off of a blocker.

And again, there's the issue of bar speed. The CrossFit Total doesn't contain a lift with enough bar speed.

WHAT ABOUT JUMPING OR THROWING?

Unweighted jumping is not useful in testing because the movement speed is too quick to develop adequate tension. There's an inverse relationship between a muscle's maximum tension and contraction speed. With a really fast movement, like unweighted jumping, the contraction speed is so quick that little tension is developed.

Tension is one of the necessary inputs for developing muscle strength and hypertrophy. You can't trigger adaptations leading to strength and power if the speed of movement is too fast. Conversely, really slow contractions develop lots of tension, but less power.

The power lifts are good for testing and training pure strength, but not power, whereas unweighted jumps are not optimal for either. For athletic power development, we want to achieve the sweet spot of tension and power. This can be achieved with weighted jumps if enough weight is applied. Many people recommend testing and training with weighted jumps for this reason.

There's research showing a correlation between weighted jumps, jerk ability, and power. However, injury is the primary limiter in weighted jumps. I've had some limited success with weighted jumps with my athletes, but found them hard to recover from and remain injury-free, which makes them hard to use long term. We inevitably end up fighting knee-pain issues. I tried for years to get around those issues with limited success. It's also difficult to apply progressive resistance in weighted jumps like we can with a barbell.

Some suggest using medicine ball throws for athletic strength and power testing. I found it hard to load medicine ball throws sufficiently to produce a movement speed optimal for producing enough power and tension.

We experimented with a two-handed, over-the-head kettlebell throw behind in a sand pit, and this can work. You can easily achieve enough loading for a great training effect, but as a measurement tool, it's not ideal. It's the kind of test that sounds good in theory, but is impractical in practice. Small changes in the release point can produce large changes in throw distance. We want a measurement that's most sensitive to athletic strength and power, and not testing technique. If you have the proper equipment and a sand pit, these can be a great and fun break from regular training that's valuable training, but are not ideal for testing.

Instead of looking for other options, let's consider the Pendlay Total, which is a simple test that avoids all of those pitfalls and limitations.

CLEAN-TO-BODYWEIGHT RATIO PREDICTS ATHLETIC TASKS

Many studies have demonstrated the relationship between the clean and athletic tasks. In 2008, researchers from Edith Corwin University in Australia tested 29 Australian football players to determine if the power clean correlated to bodyweight speed and power.

They tested the athletes in the power clean (1RM), counter-movement jump, sprint speed, and a change of direction drill and found the following significant correlations:

Clean-to-bodyweight ratio and counter-movement jump peak power
Clean-to-bodyweight ratio and sprinting speed
Clean-to-bodyweight ratio and counter-movement jump height
Clean and change of direction performance

Note that the clean-to-bodyweight ratio was especially predictive.

THE PENDLAY TOTAL

The Pendlay Total consists of:

o   Clean or Power Clean (not a hang clean)

o   Squat

o   Push Press

THE CLEAN OR POWER CLEAN

The clean or power clean are ideal lifts to include in a test of athletic strength and power. Though both lifts are good choices, I prefer the clean. Many coaches favor the power clean because they believe it's easier to teach. I've found the opposite to be true. Any good coach should be able to teach an athlete to clean in a short period of time.

The advantage of the clean over the power clean is that you can use more weight. More weight means you're getting more of a training effect with every set and every repetition. This can be important over time. The clean is also a better choice than the snatch because there's much less of a skill gap to overcome. Athletes are able to access their available strength and power with the clean faster than with the snatch.

In all of sports training, across dozens of sports, the clean and power clean have proven to be the most effective way to train speed-strength. The ratio of the clean or power clean to bodyweight has the highest correlation to athletic abilities that directly relate to athlete performance like the 40-yard dash, the pro agility test, and vertical jump than any other lift. In fact, the highest sprint correlation is with the 10-yard sprint, which is perhaps more relevant than the 40 for most ball sport athletes. An athlete with a ratio of clean or power clean to bodyweight of two or higher (a double-bodyweight clean) will be fast, powerful, and agile.

Both the clean and power clean are better than jumping because compared to jumping, the load on the bar slows the movement, allowing you to achieve optimal bar speed for power development. Cleans, unlike unloaded jumping, significantly develop the hamstrings, improving the hamstring-to-quadriceps strength ratio, which is correlated with reduced risk of knee injury.

Cleans are explosive, but the load limits the bar speed enough to produce lots of tension, unlike unloaded jumping, which produces too little tension. Optimizing tension and power is the key to power development. You simply get very little adaptation with low tension.

The use of a barbell is another advantage of cleans, which allows small incremental loading. These small increments make the barbell superior to kettlebells or medicine balls. You can precisely apply progressive overload in reasonable increments. These qualities make it an ideal lift for both training and measuring athletic strength and power.

If you can clean a lot, you can also snatch or power snatch a lot. You can deadlift a lot. The same is true for cleaning from all the positions. If you can clean a lot from the floor, you can also hang clean a lot from the hip, and hang clean a lot from the knee. The clean makes athletes strong in any exercise that requires explosive hip and leg extension.

This doesn't always work the other way around. Having a big clean or power clean means you'll also be decent at the deadlift, even if you don't specifically train the deadlift. A big clean means you'll have the power to do a big snatch. Whether you can actually do a big snatch depends on if you practice that movement, but if you have a big clean, you can at least power snatch quite a bit.

Every football coach knows that a big bench press or squat means an athlete is strong, and strength always helps, but they don't automatically mean a player is strong on the football field. But, a kid who can clean double bodyweight will be a terror on the field—he just will. And almost every coach recognizes this. The clean carries over to the field like nothing else.

WHY NOT HANG CLEANS?

The hang clean is one variation I don't recommend. It's easy to coach, but eliminates much of the value of the clean. The first part of the lift is missing: the pull from the floor.

It's well established that the strength ratio between the hamstrings and quadriceps is an important risk factor for knee injury, especially anterior cruciate injuries in women. The quadriceps and hamstrings pull on the tibia from opposite directions. This can stabilize the knee when their strength is comparable.

But when an athlete is quad dominant and has an imbalance in hamstring-to-quadriceps strength (less than 50–75%—the precise amount is subject to debate), there's an increased risk of anterior cruciate injury due to lack of stability.

The hang clean, unlike the clean or power clean, is quad dominant because the hamstring-dominant pull from the floor is missing. Training the hang clean will only exacerbate the imbalance and make an athlete more injury prone. In my opinion, using the hang clean is criminally negligent. I don't use them with my athletes.

BACK SQUAT

The basic back squat brings immense value to athletic development. This is one of the great barbell truths you only really know after spending time under a heavy bar, or having spent time getting athletes really strong.

Weightlifters know the squat is the requisite to a big total. Powerlifters know that squatting is essential to the sport. Bodybuilders know that squatting is vital for building overall body mass. As a result, squatting has become a universal standard of developing and testing hip-and-thigh strength. Because it's universally used, it provides an effective basis of comparison. This means there are literally thousands of data points across a wide variety of sports.

After having a stroke, I trained quite a bit on the rower because it doesn't require much balance. I chose the Concept 2, even though there are other brands, because it's universally used. Every rowing program in the world both trains and tests their athletes on the Concept 2. It removes the aspect of skill with an oar on the water and tests pure sustainable rowing power. It tells a coach about the fitness of an athlete and about raw potential of new athletes.

Because it's universally used, there are thousands of data points available and well-established standards. If an athlete rows a seven-minute 2K on a Concept 2 rower, it's equivalent to a seven-minute 2K on any Concept 2 rower, anywhere in the world. That can't be said when comparing times across other brands. The Concept 2 rower is a standard. Its value is in its universal use.

The squat is like that. Because everyone does it, it's a great way to compare basic strength between athletes. There are thousands of data points, and it's an ideal lift for creating standards.

The other advantages are that it's a multi-joint exercise using big muscle groups, and training the squat provokes a favorable endocrine response. The hormonal response to heavy squatting is anabolic. No other exercise can rival the endocrine response of the squat. These factors make it an ideal exercise for testing and training.

Perhaps the most important reason to include the squat is that it has great carryover. If you're strong on the squat, you'll also be strong in every other exercise involving the legs and hips. You'll be strong on step-ups, strong on split squats—name the other exercise you want to strengthen, and the squat will improve it.

These are the reasons coaches use the basic back squat as the foundation of their strength programs and why it's included in the Pendlay Total.

PUSH PRESS

Many people have argued the use of the press or military press as a universal test of upper body or pushing strength. The CrossFit Total uses the press as a standard. However, as previously discussed, the press uses small muscle groups and is not an ideal test of overall body strength and power. The sticking point is in the initial phase of the lift, a range rarely critical to athletes.

It's also problematic to judge a proper press, which is part of the reason it was eliminated from Olympic competition in 1972.

In many ways, the bench press is more optimal. It uses more muscle mass, and a good lift is easy to judge. However, the bench press removes many of the stabilizing muscles and doesn't require the athlete to produce force while balancing on the feet, the very essence of sport strength and power. This makes it much less relevant for athletes.

We need a lift that uses more muscle mass than the press, with a sticking point in a relevant range of motion, that uses more stabilizing muscles than the bench press, and that requires balance. The push press is that lift.

The sticking point of the push press is the last 10 degrees. The hardest part of the lift is the part that receives the most training effect. For the push press, this is the most relevant part of the range of motion for athletes. More weight can be used in the push press than with the press, and unlike the bench press,

it requires balance and a tremendous amount of stabilization in lockout.

The ability to lock out and balance a heavy weight overhead brings into play a large number of muscles from head to toe. This stresses the postural muscles, which are the muscles used to position the body to apply force maximally during athletic movements. On the field or court of play, weak postural muscles will keep an athlete from athletically applying strength.

The push press obviously develops the postural muscles more than the bench press, but also more than the press because more weight is used. The bar speed is also ideal for power development with the ideal balance of tension and power.

Having a plyometric component is another aspect of the push press that makes it unique. In the push press, you're dipping, then exploding. Plyometric action reverses the normal recruitment of motor units. Normal recruitment follows the pattern called "Hennemen's size principle of motor unit recruitment." Hennemen's Principle states that at low force contractions, primarily small, slow twitch motor units are recruited first.

Then, as force goes up, more, larger, and faster twitch motor units are added. However, during an explosive plyometric contraction, this recruitment order is reversed, with the largest, fastest twitch motor units recruited first. This increases the power output potential of the movement.

Finally, like the squat and the clean, the push press has great carryover to other lifts. Simply having a strong bench press won't automatically carry over to the push press. The same is true with the dumbbell bench press or incline press. But if you're a strong push presser, with minimal practice on another lift, you'll be strong at it.

When I coached in Wichita Falls, Robert McAdams was a good 94-kilo lifter who was push pressing around 170 kilos. One day, he decided to max his bench for the hell of it, without having bench pressed in several years. He found he could bench press 385 pounds and over the course of two bench press workouts, was able to bench press 405 pounds moving the bar very quickly. Two or three workouts later, he did a close-grip bench press with 405 pounds.

PLYOMETRICS

The term "plyometric" refers to the stretch-shortening cycle (SSC). The SSC involves a rapid stretch of a muscle, followed immediately by a contraction of that same muscle. The SSC can increase the force and power a muscle can produce.

The SSC involves the following steps:

- A muscle is stretched rapidly, like the rapid dip or knee bend in a push press. A special sensor in the muscle called a muscle spindle sends a message to the spinal cord.
- The elastic components of the muscle are stretched like a rubber band.
- The spinal cord sends a signal back to the muscle, increasing muscle fiber recuirtment.

The elastic components spring back like a rubber band, contributing a small amount of force. The neural potentiation from the spinal cord signal allows for more rapid recruitment of large fast twitch motor units, increasing the power of the muscle contraction.

You can demonstrate this effect yourself. Squat down and pause for two seconds, then jump as high as you can. Next, do the jump as a counter-movement jump: Dip down and immediately jump up as high as you can. You'll do this naturally without having to think about it. The second jump will be higher because it's a plyometric jump.

Phase	Action
Eccentric Phase	Stretching and loading of the agonistic muscle
Amortization Phase	Transition from eccentric (lengthening) to concentric (shortening) Any delay causes dissipation of elactic energy and overriding of muscle spindle reflex potentiation.
Concentric Phase	Shortening of the muscle Training can result in reversing the order of muscle fiber recuirtment, recruiting large, type IIx fibers first.

I started experimenting with this, and found that people like Justin Schlager, Justin Brimhall, and Brett Crossland could all bench press very impressive weights with basically no bench press training. The same went for the dumbbell bench press and dumbbell incline press.

I experimented with this while coaching at other places, and discovered the push press seems to carry over to any type of pressing exercise. I think this is because it makes athletes so strong in the supporting and postural muscles of the shoulder girdle, back, and core. The push press carries over to everything.

Another overlooked advantage of both the clean and the push press is that they not only train the body to accelerate a load, but they also train the body to receive a load and *decelerate it*. This is necessary in all field sports, whether receiving an opposing player or decelerating the body relative to the ground. Strength is specific. We must train a quality to be better at it, and this is an overlooked quality.

Finding exercises that carry over to other things an athlete might do is the trick to training athletes. It's all about carryover. I developed the Pendlay Total with that in mind.

THE TESTING PROTOCOL

With kids, I like to test the Pendlay Total as soon as they've developed proficiency in the lifts. For athletes familiar with the lifts, I try to get a total as soon as possible. With teams or individual athletes coming back after a layoff (short or long), I'll allow a week or two to refresh technique, and then test.

I like to test quickly for two reasons. First, testing provides information. It tells me where the athletes stand in the standards. Is the athlete strong and powerful, or not? It also tells me something about the athlete's abilities. For example, if an athlete is tremendously strong in the push press and squat, but has a weak clean, that athlete lacks power and explosiveness. Every coach has seen really good squatters who can't move athletically. Testing can provide those insights.

Driving progress through competitiveness is the other reason I like to test early. Athletes love to compete, especially the best athletes. Nothing will motivate an athlete more than having a measured performance

to beat. This is especially true in a team environment when competition is both with themselves and their fellow athletes.

Testing is motivating and provides great insights, but you can't do it too often. It takes too much time, and it comes at the cost of training time. It can take a whole day to test a team, so no other training is possible that day. However, you don't need to test too often to see if an athlete is progressing. The day-to-day training log will provide that information.

But testing is important. Most coaches will be able to figure out where testing fits based on the competitive and practice season. For example, the beginning and end of summer program is a good choice for football players. Testing should be done more than once per year, but once per month is probably too much.

The order of testing for the Pendlay Total is cleans first, followed by push press, and finally the squat. Each athlete gets three attempts at each lift before moving to the next.

When testing teams, simply start with the lightest weight, then slowly add weight to the bar, allowing athletes to take an attempt when their weight selection comes up. This results in somewhat varying rest periods between lifts, but that can't be avoided in a team situation. However, it generally works fine.

CLEAN

We clean from the floor. An athlete can do a power clean or a full clean. It doesn't matter as long as they are cleaning from the floor with proper form.

PUSH PRESS

We don't use racks. The athlete must clean the weight to get it into position for a push press. This is not generally a problem because most athletes can clean more than they can push press.

However, some athletes, especially some great bench pressers, may have a problem if they have to clean the weight prior to the push press. As a result, some have said that making the athletes clean the weight before push pressing just double penalizes these athletes. That's absolutely true, and it's done on purpose.

Some athletes are very strong at the bench press and squat, but still play third string. They're not explosive and can't move athletically. In fact, this happens more than most people think. Coaches know that a monster squat doesn't make a great football player. But if you can clean (especially two times bodyweight), you can jump, sprint, and change directions quickly. In short, you can move athletically and powerfully.

Double penalizing an athlete who can't clean makes sense. If you can't clean, you won't have a good Pendlay Total, and this is as it should be.

BACK SQUAT

You can use either a high- or low-bar back squat. The back squat is tested just as it is in powerlifting where three attempts are provided. Make sure the athletes are getting sufficient depth in the squat, just as you would at a powerlifting meet.

Here are some good totals produced by my athletes.

James Tatum

Bodyweight 197 pounds

- o **Back Squat:** 507 pounds
- o **Push Press:** 308 pounds
- o **Clean:** 402 pounds
- o **Pendlay Total:** 1,217 pounds

Travis Cooper

Bodyweight 169 pounds

- o **Back Squat:** 605 pounds
- o **Push Press:** 341 pounds
- o **Clean:** 451 pounds
- o **Pendlay Total:** 1,397 pounds

Jared Fleming

Bodyweight 207 pounds

- o **Back Squat:** 650 pounds
- o **Push Press:** 352 pounds
- o **Clean:** 462 pounds
- o **Pendlay Total:** 1,464 pounds

CLOSING THOUGHTS

We don't do any special build-up prior to testing. We just insert it in place of a normal training day when it makes sense. The next workout is not adjusted either. Most athletes will recover fine from testing with no real adjustments being necessary.

CHAPTER 17
BEGINNER AND INTERMEDIATE ATHLETIC PROGRAMMING

Proper physical development of kids is just as important as proper mental and social development, and it's an area where we're sorely lacking today. Physical education programs are being cut, sometimes entirely. Physical development also has to compete with video games, TV, and social media. It's gotten so bad that the Pentagon has reported that seven out of 10 kids wouldn't qualify for military service, in large part due to lack of physical fitness.

When I was a kid, physical development included PE, but also riding bikes—sometimes recklessly—running, jumping, climbing trees, wrestling, fighting, and pickup games of sports. Today, due to changes in social norms, the economic challenge of both parents working, and changes in how we live (no more "free range" kids), physical development is generally relegated to organized sports. That results in a two-tier system with regard to kids and physical activity.

The first tier are the kids who participate in every sport from a young age. They go from one season to another with very little break, or sometimes with overlapping sports.

Many of these kids are at their limits in terms of physical and mental stress and are at high risk of injury. These kids can benefit greatly from a well-planned, progressive strength training program. An effective program, properly supervised, can strengthen the ligaments, tendons, and joints, and teach effective movement patterns under load. This can significantly reduce their risk of a career-ending injury at a young age.

The second tier gets almost no physical activity. Their play time consists primarily of screen time. These kids need physical activity in order to develop normally. It's not normal to be a couch potato, especially at a young age. The body needs physical activity to develop in a normal way.

Kids have a natural affinity for physical activity if nudged in that direction. I firmly believe that just like helping kids with their homework, parents should be involved in their physical development. The kids absolutely need a physical activity program.

Programs like CrossFit Kids are phenomenal. If you have a good local CrossFit affiliate that participates in the program, it's worth sending your kids. If you don't, the program is simple, and any adult with some common sense and a little patience can employ it using the CrossFit Kids workout of the day from their website.

For those parents who have aspiring athletes, a well-planned, progressive strength training program is ideal. The beginner's program in this chapter was created with that goal in mind. It provides a dose of physical activity and also teaches sound athletic movement patterns, such as good posture and bracing the core under load. These types of movement patterns are essential for normal physical development. The time to learn them is in childhood.

People who object to putting kids as young as eight or 10 years old on a strength training program generally cite two reasons: safety and physiological capacity to gain strength before puberty. Both of these objections are unfounded and are fortunately falling out of the mainstream thinking about training kids.

People concerned about the safety of strength training haven't carefully thought this through. Young kids are just not strong enough to hurt themselves while lifting weights under supervision. Weight training is one of the activities least likely to result in injury. In a supervised weight training program, we carefully control the weight and the movements. The lifts are well below maximum capacity.

Contrast that with an activity like soccer. In soccer, the loads on the tissues are not at all controlled. Kids run into each other, step into ruts in the field, and make sudden changes of direction. These movements can place tremendous unpredictable stresses on the knees, hips, and ankles. Rather than controlled loading and movement, it's more like chaos.

I'm not saying kids shouldn't play soccer, but parents who worry about weight training injuries are misplacing their worry. In fact, because we can carefully load with weight training, we can strengthen the muscles, joints, and tissues, and can reduce the risk of injury. Fear of injury is a reason to encourage strength training, not to avoid it.

I've always believed that weightlifting is one of the safest sports because the movements are so well controlled, and so are the loads. Even the American Academy of Pediatrics recommends weight training for kids age eight and up.

THE SAFETY OF STRENGTH TRAINING FOR CHILDREN

In 2012, *The British Journal of Sports Medicine* published an extensive review of the scientific studies on the safety and efficacy of resistance training for youth. The researchers identified 27 intervention studies—an intervention study is a study in which the experimental group receives some type of manipulation; in this case, it was strength training.

The studies involved hundreds of research subjects, both male and female, from six to 18 years old. Of the 27 studies, only two studies resulted in reportable injuries. These two studies reported one injury each. The other 25 studies resulted in no injuries.

Observational studies have also shown low injury rates—observational studies observe subjects without employing manipulation. Combining observational studies of more than 5,000 adolescents showed that the injury rates for strength training were 0.0017 per 100 hours at the low end, and 0.0035 per 100 hours of training. To put that in perspective, to produce three injuries, you would need to observe about 33,000 hours of resistance training.

Injury data from tens of thousands of adolescent athletes in the US over a one-year period showed that strength training resulted in 0.7% of the injuries, while football represented 28%, wrestling 16%, and gymnastics 13%.

The second objection that kids aren't ready for strength training until puberty has been disproven by a number of research studies. A published review of the research stated, "A long-held belief by many clinicians was that strength training is not effective in children until they have significant levels of circulating testosterone, which is needed for muscle hypertrophy. Studies have demonstrated that children can improve strength by 30% to 50% after just eight to 12 weeks of a well-designed strength training program."

I've been training athletes for more than 25 years. When I look back at my best athletes, one thing most have in common is that they started lifting before they were 10 years old.

I have considerable experience in training kids in the six- to 11-year-old age group. My experience has shown me that the primary determining factor of whether they're ready to train is mental and social, not physical. As soon as kids are psychologically mature enough to accept coaching, they're ready to start a supervised training program. If they can understand and make the adjustment when I say, "Straighten your back," or "Pull to your knees," they're ready to train. Most kids will get to this point by seven or eight, but some will get there sooner, some later.

Why start them this early? Besides getting them much needed physical activity so they can develop normally, starting this early provides a lifelong advantage over their peers. Swimmers and gymnasts figured this out decades ago. Those who start later can never catch up to those who started young. Just as with learning new languages, learning motor skills is much more easily done at a young age.

For kids who may later become athletes, learning these skills early will teach them to brace the core, to better transfer force from the lower body to upper body, to be better balanced under load, to better receive impact forces, and to move more powerfully and safely. These are lifelong advantages for any sport.

A kid who arrives at puberty with a significant training history and who has already learned the basic skills is ready to take advantage of the growth spurt at puberty with a full-fledged advanced program. Those who don't will have to first go through a potentially lengthy beginner program.

THE BEGINNER PROGRAM FOR ATHLETICS

For most kids six to nine years old, I recommend training once per week, keeping the workouts under 45 minutes. It's best to stop when they still want to train, rather than stop when they're ready to stop. In some cases, twice per week may be okay, depending on the kid. You'll have to use your judgment here.

I don't recommend exceeding twice per week at this age. Twice per week is the limit for kids under 12 years old. There isn't much to be gained by training more frequently at that age.

The backbone of the beginner program is three lifts: the snatch-grip deadlift, push press and back squat. The basic beginner template can be seen below.

BEGINNER PROGRAM TEMPLATE (ONE OR TWO TIMES PER WEEK)
A short warm-up activity
Snatch-Grip Deadlift A couple of warm-up sets, followed by one challenging set of 5 repetitions
Push Press A couple of warm-up sets, followed by one challenging set of 5 repetitions
Back Squats A couple of warm-up sets, followed by one challenging set of 5 repetitions
A 5- to 10-minute conditioning drill

The initial warm-up can be anything. The real purpose is to get the kids' attention and get them in the mode of accepting coaching. Be creative, but try to pick something that's organized and forces the kids to focus, at least a little. Developing that mental focus before beginning the lifts is important. For the lifts, the warm-up sets are an opportunity to coach the movement. Make corrections as necessary to ensure they're doing the movements right, but there's no need to overdo it here. You aren't going to fix everything in one session. Gradually increase loading to the working weight. The final set should be challenging for five repetitions and performed with correct technique.

The final conditioning drill is typically five to 10 minutes, but I don't tell the kids that in advance. In reality, I never time the final drill; I just go until the kids are breathing hard. Then, I stop when they still want to go, not when they're ready to quit. You want to leave them wanting more, not dreading the next workout.

For these drills, you can do anything that makes sense. I like having the kids carry something around a cone and come back. We use medicine balls, sandbags, kettlebells, and a variety of other implements. Kids love variety. The idea is just to keep them moving, and to keep it fun and safe. You can find a lot of good ideas from CrossFit Kids.

This is the basic beginner program strength training template. If I'm training kids specifically for Olympic weightlifting, or if the kids or parents have an interest in the kids learning the Olympic lifts, I introduce the snatch early in the beginner program. Kids are so flexible and pick up motor skills so quickly that if they can overhead squat, they can learn to snatch.

One of my weightlifting athletes, Samantha Nichols, started at age seven and won every Nationals from eight until 16 years old. She got her first American record at age 12. Starting at a young age is a gift that keeps on giving.

THE INTERMEDIATE PROGRAM FOR ATHLETICS

We progress the beginner template by staying with one set of five repetitions after the warm-up sets, increasing the load by approximately one pound weekly or per workout until they reach the point where we know they're going to have to slow down the bar or compromise technique if we add more weight. This can take one to six months, depending on how well they respond to the coaching and training.

When we reach that point, we reduce the weight 10 to 20% and start using three sets of five repetitions for the lift. Somewhere along the way, we introduce dips and either glute ham or hip extensions. This becomes the intermediate program. The workout quickly progresses to what's seen in the table below.

To be clear, we're adding components and sets to the beginner template when the kids are ready. This varies based on maturity, coachability, and consistency of training. It's a judgment call, with no simple answer, but it's not rocket science either. It's clear when the kids are ready. Once the components are added, this becomes the intermediate program template.

INTERMEDIATE PROGRAM TEMPLATE (TWO OR THREE TIMES PER WEEK)
A short warm-up activity
Snatch-Grip Deadlift A couple of warm-up sets, followed by 3 sets of 5 reps
Push Press A couple of warm-up sets, followed by 3 sets of 5 reps
Back Squats A couple of warm-up sets, followed by 3 sets of 5 reps
Dips 2 sets of 10 repetitions
Glute Ham Raises or Hip Extensions 2 to 4 sets of 10 repetitions
A 5- to 10-minute conditioning drill

The dips are a great assistance exercise for the push press. They also help set up a strong foundation for the other push movements that will be added in the advanced program.

The glute ham raises or hip extensions are inserted for hamstring strength. Kids tend to increase strength rapidly in these exercises, often progressing to using a barbell behind the neck with considerable loads. This is important because we can achieve hamstring strength that matches or even exceeds thigh strength. Strong hamstrings protect the knee during contact sports or sports with rapid changes of direction. Strong hamstrings and glutes will also help with the pull exercises to be introduced later in the advanced program.

This is a really important key to the Pendlay System. A strong posterior chain is the key to injury prevention and athletic strength and power. It's best to develop it early.

We then progress by small increments using one-pound or fractional plates of one-quarter or one-half pound. Add weight when it makes sense based on when the athlete is ready. Place emphasis on the proper execution of the movement. The goal is to teach the movements, improve their coachability, provide physical activity, and build a love of training.

CLOSING THOUGHTS

This simple program is enough for preadolescents. If they're getting other activity in addition to this program, that's great. By keeping the workouts short and only training once or twice per week for beginners, and two or three times for intermediates, we can achieve those objectives. Most kids love the feeling of getting stronger.

At this point, it's okay to take summers off or take time off for the holidays or vacations. Because they started early, we have plenty of time for development. The opposite is true for those who start at puberty. Because the clock is ticking, those athletes can't afford to take summers off.

We'll cover advanced programming for athletes in the next chapter.

CHAPTER 18
ADVANCED ATHLETIC PROGRAMMING

The transition from the intermediate program to the advanced program isn't based on age. It's based on readiness to learn additional lifts. Some kids will be ready early, while others may take years. This is a judgment call based on the individual, and is part of the art of coaching. It's generally obvious when a kid is ready to progress. Having said that, it's unusual to progress to the advanced program before 12 years old.

In the intermediate program, we expanded the toolkit by introducing two additional lifts to the program at once. In the advanced program, we'll add new exercises one at a time, and train them for a few weeks before adding another. Because the lifts are added one at a time followed by a training period, it can take several months or even a year or two to fully implement the program. In general, progress is quicker for older adolescents with some strength training experience than it is for younger adolescents. With young kids, we have plenty of time, and there's no hurry to move them along to advanced programming.

THE ADVANCED PROGRAM EXERCISE LIST

The rate of adding new exercises depends on the athlete. Some will be ready quickly, while others will take months. The exercises we add to the program are:

o Deadlifts

o Cleans

o Snatch

o Bench Press

o Press

o Front Squats

When we add a new lift, we start in the same way as with the preadolescent program with a few light warm-up sets, followed by a challenging set of five repetitions. Again, we increase the load by approximately a pound each workout until it looks like form will be compromised if we increase further, then we reduce the load 10 to 20% and start with three sets of five repetitions.

The program evolves seamlessly from a two-day-per-week program with five lifts (snatch-grip deadlift, push press, squat, dips, and glute ham raise/hip extension), to a three-day-per-week program consisting of up to 11 different exercises. We do this by moving to three days per week when the athlete is ready, then slowly introducing one new lift at a time, and training it for two or three weeks, and maybe more before introducing an additional lift.

As we introduce a new lift, we don't remove the old lift. There's some flexibility intentionally built in because every kid is different. Some can handle adding a new lift every two weeks because they have good motor control, are focused, and consistent. For others, the pace may need to be much slower. This is the "art" part of the art and science of coaching.

These are the lifts used in the advanced program.

PUSH	PULL	SQUAT	ASSISTANCE
Push Press	Snatch-Grip Deadlift	Back Squat	Dips
Bench Press	Deadlift	Front Squat	Glute Ham Raises
Press	Snatch	-	Hip Extension
-	Clean	-	-

The advanced program uses a three-day-per-week template. It starts as a three-day program with one additional lift, then progresses with the addition of more lifts from the table—each added one at a time until it becomes the complete template.

The program is designed so the athletes are doing three different pushes, three different pulls, and two different squats during the week. For example, pushes (push press, bench press, and press) will be alternated, so a different push is done each training day of the week. The same approach is taken with pulls (deadlift, cleans, and snatch).

Most athletes need three days of squatting—two back squat days and one front squat day per week. Some coaches like to program more front squat days, but keep in mind that every clean is also a front squat, so one additional front squat dedicated session is sufficient.

ADVANCED PROGRAM TEMPLATE (THREE TIMES PER WEEK)

Monday	Wednesday	Friday
Push	A different push	A different push
Pull	A different pull	A different pull
Back Squat	Front Squat	Back Squat
Conditioning	Conditioning	Conditioning
Optional assistance exercises	Optional assistance exercises	Optional assistance exercises
Volume Day 3–5 sets of 5 repetitions	**Light Day** 3 sets of 5 repetitions with 10% less weight than a volume day load	**Intensity Day** Work up to a max set of 3–5 repetitions

The back squat can push heavier weights, and thus is a better overall strength builder. Back-squat strength helps drive the front squat up, as well as the snatch and the clean. That's the reason for performing two back-squat sessions per week and only one front squat.

Beginners should back squat for sets of five for the first several months, or even years. Resist the temptation to stray from this advice and attempt heavy singles immediately, or to do sets of higher reps. Multiple sets of five, while admittedly unimaginative, have probably built more strength in more people than any other squatting system. For the front squat, clean, and snatch, sets of three to five (up to five sets) are usually best because maintaining the rack position can be difficult with higher reps. Failing to keep the bar in the rack position will prevent kids from obtaining the appropriate stimulus to strengthen the legs enough to benefit the clean.

With the advanced program, we insert a testing day every two to six months. During the testing day, we work up to a 5RM on all the lifts. The goal of training after establishing the 5RM will be to work up to doing three sets of five repetitions with the new PR weight.

We want to progress to the point that the testing involves the Pendlay Total as described earlier. If one or more of the Pendlay Total lifts hasn't yet been incorporated, test with the equivalent pull or push you've been using.

The testing week has a number of benefits. It allows the kids to handle a heavier weight, so it builds a tremendous amount of confidence in their abilities. Kids love to compete and to show improvement, and testing is a great motivator and a reward for their hard work. It teaches them that hard work pays off. It allows them to set a PR, which will be the benchmark for the workouts going forward.

INTENSITY VARIATION ON THE ADVANCED PROGRAM

Perhaps the most valuable outcome of my graduate training in exercise science was that I gained an appreciation for experimentation. I learned to think like a scientist., and how to manipulate variables and observe outcomes. My 25 years as a coach has been one big experiment, always trying to find what works, then trying again to find something that works even faster. If something works, I'll use it, but I'll always keep searching for a better way. The art of coaching has allowed me to know when to change a variable and to be able to judge what outcomes are beneficial.

At some point while integrating the additional lifts, the athletes' progress will begin to stall or slow on the squat, the primary hip- and leg-strength lift. This is the appropriate point to begin to vary the intensity throughout the week, which will consist of a volume day, a light day, and an intensity day, and is a key feature of the advanced program. This may happen either before or after you've introduced all the new lifts to the program.

For most kids, the squats will stall before all lifts are introduced, and that doesn't matter. The point is, when squats begin to stall, introduce intensity variation, the final piece of the advanced template.

When you begin this intensity pattern, introduce new lifts on the volume day, typically Monday. The intensity variation is based on the Texas Method in Chapter 7 of this book, which is a nonlinear periodization template. The introduction of this intensity variation completes the evolution of the Pendlay System. At this point, the athlete has fully incorporated all aspects of the system and can continue with this program for years or decades to the collegiate or professional level.

PROGRAMMING THE ADVANCED TEMPLATE

The advanced program evolved from the Texas Method. Three days per week is the ideal frequency of training for the advanced program. Athletes are often juggling multiple commitments related to their various sports, even in the off season. Skills practice, film study, recovery, rehabilitation, school, and drills can take a significant amount of time and energy. Unlike the strength sports athlete, ball sport athletes should view the weightroom as a supplement to athletic development. It's an important, even indispensable supplement, but the primary focus is on becoming a better athlete, not just getting stronger or more powerful in the weightroom.

It's unlikely for a strength or power training program that requires more than three days per week to be sustainable for most athletes. This is certainly true during a sport season, when one or two sessions per week are more realistic.

Fortunately, three-day-per-week training programs have been used successfully by athletes for more than 50 years. They are time tested, and they work. The Pendlay System doesn't compromise effectiveness because it's a three-day-per-week program. In fact, spending only three days per week in the weightroom is an asset due to the lifts that are performed and the recovery required, and the time it allows for other athletic development.

The advanced template uses 11 lifts with the intensity pattern from the Texas Method. Again, there's a smooth transition from the intermediate program to the advanced program. The advanced program is simply a continuation of the intermediate program with all lifts incorporated, and with intensity variation throughout the week.

ROTATING EXERCISES IN THE ADVANCED TEMPLATE

Exercises are performed on the same days for a three- or four-week period. After that, the exercises are rotated. For example, you may be doing deadlifts on the volume day, snatches on the light day, and cleans on the intensity day for a training block. For the next block, you might do snatches on the volume day, cleans on the light day, and deadlifts on the intensity day. Do the same with the other lifts in accordance with the template.

Because these athletes aren't strength specialists, we can introduce this rotating variation to ensure that all lifts are progressing. The goal is to drive up the lifts in the Pendlay Total without specializing.

We aren't training for the weightroom; we're training for the field of play, and this type of rotation provides the most strength and power transfer to the field of play. The field of play involves endless directions of movement and applications of force and power.

Treating athletes like they're strength specialists is a mistake many coaches make. I wholeheartedly believe in periodic testing, and am confident that increases in the Pendlay Total indicate an athlete is stronger and more powerful, which is a good thing. However, focusing on the Pendlay Total lifts (or any other lifts) like a specialist isn't the goal.

EXAMPLE OF ROTATING LIFTS (DONE EVERY THREE OR FOUR WEEKS)

VOLUME	LIGHT	INTENSITY
Deadlift	Snatch	Clean

AFTER THREE OR FOUR WEEKS

VOLUME	LIGHT	INTENSITY
Snatch	Clean	Deadlift

For the strength specialists, like weightlifters or powerlifters, a heavy focus on the competition lifts makes sense. Their whole purpose for training is to improve the competition lifts. They aren't concerned with speed, agility, sprinting, jumping, or moving an opponent. Their focus is singular: to move more weight in the competition lifts. It's a narrow but deep focus. For sport athletes, there's a significant drawback to that approach. It compromises transfer to the field of play, which is the whole point for a non-strength sport athlete.

A strength specialist doesn't care much about strength transfer to other lifts or the field of play, and as a result can put maximum effort into a narrow range of strength skills. However, for a non-strength-specialist athlete, that narrow focus isn't optimal. Athletes benefit tremendously from a wider variety of exercises that expose them to different bar speeds, different ranges of motion, and that train different muscle groups.

This develops a wider range of strength and power application. Instead of becoming very strong and powerful at two or three movements, we focus on becoming strong and powerful at a wider range of movements. That's why I often say that athletes rarely progress beyond intermediate strength. It isn't that they can't get very strong. They certainly can, but they rarely reach advanced levels of strength in particular lifts because they don't specialize.

For this reason, the Pendlay System can be used long term, even by collegiate and professional athletes. It strikes the right balance between variety and consistency for athletes.

This isn't to say there's no transfer with the Olympic or power lifts. There certainly is, but we want more transfer and a wider strength and power base for non-strength athletes. Remember, the point with these athletes is to enhance performance on the field of play. Getting stronger in the weightroom is a means, not an end.

In the internet age, a different kind of mistake is becoming more common: too much variety. This is the opposite of our earlier problem. With a quick internet search, everyone can find articles and instructional videos showing thousands of different exercises with a variety of implements like kettle-bells, TRX, rings, bodyweight, sandbags, and more. Some athletes and their coaches want to try them all!

The problem with this approach is that too much variety results in spending too little time and effort on each lift. As a result, the athletes never get very strong. It takes a lot of time to develop high levels of strength and power, and they need to perform a lift regularly to get really strong at that lift.

This can be done without specializing in any particular lift though. In the Pendlay System, we strive to drive up the clean, push press, and squat that are the foundation of the program, but we do that without specializing in those lifts. This is achieved by training those lifts, but not exclusively. We rotate the emphasis to related lifts at the appropriate times.

We generally start beginners with cleans twice per week because they're easy to learn and are great for developing power. They might be doing deadlifting on the third day. After a time, we might use snatch-grip deadlifts and incorporate some snatch technique work on the light day. Over time, if the athlete's snatch has progressed enough, we might substitute one clean day for a heavy snatch day. This gives the athlete some additional variety—and another excellent training tool—and is also great for driving up the Pendlay Total at the same time.

We use three different pressing movements: the push press, the bench press, and the press. This provides the right balance of variety and repetition to make an athlete stronger and more powerful in the weightroom, and a better athlete at the same time. Too little variety is a problem, and so is too much. The key is to get the balance right. Getting that balance right has been a 25-year effort for me.

CONDITIONING

Conditioning requires a bit more savvy. The one thing I can say for sure is that the answer is *not* lots of running. Running too much is the biggest mistake I see coaches make with their athletes. Too much running absolutely kills leg strength and power. Many coaches believe the extra endurance work simply layers endurance on top of strength. They don't understand that excessive endurance work—even repeated 40s if done excessively—can inhibit strength adaptations. Running kills squat strength faster than anything.

There's so little time available to develop strength and power, and it's critical to optimize that time, and not compromise it with excessive running. A little running is okay, but sports practice can provide the majority of what's needed. Coaches concerned about more conditioning can get around the interference issue by employing smart conditioning.

Smart conditioning enhances game endurance, as well as strength and power. The drills I include in the advanced program come from various sources and have been tested over the years by my athletes.

Some of the simple rules I apply when developing conditioning drills:

- **Get strong first.** Strength is always the first priority. Just about any amount of conditioning will slow strength gains, but some conditioning may be necessary. No athlete is too strong. Strength is the most malleable quality. You can double an athlete's strength, but you can't cut the 40-yard time in half or double the long jump. Why compromise that effect with excess conditioning?

- **Do the least amount of conditioning you can get away with.** So many coaches, especially football coaches, think athletes have to be dead tired at the end of practice. There are no medals for working hard—getting tired doesn't help anything. Being stronger and more explosive trumps being tired after every practice. A strong and powerful athlete doesn't need as much conditioning as a weaker athlete.

- **Keep it short.** Think in terms of 40-yard repeats, rather than running a mile. Short with high intensity is what we're aiming for.

- **Don't underestimate the conditioning effect of heavy strength training.**

- **Fitness doesn't have to be aerobic.** In fact, most sports are not steady-state aerobic events; they're stop and go. The ability to recover quickly from high-intensity efforts is the type of fitness needed for these sports. That's why short, high-intensity efforts are preferable.

- o **Focus on the posterior chain.** The posterior chain is so important for sport performance that it makes sense for the conditioning work to focus on this area.

- o **Pick a time of the year to focus exclusively on strength.** Because any amount of conditioning can slow strength gains, schedule at least some part of the year devoted only to strength. Immediately after the end of the season is often appropriate. That way, the athletes can focus on maximizing strength gains. Conditioning is a quality developed quickly—unlike strength, which takes a long time—so focusing conditioning work in the month or so before the competitive period makes the most sense. Trying to stay "in shape" year-round is a bad idea. It compromises what can be accomplished with a good strength program.

These simple rules are well known and have been for a long time, but many coaches don't use them. They either haven't educated themselves, or they know better, but still insist on excessive conditioning. They think they simply must get their athletes dead tired every practice.

I hope you can see this is counterproductive if you want fast, powerful, explosive athletes.

Here are some conditioning drills I've tried, but you can create your own using the previous rules.

Sled Drags

Sled drags done right are so valuable; they're like a secret weapon for strength and power development. Few people do them effectively. I learned how to do sled drags from Louie Simmons.

When I was a powerlifter, I found that my squat improved quickly. I was a good squatter, but only a so-so deadlifter. In my first meet, I squatted 500 pounds, and my second meet, 550. Six weeks later, at my third meet, I squatted 606 pounds. In my first meet, I deadlifted 555 pounds, but it took me years to get to 600.

Out of the blue, I called Louie Simmons for advice about my deadlift. Surprisingly, he recommended sled drags, an idea he got from Finnish weightlifters.

Many of the great Finnish weightlifters were also lumberjacks. After they cut timber, they put on a harness attached to the log and dragged it to a clearing for pick up. They had to drag the logs 50, 100, or 200 yards—whatever it took because the big track vehicles weren't allowed in the forest. They did this over and over. The Finnish lifters said it was the key to their deadlift strength.

Louie incorporated this with his lifters with great success in the 1990s. I found a 200-pound dredging sled at my parent's farm and connected it to my weightlifting belt with a rope...and started to train sled drags. That's when my deadlift finally started to increase at a reasonable rate.

Long, slow strides was how Louie recommended they be done, and that's how I did them. I don't believe in sprinting or running while dragging a sled. The weight slows down the sprint too much to be effective for speed development.

We use the sled drag as a strength tool that's also great for conditioning. The idea is to take as long a stride as possible to activate and stretch the hamstrings. The athletes I've trained with sled drags have all gotten significantly faster. They got faster because their single-leg hip-extension strength in the glutes and hamstrings improved greatly.

Having no eccentric contraction is another reason sled drags work so well. The lack of eccentric contraction means an athlete can recover quickly. Even a hard sled drag workout can be well tolerated by an athlete without negatively affecting the ability to lift heavy that week.

Sled drags makes an athlete stronger, unlike running mileage—nothing makes an athlete weaker faster than running miles. I've used sled drags with high school, collegiate, and pro athletes...and it simply works. They've become a real foundation of my conditioning program.

Death March

Like the sled drag, the death march places tremendous emphasis on single-leg hip extension, and the glutes, hamstrings, and lower back. These are great for conditioning because they also produce a tremendous amount of metabolic fatigue.

Increase the load and distance over time. I've had teenagers manage almost 100 yards of smooth, unbroken stride with over 100 pounds in each hand. It takes time to get to that level, but the benefits are tremendous. See pages 174–175 for a detailed discussion of the death march.

Sandbag Stair Sprints

Stair sprints are one of my favorite conditioning drills. I had a friend who managed a local hotel with a set of stairs that were perfect for sprints. I bought several 50-pound bags of dog food and had athletes sprint up the stairs with them, then take the elevator down. They got their rest breaks in the elevator. This is a devastatingly hard workout.

Row and Snatch

Row and snatch is one of the hardest workouts I've done. The first time I did it, it took me 30 minutes, and I sweated for three hours afterward. Fortunately, after a few sessions, it took half as long.

Here's how you do it:

Row hard for 500 meters, kettlebell snatch for 10 reps left hand, then 10 reps right hand, then row hard for 500 meters. Repeat four times. Rest very little between rounds or continue on with none at all. You might want to have a bucket nearby.

CLOSING THOUGHTS

The rate of progress will be different from one youth athlete to the next. It *always* is.

Coaches should use their best judgment when progressing kids from beginner to intermediate, and finally to advanced programs.

Less is always more.

And always remember that for these young athletes, training in the weightroom is meant to drive performance on the field of play.

CHAPTER 19
IMPLEMENTING ATHLETIC PROGRAMS

My athletic template is discussed in terms of three different programs, the beginner program, the intermediate program, and the advanced program. The beginner program consists of only three exercises: snatch-grip deadlift, push press, and squats—plus some conditioning. The intermediate program adds some optional assistance exercises. The advanced program adds additional exercises until the athlete is using 11 different exercises, and eventually adds weekly intensity variation.

The program is a smooth continuum from beginner to advanced with small additions and adjustments along the way. These three divisions are provided to steer your thinking about training kids through adulthood, but there's no specific point where the beginner program ends and the advanced program begins.

It's like building a house and trying to determine when you're in the early, middle, and late phases of construction. The beginning is easy to pinpoint, and so is the end—we're finished! But where's the line between early and middle, or middle and late? Does middle start after we put in the sheet rock or after the cabinets? We have the same issue here. Just like building a house, building a strong and powerful athlete involves a lot of small additions and adjustments done when the time is right.

So why not just scrap the divisions? Because they serve a purpose. For the most part, the beginner program is where we put preadolescents, who tend to move to the intermediate program as they become adolescents. The advanced program is the final stop and is usually arrived at in the preteens or teens. It puts some context to the long-term training of kids through adulthood.

But in practice, the reality is more fluid than that. Everyone starts with the beginner program and progresses through the intermediate and then to the advanced program. This is true even for those who start training in high school...and as adults too. Those who start late will likely progress through the beginner and intermediate programs and rapidly arrive at the advanced program.

For example, a kid who begins training as a freshman may spend as little as two weeks on the beginner program before moving to the intermediate program, then maybe just two to four weeks before adding additional lifts. If kids have good motor skills, they may end up on the advanced program just a few months later.

A seven-year-old will start with the beginner program, but if the kid is very coachable and dedicated, we may quickly progress to the intermediate program and reach the advanced program by nine or 10 years old. Other kids may take much longer.

The key to the program is to progress seamlessly when the athlete is ready. For kids, readiness is generally determined by the ability to follow directions and accept coaching. For teens and adults, it's more physiological, having more to do with mastering the lifts and having the strength, flexibility, and conditioning to progress.

PROGRAMMING FOR 8 TO 12 YEARS OLD

There's a difference in how we program depending on what age someone starts the program. The kids always start with the beginner program. When an athlete starts young, I start them on snatches early during the transition to the intermediate program, even before they learn simpler lifts like the clean. Young kids are flexible and learn skills quickly, so it makes sense to take advantage of this period of development to teach the more complex skill while it's easier to learn.

You already know how this applies to languages. Kids pick up new languages easily because they have a high level of brain plasticity, while adults take much longer to learn them. The same is true of motor skills. Like riding a bike, if a kid learns to snatch at a young age, it's a skill for life.

Since they started early, they have plenty of time to develop their snatch technique. For kids who start this young, we can add the additional lifts of the intermediate program. I try to include the assistance lifts early too (dips, glute ham raises, or hip extensions) to ensure adequate posterior-chain development.

PROGRAMMING FOR
OLDER THAN 12 YEARS OLD

Kids who start much later though—for example, freshmen year—have less time for physical development. The clock is ticking. As a result, we have less time to develop strength and power. As with younger kids, we start with the beginner program, and move to the intermediate program in two to four weeks. Then we start to introduce additional exercises.

We have less time to work with than if we started at a younger age, so we go for cleans first, because they're easier to learn. Athletes can quickly get to the point where the clean technique is good enough to challenge them physiologically, which is the key to strength and power gains. It might take six months to five years to get them to that point with snatches, and we don't have that time to waste.

For athletes who start later in life, snatches are optional. If an athlete has an interest, we can introduce them, but start with cleans first so power development won't be compromised while learning the snatch technique. To introduce snatches, put them in the warm-up until the athlete has achieved sufficient proficiency to use them as a training tool.

HOW TO INTRODUCE EXERCISES

When using the intermediate template, introduce one new exercise at a time.

How long to wait before introducing another exercise is an individual decision based on an athlete's progress and receptiveness to coaching. Introduce the exercises when each athlete is ready.

If you're in a team setting, you'll have to make a judgment call based on the age of the athletes and your coaching ability.

Don't be in too much of a hurry. Much can be gained by mastering just a few exercises.

MANAGING IN-SEASON
AND OUT-OF-SEASON TRAINING

If this system is correctly implemented, you can expect all kids to make consistent progress out of season. The program works. The real difficulty is that kids may have only a few months of out-of-season training time, especially if they're two-sport athletes. In my part of the country, most of the kids who play football also wrestle. This makes it difficult to manage a training program year-round, especially in season.

An athlete who doesn't continue to train in season will significantly stifle athletic development. It takes some negotiation with the kids and parents, and a real commitment for all involved to make in-season training work. I try to negotiate for two training sessions per week in season. If I get two days per week, I try to do the posterior-chain exercises either right after a game or the day after a game or competition. That way, the athletes aren't too fatigued to perform on game day. I also abbreviate the program.

Though it varies, assuming a Friday or Saturday game, it will typically look like this:

TUESDAY	SATURDAY
Snatch or Snatch-Grip Deadlift or Cleans	Squats and Bench Press or Push Press

The rep scheme would be following the volume-day template using three to five sets of five repetitions. Kids always want to push press or bench press, and it's an effort to ensure that pulls and squats are done.

We generally don't do any conditioning drills in season. Practice and competition provide more than enough conditioning.

The goal of an in-season program is to provide work in the major movements so kids don't regress during the sport season. Some kids will even continue to improve on an abbreviated training schedule such as this. For kids with short out-of-season training time, maintaining strength with an abbreviated schedule is essential.

OVERVIEW OF
THE PENDLAY SYSTEM TEMPLATES

PUSH	PULL	SQUAT	ASSIST
Push Press	Snatch-Grip Deadlift	Back Squat	Dips
Bench Press	Deadlift	Front Squat	Glute Ham Raises
Press	Snatch	-	Hip Extension
-	Clean	-	-

BEGINNER PROGRAM TEMPLATE
(ONE OR TWO TIMES PER WEEK)

A short warm-up activity
Snatch-Grip Deadlift A couple of warm-up sets, followed by one challenging set of 5 reps
Push Press A couple of warm-up sets, followed by one challenging set of 5 reps
Back Squats A couple of warm-up sets, followed by one challenging set of 5 reps
A 5- to 10-minute conditioning drill

Add optional assistance exercises and move to three sets of five for main lifts.

INTERMEDIATE PROGRAM TEMPLATE
(TWO OR THREE TIMES PER WEEK)

A short warm-up activity
Snatch-Grip Deadlift A couple of warm-up sets, followed by 3 sets of 5 reps
Push Press A couple of warm-up sets, followed by 3 sets of 5 reps
Back Squats A couple of warm-up sets, followed by 3 sets of 5 reps
Dips Two sets of 10 repetitions
Glute Ham or Hip Extensions 2 to 4 sets of 10 repetitions
A 5- to 10-minute conditioning drill

Add the remaining exercises and weekly intensity variation.

ADVANCED PROGRAM TEMPLATE
(THREE TIMES PER WEEK)

Monday	Wednesday	Friday
Push	A different push	A different push
Pull	A different pull	A different pull
Back Squat	Front Squat	Back Squat
Conditioning	Conditioning	Conditioning
Optional assistance exercises	Optional assistance exercises	Optional assistance exercises
Volume Day 3 to 5 sets of 5 repetitions	**Light Day** 3 sets of 5 repetitions with 10% less weight than a volume day load	**Intensity Day** Work up to a max set of 3 to 5 repetitions

CLOSING THOUGHTS

A coach needs to understand all aspects of the athletes' training life when mapping out a program. How many years of training do they have under their belts? How many sports do they play in a year? How long are the sporting seasons and how much time is there pre- and post-season? What does each athlete need *right now* to be successful?

When you can answer those questions, developing a plan becomes much easier. You can more effectively progress a young athlete along the continuum of beginner to advanced and make the appropriate adjustments to the training along the way.

If the system I've outlined is implemented correctly, you can expect kids to make consistent progress and give them the best shot possible to become successful in their sports.

CHAPTER 20
EPILOGUE:
AMERICAN WEIGHTLIFTING
AND THE PENDLAY LEGACY

Those who knew Glenn are well aware that he was an intellectually driven person. He enjoyed spending countless hours reading, writing, and researching various topics he was passionate about. It's no wonder that once he discovered weightlifting, he began to seek out as much knowledge as possible and quite literally read all the books and articles available on the sport at the time.

Early on when we first started working together, Glenn gave me a list of books he thought I should own and read, telling me they would make me a better coach, and even a better person. He added to that list seemingly each time we spoke and I'm still working my way through it. Some of the books Glenn recommended included *The Lucifer Principle* by Howard Bloom, *Atlas Shrugged* by Ayn Rand, and *Guns, Germs, and Steel* by Jared Diamond. There were many books on weightlifting and training, such as Bud Charniga's translated Russian texts, Alexander Medvedev's *A System of Multi-Year Training in Weightlifting*, and *The Weightlifting Encyclopedia: A Guide to World Class Performance* by Arthur Dreschler, to name a few.

Glenn possessed a tremendous amount of respect for these authors and their literary works. He pointed out how Bloom and Diamond backed the main arguments of their text by skillfully providing layers of supporting evidence page by page. He often spoke about admiring the way Ayn Rand crafted such an epic story with deep philosophical messages. Of the weightlifting text, Glenn would remind me that the science within them was sound and time-tested. Anyone who read Glenn's blog articles in the past, and indeed this book, can see a bit of all these characteristics that inspired his own writing.

It's not surprising someone so well-read as Glenn would someday aim to write his own book…and

that book would be about his life's passion. Glenn didn't just want to write another book that resembled all the rest, but instead had a specific goal for what would eventually become *American Weightlifting*.

In our first phone conversation, Glenn explained that there were many great books about weightlifting. But, as he said, it always felt like they lacked a clear direction for the readers once they finished reading and put the book back on the bookshelf.

Glenn's goal was to do the opposite. He wanted to write a book that a "rank beginner" could use when going to the gym. After a few conversations with Glenn, it was apparent that he was a generous person who loved to share. He never held anything back—and that's exactly the approach he took with this book. Glenn's goal was to share how to apply the information in his book with all readers. He felt it was important to demystify the training process… and that there should be no secrets in training.

A major part of Glenn's overall philosophy in the creation of this book was that if you give people all the tools they need and the guidance on how to use those tools, it will greatly enhance their chances of achieving ultimate success.

He felt strongly that a weightlifter should eventually be capable of picking exercises, weight intensities for the day, and the number of sets and reps to do to achieve a training goal. This information should be known and shared between the athlete and coach. Both parties then work together to complete the training, win gold medals, break records, and make teams. He wanted to write a book that helped make weightlifters self-sufficient, a book that would have helped him when he first started weightlifting.

Many eagle-eyed readers may finish reading *American Weightlifting* and wonder to themselves, "Why wasn't X included?" or "I really wish THAT story from THAT meet was in here." Well, you're not alone! Glenn and I often discussed what should be included in the book and what he didn't feel was necessary. In the end, many topics were not included because Glenn had a very specific purpose for this book and at the time intended to write more books.

After his passing, I felt it was important to keep Glenn's purpose for this book intact. Now, that's not to say certain liberties weren't taken by including something here or there, but first and foremost, it always had to fit within Glenn's mission and vision for the book. After almost four years of working together, I'd collected countless pages of notes, emails, and well over 24 hours of audio between us as we discussed weightlifting and Glenn's thoughts on training.

As I was working to organize this mountain of information, I found myself on many occasions calling Glenn and asking him for help deciding where he wanted specific topics, old stories, or ideas to be arranged in the book. In typical Glenn fashion, he'd respond with "Y'know, I'm not sure if it should go anywhere, but I thought it'd be fun to talk about." He always answered his phone for anyone. He simply loved talking about weightlifting and could do so for an entire day if other responsibilities didn't pull him away.

While working to complete this book for Glenn after he passed, I thought a lot about the material we left "on the cutting room floor." There's definitely a lot of it that doesn't fit Glenn's purpose for this book, but there were a few things that should be included. So, in the coming pages I'll reminisce on some of the conversations I had with Glenn on topics that didn't make it into the main text. I'll also recap a few core concepts of *American Weightlifting* that are important to expand upon or mention one more time. I'll do what Glenn was so fond of doing: share just a little bit more.

ON LEARNING THE LIFTS

The first time we worked together, Glenn explained that learning the lifts is a career-long process. He said the learning process is one that starts when a weightlifter picks up a barbell for the first time and follows right through a perpetual number of reps done in a quest to "get it right." "Right," Glenn explained, never really happens or at the very least is short-lived—just when you think you have it, the next rep or training session proves you wrong.

Sure, one day a lifter accomplishes a goal by snatching 100 kilos to set a new PR, but had to walk around the platform a bit to stabilize the weight overhead or the elbows flickered on the catch—is that what "right" is? The next training session, this lifter might snatch 100 kilos again, only this time with flawless execution—was that "right?"

According to Glenn the answer to both questions is: Yes. Yes, in those moments, the lift was "right" because both represent progress. Glenn reminds us to be happy with progress. But—and he said this is a big BUT—"right" in the moment should never be enough in the grand scheme of a career.

Snatching 100 kilos is only 100% "right" if the lifters plan to unlace their shoes, leave them at the front of the platform, and retire from the sport after hitting that lift. If that's not the case, mere moments after that exhilarating feeling of setting a new record, it should become old news. At that time, anyone planning to be in the sport for an extended period should wonder next, what about 101, or 105, or beyond?

Many times, athletes load 101 kilos on the bar and everything will change…maybe physically…maybe mentally…or maybe even both. They learned how to snatch 100 and everything that came before it, including the precise timing needed to make the lift and the mental fortitude to finally pull under the bar. Now they have to do it all over again and learn to snatch 101 and everything that will come after that.

So, as Glenn explained it, no one can say they've learned everything there is to learn about weightlifting. The next weight you want to lift requires learning how to move your body and operate your mind to lift it. Saying you "got it" or "know all you need to know" is a sure sign you don't know much of anything at all. Glenn even made it a point to say that if he ever made that claim, it would mean he should retire as a coach.

Through his entire life, Glenn placed a high value on being open to learning and felt it was vital to a weightlifter's long-term success. Unfortunately, he said it's something many beginner lifters forget as they progress to becoming an intermediate lifter. Not only that, but they may even rush too quickly from being a beginner because of ego and being closed to learning. He felt strongly that new lifters should embrace being a beginner and stay there as long as possible. He often said it's valuable time no one ever gets back.

After he told me all of this, I remember laughing and saying, "Oh man, some people will definitely get upset hearing about this." Glenn quickly responded with, "Good, if they have any sense at all, they'll change their minds."

He then went on to expand on this, reminding me it's hard for many joining the sport to resist the urge to increase the weight on the bar too quickly. The ego gets in the way and this results in poor technique being developed in the early days.

Embracing being a beginner, he said, also means "Stay humble and open to learning as your abilities improve." There will always be a next level of weightlifting abilities, even for those at the top of the sport. There's always a bigger weight to learn how to lift.

Glenn felt that the best lifters are advanced in their strength and abilities to perform the snatch and clean and jerk, but at heart, they retain the wanderlust mindset of a beginner. They're on a continuous journey of discovering what they can do to improve, which is a quality possessed by those most likely to achieve major accomplishments in the sport. These athletes will be who win gold medals, break records, and make international teams. Those who don't—who think they know it all—will become frustrated with the sport and eventually quit.

Deep into our conversation, Glenn commented that each new weight loaded to the bar has the ability to humble us and make us feel like we have no idea what we're doing. I asked him how he and his lifters worked around this during hard training. He explained that while strength was something they always worked on, each of his lifters had within them the strength to reach the next level they aspired to on the snatch. But the specific technique and the removal of mental blocks needed to hit that next number was the tricky part.

Each weight represented the next level a lifter on his team desired to reach. He used Jon North as an example, saying when Jon snatched 150 kilos, 160 was the next long-term goal. Each incremental weight between those two numbers such as 151, 152, and 153, represented the short-term goal and steps needed to get to 160—all rungs of a ladder leading to dreams fulfilled.

In order to reach the next level and accomplish that long-term goal and the goals beyond it, he, Jon, and the rest of the team were always tinkering with techniques, making adjustments lift to lift, analyzing training videos, having detailed discussions about training, and reading about the sport. They lived weightlifting, practicing the basics daily by working to refine positions with a barbell, while warming up properly before going heavy.

Each lifter on the teams at Wichita Falls Weightlifting, Cal Strength, or MDUSA was as fully invested in the training process and open to learning as Glenn was, even after having won National titles and making Team USA. They remained humble in spite of their achievements.

Learning how to take technique to the next level was an obsession everyone on Glenn's team shared and was a key component of their successes.

ON PROGRAMMING

Glenn was a firm believer that programming didn't need to be complicated or flashy to produce results; he kept things simple and elegant. A coach should be able to quickly explain the program, with the lifter understanding right away what needed to be done. Better yet, a lifter should be able to look at the programming without the coach present and successfully complete the training session. If done well enough, an experienced lifter can accurately predict what the following week's training would look like.

Glenn admired those qualities about the Bulgarian system (he spoke about their programming in great detail in Chapter 4). The simplistic nature of the Bulgarian program really stood out to Glenn. Yet, he also realized it wouldn't work as written for most lifters as discussed earlier in the text. I remember him comparing the Bulgarian system to Ayn Rand's philosophy of Objectivism—I'll let you do the homework on what that is if you haven't already.

He explained that both Rand's philosophy and the Bulgarian system *should* work when seen on paper. At face value, you could probably pattern your life on one and your training on the other. But, as he was fond of saying, the devil is often in the details and you soon come to find that neither work 100% in real-world situations.

The simplicity of the Bulgarian system should be the ultimate goal. The programming stays close to the competition lifts, with very little deviation from the snatch or clean and jerk. But since we live in the real world of drug-free competition, it won't work for the long-term and we have to add to it. Adding to a philosophy creates problems because if you add too much, you stray far from the core concepts that make the philosophy work. You run the risk of over-complicating things to the point where you're even worse off. This is, as Glenn noted, where many coaches who become enamored with creating training programs get into trouble—*by adding too much*.

We've previously discussed the pitfalls of copying the programming of other countries. Copying and then adding everything a coach feels would make it better is an extension of that error. This puts you in a situation where you're running a hybrid that has strayed far from the original core philosophy of a program that was intended for advanced lifters… from countries that aren't drug-free in the first place. It's no wonder it never works out well.

For Glenn, sticking close to the competition lifts was important. That's the sport and those are the only lifts you'll do in a weightlifting meet. Beginners especially don't need any variety in Glenn's programming, but instead will work on perfecting movement patterns and getting brutally strong. That's the initial prescription for beginners. But, as you've learned in the text, as a lifter progresses through training, learning and growing in ability, training becomes more individualized.

I asked Glenn why there's a disconnect on this for many coaches. Why are they complicating their programming? According to Glenn, some coaches become more concerned with innovation than results. Being innovative for the sake of innovation is detrimental to a lifter's long-term progress. In Glenn's thoughts, some coaches seek something they know and others don't. They'll work hard to think of something different, looking for a secret edge to beat out the competition.

He acknowledged that most of the time the "secret squat program" works, but only because it's different from what the lifters were doing before—never mind if it doesn't work a month later.

Then what do you do? You keep adding and adding until eventually you come to a place where nothing works well anymore. Unfortunately, most coaches can be convinced quite easily that they know more than anyone else. Most people can be convinced their secret program will lead to big totals, but it's never the case. Coaches will often go too long before they realize the error of their ways and it's their lifters who suffer. He made a point to advise me to never go down this rabbit hole in my own coaching. Duly noted.

A SIMPLE PROGRAM

Next, I asked Glenn, how do we write a weightlifting program that's simple, stays close to the competition lifts, and isn't overcomplicated with unnecessary exercises. He said he's been working on a solution to this problem his entire career. He aimed to find a way to incorporate what he admired about other training systems, take into account the drug-free nature of American weightlifting, and accommodate beginners entering the sport at different stages of life.

His answer to the question was to incorporate his three-step top-down method into training, and pairing it with a short list of accessory exercises based on the general needs of his weightlifters first, and then progressing into the individual needs of each lifter over time.

Glenn expanded upon this by reminding me a cornerstone of his weightlifting philosophy: "There's no definitive line between learning the lifts and training the lifts."

As mentioned, learning is a part of training, and training is a part of the learning process that'll go on for as long as you're in the sport. Marrying the two into a simple program allows us to stay close to the competition lifts, meet the needs of individuals who didn't start the sport at a young age, refine technique from different positions, and provide the majority of variety one could need.

With that as a foundation, an expert programmer and coach like Glenn could easily shape programming around each individual lifter when the time came. Some will need to do more snatches from the hips, while others might need more work lifting from the knees. Although snatches done from the hips or knees aren't the competition lift of the snatch, they're still close enough to offer a high carry-over in training stimulus.

ACCESSORY EXERCISES

When he discussed accessory exercises, Glenn again made reference to the Bulgarians. As we've previously learned, their system works best for the perfect athlete built for weightlifting. This athlete has perfect limb lengths, no mobility restrictions, ideal levers and joints. A person such as this would be able to get away with training solely on the snatch, clean and jerk, and some front squats to meet training needs. Training only those exercises would develop the ideal ratio of quad strength to hamstring strength in this situation.

Everyone else who isn't perfect will have to work harder and need to modify the programming slightly. Those born without perfect body structures will have to add accessory exercises that complement the main training—complement being the key word.

For them, doing Romanian deadlifts to bring up hamstring strength and development will be necessary. That exercise stimulates more adaptation than the lifts alone and will help level those strength ratios. It's okay to add exercises like this and stray slightly from the core system, but one should avoid going too crazy with it.

For example, if you can go through an entire week's worth of training, and pulling from the floor on the snatch and clean are a small percentage of your training volume, you've gone too far. The bulk of your training should be centered around snatching and clean and jerking, with the accessory exercises filling in the gaps. Accessory exercises should complement training, not dominate it.

BELIEVING IN THE PROGRAMMING

Another discussion I had with Glenn that you'll want to know involved athletes *believing in the programming*. One of his core coaching beliefs was that when

lifters think a program is going to work, they'll make it work. When they don't think it's going to work, they'll figure out a way to fulfill that prophecy too.

Believing in one's training and one's self was big to Glenn. He told me he'd seen it a million times: When athletes really believe in something, they'll become an unstoppable force. If they believe a program will make them a champion or add 10 kilos to their snatch, they'll absolutely attack the program. They'll go to battle and fight to do the reps and make lifts. There won't be a little voice in the back of their heads whispering, "Why are you trying so hard? It's not going to work."

When he told me this, I asked, "How do you get a lifter to that level of belief?" His answer, like most of his teaching, was simple: First, you have to gain their trust in you as a coach. That trust doesn't come on day one. You have to build it up over time.

For example, I might have lifters who need to adjust their grip width on the snatch. This prompts me to suggest taking the grip out wider and then explain that they may not be able to hit their regular numbers right away, but with practice, they'll quickly get back there.

As a coach, that's a decision I have to make based on what I see. If it turns out to be true and works, then score one for me in the trust category. Moments like that will help my lifters decide if they think I know what I'm talking about... or not.

It will take repeated moments like this to earn trust. Glenn's point to coaches is to make sure when you say something, it's meaningful and not a bunch of fluff or technical jargon for the sake of sounding smart. Your athletes need to feel you care about them, not that you're a weightlifting genius.

On the other hand, if I say "Go light today and tomorrow you'll do great," and the next day is a rough training session, it'll be a mark against me.

Be honest. Training will go through ebbs and flows of great and downright agonizing. Avoid feeding your athletes a bunch of nonsense or massaging their egos. Tell them the truth—that you're seeing them struggle on front squats today and that could negatively affect another day's training session when you get to clean and jerks. Explain the reality of hard training opposed to trying to hide it. Lifters can sense when a coach is artificially trying to build them up. Be real, be honest, and be truthful.

ON BEING A WEIGHTLIFTER

The lion's share of this text focuses on weightlifters as individuals. It's from the perspective of Glenn talking to you as he would one of his lifters, trying to teach you all he knows. Here and there, training partners and teams were mentioned, but not really expanded upon. However, Glenn did have some thoughts about training alone versus training in a group.

According to Glenn, a team adds a lot for a lifter. Training in person is best, but these days, online teams are also common and beneficial in their own way. People are social animals. Some lifters are more social than others, but if you have five people watching you lift, you can almost always lift more than you can when alone. If those five people are cheering for you, you can almost certainly do more.

In a team dynamic, not everyone will have a bad day at the same time. At least one person will be having a good day and will raise up the others. You'll always have better training sessions being a part of a team than on your own. The push from the team is that powerful.

Glenn also felt that even as a coach, he did better coaching in a team atmosphere. Weightlifting is a hard sport, and it can be a lonely sport when you train alone. The shared misery of training with others makes it easier to bear that suffering. You can get into a rhythm with your training partners as well as trading lifts back and forth. Pretty much everywhere Glenn went, he emphasized the team atmosphere.

When I asked him about people who have no choice but to train alone, Glenn advised watching training videos while lifting. I remember laughing when he said, "If I had a dollar for everyone who told me they watched Cal Strength videos when training…I'd have a few dollars" in his normal matter-of-fact way. He went on to say people would tell him they'd play those videos and imagine training with Donny, Jon, Spencer, and Caleb. It's an excellent strategy to make the sport a little less lonely if you're a garage lifter. He said anything you can do to generate excitement in your training is better than nothing.

A LIFTER'S RESPONSIBILITY

Glenn was adamant about developing a lifter from head to toe. That goes beyond just teaching athletes how to lift, writing their programming, and going to meets. We had many conversations on what qualities Glenn tried to develop in his athletes so they could find long-term success.

On one particular day, the topic revolved around weightlifters taking responsibility for themselves and their training. According to Glenn, helping to develop the ability of athletes to take care of themselves is one of the most important things a coach can do. Almost anyone can teach someone how to snatch if they know the steps, but helping someone become an independent individual is not easy. He felt strongly that if lifters are able to take ownership of their performances, it will translate to major accomplishments in the sport and success in life.

I remember him saying when athletes get out on the competition platform, they have to do everything for themselves. He saw it time and time again: When athletes were used to handling things on their own, it led to superior performances. He also frequently noted that a major pet peeve of his involved lifters never learning to evaluate their own lifts and understand what they did wrong on a lift.

He'd seen many lifters miss a competition snatch and immediately come off the platform and ask their coach, "What did I do? Tell me what I did wrong." They had no idea what happened. That's more of a reflection on the coach than it is the athlete. When someone is new to the sport, of course that situation will occur.

But Glenn was very clear that if a coach has been working with athletes for a couple of years and they still don't know what went wrong on a lift or how to fix it, it's just shameful. Those coaches were ineffective and didn't do the job. What happens when their lifters are at a competition and the coach can't be there? He never wanted his lifters to be in a place where they'd say, "My coach isn't with me today so I can't lift," or to be in a situation where they're desperately looking for help weeks, days, or even during a competition.

Lifters should learn the lifts. They should train the lifts and learn how to snatch and clean and jerk progressively heavier weights. They should also learn how to handle themselves as athletes in training and at a competition.

It should be no problem for lifters to go to a competition without their coaches, read the schedule, warm up, count their own cards, and make meaningful decisions about their attempts.

When the coach is present, the cooperation and teamwork enhance the performance because now there are fewer things the lifter needs to worry about. To Glenn, anything else was just bad coaching.

WEATHERING STORMS IN TRAINING

Everyone who's been involved in the sport very long understands there will be great days in training… and then days that make them want to quit weightlifting altogether. There will be days where lifters even miss all their prescribed lifts. According to Glenn, that's completely normal. He never found an athlete who trained on what he called "the razor's edge," which was discussed in Chapter 14, who didn't have bad days. When you're training on the razor's edge, you're in the process of adapting to training and your body is going to respond to training differently day to day. There's simply no way around it.

When I asked him what advice he had for lifters that would allow them to mentally handle the bad days in training, he said lifters should welcome those days and to not fight them. The example he gave was to take someone lifting three days a week. For this theoretical lifter, Monday's training session was sensational. Wednesday's training was brutal and the athlete seemingly couldn't make a lift. Friday was a so-so day of training. The following Monday is just "all right" and then on Wednesday, the lifter makes all new PRs on the lifts…but that Friday is a horrendous day of training. This lifter should welcome this modulating experience from one training session to the next— and welcome it like crazy because the person is indeed making progress, although it may not feel like it in the moment.

Athletes progressing like this are making changes week to week and placing various stresses on the body… and their body is adapting. If their capabilities are wildly varying every day, going up and making PRs, but then in the same week, they have a day when they can't lift anything, they're walking on the

razor's edge of hard training and are making progress. This is a reality of training and a point where many lifters hit the emergency brake and take a week off or change the program. That's a mistake.

This is not to say the goal is to have sessions where you completely miss all your lifts. You want to make lifts. After you've gone through the process a few times, as a lifter, you should learn how to adapt the programming day to day based on how you feel.

If a program says to perform five snatch singles at 90% and you miss the first three singles, of course you should reduce the weight. Go down to 80% and if you make a lift there, bump it up to 85%, and if successful, try 90% again.

According to Glenn, your body will adjust the training program for you; you just have to learn how to listen to it and adapt the sets and reps from there.

ON COACHING

Glenn's coaching philosophy is tightly interwoven into every word, sentence, and paragraph of this book. It's presented in a conscious and continuous flow of information geared toward teaching his methods to weightlifters. While that may be the case, experienced coaches will be able to read between the lines and pull deeper insight from Glenn's thought process.

When reading *American Weightlifting,* we need to keep in mind Glenn's original purpose of the book. It's a manual weightlifters can use to learn how to lift and train, coaches can gain ideas to incorporate with their athletes, and now, with his passing, it's an anthology that documents his legacy.

While an expansion of the topic of coaching wasn't something Glenn intended to include in the main text, I feel that now would be an appropriate time to take a deeper dive into some of the finer points of coaching we only briefly touched upon earlier.

Here I'll discuss Glenn's thoughts on the concepts of the role of a coach, when and how a coach should offer advice, and some insight into how Glenn continued to learn and grow as a coach.

A COACH'S ROLE

One day, I asked Glenn about the role of a coach in the athlete-coach relationship. This topic and his answer were one we discussed later in countless meetings…and his thoughts were always the same. Every time, Glenn answered the question by saying his ultimate goal as a coach was to one day work himself out of a job.

Glenn despised coaches who work to make athletes dependent on them for job security. Glenn was vehemently passionate about this, and even had several heated debates both in person and over the internet with other coaches who felt differently. Ever the contrarian, Glenn worked tirelessly to make his athletes as independent as possible.

Now, when taken literally, one can see how some coach's feathers would get a little ruffled. But as Glenn elaborated, it all made a little more sense. While he worked toward his athletes not needing him anymore, he also acknowledged it would never truly happen if the relationship is strong and there's a foundation of trust within it.

He wanted to build his athletes up and push them to the point where they didn't need a coach, but chose to have one. Smart athletes will choose to have a coach help them with their training because athletes struggle to be honest with themselves. A coach is needed to offer completely unbiased feedback on lifts and training.

In the beginning, a young kid just starting the sport will be 100% dependent on the coach to do everything, and that's fine. But over time, athletes should need the coach less and less, or Glenn felt he hadn't done right by them. They need to learn how to become independent and capable of taking care of themselves. When that happens, if the relationship is strong enough, they'll continue to work together. In the grand scheme of things, the dynamic Glenn wanted was to someday shift from being one of teacher and student to one of partners with a shared goal.

ON COMMUNICATION

You've read so much diving deeper and deeper into the mind of Glenn Pendlay. From learning the lifts to programming for different experience levels all the way to what a weightlifter should eat, this is everything he thought would be helpful for a weightlifter to know.

In reflecting on the book, I'm reminded about a conversation I had with Glenn while visiting him in Kansas. We were sitting in his living room, both with laptops propped on our thighs. While working on the intermediate programming chapter, I said, "We already talked about why it's important not to teach beginners how to do power snatches in Chapter 1." To which he replied, "You're right, but why not say it again if it's important?"

Being a weightlifting coach myself, I always appreciated Glenn taking the time to teach me about coaching. In addition to teaching me about the methods discussed in the book, he'd often go into details on the method behind the method. He put effort into helping me become a better coach, and that's something I'll never forget.

In that moment, he was teaching me something important about communicating as a coach. Glenn went on to explain that he repeats himself a lot when coaching because over the years, he found that people either weren't listening the first time around or because some topics are worth repeating to drive the message home.

That's why throughout the book, Glenn says repeatedly that beginners should learn the full lifts before they learn the power variations. It's an important message he hoped coaches and lifters take to heart because the ramifications of learning poor motor patterns in the power snatch could possibly be felt negatively throughout the rest of a lifting career. Or, at the very least, it will waste precious training time when a lifter inevitably has to take weight off the bar to relearn the lifts.

Glenn felt repeating himself was an effective way to emphasize what he thought was important, and to communicate to his lifters where their focus should be directed. At the time, I hadn't thought about it that way. Having less experience than Glenn, when teaching, I'd often say something once and move on.

After that conversation, I changed my approach and indeed found it to be much more effective. I may even sound a bit like a broken record at times, but that's because what I'm focusing on is the one thing out of thousands of things I feel is important for a lifter in the moment.

Ultimately, what I learned from Glenn was that a good coach doesn't say things once because people should listen when they speak, but instead, repeat what's important because they care enough to take the time to say it again.

OFFERING ADVICE

Obviously, in competition lifters need someone they can depend on. But if no one is available, they need to have the confidence that they can depend on themselves. That skill starts in training and Glenn was confident that his style of coaching fed into his lifters being able to take responsibility for their training.

He told me he worked tirelessly to build his athletes to the point where they could come off the competition platform and say to him, "You know what? I didn't finish that pull." Glenn knew they didn't finish the pull, but more importantly, the lifters could feel and realize they didn't finish the pull. From there, a validation of how they felt about it was all the coaching they needed.

After Glenn told me this, I asked, "So when do you correct someone or offer advice on their technique?" He told me he never really wanted to do that until they'd made the same error two or more times. If someone misses one snatch by dropping the barbell behind at 100 kilos, Glenn wasn't going to immediately jump in with cues and fixes. He had no way of knowing if that miss was an anomaly. After he'd seen athletes miss a lift the same way multiple times, he could accurately say what they were doing incorrectly.

Often, his first move would be to ask the lifter, "What do you think you're doing wrong?" He wanted athletes to think and wanted to prompt a meaningful conversation as opposed to solving the problem for them outright, offering a fix, and walking away. If he and the lifter were able to correct the error, training continued, but if they're unable to, a new goal of the day's training session had just presented itself to both of them. Whatever the issue may be, THAT'S what they needed to work on that day.

During this conversation, Glenn said that if a coach has a knee-jerk reaction and fixes errors immediately, it opens up the risk of playing Whac-A-Mole with technical errors. I may tell lifters to move their feet on the snatch. On the next lift, they move their feet,

but cut the pull short and miss again. If they miss the lift another time, it will be for a different reason.

If the reason they're missing the lift is different each time they snatch, why even bother correcting them? At this point, it'd be better to take weight off the bar and build back up from there. It's useless to correct technique when the technique changes every rep.

DEVELOPING A LIFTER'S CONFIDENCE

Anyone who knew Glenn knows he wasn't about fluffing egos. He was logical in his thinking, patient in his coaching, and direct with his opinions. Those qualities certainly helped him develop countless lifters to achieving their ultimate potential.

He often found if he gave his lifters a chance to figure out an error on their own, they'd correct it without needing to be prompted. Sometimes a part of coaching is just giving lifters enough space to breathe and lift weights. This, Glenn said, is how a coach helps lifters develop REAL confidence. If they discover they need to pull a little harder and then do that and make the lift, it's a huge psychological win.

With this approach, athletes begin to learn they're responsible for what that bar does. A lot of lifters get in a rut where they don't believe what they're doing is causing the problem. They may say something like, "I don't know why I'm missing; I'm pulling straight." That's when they need a coach to say, "No, you're not." They'll often act like it's out of their control and that's a bad place for them to be in.

As a coach, Glenn wanted to guide athletes to the point where they could identify a problem, fix it for themselves, and make lifts. He said his job was to help them achieve that… and not to do it for them. That gives them real confidence instead of a fake confidence by fluffing egos.

To Glenn, a lifter is in a good place when he or she can say, "I'm who's making me miss this lift. I'm the one who's overpulling. The bar does whatever I do to it—no one else." This is along the lines of people taking responsibility for their own lives: Weightlifters need to take responsibility for their own lifting.

ALLOWING WEIGHTLIFTERS TO BE WEIGHTLIFTERS

Good weightlifters have a need to push themselves. Glenn didn't want to take that away from his athletes.

He said too many coaches are control freaks; they want to make an athlete do what THEY want to do. A lot of coaches are too focused on controlling their athletes almost to the point where they seemingly get joy out of telling them they can't go heavy because "this week is light."

Glenn acknowledged that there are times when an athlete is peaking or taking a break where controlling the programming is necessary. But he always wanted to be open-ended with his coaching. He wanted to challenge people and he didn't want them to come to a training session and say, "This is all we can do today." He wanted training to be fun and exciting… and what's more fun and exciting than going heavy?

According to him, a great question for lifters to ask themselves is, "I wonder if I can lift that?" That kind of wonder is inside all of us, and because of that, he felt that weightlifting should be the most popular of sports. He reminded me that every 10-year-old wants to see how much they can lift over their heads. We don't have to instill that in them or develop that quality; it's already there. And there's a 10-year-old inside of all of us who wants to see what we can do today.

It's up to coaches to facilitate their lifters, not put a roof over their heads. Glenn didn't like closed-off workouts and preferred open-ended workouts that give people an opportunity to challenge themselves.

Of course, coaches need to rein things in so people don't miss 20 times in a row. And we also need to be creative with it by programming complexes, lifts with pauses, doubles, triples, and other ways of going heavy opposed doing only singles. That allows us to facilitate hard training, not burn out our lifters, and allows their inner 10-year-old to thrive. That makes training more fun and keeps them coming back.

LEARNING FROM OTHER COACHES

Even when he was a USAW Level 5 coach and had accomplished so much in the sport, Glenn always sought out learning from others. Glenn mentioned once how he admired a coach by the name of Lou DeMarco. He admired the way Lou psychologically handled lifters. Glenn called him a "good competition coach," and said it always seemed like he had a special way of communicating with lifters, a good way of earning their trust. Glenn noted that in coaching, trust is everything.

Glenn wanted to be the best coach he could be, so much so that he'd try to get to the warm-up room so he could watch others coach. Lou was a guy Glenn would quite frequently try to watch to see what he said and did. Glenn always learned something new from these experiences.

Glenn also wasn't above asking other coaches for help. Several times over the years, he asked John Thrush and others for assistance coaching one of his athletes. It was for the betterment of the athlete, and so he could learn. I thought it profound when he said that if a coach puts aside the ego and asks another coach for help, it's a win for everyone involved.

PAYING IT FORWARD

Glenn Pendlay was immensely accessible. Many high-profile athletes and coaches put up walls and don't have time for people they're not directly working with, but that wasn't Glenn's style. If you wanted to talk about weightlifting, he was game regardless of who you were or if he was your coach. It could be through email, on a forum, or even a phone call—he was never shy about giving out his phone number. He would have been thrilled to hear your thoughts on weightlifting, to give you advice on your programming or technique, and to listen to your experiences in training and competition. Sadly, it's not possible for any of that to happen anymore. It's still difficult to believe he's gone.

There's no questioning it, Glenn loved weightlifting and he loved his athletes. This text is a reflection of that affection and the passion he had for the sport that can hopefully be felt through every word, sentence, and page of the book. While Glenn may no longer be with us, the countless stories of lifters and other coaches, his writings on training, and this book will help keep his memory alive.

I'll never forget hosting Glenn in Albany, New York, when he visited to teach a seminar. After the first day of the seminar concluded, we went back to my apartment and began to work on the book. Glenn always had a habit of pacing around a room when he spoke; he said it helped him think through concepts he was explaining. As I was typing, I noticed he had gone silent and was leaning up against the wall while holding Jon North's book, *The Dark Orchestra*. As he clutched the book to his chest, he said, "James,

I think this book we're working on can be something special. I think this might be what helps people remember me."

Publishing his book was immensely important to Glenn. As I think back on it now, he was right, as was often the case. This book is indeed something special in that it's a physical and portable collection of the methods of Glenn Pendlay. I absolutely agree with Glenn's statement because many who read through these pages will hear Glenn's voice speaking to them. It's special and this book will no doubt help to preserve the legacy he built.

I'd like to expand on his statement, however, and add that it takes more than a book to carry on a legacy. This book is a small snapshot, a glimpse if you will, into one of the greatest minds in weightlifting history. He left it all out on the field, yet still had so much left he wished to accomplish. Glenn had goals and dreams he shared with many others, and I believe his legacy will carry on through those who have so much more to share about Glenn. Putting more than 25 years of knowledge and experiences in one book is impossible. A book alone could never carry the weight on its back of such an enormous task.

So how do you find out more? Well, that's easy: Just talk to the people who knew Glenn. Donny Shankle, Jon North, Travis Cooper, Trey Goodwin, and Caleb Ward all no doubt have hours worth of stories from training, competition, and life with Glenn. They're also just the tip of the iceberg of people you could gain more insight from. Once you absorb the knowledge in this book and put it into practice, speaking to these people is how you'll get to another level of understanding Glenn and his methods.

I personally learned a lot about Glenn from conversations with Trey Goodwin that are great examples of insight you can gain from talking to those who knew Glenn. According to Trey, when Glenn was a younger man, he'd be right there training and competing with his athletes. His shoes would be on; his knees tightly wrapped, icy hot covered his elbows, and he led strongly by example.

It was inspiring to his athletes to see their coach lifting huge weights and sharing in the misery of the hard training. Trey said that everyone on the team in Wichita Falls, Texas, knew Glenn soundly understood

the science of training, but that science was backed up by experience and time spent under the bar.

Trey also told me how charitable Glenn was with his time and investments into his athletes. At the time, Trey had been in Glenn's program for several years and was now in college at Midwestern State University. Like any college kid on a Friday night, he wanted to hang out with his friends. Trey said he attempted—attempt being the key word—to skip training that was supposed to start at 6:30 p.m.

Little did he know Glenn wouldn't stand for this and proceeded to call Trey's parents, grandparents, and numerous other people to track him down and find out why he wasn't at weightlifting practice. Glenn managed to get the phone number of a buddy of Trey's, one he'd never met, and was finally able to contact Trey. That's when Glenn informed Trey he was still at the gym and would be there waiting for him to come in and train.

So, Trey arrived at the gym sometime around 9:00 p.m. Everyone else had gone home and it was just he and Glenn that night. Trey said he wanted to finish the training session as quickly as possible in order to enjoy the rest of the evening with his buddies, so he made a bet with Glenn. The workout was supposed to be five sets of five reps at a prescribed weight on the back squat. In an effort to end the workout early, Trey proposed a deal where if he set a new PR on his five-rep-max back squat, he could go home. Glenn agreed to the wager…and Trey set a new back squat record to finish the session early. Trey told some of the other lifters about it the next week and soon they also started making deals with Glenn to get out of doing the Friday evening back squat work sets—this would set the wheels in motion for what would later be known as the "Texas Method."

Now, besides Glenn masterfully turning his lifter's attempts to get out of doing work into a time-tested training program, a story like this really shows the type of person he was. Many others would have trained whoever showed up at 6:30 p.m. and then go home, but not Glenn. He cared that much about all of his lifters.

Time is one of our scarcest resources in life and Glenn was no stranger to sacrificing time for Trey and the other athletes on the team—time he could have spent with his family or working on other projects. That's how much Glenn wanted to see his athletes be successful. Glenn knew that when Trey finally achieved his dreams in the sport, the feeling of accomplishment and success outweighs one night out with friends. He knew that when Trey was standing with a gold medal lift over his head, coming in at 9:00 p.m. that night was worth it.

Another story Trey told me is a little more comical, but also shows how committed Glenn was to his athletes excelling in competition. According to Trey, this Glenn Pendlay stunt occurred at the Texas State Championships sometime between 2002 and 2003. There were a few guys in the heavier weight classes on the team attempting to qualify for bigger meets. 105 kilo and 105+ lifters need a little more rest between big lifts compared to their lighter counterparts. Glenn, being a big guy himself, knew this all too well, so he registered for the competition in order to be in their lifting session with a very specific goal: get his lifters rest when they needed it.

His strategy was simple. If one of his guys lifted a first attempt on the clean and jerk and needed more rest, Glenn would request his own weight a few kilos below the athlete's next lift. As the lifter, Glenn would go out and use the majority of his one-minute clock before performing the clean. He'd then sit at the bottom of the squat for an extended period before standing, and pause for a few seconds before performing the jerk. Then he'd declare the next lift to a weight still under his lifter's and proceed to run out his entire two-minute clock if need be. Glenn's commitment, creativity, and willingness to do whatever it took to help his lifters was like none other.

These are just a few examples of what you can learn by talking to people who spent time with him. If you're one of those people—someone who knew Glenn and had experiences with him—I encourage you to share your stories so the generations of weightlifters coming up after you can learn. As time carries the memory of Glenn Pendlay into legend, it'll be our responsibility to verify that the stories are truth opposed to myth. We'll keep his legacy alive.

CLOSING THOUGHTS

As *American Weightlifting* draws to a close, I find myself filled with a litany of mixed emotions. I'm happy

the book has finally made its way to the calloused chalk-covered hands of weightlifters all over the world. I'm also sad Glenn is no longer with us to flip through the pages himself and relish in the reality that his dream of publishing a book has finally been fulfilled. Regardless of how I feel, I'm confident Glenn would be proud of the work we've done.

In the final days of completing the text, I also found myself thinking of Glenn often. I think about the mind-boggling number of hours we stared at our computer screens obsessing over every single word in this book. Line by line, we worked meticulously to ensure everything was exactly as he wanted it. We always tried our best to stay on task, but inevitably a topic in the book would prompt a story from Glenn's life. Other times, we'd hop on a call and get no book work done because we spent an hour or two talking about current politics, a new gun Glenn bought, or the golden eagles being used to hunt grey wolves in Mongolia. I'm grateful to have had the opportunity to get to know him and to have shared time together.

I have a lot of great memories of Glenn, but I'm certainly not alone in that. I was able to see firsthand the impact he had on others. As his health began to take a turn for the worse, Glenn's hometown gym, Mac-Town CrossFit, decided to host a weightlifting camp for him. Being around a bunch of weightlifters who were snatching and clean and jerking heavy weights, eating tons of food, and sharing battle stories from training and competition was Glenn's idea of a good time. Unfortunately, he passed away the day before the camp. What was meant to be for many, including me, one last time to see him turned into a memorial.

Travis Cooper, Addison Jones, Jon and Jessica North, and a few of Glenn's childhood friends were in attendance. The rest of the group was rounded out by more than 30 weightlifters. In speaking with them, I discovered each person there knew Glenn in a different way. Some were athletes who trained under him at some point; others had taken a seminar, listened to podcasts, read blog articles, watched old Cal Strength or MDUSA YouTube videos, or met him at a weightlifting meet.

Glenn impacted so many people in so many different ways. It was beautiful that those whose lives he touched even in the smallest of ways flew or drove from all over the country to pay their respects. During the camp, we gathered in a large circle at one point to share how we knew Glenn.

Each person who spoke presented another layer of Glenn. Some spoke of the stoic coach who fearlessly led them to championships. Others made mention of the mad scientist who studied the inner workings of the human body and used the gym as his laboratory. Those who grew up with him spoke of the teenage rebel who got into all sorts of trouble.

Hearing each person speak gave me a new perspective and revealed more of the man Glenn was. It's not often you find yourself in this sort of situation, where you're around a massive group of people who open up their hearts about someone they love. That day, I learned so much about my friend and mentor. I gained an even deeper appreciation for him with every story told. After it was all said and done and I was on a plane back home, I started to think about the day I'll be asked by a new weightlifter, "Who was Glenn Pendlay?" A surface-level answer would be that he was a world-class weightlifting coach. But he was so much more than that.

For decades, the name "Pendlay" towered over weightlifting and strength and conditioning just like the man himself towered over most people. Although he was brutally strong and could lead others to elite levels of strength, he was kind, gentle, and compassionate. He was just as relentless in his pursuit of building better human beings and future generations as he was in building champions. He became a teacher to many, but never forgot how to be a student. He was indeed a coach, but he was also an entrepreneur, an academic, an author, an innovator, a father, a son, a brother, a friend to many, and a competitor to many more.

Glenn took on an untold number of challenges, yet also enjoyed the gift of life to its fullest. Along the way, he impacted the lives of countless people. He generously gave them his time, and his charitable nature knew no bounds. One might wonder what drove him to do all the amazing things he did. What gave him that incredible strength?

The answer to those questions is a simple one. Glenn Pendlay was a renaissance man who possessed many talents. He was clever in the way he thought about the world, and displayed great strength, whether it be with a barbell in his hands or by his mere presence in the room while his athletes trained.

However, what many may not know is that he was also a man of faith. That faith guided Glenn's hand and heart in all he did. It filled him with empathy and compassion as he packed his house with broke weightlifters, never asking for anything in return. His faith fueled his generosity as he gave away barbells, plates, lifting shoes, and his time to those who couldn't afford any of it. Faith led him to success with a great number of champions and gave him strength in overcoming the challenges of failed ventures and relationships. His faith no doubt lit the fire within him to aspire to the highest levels of his pursuits, to achieve excellence, and find the will to win.

The legacy that Glenn left behind motivates me, just like it undoubtedly does for many others, to aim for just as high a level of excellence. His example inspires me to be a better person, to be in the service of others, and live a life guided by faith. It has been an absolute honor to have been able to take this journey with Glenn.

"For I can do everything through Christ, who gives me strength." – Philippians 4:13 NLT

APPENDICES

APPENDIX 1
AMERICAN WEIGHTLIFTERS

Glenn began this section with a plan to discuss the attributes of some of the athletes he worked with, thinking the readers might learn some inside tips for success in weightlifting. However, he was unable to finish before he passed, so you may notice people missing who would surely have been included had Glenn had time to collect more material. For example, Trey Goodwin, who wrote the introduction to this book and for whom Glenn had great admiration, is notably missing from this section. I know Glenn would be disappointed in this gap. ~ James McDermott

Photo A1.1—Team photo, 2011 Muscledriver USA Grand Prix
From left to right: Kevin Cornell, Lindsay Bachinski, me, Spencer Moorman, Caleb Ward, and Jon North

I *love* weightlifting. I love everything about the sport, but most of all, I love coaching and helping athletes perform the snatch and the clean and jerk at the highest possible levels. Many coaches relate to the way I feel when I see athletes smile after doing something they never thought they could do. It's times like those that make us feel all warm and fuzzy inside.

Yet, over the last 25 years of coaching, I've found the lifts, personal records, programming, and competitions still don't encompass the whole sport for me. What's ultimately most important are the little things like the long road trips to competitions, the philosophical conversations or debates on the way the world works, the meals shared, and the sometimes-unexpected humor in the training hall.

Simply put, it's about the people; it's about the relationships—they're more important than the lifts.

In this sport, I've met some incredible human beings

who have deeply affected my life. I mention that quite a bit in the coming pages, and that's because of how profoundly each individual has contributed and continues to contribute to my personal journey as a coach and a person. Trey Goodwin, Justin Brimhall, Donny Shankle, Caleb Ward, Jon North, Travis Cooper, and Mary McGregor, to name a few—these are some of the best friends I've ever had.

It's just crazy to think we met through our shared love of lifting barbells.

Photo A1.2—Cal Strength team meeting of Rob Blackwell, Jon North, Donny Shankle, Kevin Cornell, Spencer Moorman

There are others with whom I may not have as close a relationship with today, but I still appreciate the time I spent with them. It seems to be either we get along and the pressure of competition forges a closeness within our athlete and coach relationship, or it put us at odds.

Whatever the case may be, I hope they all know, even those not discussed here in the text, that even though we don't see each other as often or speak on a regular basis, I still cherish every moment spent with them. I also hope each and every one of them knows that for every single thing they learned from me, I learned 10 things from them, and I'm forever grateful.

While this section might initially appear to be about the athletes, what I want you to gain from this are the lessons I learned from them. The insights and nuances will enhance your athletic or coaching career if you take the time to ponder the ideas that follow.

CALEB WARD

Photo A1.3—Coaching Caleb back in the Cal Strength days

My experiences coaching Caleb Ward were monumental, and I wholeheartedly believe I learned more about weightlifting from him than any other resource in my career. Sure, he learned some things from me, but overall, I received the better end of the exchange. Every lifter I've coached since Caleb benefited from the relationship we shared and the knowledge I gained as his coach.

Caleb was a unique lifter, first because he decided to devote himself to weightlifting at a young age—before the CrossFit boom and the huge rise in popularity of the sport that arose from that. Second, even from the ages of 12 through 20, he maintained an unwavering laser focus on his weightlifting goals. This is the most useful trait a young lifter can have—and Caleb Ward had it in spades.

I met Caleb through his older brother, Josh, whom I coached for a couple years. Josh was a physically

talented lifter—actually, the first lifter in our club to clean and jerk 300 pounds.

One day during his training, Josh mentioned he had a little brother who might be interested in weightlifting. He also insisted that little brother was somewhat of a cry baby who was likely to quit as soon as training became hard or uncomfortable.

At some point, Josh brought Caleb to the gym— "Tank," as we all came to know him—and after a week or two, it was obvious he had a talent for the sport. At first glance, Caleb didn't look very athletic. He was a chubby kid who had eaten too many chips and spent too much time on the couch.

But he also had huge thighs, elbows that slightly hyperextended, and in general, great joint mobility. I didn't know it then, but Caleb was also extremely explosive, and by the time he was 15, would have no problem doing multiple standing backflips weighing 270 pounds at 5′9″.

Caleb was an extremely determined young man. Over his first several years of training, he surprised his older brother and me by displaying a maturity that was downright shocking for someone his age.

When he was 14 and had been training for a couple of years, I remember a conversation that involved him thinking about taking a month or two off from training during the summer. He told me he felt he could definitely continue without a break, but he was worried if he didn't take at least a little time off, it might negatively impact his long-term desire to stick with the sport. We discussed it, and he decided to take a month off from training. He came back four weeks later, chomping at the bit to train.

Now, what other 14-year-old would display that kind of maturity?

In many ways, he was displaying more maturity than I had. I was coaching a group of teenagers and was mainly concerned with keeping them in the sport and enthusiastic about weightlifting. I was more anxious about what would happen the following month than looking forward years into the future of an athlete's career.

Besides determination, his almost insane attention to detail was his most useful trait. Even at age 12, lifts that even I could find no fault with were not acceptable to him. Seemingly, nothing escaped him. He picked apart joint angles at different positions, the relative speeds of different parts of a lift, and even the slightest hesitation during a snatch or clean. Many of the coaching points I still cover during my seminars originated during seminars many years ago when I used Caleb to demonstrate the lifts.

Things I can confidently say I did "right" while coaching Caleb were to focus more on movement patterns, the rhythm of the lifts, and speed rather than on strength.

Through the first seven or eight years of his career, Caleb focused almost exclusively on squats and the competitive lifts in training, rarely doing any other pulling exercises. I didn't try to increase his squatting strength at any cost. Caleb usually limited his back-squat training weight to a weight he was capable of clean and jerking. When he could clean and jerk 160 kilos, he was able to comfortably back squat 160 for a set of five, and do so with a bar speed that was very near the bar speed of his max clean and jerk. His best front squat triple usually didn't exceed his clean and jerk, and if it did, it wasn't by much.

My belief was that Caleb should develop a lifting technique that utilized his strength in the most efficient possible manner. Once he did that, there would be plenty of time to worry about strength. I still believe efficient technique is the proper focus for a lifter or coach who has the aim of becoming an elite weightlifter, or developing them.

I owe so much of my coaching career to Caleb and athletes like him that it's difficult to talk about any of them without the conversation veering off into training and coaching theory. But when I think back on Caleb and that group of kids I coached in Texas, the main thing I remember is that we had a lot of fun. We had a blast in training, at meets, doing car washes and other fundraisers—in fact, in everything we did.

When I look back at that time in my life, I don't think about the politics of the sport, about the financial stresses of paying for travel, or any of the negatives.

I think about the fun we had, and how lucky I was to coach lifters like Caleb. It was a hell of a ride.

KEY LESSONS

1. To be successful, you need to think about long-term development and how what you're doing now will affect you positively or negatively in the next five to 10 years.

2. Paying attention to details is an important quality for athletes at any level. Be as invested in the training process as your coach.

JAMES MOSER

"Fearless" is the word that best describes James Moser. James approaches every bar with a total disregard for the weight and with an unshakable belief he'll make the lift. This is not cockiness or arrogance; in fact, James is a humble guy. Instead, this quality is an absolute belief in himself and what he can do that goes so deep, it's almost scary.

James's father, Jim Moser, had been his coach since he started in the sport at a young age. Jim always wanted more for his son than the typical status quo, and set James's sights higher than they were for most American lifters.

I remember talking to him about how he wouldn't allow James to have any weightlifting posters unless the lifter pictured was clean and jerking over 500 pounds, or how he never wanted the focus to be on breaking American records, but instead wanted it to be on world records.

I was fortunate to have James live with me for a few months as he finished high school before the 2008 Olympic Trials. I won't claim to have coached James or programmed for him—his dad was responsible for those duties—but having James in the room with Caleb, Justin Brimhall, and other lifters was a great experience for all involved. His confidence and work ethic rubbed off on the lifters around him, and the training atmosphere pushed everyone to rise to another level. It made all of us better.

Jim Moser is a big believer in two things: the Bulgarian system, and using heavy snatches and clean and jerks to build the strength needed to perform even heavier snatches and clean and jerks. I differ somewhat from him in training philosophy, but the difference is one of degrees, not of direction.

I remember conversations when we discussed coaching James. He felt the goal was always to minimize the amount James would have to back and front squat, while still eventually being able to clean and jerk 500 pounds. That James would someday squat 500 pounds was assumed from the beginning.

But the underlying premise was that if James developed the sincere belief that clean and jerking a weight was actually easier than front squatting it, that belief would go a long way toward ensuring his future ability to clean and jerk that weight.

Jim convinced me of the validity of this line of thought. The philosophy became the basis for my belief that when learning the lifts, it's an advantage to do the initial learning when still weak.

Greater strength allows the lifter to lift inefficiently, yet still make the lift. If you don't have an abundance of strength, you're forced to lift efficiently to make the lift. Of course, one has to become very strong to be a great weightlifter. But the lifter who waits until technique is firmly ingrained before attempting to build strength will have a big advantage in the end.

James trained with a Bulgarian-inspired program using mostly singles on both the competition lifts and the front and back squat. The only other exercises I ever witnessed him perform were the power versions of the lifts. I've seen James accomplish jaw-dropping feats of strength, such as missing a 175-kilo front squat several times across multiple workouts leading up to a meet, only to then clean and jerk 180 kilos in competition. We can all agree that it takes enormous mental fortitude to pull that off.

His mental strength in training and his absolute fearlessness on the competition platform aren't the only things that come to mind when I think about James; he also had a tender side.

I have fond memories of the 17-year-old high school kid who took my eight-year-old son to the park to play and go down the slides when I was too busy with work. He was the only lifter I've ever had live with me—and there have been many—who helped out around the house, taking the trash out or doing the dishes without being asked.

KEY LESSONS

1. Not everyone is born with a high level of mental toughness or the fearlessness that produces champions. But these qualities can be developed like any other skill in training. If the training is hard enough and you put in the effort, you can get there too.

2. Coaches should frequently talk to one another. We have the shared goal of producing the best possible results for our lifters and for raising the standards in this country. We can't accomplish any of that if we never speak or share ideas.

TRAVIS COOPER

Photo A1.4—After Travis Cooper won the 2015 National Championships, he presented me with the Coach's Medal

In the years prior to becoming his coach, I was already a big fan of Travis Cooper. Our first conversations concerning weightlifting occurred when I was coaching at Cal Strength, and were about his snatch.

At that time, Travis had a flaw in his technique that was holding him back. He'd learned and practiced starting the second pull about three inches too far down his thighs, which limited his performance and caused his snatch to lag far behind his clean and jerk numbers.

Travis is open to learning, and will do what needs to be done to improve, which is why he was willing to come to Cal Strength for a month to focus on correcting his snatch pull. During that time, Travis stayed at my house and undertook the slow and frustrating process of changing a deeply embedded motor pattern.

This is always a difficult process, and it was no different for Travis. In one month of work, he was able to start the second pull at the crease of the hip with about 50 kilos when lifting at top speed, but when the weight increasingly became heavier, he'd revert to starting the second pull with the bar on his thighs. Old habits die hard.

Travis had previously snatched over 130 kilos at that point in his career. During that month in California, he improved to being able to correctly do 100 or 110 kilos, but anything over that, he'd fall back on his old technique.

Then Travis went home to Georgia, continued to work on his snatch, and sent me videos and updates on his progress over the next few months. The whole process of adopting the improved positions took between six months to a year. He was patient, and finally made it happen. By the time I moved to South Carolina and started coaching him full time, he was bringing the bar all the way into his hips before the second pull, even with maximum weights.

Travis is probably the smartest lifter I've coached, and I have a tremendous amount of respect for him. This made it difficult—maybe even impossible—to have a normal coaching relationship. To be honest, our relationship was more as colleagues than coach and athlete. In fact, in a lot of situations, Travis is probably a better coach than I am, and because of this, coaching him was a little intimidating. If I screwed up, it would immediately be obvious to him.

In trying to write a few paragraphs about Travis, I find each time I attempt to relate an experience with him or explain something about him, I feel like I'm diminishing our friendship or Travis as a person—and I don't want to do that. Travis is one of the true friends I've made through weightlifting. The sport is better with people like him involved in it.

Maybe the best thing I can say about him is that Travis Cooper is already a great coach and will continue to grow better and better as a coach.

KEY LESSONS

1. Taking weight off the bar and starting over is one of the most difficult things to do in training. It can also be one of the most rewarding, and Travis is proof of that.

2. Coaches should never forget that their athletes are their students, and are potential coaches of the future. If you're a coach, educate your athletes. Teach them the "why" behind their training.

JAMES TATUM

Photo A1.5—James Tatum and me: On this day, he used only yellow plates to build 215 kilos for back squats

James Tatum is an unusual guy. To start, he lived on a sailboat as a child and was mostly homeschooled. But the thing that really sets him apart is his incredible level of patience and his almost-intimidating intelligence.

"Patient" is not a word I use to describe most weightlifters. One thing that will drive almost any coach crazy is lifters who change six things at once in training. When you change more than one thing, how do you know which change helped…and which hurt?

James understands the training process in a way that can't be taught. He's focused, patient, and smart enough to learn—qualities that make him similar to Caleb Ward.

When a lifter is patient and smart, we can plan for the long term. A lifter who can look ahead to what will happen two, three, or even 10 years in the future is much easier to coach and is easier to help along the road to the top.

Too many American lifters are only concerned with what will happen next week, month, or at the next competition. A lot of the training that will turn an athlete into a champion has a negative effect on performance in the short term. For instance, heavy squats usually hurt performance in the competition lifts for at least a day or two, but are absolutely necessary for long-term progress.

When I first met James, he was pretty tall and thin for a weightlifter. He weighed a little over the 77-kilo weight-class limit, and in fact, he competed at 77 for several years before eventually moving to the 85-kilo class.

Like many lifters who are tall for their weight class, he was a strong puller who had an easier time racking the weight for cleans, but a lot more trouble standing up and jerking it. At about 5′9″, James would probably have to move up another weight class before the pull was his limiting factor—and even then, I'm not sure it would.

James is a talented puller, whether the pull is a deadlift, snatch, or clean. There are a lot of lifters who are physically talented, but his ability to make the lift that matters is what sets him apart from the crowd. Often in a competition, James is the wild card in the deck. With many athletes, you know approximately what they're capable of. I don't think anyone really knows what James is capable of, even now that he's been a top-ranked lifter for many years.

He could have a bad snatching day, or he could make an American record. His absolute belief in himself is one of the things that gives him the ability to do the unexpected.

Many athletes walk up to most lifts wondering whether they can make the lift. Whether the weight on the bar is well within his capability or is a new record, when James grips the bar, he really believes he can make the lift. This makes him very dangerous to any other lifter in his weight class.

You have to believe.

The same can be said about the athlete-coach relationship. Athletes should know the coach believes in

them, and in turn, the coach gains buy-in from the athletes. At that point, it almost doesn't matter how the programming is written.

KEY LESSONS

1. You have to take a few steps back in training to make leaps and bounds later. It's critical to have the patience to let the training process play out.

2. Belief is a powerful training tool for both athlete and coach. If an athlete doesn't believe in the training program, it doesn't matter how scientific or well-thought out it is: It won't work.

DONNY SHANKLE

Photo A1.6—Donny Shankle

Donny Shankle and I first crossed paths at the 2003 American Open in Atlanta, Georgia. He was at the meet with his first coach, Mike Burgener, and almost bombed out in the snatch before he finally lifted 125 kilos for his third attempt. He finished the competition with a 175-kilo clean and jerk, which is a tremendous weight for a beginner.

Just prior to the competition, Burgener called to discuss the future of his newest student. Mike said something along the lines of, "Glenn, I have this guy who's going to be a great lifter, but he just won't listen to me. He recently got out of the Marine Corps and needs an education. Can you take him to Wichita Falls and coach him?" Of course, I said yes.

Soon after, Donny made the trip from California to Wichita Falls, and I set him up in an apartment, where he stayed until a more permanent place could be found. I helped out where I could, getting him set up with the necessities of life so Donny could begin his training.

Coaching Donny was never easy. Donny has his own ideas about how to train, and he can be an immensely stubborn man. We butted heads about a number of topics, most notably how much rest he needed, and when to end a training session that wasn't going well. It took considerable work convincing him that what I wanted him to do was the right choice.

It's funny to think about now, but the first thing Donny said to me was, "I don't need all this technique stuff. I just need you to show me how to get strong." I told him, "Donny, that's just not how it works. Learning how to snatch and clean and jerk *is* weightlifting. Just getting strong is not enough."

But he was adamant he could figure all that out by himself, and that he just needed to get stronger. While certainly frustrating, the stubborn streak that made him difficult to coach was also his strongest asset as a competitor.

At that early point in his career, Donny jumped forward about a foot when he snatched. I tried to correct this in our first workout by having him take some weight off the bar. I quickly realized that in the whole sport of weightlifting, there's nothing quite as hard as trying to convince Donny Shankle to take weight off a bar. That's a fight that started our first workout together, and has lasted to this day.

I wanted him to work with 90 kilos, which he eventually yielded to after a lot of heartache and gnashing of teeth. By going lighter, his forward jump was reduced to about three inches. After that, he put weight back on the bar and went back to jumping forward 12 inches. That was my first experience coaching Donny, and would be the start of a long relationship that we still hold today.

What started as the relationship between a coach and an athlete eventually became the mutual respect of two close friends. Through the years, it was often a combative relationship, maybe made more combative because of our friendship and mutual respect.

Above all else, I always wanted Donny to make the Olympic team and break an American record. When he did things I felt were hurting his chances of achieving those dreams, I sometimes took it personally. I love Donny like a brother, but fights between brothers are often the worst fights of all.

Donny has never just gone along with what I or anyone else wanted until he was absolutely convinced we were right. I've never had another weightlifter who was as challenging to coach as Donny, but in spite of that challenge, I discovered a person who thought more like I did than anyone I know.

He and I share a love of both history and philosophy, and in fact, when we get together, we're as likely to discuss history as weightlifting. With nobody but Donny Shankle could I discuss both Ayn Rand, and the importance of pulling under aggressively in the snatch.

Some of my best memories of weightlifting are from driving to weightlifting meets with Donny. He and I have solved all of the world's problems and then some in our discussions while traveling to events. We've driven across the country for Collegiate Nationals, the American Open, and the National Championships…and those drives were never boring, even some that were longer than 12 hours.

Donny was a lifter who had so much raw potential, I still can't believe he didn't make the Olympic team. He was, and is, one of the hardest working lifters I've ever seen—the opposite of lazy is a good way to describe him.

I think it was his work ethic that eventually ended his career as a competitive lifter. Of course, hard work is a good thing, but Donny often took it too far—to the point where it caused injuries.

Habitual overwork can cause the body to break down. But asking Donny to train without pushing to the absolute limit again and again and again was impossible. It would have been like asking him to become a different person.

Donny just didn't have the ability to back off; it was pedal to the metal 100% of the time. I remember one snatch workout while we were living in Texas where Donny was trying to snatch a pretty big weight—around 160 or 165 kilos. After the first couple of misses, I told him to stop—and he kept going. Eventually, I was practically begging him to stop. On his 12th or 13th miss, he injured his calf and ankle. It ended up not being as bad as we first thought, but this episode and many like it perfectly describe Donny. Even after more than 10 misses, he was still going after the lift, not clarking it, but getting under the bar and just not quite catching it. That tenacity makes Donny who he is, and it ultimately cut his career short.

With Donny and me, the learning definitely went both ways. I hope I taught him a few things about weightlifting, as well as a few things outside of weightlifting. He taught me a lot about the sport and about life. Knowing Donny Shankle made me a better weightlifting coach and a better person.

KEY LESSONS

1. Athletes and coaches will test each other. It's not a one-way street. Coaches should never steamroll ideas for their athletes, but guide them in the right direction and allow room to learn.

2. A coach has the task of earning their athletes' trust and respect. Sometimes it comes quickly, but other times it requires patience—as do all things worth having.

JON NORTH

Photo A1.7—Helping Jon North pose for a weightlifting poster. Photo courtesy of Mark Hazarabedian

I first met Jon after moving to California to coach at California Strength. I was excited to relocate to reconnect with Donny Shankle, whom I'd coached for several years before he went to the OTC, and to continue coaching Caleb Ward, whom I was bringing with me to California. I knew going into the job that I'd be in the company of these great friends and lifters, but I'd never met Jon, and I certainly never suspected that this cocky young kid would end up playing such an important role in my life. It was a different role than those played by Donny and Caleb, but just as important.

My first impression of Jon was that he was extremely talented. He'd just bombed out of three meets in a row—in each case with the same relatively light snatch, but it hadn't affected his confidence at all. He was loud, even brash, and I liked him immediately. It was obvious he absolutely loved being in the gym and lifting weights. Jon has a big personality; being the center of attention wherever he goes comes naturally to him, and he thrives on it. When I arrived at California Strength, Jon reminded me of an overly enthusiastic kid, but now with a wife and two kids of his own, he's certainly not a kid anymore.

Everyone involved with weightlifting in the United States knows Jon, or knows of him. Some people hate him and others love him—but very few are ambivalent. Most who don't like Jon dislike him because of a view of the sport that's at odds with what they think Jon represents. Jon wants loud gangster rap to play when he lifts at a competition. He wants to put on a show for the audience. And he wants audience participation. He'll demand that the audience cheer louder and louder for every lift. Even if you dislike him, you have to admit he makes a competition exciting.

I'll be the first to admit that sometimes in the past, Jon has gone too far. Anything that interferes with the lifters after him doing their best is crossing the line as far as I'm concerned, and I've seen Jon do things that interfered, or could have interfered, with other athletes. I've been vocal about some of his antics with chalk dust and especially with extended stays on the competition platform after his lift.

I love to watch Jon lift, as almost everyone else loves to watch Jon lift. You can so plainly see the pure joy on his face when he makes a lift. Even if you think you don't like him (or just don't admit to liking him), he still has a unique ability to transfer some of the joy he's feeling to the audience. And that's what entertainers do. They have the ability to transfer some of their emotion to the audience…to you.

When I started writing about Jon, I assumed this would become a description of the weightlifting meets he and I attended together as coach and athlete. And there's plenty I could write about that; we certainly had some exciting and interesting times. We shared memories I love to relive.

But there's so much more to our relationship than just the sport of weightlifting. I've watched him grow up, going from a cocky young kid to an adult. I have to smile as I think about the times I poked fun of his "Attitude Nation" slogan, and told him his "nation" was so small that a more apt name would be "Attitude Village."

He's taken that "village" and grown it to the point where he and Jessica are not only making a living from it, but also raising a family. And just like there's more to our shared relationship, there's so much more to Jon than just weightlifting. I think that's why so many misunderstand him. They don't see the whole picture—and they should certainly look harder.

KEY LESSONS

1. There's nothing wrong with being cocky or fueled by emotion. When you properly figure out how to use those qualities, they can help you become a champion.

2. Whether you're an athlete or a coach, there will be people who struggle to understand who you are, and as a result, will jump to conclusions about your character. It's on you to help them understand that you mean well.

Photo A1.8—Podcasting with Jon North

SPENCER MOORMAN

Photo A1.9—Spencer Moorman breaking the Junior American Record with a 204-kilo clean and jerk

I started working with Spencer a few months after Caleb Ward broke the Junior American clean and jerk record in the super heavyweight class—the same weight class Spencer competed in. I'd previously seen Spencer lifting a few times at School-Age Nationals and again at Junior Nationals, and I was aware of his talent. It seemed like every time Caleb made progress, Spencer was right there behind him improving as well.

In truth, my having coached Caleb was a major factor in Spencer and his family deciding that California Strength was the right place for him to train, and that I was the right coach for him.

In spite of them both breaking the same record—Caleb first with a 203-kilo clean and jerk, and then Spencer a year later with a 204-kilo lift that still stands as of this writing—they were almost complete opposites when it came to lifting style.

Where Spencer was naturally brutally strong, Caleb was not. Where Caleb was precise in his movements, Spencer wasn't. Spencer was extremely tight, and Caleb extremely flexible. While Caleb was prone to small sprains, Spencer was durable and rarely injured. Being two of the nicest athletes you could imagine was about the only thing they had in common. I consider myself lucky to have coached two of the best young American supers in a long time.

When Spencer first arrived at Cal Strength, he seemed to break his PR snatch, clean and jerk, and total records almost daily. He was already enormously strong, and being in that competitive environment with Caleb, Donny, Jon, and several other lifters was like putting an engine on nitrous. At one point, he increased his snatch PR by something like 16 kilos in about 10 days.

The story of me coaching Spencer is less about coaching, and more about me just being smart enough to get out of his way. I've made no secret of the fact that what most American lifters need is less reliance on coaches, and more on good training partners. In a situation like Cal Strength where we always had three or four talented athletes in the same room, sometimes the best thing a coach can do is just stand back and watch.

I put Spencer in this category. He had originally been taught to lift by his father. I might have corrected a few rough edges, but certainly nothing more than that. Spencer, Shankle, Ward, and North fed off each other. At least one of them would have a good day, and brought the others up to his level that day.

The time I spent as Spencer's coach was special. I may never coach another guy who's as brutally strong as he was, or one who can put himself in that special place where an athlete just knows beyond a shadow of a doubt that he can make a lift.

There are a handful of lifters who really affected me at least as much as I affected them, and Spencer is part of that group.

KEY LESSONS

1. Figuring out how to maximize athletes' natural gifts…and then stepping aside to let them do what they do best is an important coach's skill.

2. Athletes should actively seek training environments that push their limits.

KEVIN CORNELL

Photo A1.10—Kevin Cornell
Photo courtsey of Nat Arem, Hookgrip

Originally from Pittsburg, Pennsylvania, Kevin Cornell was introduced to me back in 2008 by his coach, who thought Cal Strength was where Kevin needed to be to improve in the sport. Back then, Cal Strength was actively recruiting and paying out stipends, which was monumental in American weightlifting in those years. It was a perfect situation for an up-and-coming lifter who possessed the kind of talent Kevin did.

After the arrangements were made, Kevin flew out to California, and stayed with me for a week while trying out for a spot on the team. It's an understatement to say I was immediately impressed with his lifting abilities. Kevin was fast, had a refined technique, and displayed great strength—a great foundation to build on with very few rough edges.

One of his first workouts with the team was a 15-minute EMOM of clean and jerks during which he managed to build up to a new personal record of

182 kilos for his last lift. That's a difficult thing to do in a workout like that, and the feat certainly helped highlight Kevin's potential.

I saw a lot of great things in Kevin's future. As a coach, when you see someone who's as talented as Kevin, it makes you start thinking, "This could be the one who goes the distance." You think to yourself, if this kid does everything he needs to do, he could be an Olympian.

It's a great notion, but coaches at times need to reel themselves in, and ask an important question: Is this what the athlete wants, or just what I want? At times during my career, it's been difficult to take a step back and tone down my vision for an athlete. I love helping athletes reach their highest potential in the sport, and it's not something I can do halfway. I'm always all in—100% committed.

While I coached Kevin, I was certain he'd perform best as a 94-kilo lifter. I thought if he could just maintain that weight, he wouldn't only have been the best 94 on the team, but in the entire country. That's what I thought was best, but it wasn't what Kevin wanted, and his weight would often drift into the 105-kilo class, or even above and into the supers.

While it didn't negatively affect our relationship, the lesson I learned was that a coach needs to look at the whole situation and stay on the same page as the athlete. A coach can't want something for athletes that they don't want for themselves; instead coaches and athletes need to share something together.

While I may not have agreed about Kevin lifting in a higher weight class, he was always a tremendous joy to coach. Part of that is because he's one the funniest people I know.

Weightlifting is not an easy sport, and decades of coaching taught me it takes a special type of person to be a weightlifter. The years of monotonous training are just too high a price to pay for most people. It's important to have the camaraderie that comes with being on a team where you can be around people who will not only push you, but will make training enjoyable as well.

Kevin was that bright spot on our team, always making everyone laugh and smile day after day, regardless of how beat up they felt while training. Kevin made

Cal Strength and MDUSA better places. He just has a way of saying things in silly ways that make people laugh no matter how hard they try not to. There were many times he had me laughing to the point of tears streaming down my face.

I can't say enough about what a great guy Kevin Cornell is, and am grateful for having had the opportunity to have coached him.

KEY LESSONS

1. An athlete's vision for life and career is more important than the coach's. Many will learn this the hard way. To spare yourself and your athletes some heartache, have difficult conversations sooner rather than later. Put the athlete's voice and opinions first. Then move on together from there.

2. Training should be fun. Seek training partners who keep you looking forward to returning to the weightroom.

JUSTIN "MOPPY" BRIMHALL

Photo A1.11—Justin Brimhall
Photo by Bruce Klemens

Justin Brimhall is another lifter who made coaching fun. The first time I saw him and his brother Zack was at a high school football game. At the game, I noticed them walking down the aisle to find seats, and I can't really tell you what made me think this, but I immediately thought, "Those guys would make good weightlifters." I was sitting with one of my lifters, and sent him over to them to ask if they were interested in trying weightlifting, and if so, to come over and talk to me.

As luck would have it, they were, and they did, and I invited them to come to MSU to check it out. When Justin and Zack showed up at the gym, it was immediately apparent they both had natural talent for the sport. I wondered if it was because their mother was Turkish, and lived pretty close to the Turkish training center growing up—who knows for sure. Zack was a pretty good lifter and a great guy, but it was Justin who took to weightlifting like a fish to water.

Justin showed up with a ton of curly hair and was skinny as a rail. The combination of the skinny body and this huge mop of hair prompted me to comment at his first practice that he was so skinny we could turn him over and use his head for a mop—and the nickname stuck. I gave it to him when he was 14 years old, and even after he graduated from college and became an officer in the United States Marine Corps, I still called him "Moppy," and so did most of those who lifted with him.

Moppy is one of those guys who had so many interesting quirks to his personality, I could write a book about him. I can't so much as think about him without a big smile spreading across my face.

He had a unique ability he called "The Turkish hop." It displays a unique combination of athletic ability, balance, and explosive leg strength I'd never seen demonstrated by another human.

To perform the Turkish hop, you first do a pistol squat. Then you stand from the squat so fast that you're able to jump about five feet forward, landing on the other leg. Without any hesitation, perform another pistol with that leg, and then proceed to do the same by going into another jump. Moppy could do this for 40 yards with absolutely no hesitation whatsoever—just leaping from a pistol on one leg to a pistol on the other.

But the real kicker is that he could do this while holding a 25-kilo plate at arm's length…overhead. I've never met another person who could come anywhere near being able to reproduce this feat of athletic ability.

Moppy also did some amazing things in training, such as jerking 170 kilos for a double as a 16-year-old weighing 75 kilos.

Unfortunately, he had trouble transferring his talent to competitions. He was one of those lifters who got so nervous, he'd often throw up between the weigh-in and the warm-up. Partly because of this, when it counted, he wasn't able to do the lifts he was physically capable of.

I know I speak for everyone who ever came into contact with Justin Brimhall when I say we're all lucky to have known him. He's one of those unique people who just made lifting and life more interesting.

KEY LESSONS

1. Not everyone will be able to perform in competition, but they still deserve coaching. This is especially true for kids and teens. Their future waits for them beyond the platform. Making them physically and mentally strong for anything they might experience in the world is just as important as medals and records—probably even more.

2. Coaches can find potential weightlifters almost anywhere. You just have to keep your eyes open and be willing to offer people an opportunity.

CLOSING THOUGHTS

From the outside looking in, the casual observer might think weightlifting is just about lifting heavy weights. They may flip through the pages of a book like this and think the sport revolves around training programs for the snatch and clean and jerk.

However, should they begin to immerse themselves in the sport, they'll quickly find those original assumptions to be wrong.

While the lifts are all we seemingly talk about, weightlifting is not about the snatch or clean and jerk; it's about the person under the bar—and the people around during the lift.

The sport is comprised of the stories behind what drove each person to pull on a singlet, lace up lifting shoes, and pick up a barbell in the first place.

We think of the thoughts that race through athletes' heads while they rub chalk on their hands and what they're thinking as they look at a loaded barbell before a big lift.

The sport is about their relationships with their coaches, teammates, and everyone else who decided to make weightlifting a major part of their lives.

If you're new to the sport, you may not believe me yet. Chances are you're more concerned with learning the snatch or worried about your nerves leading up to your first meet than you are about relationships with the people around you. But over time, you'll notice that awareness changing. You'll start to remember moments with good friends and competitors more than you do the training program you were on your second year in the sport.

Those memories are the greatest gifts the sport can give you. My advice is to talk to people early on and start forming relationships. Learn from everyone around you. That goes for athletes and coaches alike, because learning and sharing experiences is a two-way street.

Cherish the car rides to meets, the crazy antics of teammates in training, and the conversations at the dinner table. Those experiences will play a bigger part than you realize in who you become as an athlete or coach.

Photo A1.12—Wichita Falls Weightlifting Club 2003

APPENDIX 2
THE PENDLAY ARTICLES

Glenn's quest for knowledge was constant, and he frequently amended his methods when he learned something new, which aligns with his philosophy of "Once you think you know everything, you really know nothing at all." Throughout his career, Glenn was an avid writer, frequently posting articles and musings in his blog, *Glenn Pendlay: Deep Thoughts and Some Not So Deep!* This appendix is a compilation of some of his memorable training material from 2006 to 2018.

Additional Thoughts on Weightlifting

Additional Thoughts on Squat Training

Additional Thoughts on Deadlift Training

Guideposts

The Training Log

ADDITIONAL THOUGHTS ON WEIGHTLIFTING

There's a common theme that American weightlifters aren't strong enough, and "stupid" American coaches don't work hard enough at improving maximal strength. It's enlightening that most of the critics have never produced a high-level lifter, and the foreign coaches they idolize have the opposite opinion.

Most comments from foreign coaches are similar to, "They pull the bar well, but can't catch it, and they drive the bar well in the jerk, but can't get under it," or "Americans can do pulls and squats, but not the competition lifts. They should concentrate more on the competition lifts and less on the slow lifts that don't translate over to bigger snatches." Both comments express the opinion that what we need is less strength work and more practice at the competitive lifts.

MAXIMAL STRENGTH AT THE OLYMPIC TRAINING CENTER

The central assertion was that the Olympic Training Center had been unsuccessful in producing consistent progress among the lifters who trained there, that they flogged technique to death, and had no interest in increasing maximal strength. This had been said again and again, and there are always arguments over the validity of this claim.

Let's look at the claim that the OTC didn't work on maximal strength.

Among the athletes who were actually there, what were the reported changes in training from the training that got them to the point of an invitation to be there? I haven't talked to all of them, but enough to have a good idea.

They reported a reduction in technical work on the competition lifts, especially the full lifts. There was an overall increase in training volume—a very high increase for some athletes—with the volume made up of much harder work on pulls of various types, all the way from clean-grip deadlifts with heavy weights,

Romanian deadlifts, partial clean pulls, and snatch or clean deadlifts from various boxes. There was an overall increase in squatting volume, using heavy exercises like partial squats in some cases.

These athletes experienced the opposite of what most internet "experts" claim—an overall increase in strength exercises and a decrease in the full competition lifts, especially the lifts done at higher weights or higher percentages of max.

What was the single biggest reported change in physical ability for athletes who spent the first year at the training center? I'd have to say it was an increase in the squat. Almost every person who went to the OTC made squat gains. The complaint I most often heard from athletes at the OTC or the personal coaches of these athletes: They got stronger at the expense of the competition lifts. In other words, the squat went up, but the snatch and clean didn't, or at least didn't go up as much as expected.

If one were of the opinion that successes or failures are never so limited as to be entirely the fault of the training program, based on the opinions of people who've actually either been there or coached athletes who've been there, it's for the opposite reason the critics propose. The error is too much time and effort spent on strength and too little on competition lifts.

If the assertions of what went on at the OTC are so far off the mark, it lowers the value of some of the other things they have to say about American weightlifting.

Even disregarding those who are either not involved in weightlifting or only peripherally involved still leaves disagreement among actual coaches as to the relationship between the strength exercises and the competitive lifts.

RESERVE STRENGTH

The idea of reserve strength is one of the concepts I disagree with. I've heard respected people pose the rhetorical question, "What's wrong with pushing the squat and pull-up to the point where the athlete has a little reserve strength?"

With a little strength in reserve, the athletes can hold onto weights not lifted with perfect technique, don't land in exactly the right spot, or make their expected lifts if they're slightly tired or off that day. On the surface, this sounds reasonable, but the concept doesn't hold up under scrutiny.

The first aspect to fall apart is that pushing the squat up or increasing back strength isn't already being done as vigorously as possible, and that it's easy to do if the effort is made. I don't personally know of any weightlifters who don't already put great effort into pushing up their squat numbers. If pushing up the squat was easy, everyone would have a huge squat—but everyone doesn't have a huge squat.

Another assumption buried within the reserve strength argument is that extra effort put toward increasing squat strength will have no effect on other parts of training. Weightlifters are training primarily to do more on the snatch and clean and jerk. Many or even most lifters could increase their squat numbers if they ceased training the snatch and clean, but that wouldn't result in better weightlifters.

Let's play devil's advocate for a moment, and assume an athlete has decided to develop some reserve strength, and has been successful with no detrimental effect to the competition lifts. Suppose a male athlete had front squatted 190 kilos, and clean and jerked 182. He has now added 20 kilos to his front squat; he now front squats 210 kilos and retains his skill in the clean and jerk.

He used to have to catch the bounce perfectly with 182 kilos to stand up. Now, it's true that even with a sloppier catch or a pull that doesn't put the bar in exactly the right place, he can still stand, whereas he couldn't before. However, if he still has the same skill he used to have, what's to prevent him from pulling perfectly and catching the bounce just right with a 200-kilo clean?

Adding reserve strength assumes the athlete either subsequently lifts only submaximal weights, or loses efficiency and skill as a weightlifter. Without one of these, there can never be any "reserve strength."

HOLDING BACK

Another variation of the reserve strength argument applies to developing lifters. Weightlifting coaches are accused of basing squat numbers on snatch numbers, or more often, clean numbers, thus "holding back" strength development and the overall development of the lifter. Progress would happen more quickly if the coach just put weight on the squat bar, figuring the quick development of strength and higher snatch and clean numbers would quickly follow.

Again, the assumption is that coaches are intentionally holding back squatting numbers. This could be so in some cases, but it's not as simple as it sounds. Take a developing lifter who squats 100 kilos, but only clean and jerks 50. The technique is inefficient enough that the leg strength is not being used anyway.

We only have so much time and recovery ability to apply to training. The quickest way to increase results is to improve technique, not to build more strength when what's already there is not even being used.

Even if there are cases where squats are deemphasized, it's not simply to hold back the strength levels; it's to prioritize the components of training that yield the fastest progress.

But this situation rarely exists. After the initial learning, a young lifter has to work quite hard on both the lifts and the strength exercises to progress, and there's rarely intentional holding back of a certain component of training. Most developing weightlifters do a higher volume of squatting than the average powerlifter, a sport where the squat itself is a competition lift. This doesn't constitute a "holding back" of strength levels.

Let's assume we have a young male weightlifter who's clean and jerking 100 kilos and squatting 140. He has the genetic ability to increase his squat 60 kilos over the following year, but because of the mental challenges of the clean and jerk—as well as physical components not related to strength—he can't increase his clean by more than 20 kilos.

This is the situation the internet "coaches" assume always exists. If it were true for our imaginary athlete, would it be wise to have an athlete who could squat 200 kilos and clean 120, assume the clean would eventually catch up, and that it would increase faster in the future…and the athlete would reach his top potential sooner?

TECHNIQUE, HABITS, AND MISTAKES

Imperfect technique is one of the components of being a developing lifter. A novice can have great technique with light weights, but get sloppy with heavy weights. Often, maximal attempts will be downright ugly. As skill increases and the competitive lifts go up on an absolute basis and also as a percentage of the strength lifts, better technique is mandatory to achieve new personal records. This is one of the driving forces behind improving technique—that smaller margins of error can be made and still make a maximal or near-maximal attempt.

Bad habits or mistakes must be eliminated, or bigger weights won't go overhead. If the margins for error don't get smaller, the errors won't get smaller.

If an athlete goes through the first few years of training with the ability to continually lift heavier weights with sloppy pulling, bad timing, and slow movement, these won't go away and will over time become ingrained. We'd have an athlete who would eventually develop into a strong but sloppy lifter who lifts average weights…and looks ugly doing it.

Lifters differ in the relationships between the squat and front squat and the competitive lifts. Some need to back squat 140 kilos to clean 100, whereas some only need to back squat 120 kilos to clean 100. For most lifters, these relationships should stay the same over the course of their careers.

As a novice, the competitive lifts usually progress faster and efficiency improves. Elite champions in their prime often continue to develop squat strength even after their lift increases cease…and efficiency actually decreases. But for the majority of a career, the relationships should be constant, and the coach should take care that the gap between strength exercises and competitive exercises doesn't continually widen.

If this means decreasing squat training to dedicate more time toward the competitive lifts, that's what should be done.

ADDITIONAL THOUGHTS ON SQUAT TRAINING

People always want advice on how to balance training for weightlifting or training specific to some other strength-related sport, while also trying to increase the squat.

In strength sports other than powerlifting, the squat isn't a competitive event. But even in the role of an assistance exercise, squats are so effective at building strength, they're absolutely necessary for success. Most of us must include them in our training.

Yet, the squat is a taxing exercise that can interfere with sports-specific training. And sports training can definitely interfere with success in building the squat and raising basic strength levels. We balance the two with daily maximums in the front squat and low-volume work for some people. Squatting four or five days a week with sub-maximal weight slowly titrated up can work.

This method is mostly geared toward those who are past the quick initial gains that come in the first six months or year of training but aren't yet at the point where PRs come more slowly, if at all. This might be someone who has trained eight to 10 years in a sport and for all practical purposes is at the height of athletic potential.

SCHEDULING THE SQUAT WORKOUTS

We squat three times per week. It's structured to interfere as little as possible with training on the competition exercises, and to let the competition exercises interfere as little as possible with increasing the squat.

On Monday, we have one or two training sessions on snatch and clean and jerk or related exercises. The athletes squat after these two sessions. They're too tired to produce maximal effort, and I ask them not to. They usually do three to five working sets of three to five reps on the back squat.

Three sets of five reps are common, using a submaximal weight. If the best set of five is 240 kilos, 210 kilos to 220 kilos for multiple sets of five wouldn't be unusual. The one or two training sessions consisting of the snatch-related and clean-and-jerk-related exercises will definitely lower the weight in the squat. It's still producing a powerful training effect.

On Tuesday, the training is easier, and we don't squat. Training consists of exercises that reinforce good technique in the competitive lifts, but where less weight can be used than on the competitive lifts. We still go to a daily maximum, but the exercises themselves are easier—think power snatch, or snatch with no hook grip and no foot movement.

We also use power cleans, push press or push jerk, or presses and jerks from the split position. In general, this is an easier day than Monday.

Wednesday is back to another hard day—one or two sessions, depending on the lifter. This is hard training on the snatch and clean and jerk, or related exercises where roughly the same weight can be used as the competition lifts. Think clean and jerk, or cleans from a block, snatches, or snatches from the hang or off a block.

We're again squatting after the hard training, but this time it's front squats, usually three working sets with the reps ranging from one to three. Yes, the lifter is tired, but these front squats are less strenuous than the back squats from Monday and the recovery is easier.

Thursday is either no training, or is a fairly easy session. Like Tuesday, we use exercises that help reinforce good technique, but let us recover from the beginning of the week so we're as fresh as possible on Friday.

Friday is either a light session in the morning, or perhaps no session. The athletes who do Friday morning training will do the competition lifts, but at lower percentages. It's mostly a tune-up for Friday afternoon, when they go to max on the competition lifts.

It's the day the athletes are most recovered and are able to do the biggest weights given Thursday's lighter training.

On Saturday, we begin the session with squats and try to make new PRs. The athletes have fresher legs on Saturday because it's been two days since they squatted, and Friday's training, although it was high in intensity, was low in volume compared to earlier in the week. After squatting, we do overhead strength work, and sometimes pulls.

Sundays mean no formal training, which is another reason doing our most difficult squatting on Saturday works well. Doing the hardest squatting prior to a day off helps limit the interference that being sore or tired from heavy squats can have on training the competitive exercises.

CYCLING THE INTENSITY

We cycle the squat intensity by programming for a month or several months in advance, but I don't really plan this; I just let it happen. As an example, maybe a lifter has PRed a best set of five on the back squat for four weeks in a row, and the weights on Monday and Wednesday have followed along, going up each week.

It's normal for a lifter to run out of recovery ability simply from consistently handling higher-than-normal weights. The squatting will start to interfere

with the training of the competitive lifts. And this is fine, because you have to get your squat up if you're a weightlifter.

When the string of PRs end, we don't bash our heads against the wall, continuing to challenge maximal weights and new PRs. Instead, I back the weights down a bit—a reset, so to speak. Backing the weights off eight to 10 percent is a good rule of thumb; in some cases, even more is appropriate.

Then we start systematically raising the weights week by week, hoping that in three to four weeks, the athletes will pass the old PRs.

After a reset using less-than-maximal squat weights is often when we see the best training in the competitive lifts because the legs are more recovered.

This is reliable and effective, and the general principles can be followed while allowing quite a number of tweaks and modifications. These principles also work well for strength sports other than weightlifting.

Here's the lesson: Do most of your high-volume and difficult work on the competitive lifts early in the week, with moderate intensity but higher-volume squatting at the end of the workout. Allow some rest on Thursday; do your highest-intensity work on the competitive lifts on Friday, but keep the volume down. Then pound the squat PRs on Saturday when fresh.

ADDITIONAL THOUGHTS ON DEADLIFT TRAINING

Some coaches don't program deadlifts, preferring to use the clean or snatch pull. For much of my career, I used mostly the snatch and clean to build pulling strength, without using either pulls or deadlifts.

What changed my opinion? To put it simply, drugs. Many of the elite lifters we admire use them. For a variety of reasons, American weightlifters don't. I don't intend to discuss the reasons behind this double standard, or how or why it came to be, but this is the reality of the situation as it now stands.

Performance-enhancing drugs assist one thing: strength. They don't help build great motor patterns or technique; they simply make people stronger. For many lifters using PEDs, simply doing the correct number of snatches and clean and jerks ensures that strength will never be the limiting factor in their lifts.

This isn't true for most "clean" lifters. Strength is almost always the limiting factor for lifters not using PEDs. And if you don't think you could snatch more weight if both your snatch-grip deadlift and your back squat were 20 kilos higher, you're lying to yourself.

Once you arrive at the conclusion that being stronger on the pull will assist in snatching and cleaning, ask yourself what will build that strength faster, the snatch-grip deadlift or the snatch pull?

PROGRAMMING SNATCH-GRIP DEADLIFTS

Snatch-grip deadlifts are generally done heavier and with a slower bar speed because they're based on the snatch deadlift max. Snatch pulls are usually based on the snatch max, which for many lifters is nearly unrelated to the maximum snatch-grip deadlift.

An efficient lifter might be able to snatch 70% of the snatch-grip deadlift, while many beginners might not be able to do 40%. Basing the programming of one of your most important strength exercises on a guess is asking for failure.

It's true you could do the same motion of the snatch pull with weights far in excess of the snatch and achieve the same amount of tension and the same bar speed as the snatch deadlift. But why rely on a guess? Why not just accept that it's a deadlift? It's just a slower, heavier movement than the snatch or snatch pull.

Snatch-grip and clean-grip deadlifts are programmed similarly to the back squat. The main difference is that we use less volume for the deadlifts, and generally limit their use to the first half of a training cycle. In an eight-week cycle, you'll use the snatch deadlift for the first four weeks, and switch to the snatch pull usually with far less weight for the second four weeks.

Deadlifts aren't for those only interested in quick progress. Deadlifts take a while to recover from, and adding deadlifts to a routine probably won't increase a maximum today…or tomorrow. But if you're willing to put in a few weeks of work—and then recover from it—they'll make that total go up.

Getting stronger always does.

USING THE DEADLIFT FOR PULLING STRENGTH

Most weightlifters do lots of snatches and cleans. After all, you have to practice to be good at your sport, and cleans and snatches *are* the sport. But many lifters do even more snatch and clean pulls.

I've never been a big fan of pulls. It seems as though they take out the most important part of the movement, the timing of that instant when you cease to pull up on the bar and begin to pull yourself under.

Timing it correctly and the speed at which you can switch off the muscles of your legs and hips and switch on the traps, shoulders, and arms to pull yourself under is what makes a great snatch or clean. Pulls leave that part out.

Many lifters believe they're doing pulls for strength, and I'd agree they do improve strength in the pull. But there's a better way. The signal to the muscles to grow stronger is based on muscle tension, and tension is highest when moving a heavy weight. That sounds like a deadlift to me.

Many coaches insist that the motor patterns reinforced by the pull done with a weight near to the weight used on the snatch or clean are so important that replacing pulls with deadlifts is a bad strategy.

But what's to guarantee that the snatch or clean deadlift won't be done with a motor pattern similar to the snatch or clean? You can even do a double knee bend, and add an explosive shrug at the top. At that point, the only difference is the load and bar speed.

But if the bar speed will only be significantly different if the load is significantly different, and if the load is that different, wouldn't that mean the snatch pulls would be just as ineffective at building strength as the deadlifts are for building good motor patterns?

Every athlete should use the best tool for the job. For building good motor patterns in the snatch, nothing is as effective as snatching. And for building strength in the snatch pull, nothing is as effective as snatch deadlifts done with weights based not on the snatch, but on the capabilities in the snatch deadlift.

Lifters should follow the motor patterns of the competition lifts as closely as possible. That means starting with an extended spine and hips in the same place they'd be in for a snatch or clean, and making sure the hips and shoulders rise at the same rate when possible.

A double knee bend is great if you're able, as is a shrug at the top. But if an athlete is doing five sets of two with 90%, and on the second rep of the fourth and fifth set, the spine rounds, or a double knee bend is impossible, I wouldn't stop the set or the workout.

We have to remember the reason we're doing the exercise: The purpose is to develop pulling strength. Many lifters and coaches get caught up in skill development. They concentrate on that aspect so much; they forget that weightlifting is a strength sport.

When a weightlifter does either a deadlift or a pull, the movement is to aid in pulling strength. This pulling strength will be used in the snatch or clean, so it makes sense to do either the pull or deadlift with a movement as similar as possible to the competitive lifts. The more the deviation from the line of pull, speed, and rhythm of the snatch or clean, the less the strength gain will carry over to the snatch or clean.

In weightlifting, athletes often call this movement a "pull" when the load it's based on is a max snatch or clean, and call it a "deadlift" when it's based on the maximum weight that can be moved from the floor to standing erect.

Usually, when the movement is called a pull, more attention is paid to following the movement patterns of the clean and snatch, and when the movement is called a deadlift, the main goal is just to get the weight to lockout. I call these clean-grip deadlifts or snatch-grip deadlifts, although I prefer the line of pull, speed, and rhythm that follow the snatch or clean as closely as possible.

PROGRAMMING AND CALCULATING THE LOAD

The problem with basing the load on the snatch or clean is that using the same percentage of the snatch can give one athlete a training session almost impossible to complete, and another a load that's too light to lead to any adaptation at all.

For an efficient lifter, a load based on a high percentage of the snatch might be too heavy, while for a beginner just learning the lifts, the same percentage-based load will almost certainly be too light.

I don't like the idea of basing the training of one lift on a different lift, even if they're related. No one would base the bench press training on results in the military press, even though they're related. They use similar muscle groups, and they both use the pressing motion, but even so, basing the training of one on results of the other isn't ideal.

Many lifters consider the pull or deadlift useful for both strength and technique. This sounds good, but it can mean that trying to keep the movement as close to the competition lift as possible means it's never done with enough load to increase strength.

However, by its very nature, it'll never mimic an actual snatch or clean well enough to help improve technique. The snatch is the only thing that makes people better at the snatch, and the clean is the only thing that builds a better clean. Why not use the snatch and clean for technique work for the snatch and clean, and program the deadlift for strength and base the load on the snatch- and clean-grip deadlift?

That doesn't mean you can't do them as closely as possible to the movement pattern used in the snatch and clean. The snatch- or clean-grip deadlift should start with the hips in the same position as the competition lift, with the hips and shoulders rising at the same rate, just as in the competition lifts.

The deadlifts should be quickly pulled with a bar speed as close as possible to the snatch or clean. The bar won't move as fast with the heavier weight, but you should try.

When the deadlift is programmed like the strength exercise it is, it's harder to recover from than a pull with a much lighter load. Because of this, it would be very difficult to do five or six days a week the way many athletes program the pull. One or two days a week is probably tops for most.

It's also hard to use as many reps as are normally used for an exercise like the squat. Deadlifts also have to be lightened or eliminated when peaking for a competition. It's smart to lower the load to something close to what you can snatch or clean a few weeks out.

Many athletes should eliminate them altogether the last week, or at least severely curtail the volume.

If there's one truth in the fitness field, it's that every untrained person who walks into a gym will be best served by gaining basic muscle and strength before concentrating on anything else. Muscle makes losing fat easier. Muscle and strength not only make us more fit and healthy, they make every other training modality used in the pursuit of fitness more effective.

Unfortunately, how to correctly begin down the road to getting stronger and building muscle has been made more complicated than it needs to be.

This is partly because of idiots giving out advice when they have no business doing so, and partly because there are many "gurus" who point to their proprietary methods as the best way or sometimes even the only way to be successful.

But this doesn't have to be hard or complicated, and you don't need to buy into one particular cookie-cutter program. There are a few simple guideposts every beginner should be familiar with. Just as with hiking, it's prudent and safe to stay close to the well-marked trail. Although the challenge and excitement of blazing your own trail is satisfying to the experienced mountaineer or strength athlete, it isn't appropriate on an initial hike, or the first month in the gym.

The following are general recommendations that will serve beginners well when choosing a prewritten strength program, or later, when planning their own.

Training three times per week with whole-body workouts is a good place for beginners to start—staying close to this will serve most people well. Training two times per week with whole-body workouts has worked for many people and is a viable option.

While whole-body workouts are a proven method, a simple split that still allows big multi-joint exercises also works. Squatting and pressing exercises on Monday and Thursday and pulling and rowing exercises on Tuesday and Friday is a practical schedule. With either a two-day-a-week whole-body workout or a four-day split routine, you might not be walking down the middle of the trail, but you're close enough, and won't be getting into any trouble.

However, if you decide on a six-day bodybuilding routine with chest on Monday, biceps and hamstrings on Tuesday, and shoulders on Wednesday, you're 20 miles off the trail with no food or water; your compass doesn't work and you've lost your map.

And it's starting to snow.

Beginners should mostly select exercises that are multi-joint in nature and that work large parts of the body at once. Squats, front squats, bench presses, incline presses, military presses, push presses, deadlifts, power cleans, chin-ups, pull-ups, and barbell rows are all great exercises for beginners.

Beginners should squat each time they train legs. One major exercise is appropriate per muscle group per workout when training the whole body at once; one or two exercises per muscle group is appropriate when using a split routine.

There's wiggle room, of course. Throwing in a couple of sets of curls for the girls isn't going to derail you. Fascinated by all the big plates the bros are throwing on the leg press? If you're training legs three days a week, leg pressing on Wednesday isn't going to kill you as long as you keep squatting on Monday and Friday.

But if you find you're doing more side laterals than presses, more leg extensions than squats, or you're doing four exercises for your chest on Monday, you're trapped at the bottom of a canyon with walls too steep to climb; it's raining, and that little creek at the bottom is flowing faster and faster.

Beginners are usually best served using four to six reps. A set of three or going for a max single isn't going to kill you, nor will a set of 10. Doing a drop set with lighter weights and higher reps after your heavier sets is popular in some circles, and this won't kill you either, but it's also not going to speed up your gains.

But if the majority of your work isn't within a medium-rep range, you're heading in the wrong direction. Not including warm-ups, three work sets for each exercise is a good starting point for most people.

As few as one set or as many as five or six can initially work, but often we find a regression to the mean when we start with too few or too many work sets. Start with only one and you may soon find you have to increase the workload to progress; start with five or six, and you may have to decrease the workload to recover properly.

Starting with three sets of five on an exercise with weights picked to make the last rep on the third set only slightly slower and harder than the first rep of the first set is a proven way for a beginner to progress. This is lighter than the possible weight, but don't worry—it's heavy enough to provide stimulation for growth in a rank beginner.

From here, simply add five pounds to the bar each successive time you do the exercise if it's an upper-body exercise, 10 pounds if it's a lower-body exercise. The rate of progress can be lower for a small woman, or greater for a large man. But for most people, progressing slower than that means progressing slower than your capability, and progressing faster means the initial easy strength gains all beginners get will prematurely stall.

There's some wiggle room on this one. You can get fancy and change the reps. This could be three sets of four with 100 pounds one day, three sets of five the next day, three sets of six the following day, then add 10 pounds and drop back to three sets of four the next day.

Even complicated schemes can work—something like this: Establish a maximum set of three. Do two workouts of three sets of five at a certain percentage of that set of three. The next workout, attempt a new maximum set of three with five or 10 pounds more than the old max.

The further you get from the simple act of adding weight to the bar each workout, the slower the initial gains are likely to be. But the further you get from that first month or two of training, the more appropriate it is to complicate or change and slow down your method of progression.

There are several very good and well-explained programs available on the internet that are virtually guaranteed to work that will keep you in the middle of a well-traveled path.

But we're not all alike, physically or mentally. And some of us get almost as much enjoyment in planning our training as actually doing it. Often, planning our own training increases ownership of what we're doing, increases our enjoyment, and makes it more likely we'll continue to train. Plan away!

If you keep these guideposts presented in sight, you're likely to get to your destination. And never find yourself halfway up a cliff wall in a thunderstorm…with no safety rope.

If you want to know if you're heading in the right direction, ask yourself two questions:

o   Do I have a plan that includes raising the weight on the bar for each exercise in a logical and stepwise manner?

o   Do I know what weight I'm going to put on the bar for each exercise before I get to the gym?

If your answers are yes, then rest easily.

Even if you've gotten off the beaten path, your socks are dry, your compass works, and your canteen is full. Your route might not be the fastest, but you'll get to your destination. If your answer to either question is no, keep your matches dry, because you're probably going to need them.

THE TRAINING LOG

That so many lifters are resistant to keeping a training log is a longstanding pet peeve of mine.

Why wouldn't they?

I know we live in an instant-gratification world. Maintaining a training journal won't give you a new body today, not even this week. But if you decide NOT to keep a journal, you almost certainly begin the process of getting bigger or stronger with a huge handicap.

Recording your workout every training session isn't hard, but it's work. Not physical work—mental work. Squatting is work. LOTS of work. And if you aren't willing to write your workouts down, some of that work will be wasted.

It's about discipline.

Planning your training and recording that training go hand in hand. One doesn't work without the other. It's a sad fact, but most lifters have no plan. They go into workouts with "get a good workout" as the main goal.

The goal should be to *make progress*. If you made progress toward your physical goal, the workout was a good workout. If you didn't, it wasn't.

Progress is an integral part of *progressive* resistance training. And it's hard to make progress if you don't keep a training log. You have to know what you did the previous workout to know what you should do the next workout.

There are a few things necessary for keeping a training log. One is the notebook you'll use to hold the information. I know a lot of people are in love with using a smart phone for everything and I'm sure tracking their workouts is one of them. You might call me old-fashioned, but I don't like that. You drip sweat on that phone one too many times and you just lost months or years of your training log. Then there's the problem with compatibility and the speed with which platforms and systems change in the electronic universe. But mainly, I think something happens in the brain when we handwrite on paper. For

these and other reasons, I continue to use a pen and paper and recommend it for you too.

Many types of notebooks work, but I like the cheap composition pads that can be purchased at most grocery and big-box stores. The last one I got had 100 pages in it, which is about right. Get the college-ruled version because it has more lines per page—enough that you'll get an entire week on one page. This is important.

Each entry should have the date first, including the year. If you don't include the year, at some point in the distant future, you'll be looking at old training logs from a dozen years earlier and won't have any idea what year the training was done.

For each day, write the date, then indent the first exercise a bit. Write the warm-up sets first, then the work sets. I always try to write small enough that each exercise will fit on one line. If you're doing sets across, you can either write out "squat 200kg for 5 sets of 5" or you can write "200kg x5x5x5x5x5." If you're doing ascending or descending weights, you'll have to use the second method.

If your training is programmed in a reasonable fashion, you'll usually have three to five exercises in a workout, and three to five workouts per week. That will all fit on one page.

Photo A2.1—Glenn's sample training log sheet

I use the front of the page for the actual workout, and if there's anything else I want to make a note of, that goes on the back of the page. I like to use one sort of notation for work sets and another for PR sets. I usually underline work sets, and put a circle around new PRs. If it's a particularly noteworthy PR, I've been known to also put a star by the set.

That's my system. Use it or design another one that works for you.

Once you've kept this log for a few weeks or months, you'll find that future workouts are much easier to plan. You'll begin thinking about the last set of your warm-up progression before you do the first set, and planning the best jumps to take so you're optimally warmed up and not tired before your work sets.

You'll have a record at your fingertips of what you did for warm-ups the previous couple of workouts and how it worked out. This is the kind of information that can add pounds to your squat or inches to your arms. You'll know the plan before you walk into the gym. And then you'll be able to start stringing together the staircase of small steps that will take you from a 100-kilo snatch to a 130-kilo snatch, or from a 150 clean and jerk to a 180-kilo clean and jerk.

Getting into the habit of keeping a training log will have such a huge positive effect on your training. It's a *transformative* experience.

I hear lots of people talk about why they can't make progress. Lots of excuses. Too many.

I've never heard anyone come right out and say I can't bench press 300 pounds because I'm unwilling to keep a training log.

Keep a training log.

Formulate a plan. Stick to it. *Progress.*

ABOUT THE CO-AUTHORS

Photo CO.1—James McDermott and me

JAMES MCDERMOTT

James McDermott earned his BS degree in kinesiology—fitness development from SUNY Cortland. As a requirement for earning his degree, James interned at Albany CrossFit in Albany, New York, eventually becoming a full-time coach, and was promoted to the gym's head coaching position. While coaching at Albany CrossFit, he prepared athletes to compete in the CrossFit North East Regionals, earned the Certified CrossFit Trainer (CCFT/Level 3) credential, and taught over 1,000 beginners how to snatch and clean and jerk through the gym's On Ramp program and CrossFit classes.

In 2014, he founded the Albany CrossFit Barbell Club. Later he went on to earn his USA Weightlifting Level 2 credential. As an athlete, he regularly competes in weightlifting meets. As a coach, he's led seminars, and has taken over 40 individual athletes to their first competitions. Through the barbell club, he's produced a Masters National Champion, two Masters Pan American Champions, and a Masters World Champion.

James has also authored multiple books and is the host of *The Barbell Strikes Back!* podcast.

Visit *jamesamcdermott.com* for information on his other works.

Photo CO.2—Mike Prevost

MIKE PREVOST

Mike Prevost earned his BA in natural science and behavioral science from the University of Louisiana, Lafayette, his MBA from the Naval Postgraduate School, and his Ph.D. in exercise physiology and kinesiology from Louisiana State University. He trained as an Aerospace Physiologist at the Naval Aerospace Medical Institute, and served 21 years as an active-duty aerospace physiologist.

Mike completed a basic flight syllabus with the Navy, and has flight experience in a variety of Naval aircraft, including fighter jets, transport aircraft, and helicopters. While serving, he employed the newest research to provide real-world human performance solutions for military operational forces including aviation, USMC ground forces, Navy Rescue Swimmers, and Special Operations Command.

During his Navy career, he served as a research scientist, applied physiologist, curriculum manager, instructor, faculty member at the US Naval Academy, procurement program manager, and deputy director of the Naval Survival Training Institute. He was the staff exercise physiologist for the US Naval Academy, charged with directing the human performance laboratory, serving as a consultant to the athletic department, and managing the remedial fitness programs.

Mike retired from the Navy at the rank of captain. Upon retirement, he taught exercise physiology, anatomy and physiology laboratory, and strength and conditioning at Loyola Marymount University, and studied clinical nutrition at Bastyr University.

ACKNOWLEDGMENTS

Many people contributed to the formation of this book. Whether it was through a student-mentor relationship, making suggestions, or proofreading the manuscript, every bit of support throughout the process is greatly appreciated.

SPECIAL THANKS TO:

DR. MICHAEL HARTMAN
WITCHITA FALLS WEIGHTLIFTING CLUB

Michael Hartman attended Midwestern State University to earn his master's degree in exercise physiology; while he was there, he also served as my assistant coach for the MSU weightlifting team. In the beginning, it was supposed to be an internship for one semester, but before the semester was complete, Michael and I had become good friends, and he proved to be indispensable to the team. He continued to assist with coaching until he moved to Oklahoma to pursue his Ph.D.

Michael continues to be a good friend, and is someone I respect immensely. If one of my lifters ever had to lift at a meet where doing well was important and I couldn't be there for some reason, Michael would be my first choice as a replacement. He can make the right decision quickly and under pressure every time—I trust him.

Many of my best memories are of driving in one of the MSU vans to various meets. Whether the meet was in L.A., Chicago, or somewhere closer, we almost always drove. It was cheaper that way, and money is always an issue for broke weightlifters. It's hard to write about Michael without getting sidetracked thinking of old stories that happened during those trips.

From a gun that shoots around corners to pumping the gravity out of a room, Michael and I discussed everything you could possibly imagine while on those long drives. That time shared with him is very dear to me, and I wouldn't trade it for anything.

DR. LON KILGORE

I first met Dr. Kilgore at Kansas State while he was obtaining his Ph.D. Our paths crossed in the rec center where he was training for weightlifting and I was competing in powerlifting. While we didn't instantly become close friends, I thought he was a pretty smart guy.

In one of those chance-in-a-million circumstances, years after meeting Kilgore and after I'd started and then dropped out of a graduate program in Montana, I learned he was teaching at Midwestern State in Wichita Falls, Texas. This was a huge coincidence because immediately after I left Kansas State, I'd moved to Wichita Falls and bought a house I still owned, although I was living in Kansas.

Kilgore discovered I was looking for a place to finish my graduate degree, and that I still owned a home in Wichita Falls...and invited me to come back to Texas to finish my degree. The years I spent at MSU were some of the most productive years of my life.

Dr. Kilgore was a mentor to me in a lot of ways, both personally and professionally, and I owe him a lot. In fact, I owe him so much that to even try to list the ways he's been instrumental in my life would belittle the effect he's had.

I will just leave it at the statement: If it weren't for Kilgore, you wouldn't be reading this right now, and you would probably have never heard the name "Glenn Pendlay."

COMMENTS FROM JAMES

Having an abundance of great photos in the book was important to Glenn, and many people made achieving that goal possible. Thank you, Addison Jones and Nicole Deines for volunteering to be athlete models in the book. The time we spent together in Kansas for the photo shoot is something I'll never forget. Thank you to Micah Gilbert and Derek Selles for your photography work. Thank you to Mark Hazarabedian for contributing many great photos from Glenn's past. Thanks to all the athletes and coaches who allowed the use of their photos to contribute to the overall learning experience of the book.

Thank you to Chris LeRoux not only for volunteering to be an athlete model in the book, but also for being such a supporter and good friend of Glenn's. He spoke often of your friendship and of how much he respected your opinions.

Thank you to Travis Cooper for being a sounding board during the final days of the writing process. Glenn always mentioned you as one of the most knowledgeable people in American weightlifting, and I agree. When he passed, I knew I could count on you to answer questions or to confirm the accuracy of the text and Glenn's methods.

Thank you to Laree Draper for being a driving force behind completing this project. I still remember the day Glenn called me to discuss working with you and On Target Publications. He was so excited by the opportunity. Glenn had tremendous respect for you and assured me it was a good idea. As usual, he was right. I don't know where we'd be right now without you and I'm incredibly thankful for all you've done. Glenn would be too.

Thank you to Kim Seevers for proofreading the manuscript. Your friendship means a lot to me and I'm honored to coach you. I'll never forget the opportunities you've given me to become a better coach.

Thank you to all the athletes in the Albany CrossFit Barbell Club both past and present. When I first started working on this book, I realized if I was going to help Coach Pendlay write about his methods, I'd first have to coach using them. Our training room became a laboratory so I could see firsthand how those methods worked and how each of you responded to the training. Working with you in the gym and at competitions helped me understand the methods and coaching on a deeper level so I could authentically write about them. I'm immensely appreciative to have your trust and confidence every day we step into the gym together.

A special thank you to Joanna Toman for proofreading the manuscript as you have so many others over the years. Finishing this book was not easy for me, and I know living with someone obsessed with weightlifting is not easy for you. I couldn't do any of this without you. You're the firmly clamped collars that keep all the plates on my barbell from falling off as I stumble around after a wobbly lift or when life gets crazy. A few words typed on a page could never come close to describing how much I love you and how wonderful you truly are.

ATHLETE MODELS

This book is filled with terrific competition and snapshots from training sessions from Glenn's collection. However, *American Weightlifting* would not have been possible without the generosity of the athletes who offered their time and expertise during many long and difficult photo sessions.

Thank you to to the following athletes for their contributions to Glenn's legacy work.

TRAVIS COOPER

ADDISON JONES

NICOLE DEINES

CHRIS LEROUX

JAMES TATUM

LOUIS VIDAL

PHOTOGRAPHER CREDITS

Glenn greatly valued the photographers who contribute to the sport and history of weightlifting and would have wanted to personally thank them for their contributions to his book. On his behalf and on behalf of the athletes pictured, we thank you for the use of your wonderful photos.

FRONT MATTER

Glenn Pendlay Collection

Photo 1—Glenn Pendlay
Photo 2—Glenn and Medvedev, August 11, 1992
Photo 3—Glenn at work
Photo 6—The Glenn Pendlay
Photo 7—Donny Shankle, 200-kilo Clean
Photo 10—Donny Shankle lifting at the Wichita Falls Athletic Club

Bruce Klemens Photo 8—Trey Goodwin snatching 140 kilos

Jason Brazie Photo 9—Glenn coaching James through jerk steps at a seminar held at Albany CrossFit

Mark Hazarabedian Photo 4—Glenn utilizing the coach's head tilt while watching a lift

Photo 5—Glenn and Jon North

SECTION A: LEARNING THE LIFTS

Glenn Pendlay Collection Photo 10—Caleb Ward snatching while teammates Donny and Jon watch

CHAPTER 1: LEARNING THE SNATCH

Glenn Pendlay Collection

Photo 1.7—Correct Overhead Position
Photo 1.8—Jared Fleming Holding the Bottom of a Squat
Photo 1.9—Stretching the Achilles Tendons with a Bar

Derek Selles

Photo 1.1—Correct Grip Width
Photo 1.2—The Grip is Too Narrow
Photo 1.3—The Grip is Too Wide
Photo 1.21—Bar Held Correctly to Begin Step One
Photo 1.22—Bar Is Held at the Crease of the Hip
Photo 1.23—Side View of Step One, Slight Knee Bend, Vertical Torso, Shoulders Neutral
Photo 1.24—Bar Held Correctly to Begin Step Two
Photo 1.25—Side View of Step Two. Shoulder Should Be Slightly Ahead of the Bar.
Photo 1.26—Bar Held Correctly to Begin Step Three
Photo 1.27—Side View of Step Three
Photo 1.28—Proper Start Position from the Floor
Photo 1.29—Side view of start position

Micah Gilbert

Photos 1.10–1.16—Shoulder Dislocate Sequence
Photos 1.17–1.18—Sots Press, Clean Grip
Photos 1.19–1.20—Sots Press, Snatch Grip
Photos 1.30–1.39—Full Snatch Sequence

James McDermott

Photo 1.4—Grabbing the bar
Photo 1.5—Tuck the thumb
Photo 1.6—The Hook Grip

CHAPTER 2: LEARNING THE CLEAN

Glenn Pendlay Collection

Photo 2.7—Front Squat Start Position
Photo 2.8—Front Squat Bottom Position

Derek Selles

Photo 2.1—Front Rack Position
Photo 2.2—Close-up of the Front Rack Position
Photo 2.9—Correct Grip Width with the Bar One-Third Down the Thighs
Photo 2.10—Side View with the Bar Held on the Thighs
Photo 2.11— Bar Held Correctly to Begin Step One
Photo 2.12—The Shoulders are Neutral, Knees Slightly Bent, and the Bar is Held High on the Thighs
Photo 2.13—Bar Held Correctly at the Patellar Ligament to Begin Step Two
Photo 2.14—The Knees Have Moved Back Until the Shins Are Vertical
Photo 2.15—Bar Held Correctly at the Mid-Shin to Begin Step Three
Photo 2.16—Side View—After the Bar Passes the Knee, the Knees Are Flexed Further
Photo 2.17—This is the correct start position from the floor
Photo 2.18—Side view of the start position with plates loaded on the bar

Micah Gilbert

Photos 2.3-2.6—Partner Front Rack Stretch Sequence
Photos 2.19-2.28—Full Sequence of the Clean

CHAPTER 3: LEARNING THE JERK

Derek Selles

Photo 3.1—Press Starting Position
Photo 3.2—Pressing motion
Photo 3.3—Press Lockout and Overhead Position
Photo 3.4—Push Press Starting Position
Photo 3.5—Push Press Dip Position
Photo 3.6—Push Press Drive and Pressing Motion
Photo 3.7—Push Press Lockout and Overhead Position
Photo 3.8—Power Jerk Starting Position
Photo 3.9—Power Jerk Dip Position
Photo 3.10—Power Jerk Drive
Photo 3.11—Power Jerk Catch Position
Photo 3.12—Power Jerk Full Lockout
Photo 3.13—Starting Line
Photo 3.14—Walk Heel to Toe to Find Split Stance Length 1
Photo 3.15— Walk Heel to Toe to Find Split Stance Length 2
Photo 3.16— Walk Heel to Toe to Find Split Stance Length 3
Photo 3.17—Full Split Position
Photo 3.21—Jerk from Split Start Position
Photo 3.22—Jerk from Split Position Dip
Photo 3.23—Jerk from Split Position Drive
Photo 3.24—Jerk from Split Receiving Position and Lockout
Photo 3.25—Jerk Start Position
Photo 3.26—Jerk Dip Position
Photo 3.27—Jerk Drive
Photo 3.28—Jerk Receiving Position
Photo 3.29—Jerk Recovery, Front Foot Back First
Photo 3.30—Jerk Finish Position and Lockout

SECTION B: TRAINING FOR AMERCAN WEIGHTLIFTERS

Glenn Pendlay

Photo 1—Everything a weightlifter could possibly need

CHAPTER 5: HOW TO WRITE A WEIGHTLIFTING PROGRAM

Glenn Pendlay

Photo 5.1—John North Preparing to Snatch
Photo 5.3—Travis Preparing for a Clean and Jerk in Training

Derek Selles

Photo 5.2—Jared Fleming with the Focus of a Champion

CHAPTER 6: PROGRAMMING FOR BEGINNERS

Glenn Pendlay

Photo 6.1—Travis Cooper has always been a big squatter

Photo 6.2—James Tatum warming up his snatch at the 2015 World Championships in Houston, Texas

Photo 6.3—Jon North

Photos 6.5–6.9—The Back Squat Sequence

Photo 6.10—James Tatum Ready to Back Squat 240 Kilos

Photos 6.11–6.13—The Deadlift Sequence

Photos 6.14 and 6.15—The Back Extension Sequence

Micah Gilbert

Photos 6.16 and 6.17—The Hip Extension Sequence

Photos 6.18–6.23—The Glute-Ham Raise Sequence

Mark Hazarabedian

Photo 6.4—Kevin Cornell Racking a 150-kilo Clean during Training

CHAPTER 7: PROGRAMMING FOR INTERMEDIATES

Glenn Pendlay

Photo 7.1—Travis Cooper in Deep Thought before Snatching

Photo 7.8—Travis Cooper Resting between Lifts during Training

Photo 7.10—Rob Blackwell Snatching 120 Kilos

Photo 7.38—Spencer Walking the fine line between full and power snatch.

Micah Gilbert

Photos 7.2–7.4—Lifting from Blocks at Knee Height

Photos 7.5–7.7—Lifting from Blocks above Knee Height

Photos 7.11–7.14—Snatch Pull Ending with a Shrug

Photos 7.15–7.18—Clean Pull Ending with a Shrug

Photos 719–7.22—Snatch High Pull

Photos 7.23–7.27—Clean High Pull

Photos 7.28–7.32—Snatch Panda Pull

Photos 7.33–7.37—Clean Panda Pull

Photos 7.39–7.44—The Power Snatch

Photos 7.45–7.52—The Power Clean

CHAPTER 8: PROGRAMMING FOR ADVANCED WEIGHTLIFTERS

Glenn Pendlay

Photo 8.1—Spencer Moorman Snatching

Photo 8.10—Snatch Deadlift Isometric Hold One Inch off the Floor

Photo 8.11—Snatch Deadlift Isometric Hold at the Knees

Photo 8.12—Snatch Deadlift Isometric Hold at the Hips

Photo 8.13—Clean Deadlift Isometric Hold One Inch off the Floor

Photo 8.14—Clean Deadlift Isometric Hold at the Knees

Photo 8.15—Clean Deadlift Isometric Hold at the Hips

Photo 8.21—Jared Fleming

Photo 8.22—Jared Fleming Holding the American Record Overhead

Photo 8.23—Kathleen Winters

Micah Gilbert

Photos 8.2 and 8.3—Snatch Isometric Hold Just off the Floor

Photos 8.4 and 8.5—Snatch Isometric Hold at the Knees

Photos 8.6 and 8.7—Snatch Isometric Hold above the Knees

Photos 8.8 and 8.9—Snatch Isometric Hold at the Hips

Photos 8.16 and 8.17—Isometric Squat Hold Low Pins

Photo 8.18—Isometric Squat Hold Against High Pins

Jenny Arthur Vardanian

Photo 8.19—Jenny Arthur

Photo 8.20—Jenny Arthur

CHAPTER 9: WESTSIDE FOR WEIGHTLIFTERS

Glenn Pendlay

Photos 9.1–9.3—Using Bands
Photos 9.4 and 9.5—Using Bands in a Squat Rack
Photos 9.6–9.8—Seated Good Morning
Photos 9.9–9.13—Jerk Steps
Photos 9.18–9.22—Romanian Deadlift
Photos 9.46 and 9.47—Pull-Up
Photos 9.48 and 9.49—Clean Grip Overhead Squat
Photos 9.37–9.41—Suitcase Deadlift

Micah Gilbert

Photos 9.14–9.17—Round-Back Good Morning
Photos 9.23–9.27—Pendlay Row
Photos 9.28–9.36—Death March
Photos 9.42–9.45—One-Arm Kettlebell Swing
Photos 9.50–9.54—Muscle Snatch
Photos 9.55–9.59—Jerk Recovery
Photos 9.60–9.64—Split-stance Good Morning
Photos 9.65–9.67—Arch-back Good Morning
Photos 9.68–9.75—Step Up

James McDermott

Photos 9.76 and 9.77—Yoke Grip One
Photos 9.78 and 9.79—Yoke Grip Two

CHAPTER 10: PROGRAMMING FOR YOUTH, JUNIOR, AND MASTERS WEIGHTLIFTERS

Glenn Pendlay

Photo 10.1—Coaching Caleb Muehler
Photo 10.2—Correcting Landon Thompson's Bench Press Technique
Photo 10.3—William Pendlay Snatching
Photo 10.4—William Pendlay Cleaning
Photo 10.5—With Landon Thompson and Cory Muehler
Photo 10.6—Landon Thompson Training Weighted Pull-ups
Photo 10.7—Cory Lifting under the Watchful Eyes of Landon, Donny Shankle, and Me
Photo 10.8—Discussing the Game Plan with Landon
Photo 10.9—Landon Back Squatting 60 Kilos
Photo 10.10—Neiman Wickline

SECTION C: ESSENTIALS FOR AMERICAN WEIGHTLIFTERS

Glenn Pendlay

Photo C1—Pendlay Change Plates

CHAPTER 11: COMPETITION GUIDE

Glenn Pendlay

Photo 11.1—Spencer in the Warm-up Room at a Competition
Photo 11.2—James and Travis
Photo 11.3—Coaching in China
Photo 11.4—Caleb Ward celebrating a successful clean and jerk of 198 kilos
Photo 11.5—James Tatum Lifting in the Training Hall in China
Photo 11.6—Jared Fleming Snatch Pull
Photo 11.7—Jared Fleming Snatch Pull

CHAPTER 13: THE WEIGHTLIFTER'S KITCHEN

Glenn Pendlay

Photo 13.1—Jared and I Showing Off Our Premade Paleo Meals
Photo 13.2—Travis Cooper Approves of Putting in the Reps While in the Kitchen

SECTION D: THE PENDLAY SYSTEM FOR ATHLETIC DEVELOPMENT

Glenn Pendlay   Photo 1—A loaded bar often yields good results.

APPENDIX 1: AMERICAN WEIGHTLIFTERS

Glenn Pendlay

Photo A1.1—Team photo from the 2011 Muscledriver USA Grand Prix

Photo A1.2—Cal Strength team meeting

Photo A1.3—Coaching Caleb Back in the Cal Strength Days

Photo A1.4— At the 2015 National Championships, Travis Presented me with the Coach's Medal after he won

Photo A1.5—James and Me—on This Day, He Used Only Yellow Plates to Build 215 Kilos for Back Squats

Photo A1.6—Jon North at the 2010 Arnold Classic, after Clean and Jerking 184 Kilos to Qualify for the Pan American Championships

Photo A1.7—Jon and I Podcasting.

Photo A1.9—Spencer Breaking the Junior American Record with a 204-Kilo Clean and Jerk

Photo A1.10—Wichita Falls Weightlifting Club 2003

Mark Hazarabedian   Photo A1.8—Helping Jon North pose for a weightlifting poster

Bruce Klemens   Photo A1.11—Justin Brimhall